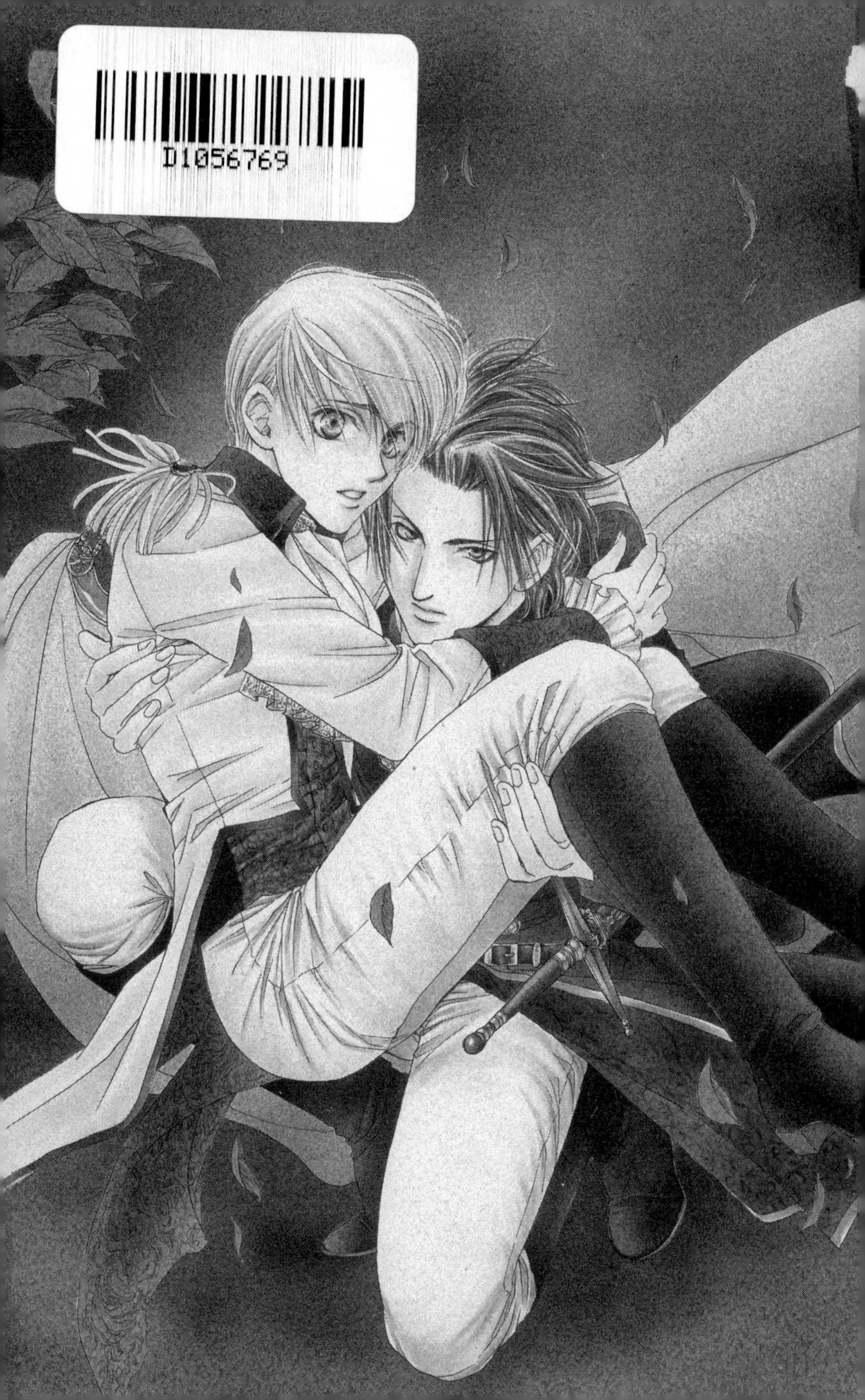

CONTENTS

BLACK KNIGHT _____3

BLACK KNIGHT 2 _____37
  Far-off Dawn

BLACK KNIGHT 3 _____69
  Private Darkness

BLACK KNIGHT 4 _____101
  Home of the Heart

BLACK KNIGHT 5 _____133
  The First Cry of Light

DEADLY SIN _____167

AFTERWARD _____193

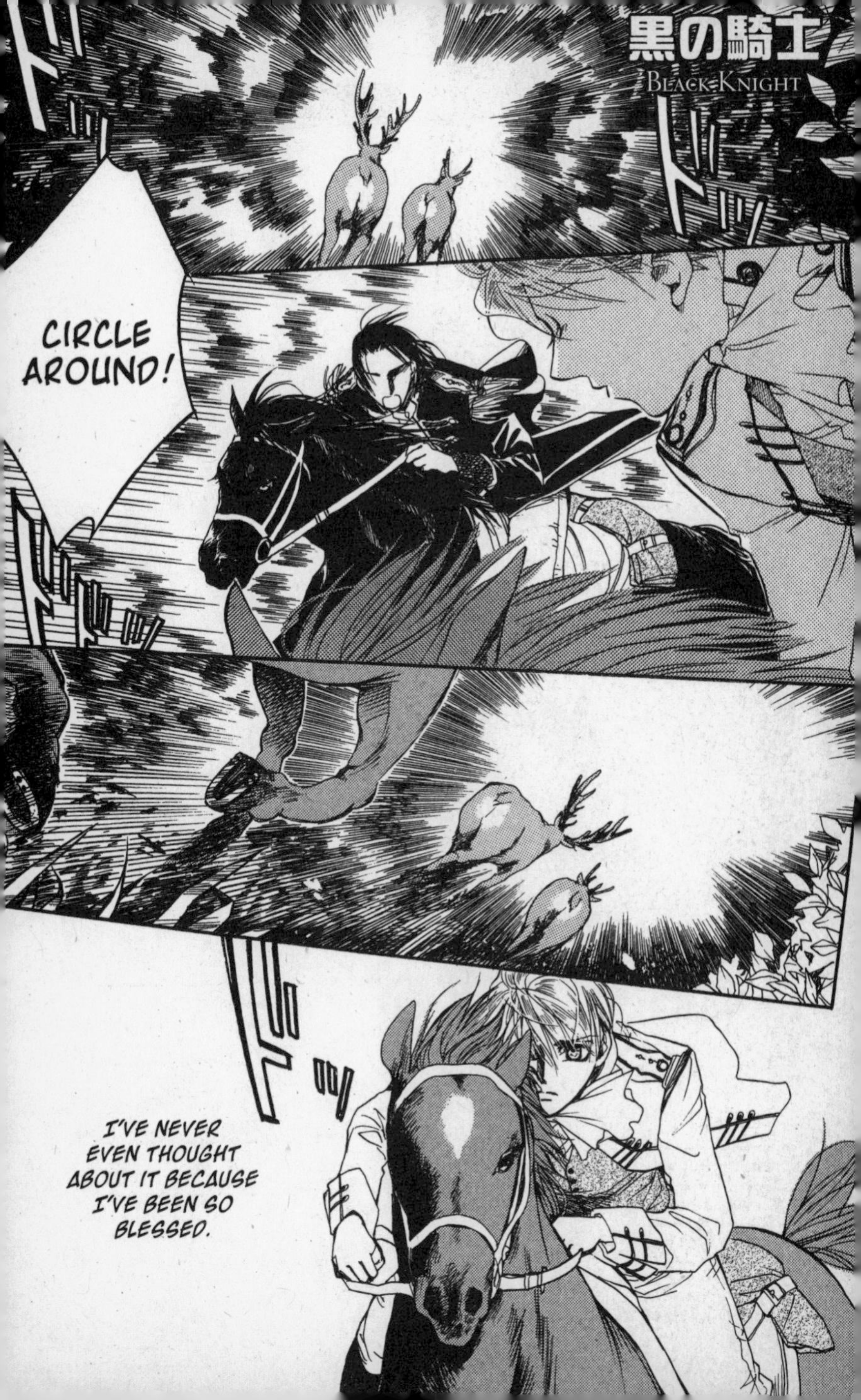
CIRCLE AROUND!
I'VE NEVER EVEN THOUGHT ABOUT IT BECAUSE I'VE BEEN SO BLESSED.

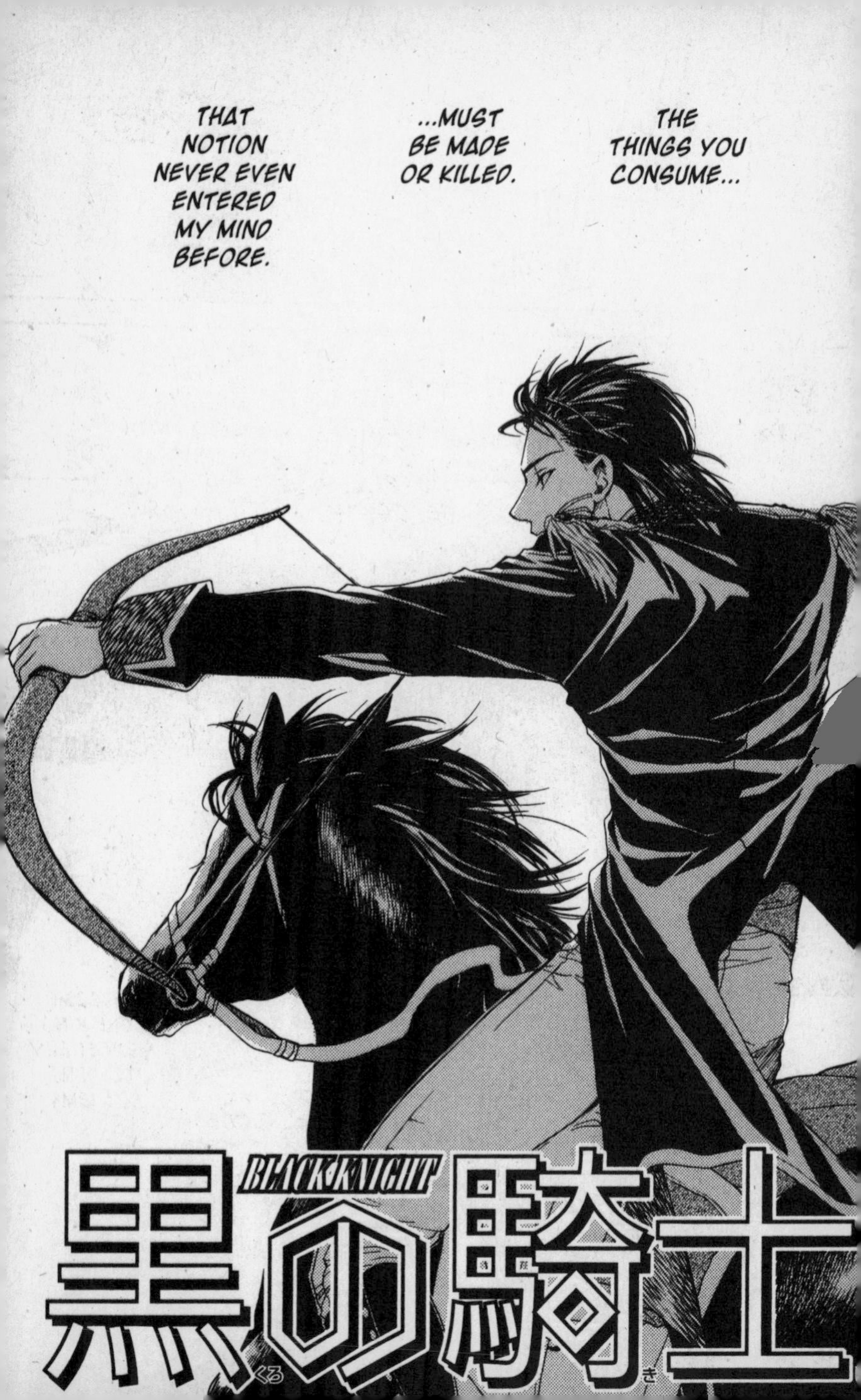
THE THINGS YOU CONSUME...
...MUST BE MADE OR KILLED.
THAT NOTION NEVER EVEN ENTERED MY MIND BEFORE.
BLACK KNIGHT
黒の騎士
くろ
き

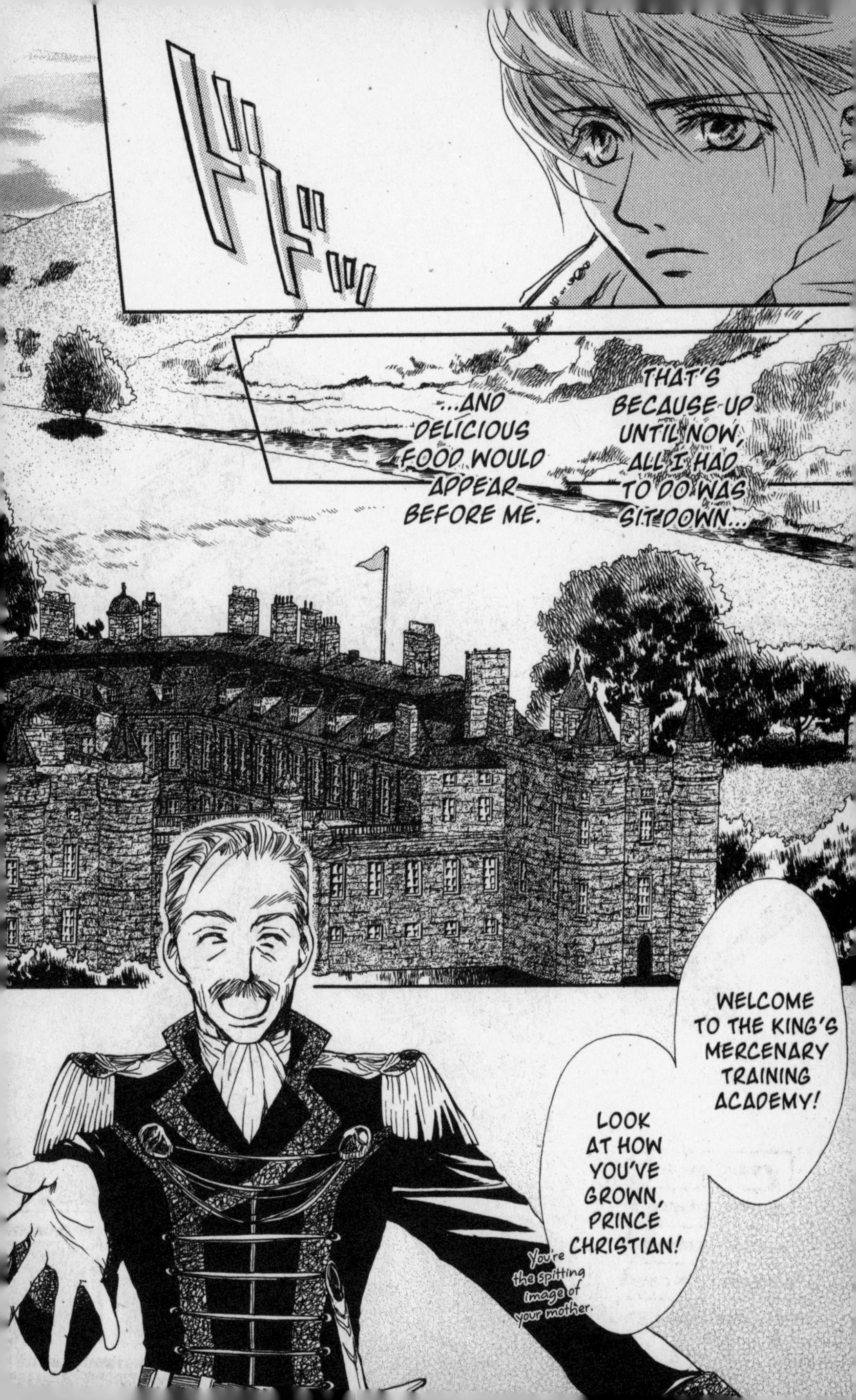
THAT'S BECAUSE UP UNTIL NOW, ALL I HAD TO DO WAS SIT DOWN...
...AND DELICIOUS FOOD WOULD APPEAR BEFORE ME.
WELCOME TO THE KING'S MERCENARY TRAINING ACADEMY!
LOOK AT HOW YOU'VE GROWN, PRINCE CHRISTIAN!
You're the spitting image of your mother.

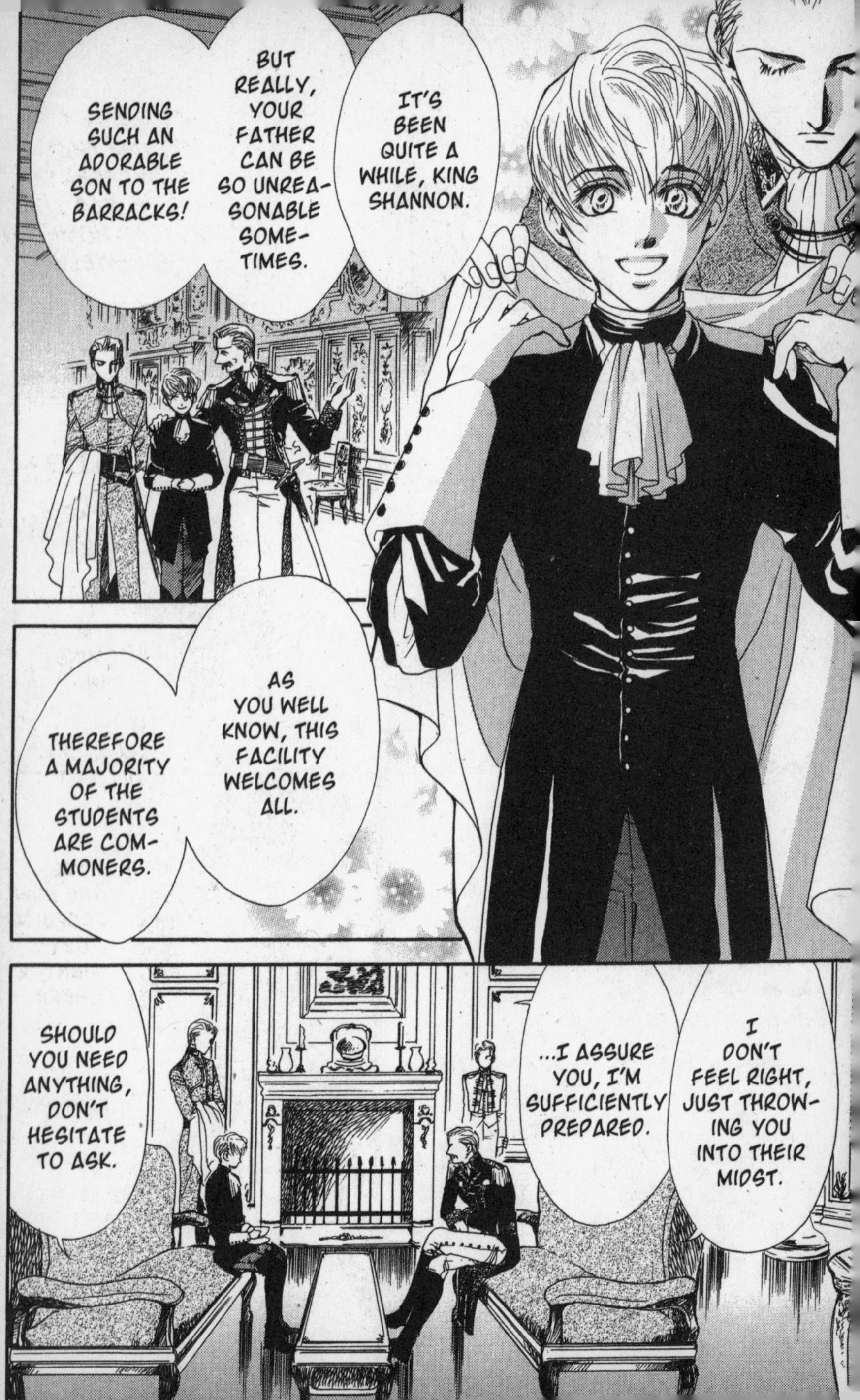

IT'S BEEN QUITE A WHILE, KING SHANNON.
BUT REALLY, YOUR FATHER CAN BE SO UNREA-SONABLE SOME-TIMES.
SENDING SUCH AN ADORABLE SON TO THE BARRACKS!
AS YOU WELL KNOW, THIS FACILITY WELCOMES ALL.
THEREFORE A MAJORITY OF THE STUDENTS ARE COM-MONERS.
I DON'T FEEL RIGHT, JUST THROW-ING YOU INTO THEIR MIDST.
...I ASSURE YOU, I'M SUFFICIENTLY PREPARED.
SHOULD YOU NEED ANYTHING, DON'T HESITATE TO ASK.

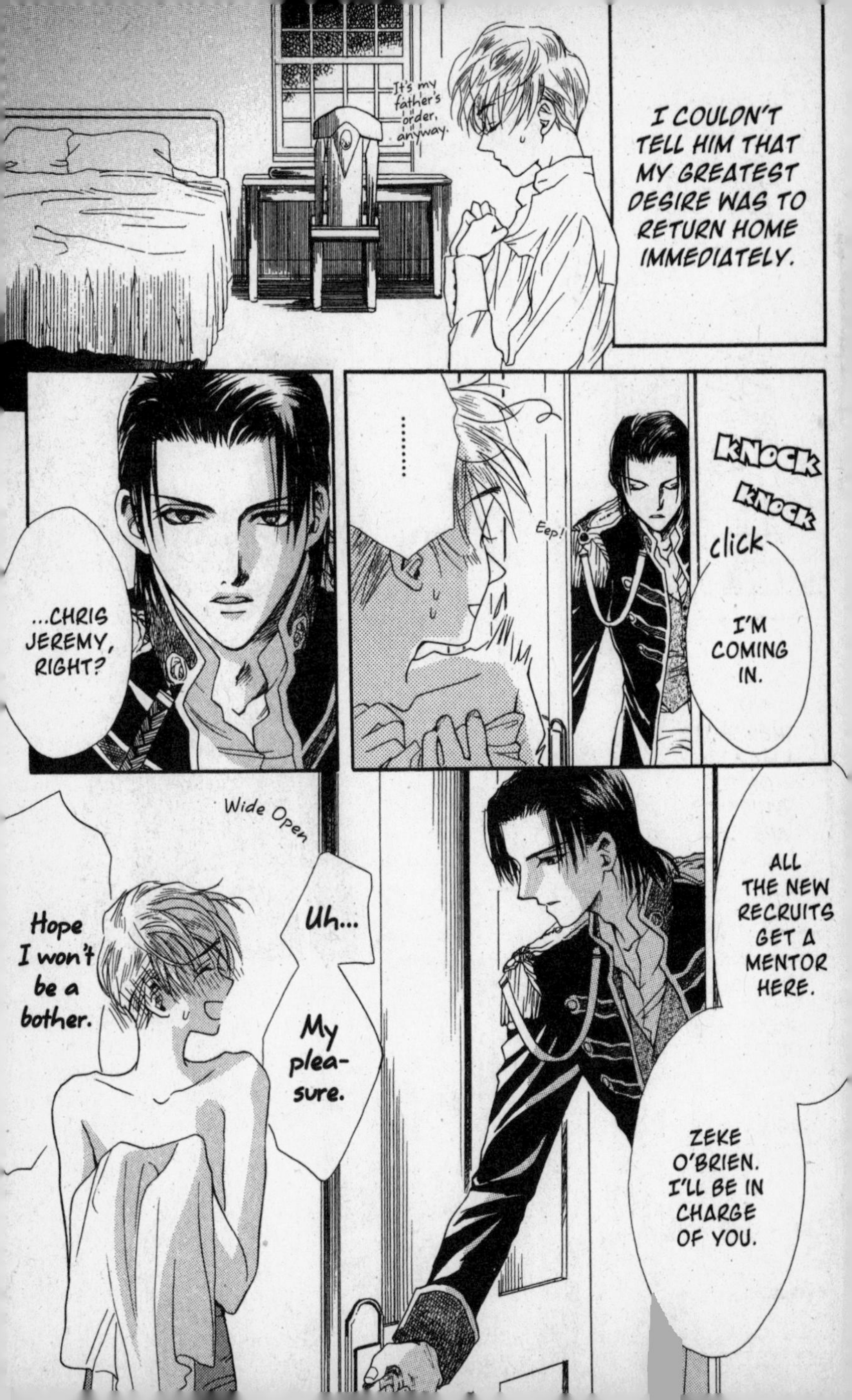

I COULDN'T TELL HIM THAT MY GREATEST DESIRE WAS TO RETURN HOME IMMEDIATELY.
It's my father's order, anyway.
KNOCK
KNOCK
click
I'M COMING IN.
......
Eep!
...CHRIS JEREMY, RIGHT?
ALL THE NEW RECRUITS GET A MENTOR HERE.
ZEKE O'BRIEN. I'LL BE IN CHARGE OF YOU.
Wide Open
Uh...
My plea-sure.
Hope I won't be a bother.

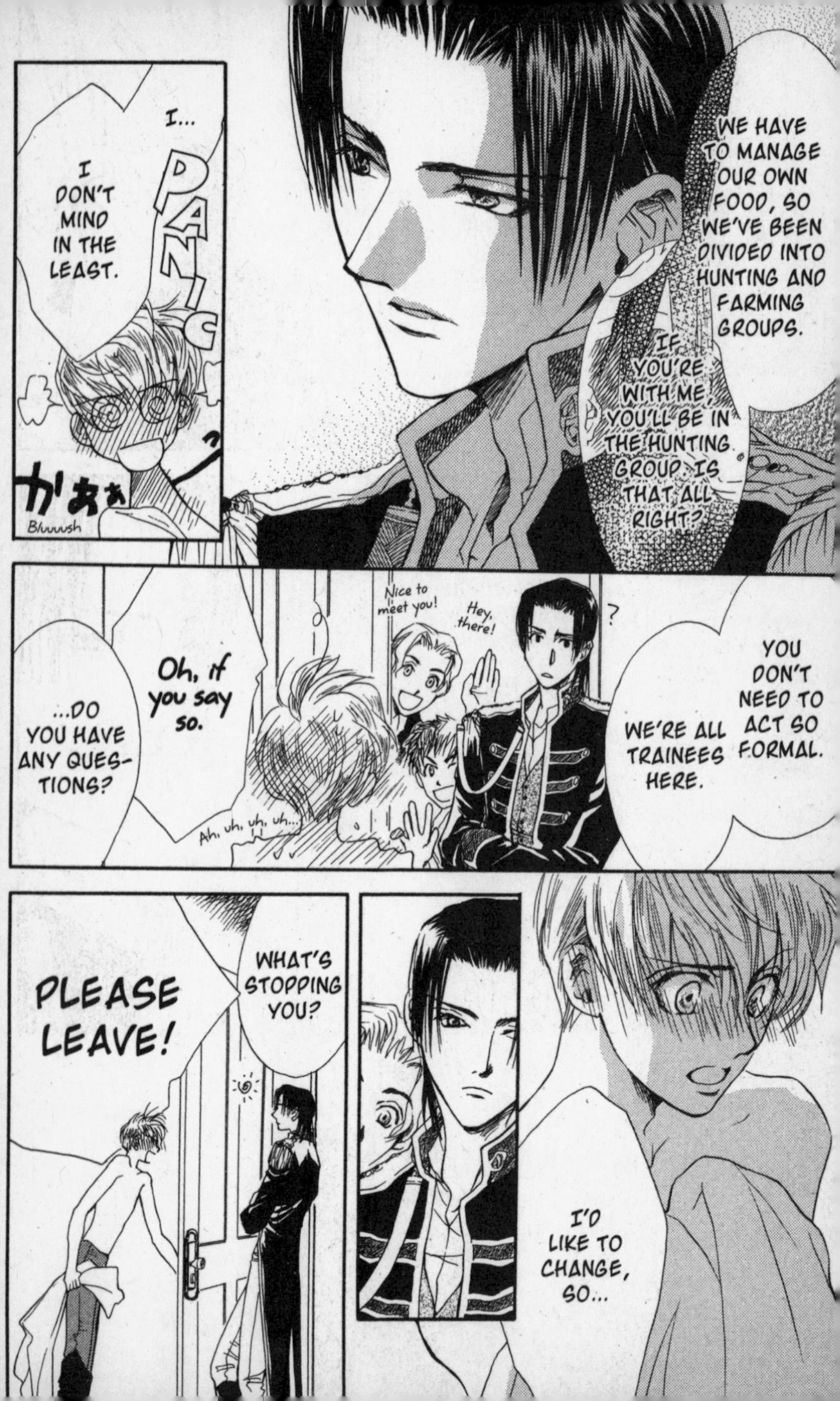
WE HAVE TO MANAGE OUR OWN FOOD, SO WE'VE BEEN DIVIDED INTO HUNTING AND FARMING GROUPS.
IF YOU'RE WITH ME, YOU'LL BE IN THE HUNTING GROUP. IS THAT ALL RIGHT?
I...
PANIC
I DON'T MIND IN THE LEAST.
かあぁ
Bluuush
YOU DON'T NEED TO ACT SO FORMAL.
WE'RE ALL TRAINEES HERE.
?
Hey, there!
Nice to meet you!
Oh, if you say so.
...DO YOU HAVE ANY QUES-TIONS?
Ah, uh, uh, uh...
I'D LIKE TO CHANGE, SO...
WHAT'S STOPPING YOU?
PLEASE LEAVE!

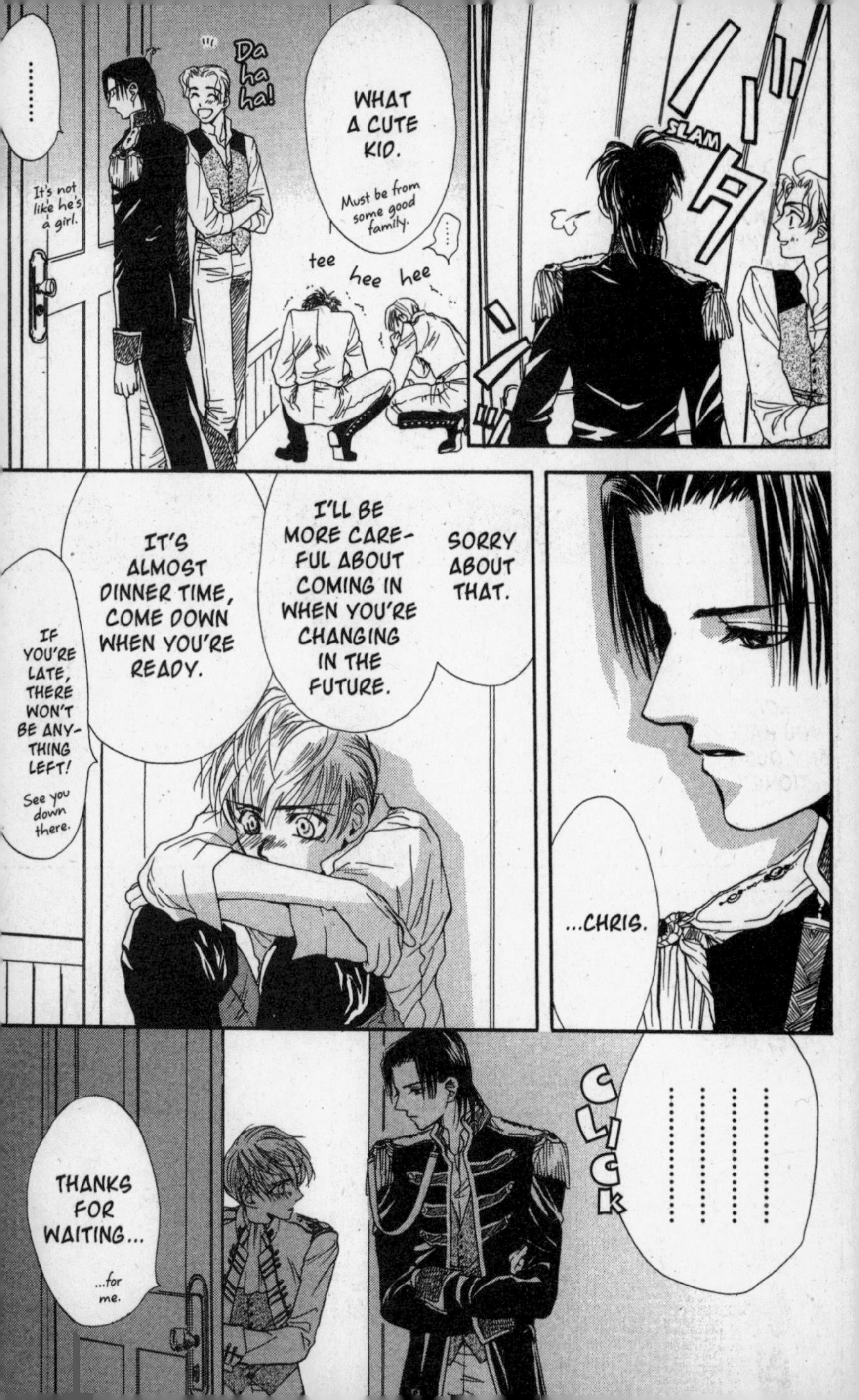
SLAM
WHAT A CUTE KID.
Must be from some good family.
....
Da ha ha!
!!!
tee hee hee
......
It's not like he's a girl.
...CHRIS.
SORRY ABOUT THAT.
I'LL BE MORE CARE-FUL ABOUT COMING IN WHEN YOU'RE CHANGING IN THE FUTURE.
IT'S ALMOST DINNER TIME, COME DOWN WHEN YOU'RE READY.
IF YOU'RE LATE, THERE WON'T BE ANY-THING LEFT!
See you down there.
CLICK
....
THANKS FOR WAITING...
...for me.

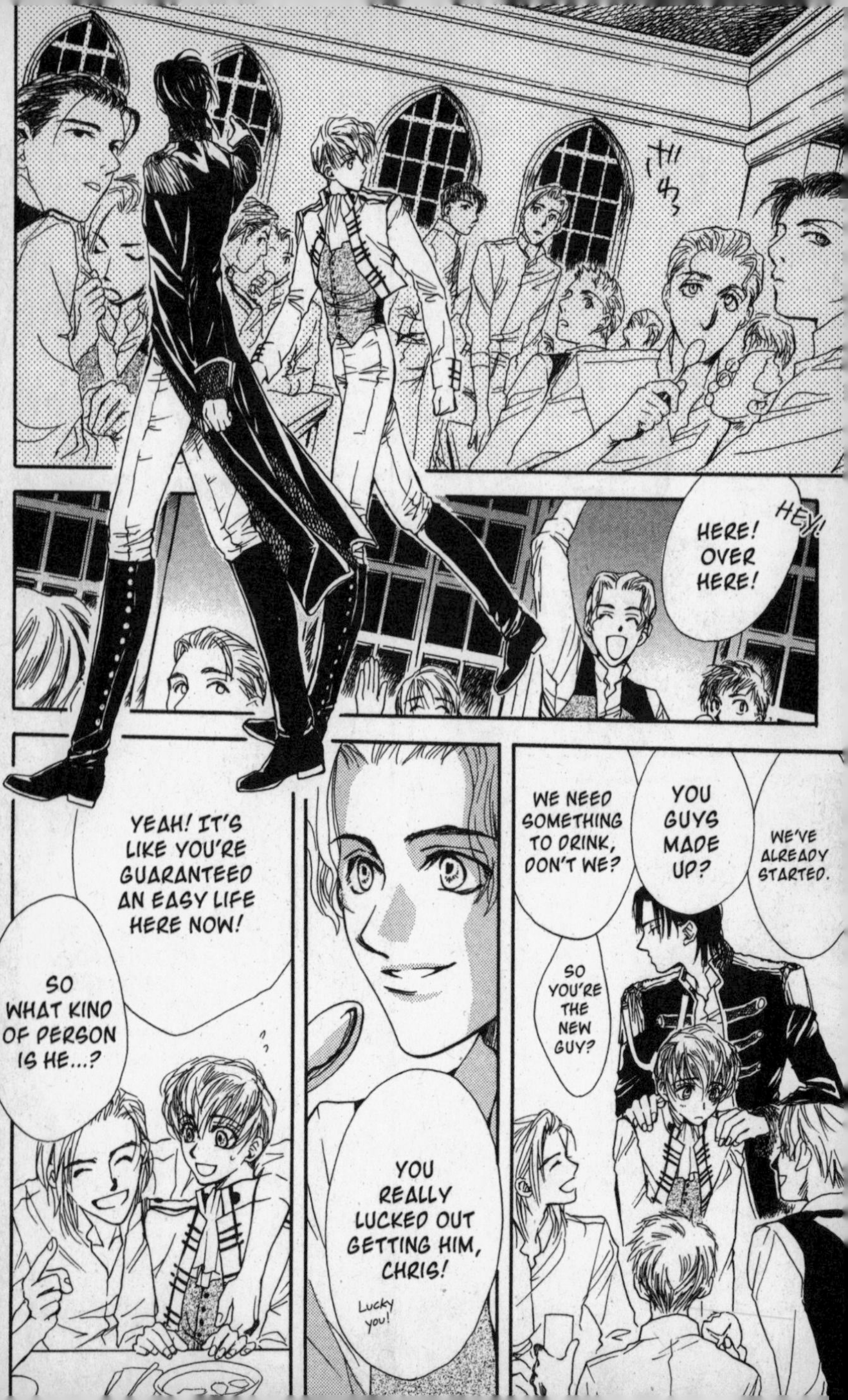
HEY!
HERE! OVER HERE!
WE'VE ALREADY STARTED.
YOU GUYS MADE UP?
WE NEED SOMETHING TO DRINK, DON'T WE?
SO YOU'RE THE NEW GUY?
YOU REALLY LUCKED OUT GETTING HIM, CHRIS!
Lucky you!
YEAH! IT'S LIKE YOU'RE GUARANTEED AN EASY LIFE HERE NOW!
SO WHAT KIND OF PERSON IS HE...?

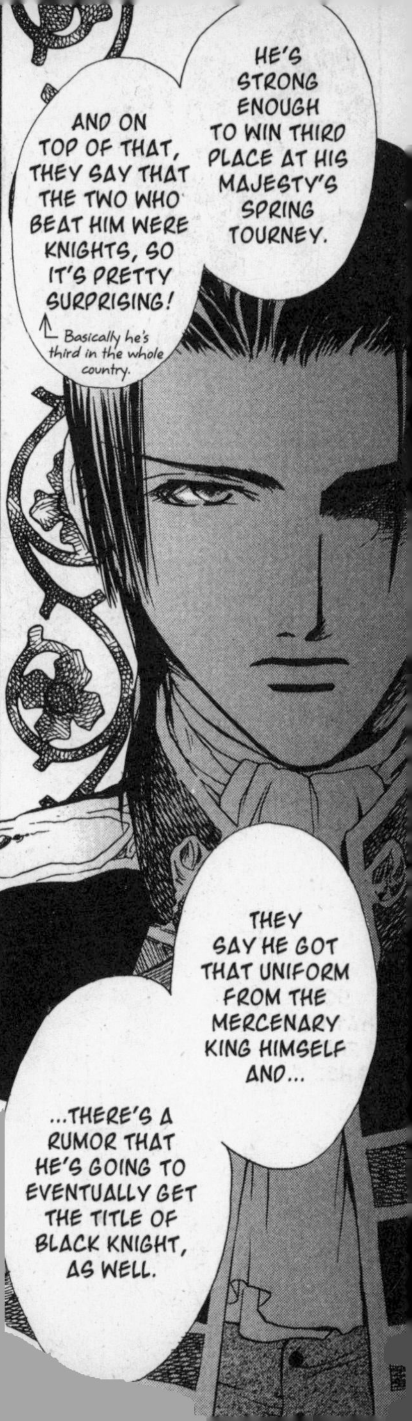
HE'S STRONG ENOUGH TO WIN THIRD PLACE AT HIS MAJESTY'S SPRING TOURNEY.
AND ON TOP OF THAT, THEY SAY THAT THE TWO WHO BEAT HIM WERE KNIGHTS, SO IT'S PRETTY SURPRISING!
Basically he's third in the whole country.
THEY SAY HE GOT THAT UNIFORM FROM THE MERCENARY KING HIMSELF AND...
...THERE'S A RUMOR THAT HE'S GOING TO EVENTUALLY GET THE TITLE OF BLACK KNIGHT, AS WELL.
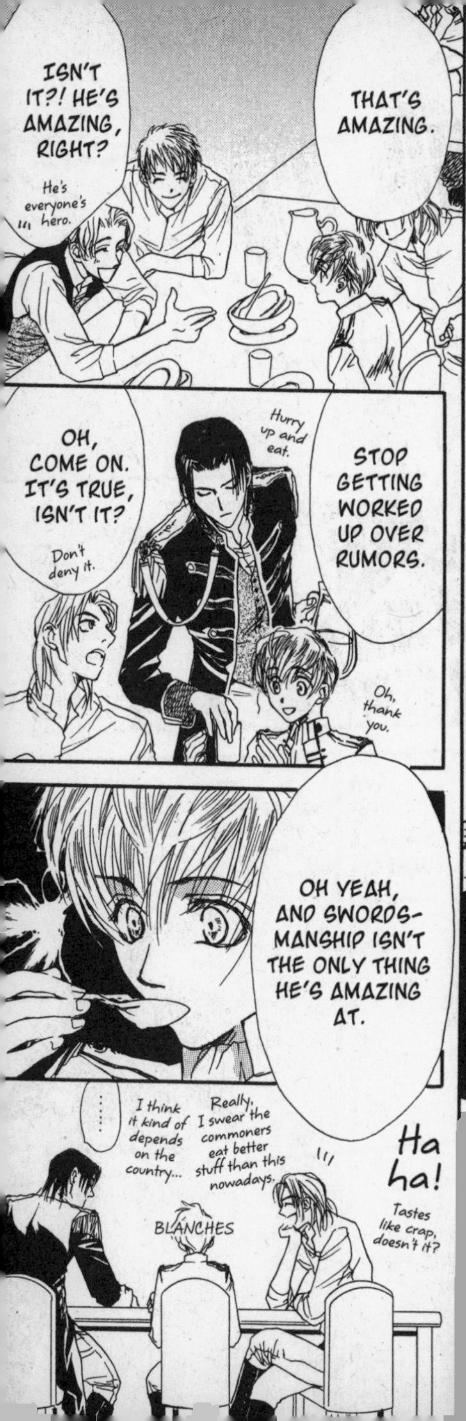
THAT'S AMAZING.
ISN'T IT?! HE'S AMAZING, RIGHT?
He's everyone's hero.
STOP GETTING WORKED UP OVER RUMORS.
Hurry up and eat.
OH, COME ON. IT'S TRUE, ISN'T IT?
Don't deny it.
Oh, thank you.
OH YEAH, AND SWORDS-MANSHIP ISN'T THE ONLY THING HE'S AMAZING AT.
Ha ha!
Tastes like crap, doesn't it?
Really, I swear the commoners eat better stuff than this nowadays.
I think it kind of depends on the country...
......
BLANCHES

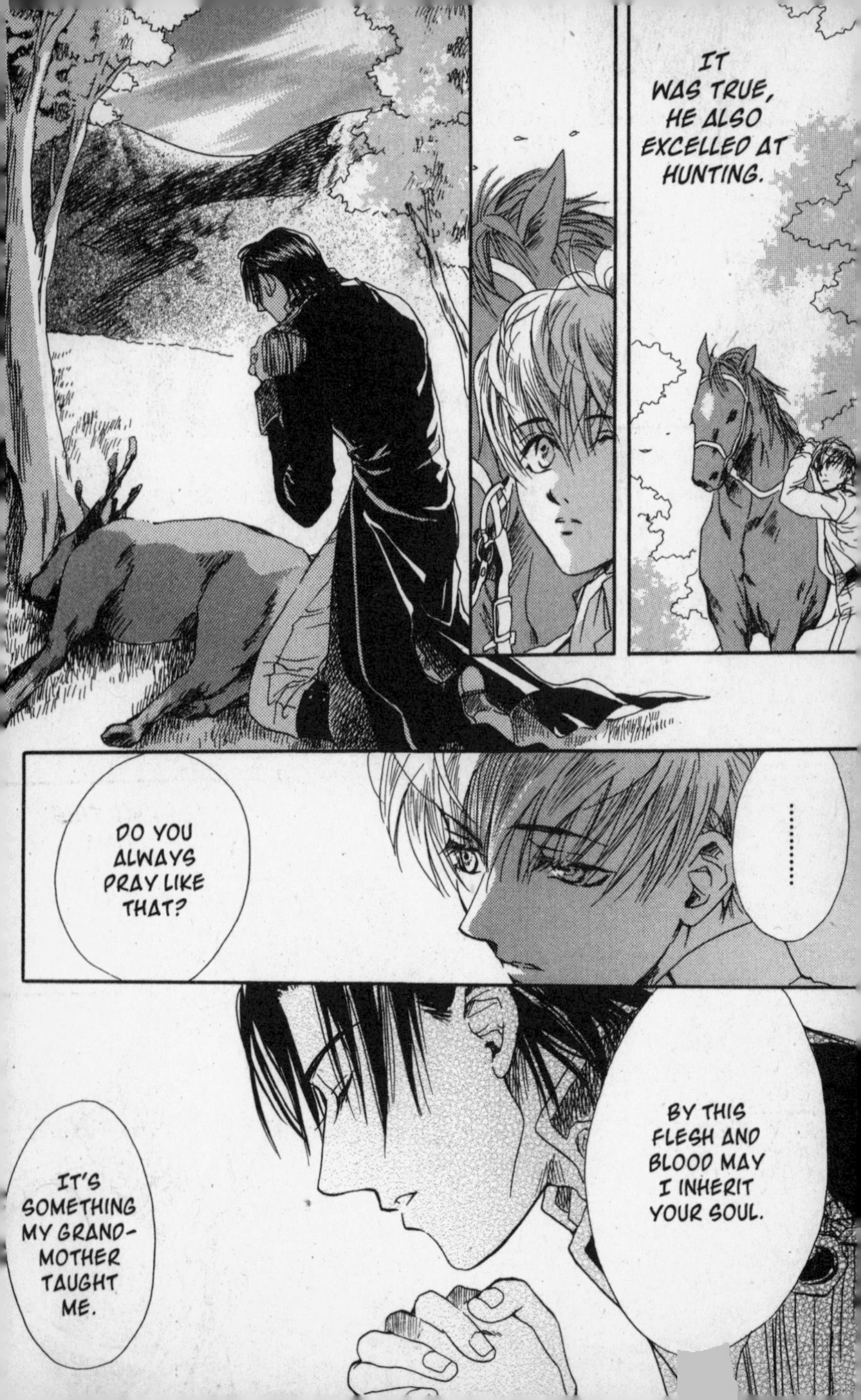
IT WAS TRUE, HE ALSO EXCELLED AT HUNTING.
......
DO YOU ALWAYS PRAY LIKE THAT?
BY THIS FLESH AND BLOOD MAY I INHERIT YOUR SOUL.
IT'S SOMETHING MY GRAND-MOTHER TAUGHT ME.

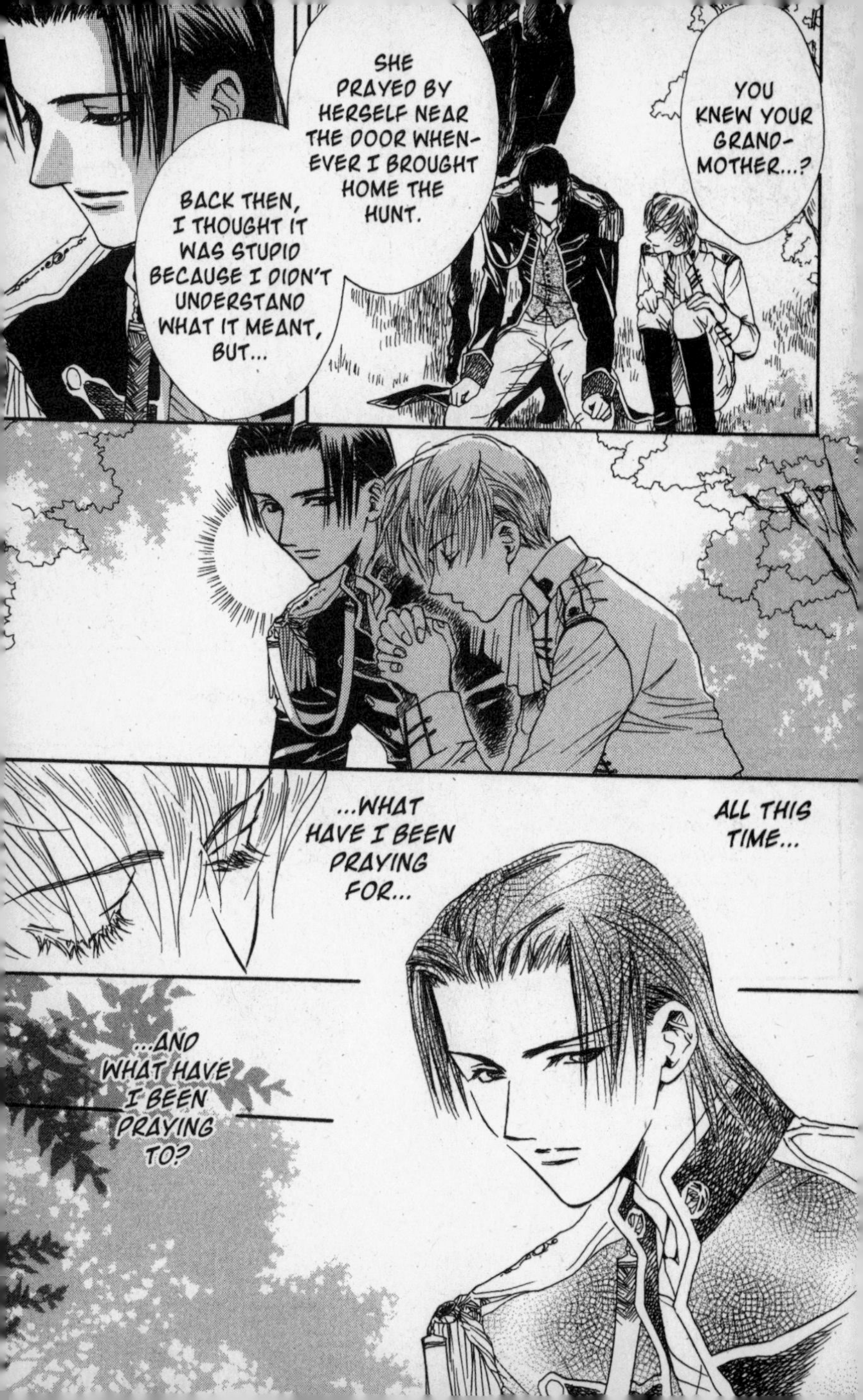
YOU KNEW YOUR GRAND-MOTHER...?
SHE PRAYED BY HERSELF NEAR THE DOOR WHEN-EVER I BROUGHT HOME THE HUNT.
BACK THEN, I THOUGHT IT WAS STUPID BECAUSE I DIDN'T UNDERSTAND WHAT IT MEANT, BUT...
ALL THIS TIME...
...WHAT HAVE I BEEN PRAYING FOR...
...AND WHAT HAVE I BEEN PRAYING TO?

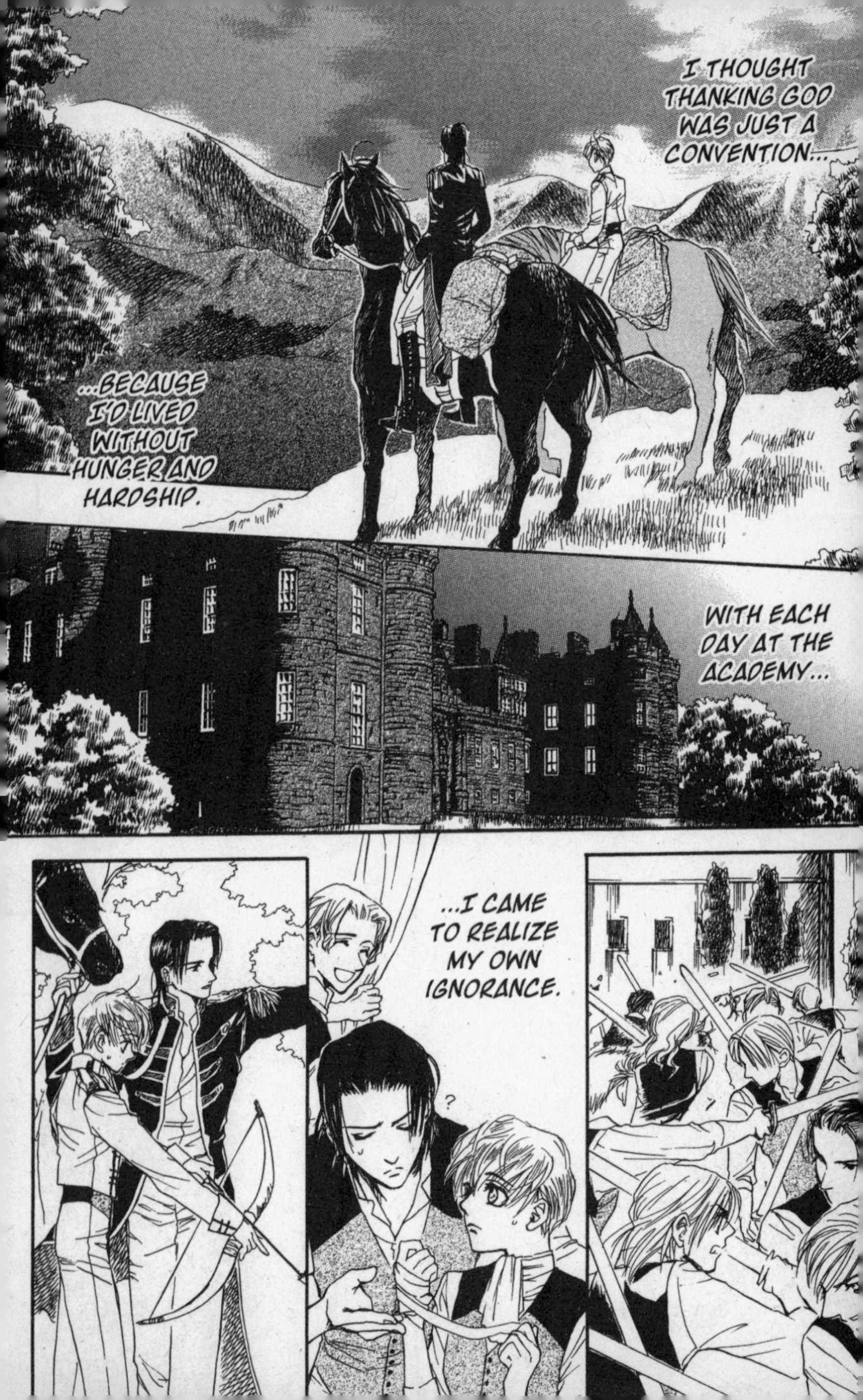
I THOUGHT THANKING GOD WAS JUST A CONVENTION...
...BECAUSE I'D LIVED WITHOUT HUNGER AND HARDSHIP.
WITH EACH DAY AT THE ACADEMY...
...I CAME TO REALIZE MY OWN IGNORANCE.
?

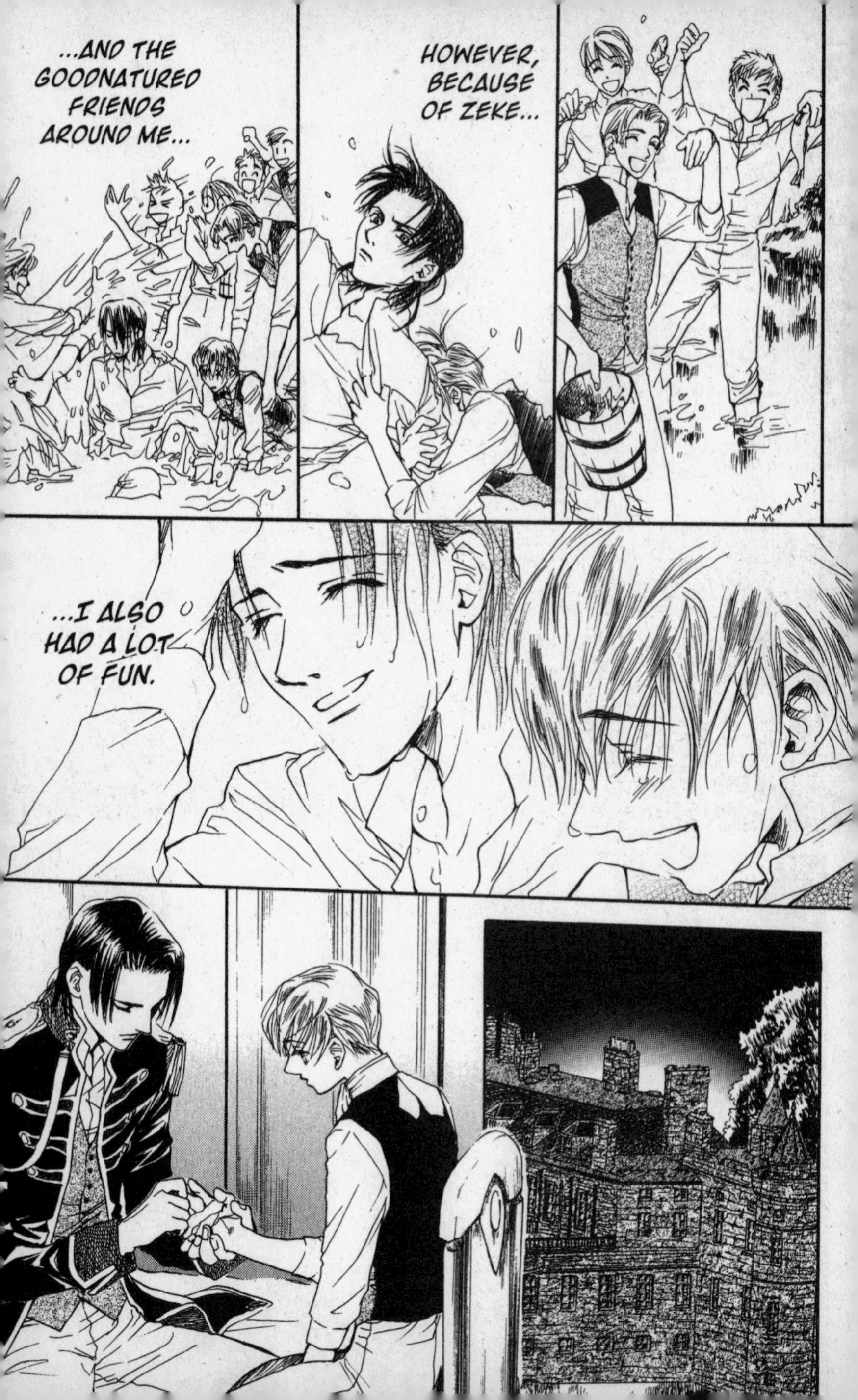
HOWEVER, BECAUSE OF ZEKE...
...AND THE GOODNATURED FRIENDS AROUND ME...
...I ALSO HAD A LOT OF FUN.

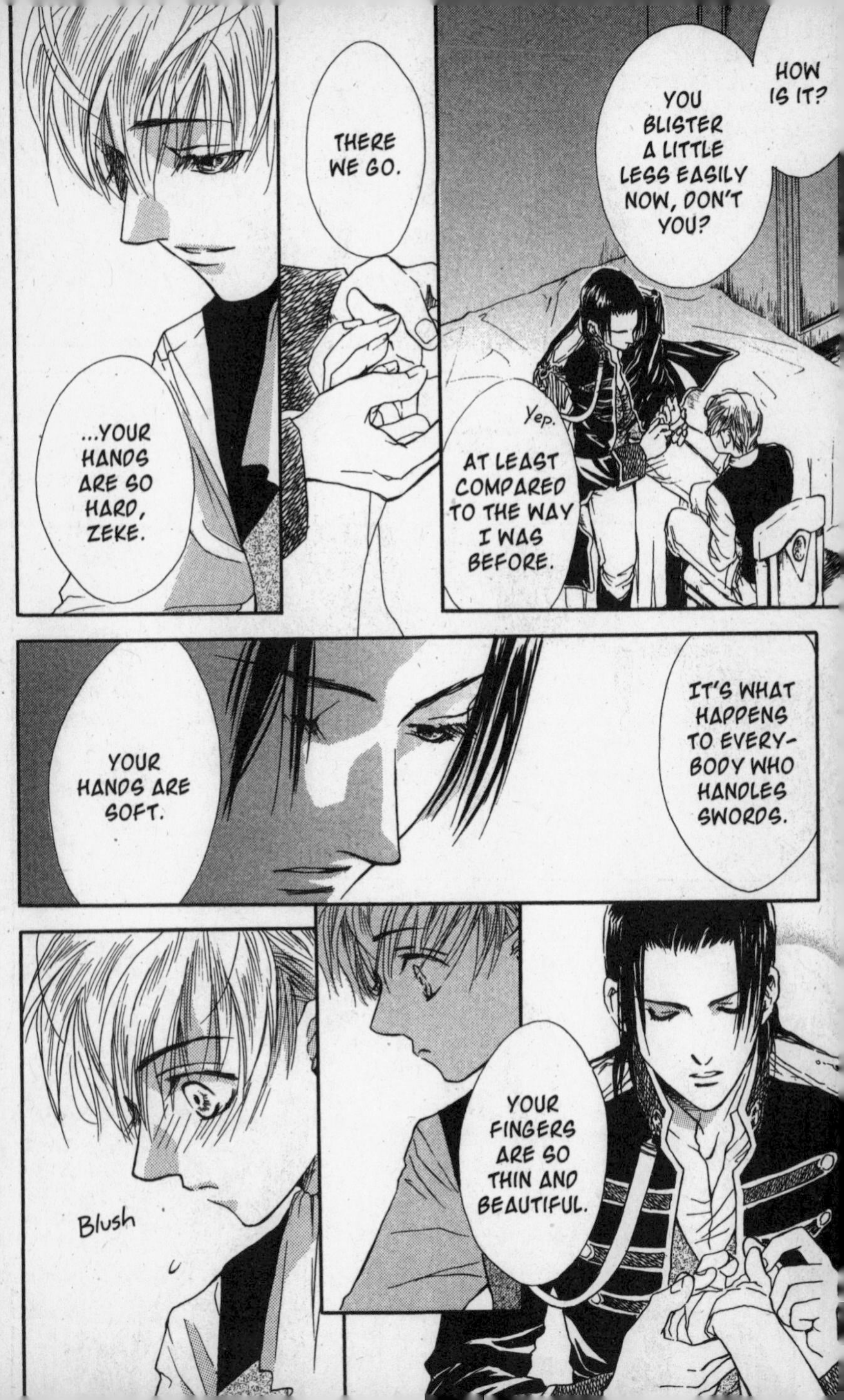
HOW IS IT?
YOU BLISTER A LITTLE LESS EASILY NOW, DON'T YOU?
Yep.
AT LEAST COMPARED TO THE WAY I WAS BEFORE.
THERE WE GO.
...YOUR HANDS ARE SO HARD, ZEKE.
IT'S WHAT HAPPENS TO EVERY-BODY WHO HANDLES SWORDS.
YOUR HANDS ARE SOFT.
YOUR FINGERS ARE SO THIN AND BEAUTIFUL.
Blush

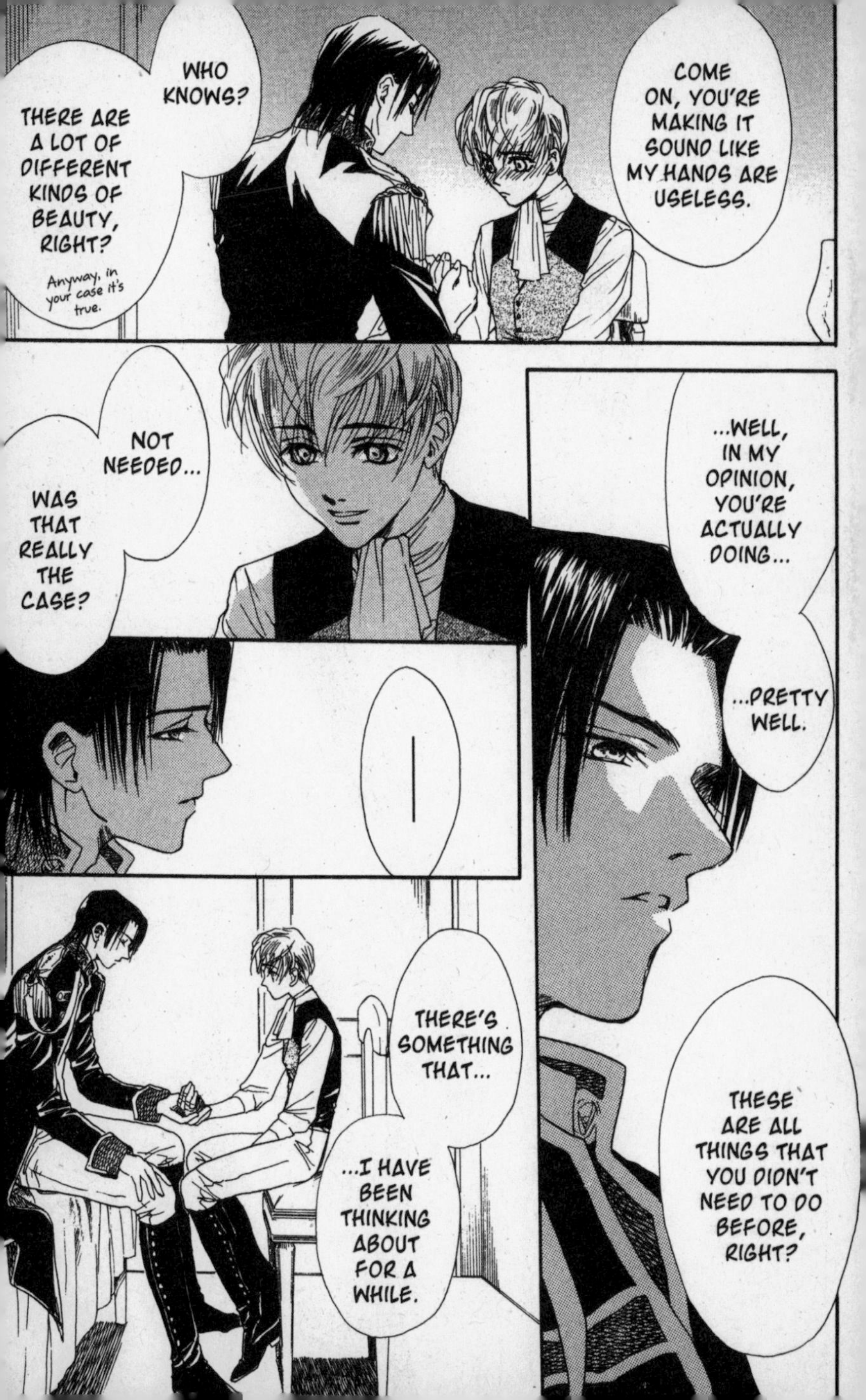
COME ON, YOU'RE MAKING IT SOUND LIKE MY HANDS ARE USELESS.
WHO KNOWS?
THERE ARE A LOT OF DIFFERENT KINDS OF BEAUTY, RIGHT?
Anyway, in your case it's true.
...WELL, IN MY OPINION, YOU'RE ACTUALLY DOING...
...PRETTY WELL.
THESE ARE ALL THINGS THAT YOU DIDN'T NEED TO DO BEFORE, RIGHT?
NOT NEEDED...
WAS THAT REALLY THE CASE?
THERE'S SOMETHING THAT...
...I HAVE BEEN THINKING ABOUT FOR A WHILE.

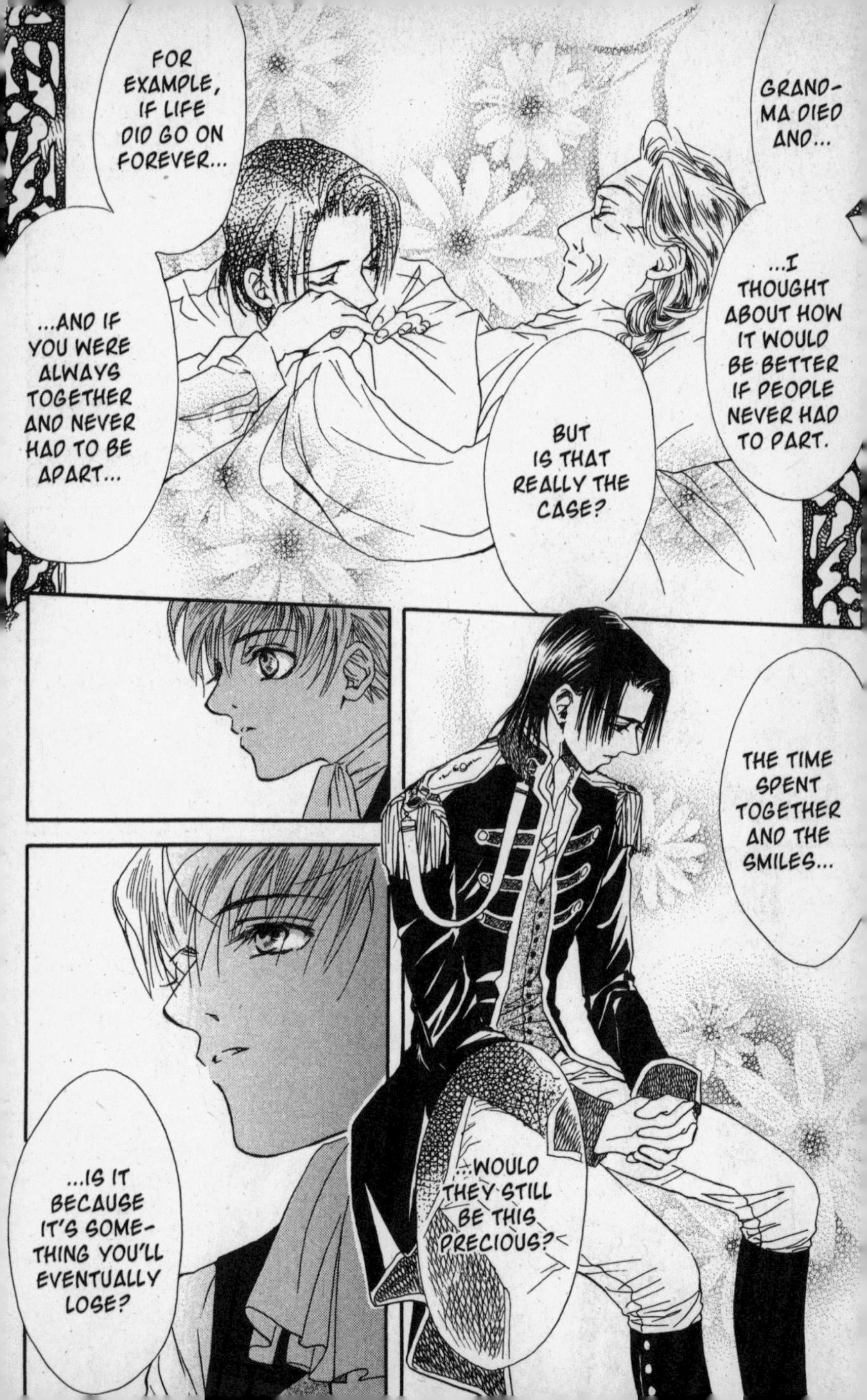
GRAND-MA DIED AND...
...I THOUGHT ABOUT HOW IT WOULD BE BETTER IF PEOPLE NEVER HAD TO PART.
BUT IS THAT REALLY THE CASE?
FOR EXAMPLE, IF LIFE DID GO ON FOREVER...
...AND IF YOU WERE ALWAYS TOGETHER AND NEVER HAD TO BE APART...
THE TIME SPENT TOGETHER AND THE SMILES...
...WOULD THEY STILL BE THIS PRECIOUS?
...IS IT BECAUSE IT'S SOME-THING YOU'LL EVENTUALLY LOSE?

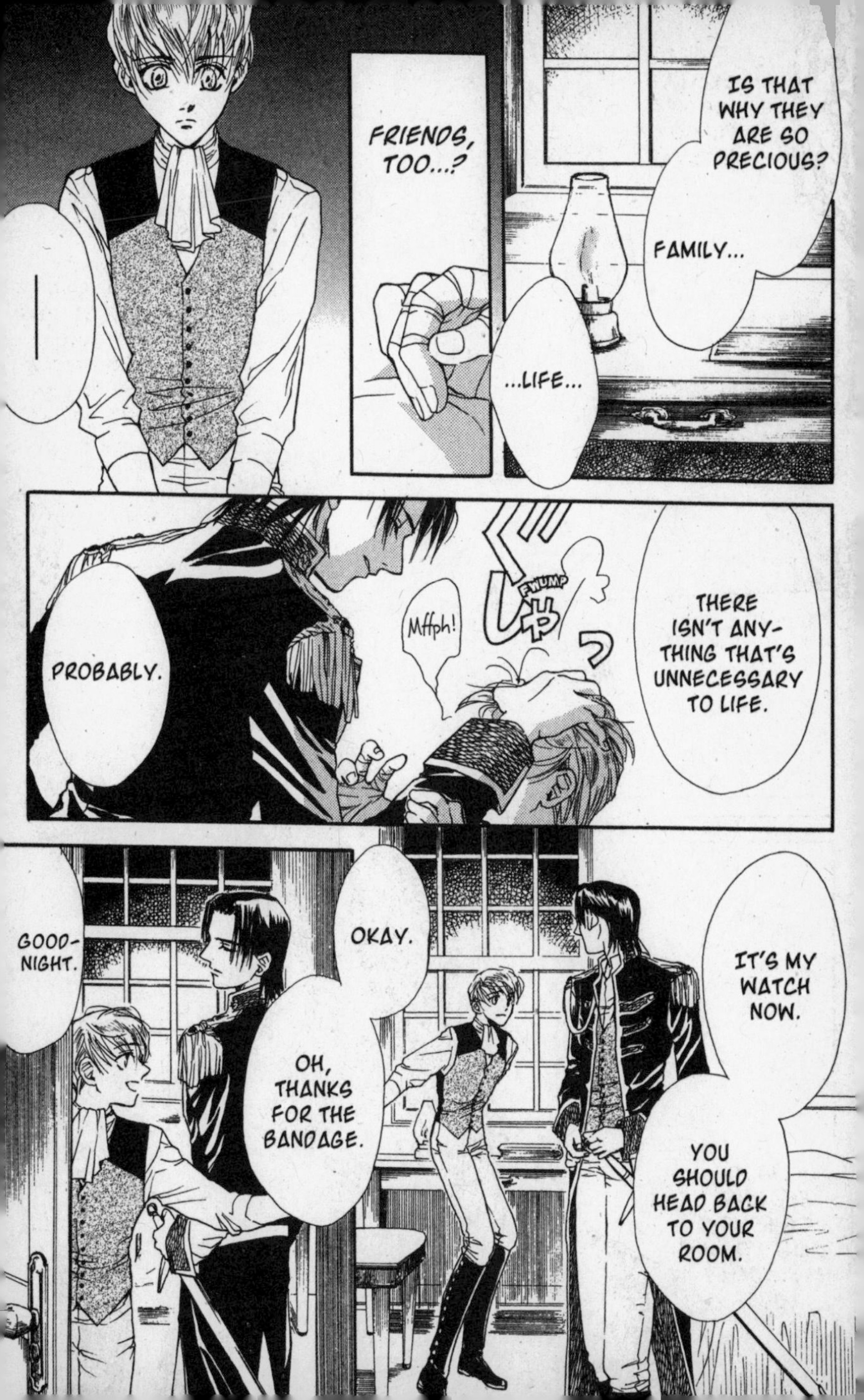
IS THAT WHY THEY ARE SO PRECIOUS?
FAMILY...
...LIFE...
FRIENDS, TOO...?
—
THERE ISN'T ANY-THING THAT'S UNNECESSARY TO LIFE.
FWUMP
Mffph!
PROBABLY.
IT'S MY WATCH NOW.
YOU SHOULD HEAD BACK TO YOUR ROOM.
OKAY.
OH, THANKS FOR THE BANDAGE.
GOOD-NIGHT.

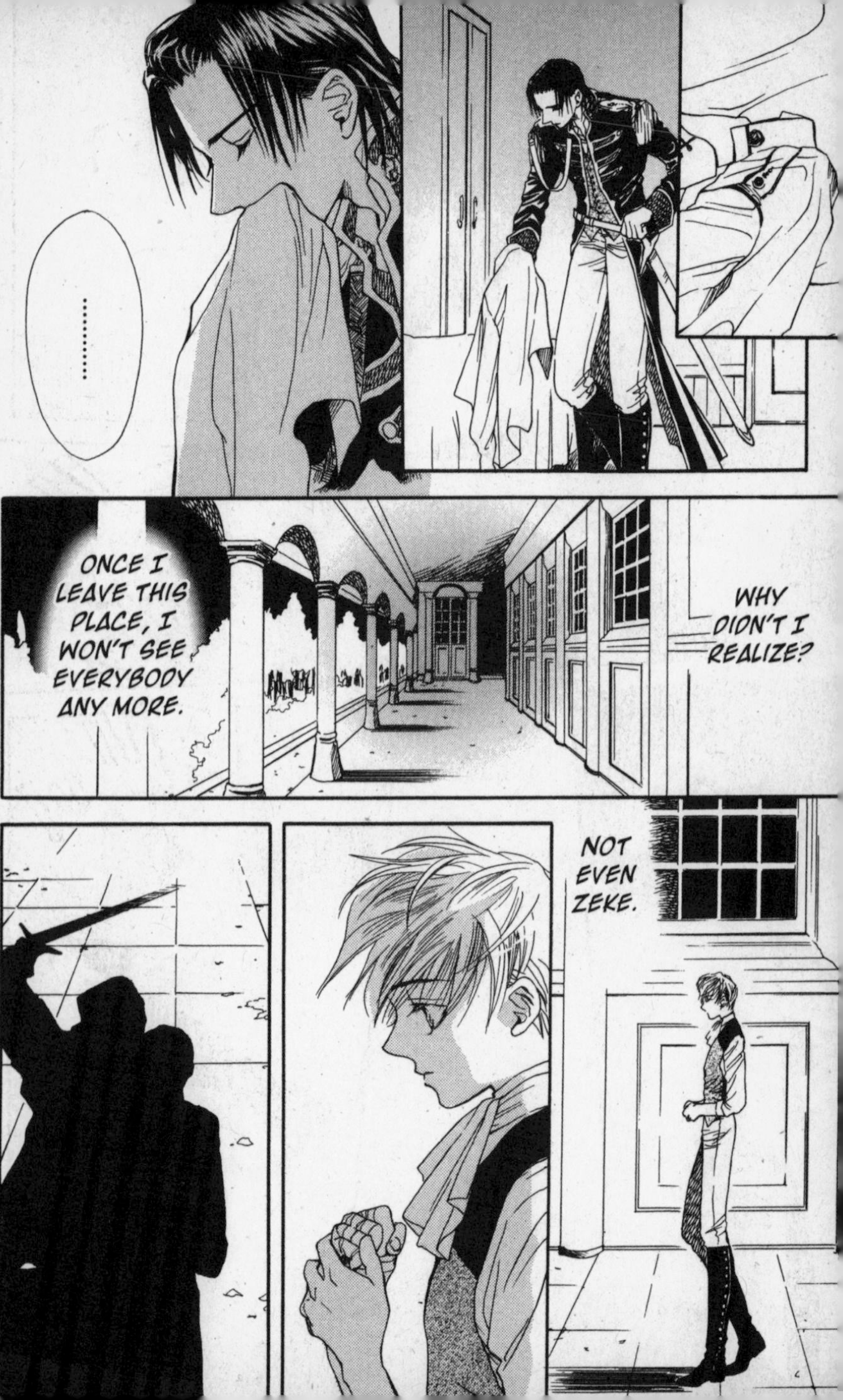
......
WHY DIDN'T I REALIZE?
ONCE I LEAVE THIS PLACE, I WON'T SEE EVERYBODY ANY MORE.
NOT EVEN ZEKE.

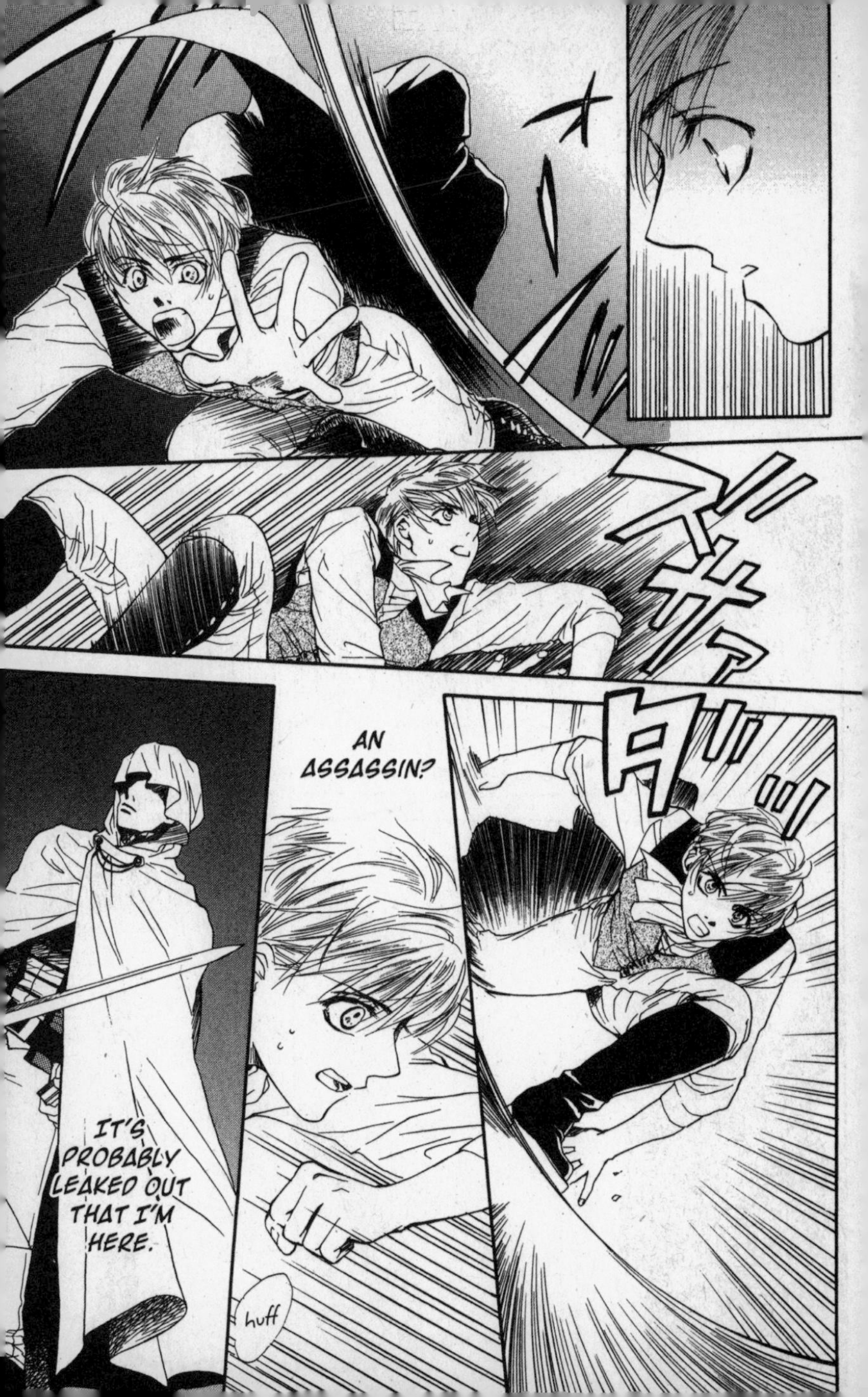
AN ASSASSIN?
huff
IT'S PROBABLY LEAKED OUT THAT I'M HERE.

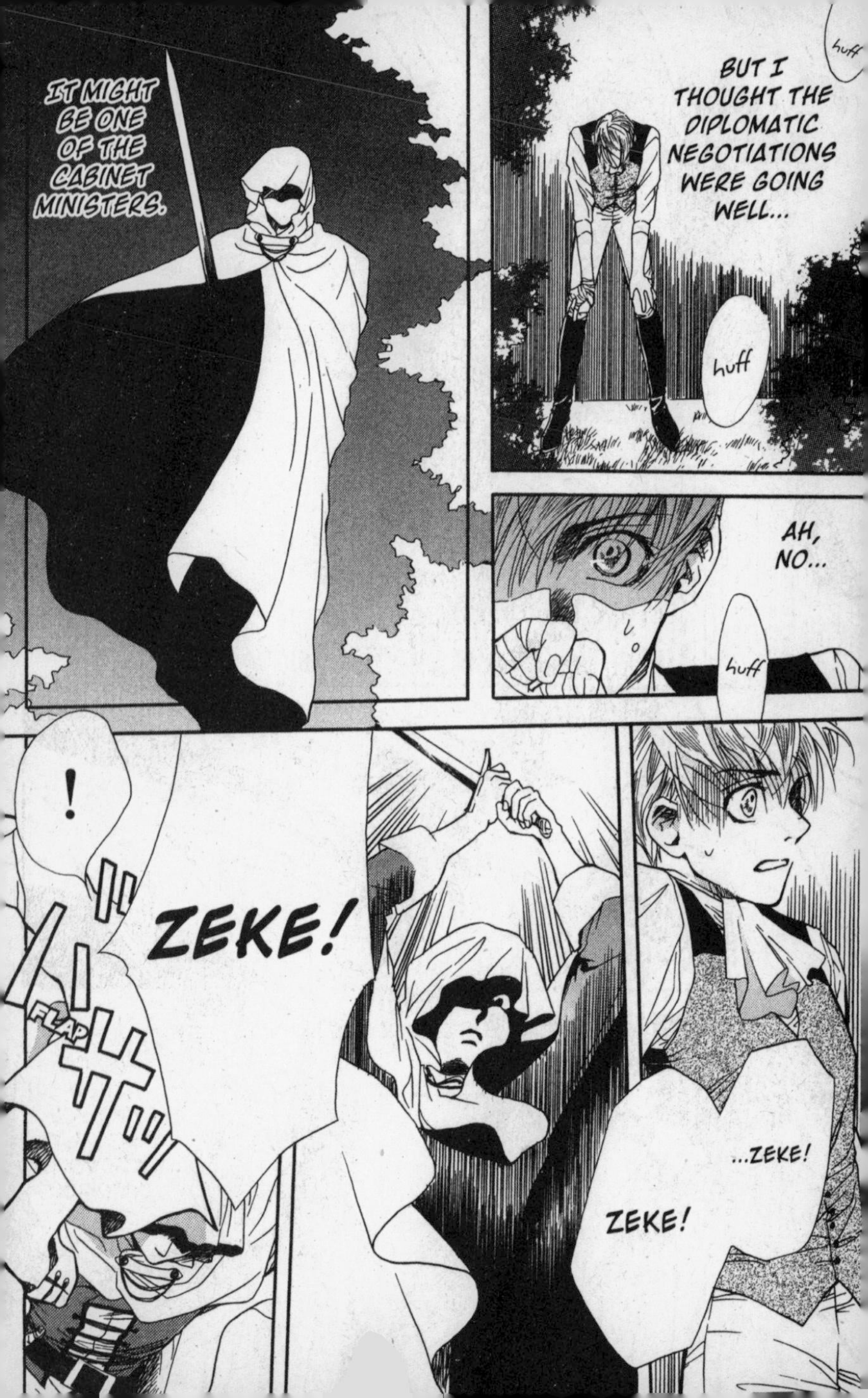
huff
BUT I THOUGHT THE DIPLOMATIC NEGOTIATIONS WERE GOING WELL...
huff
AH, NO...
huff
IT MIGHT BE ONE OF THE CABINET MINISTERS.
...ZEKE!
ZEKE!
!
ZEKE!
FLAP

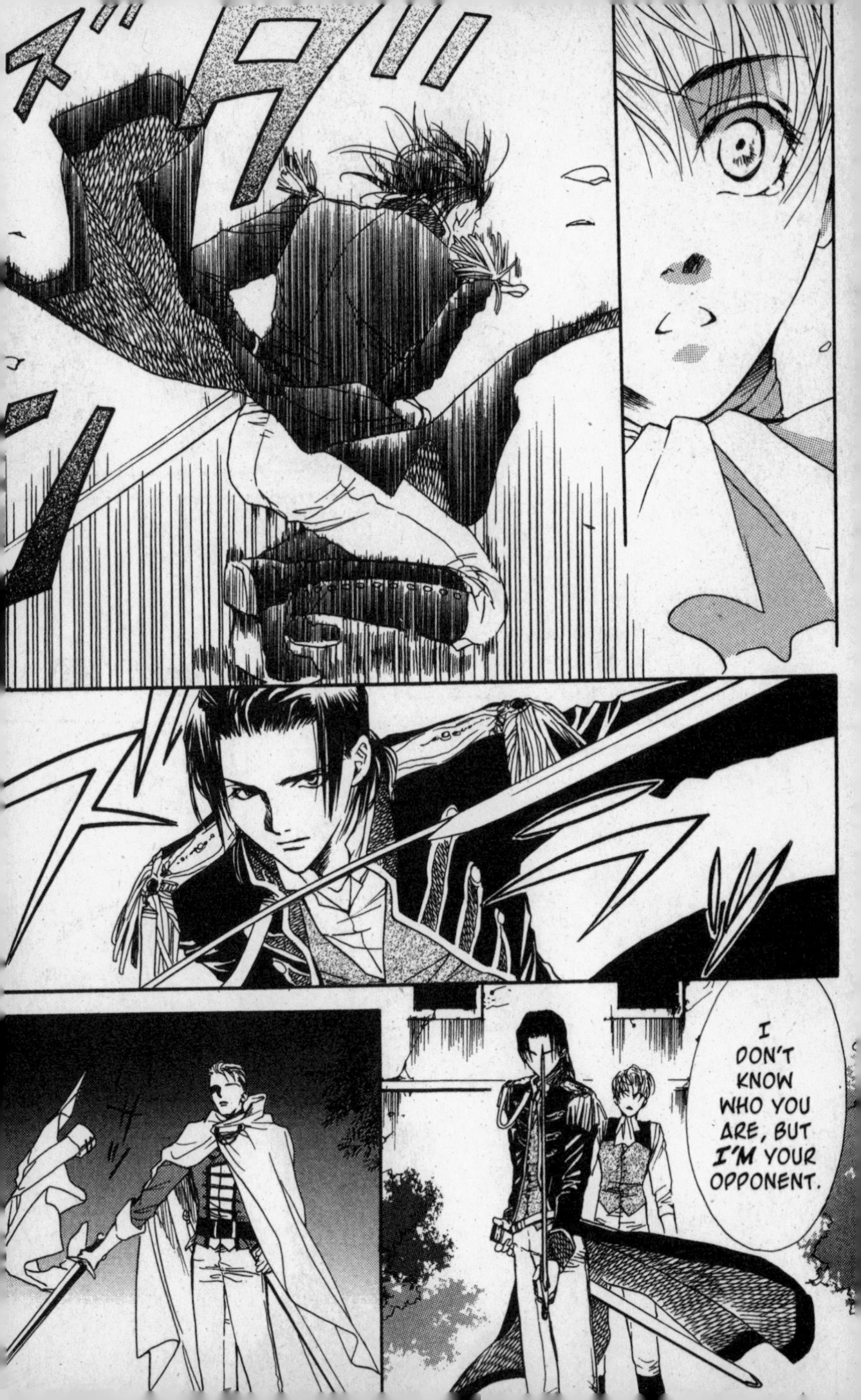
I DON'T KNOW WHO YOU ARE, BUT I'M YOUR OPPONENT.

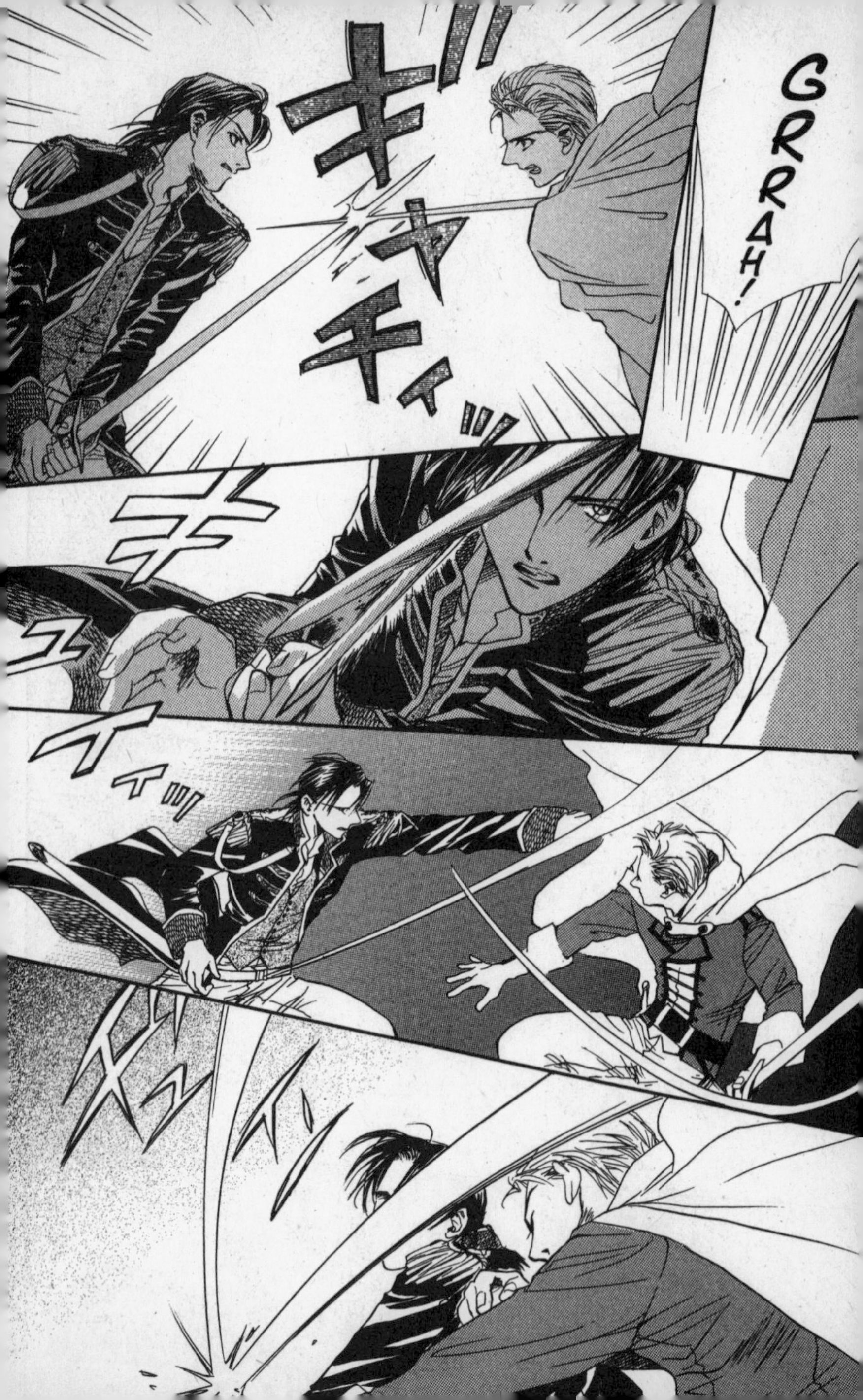
GRRAH!
ギャチィッ

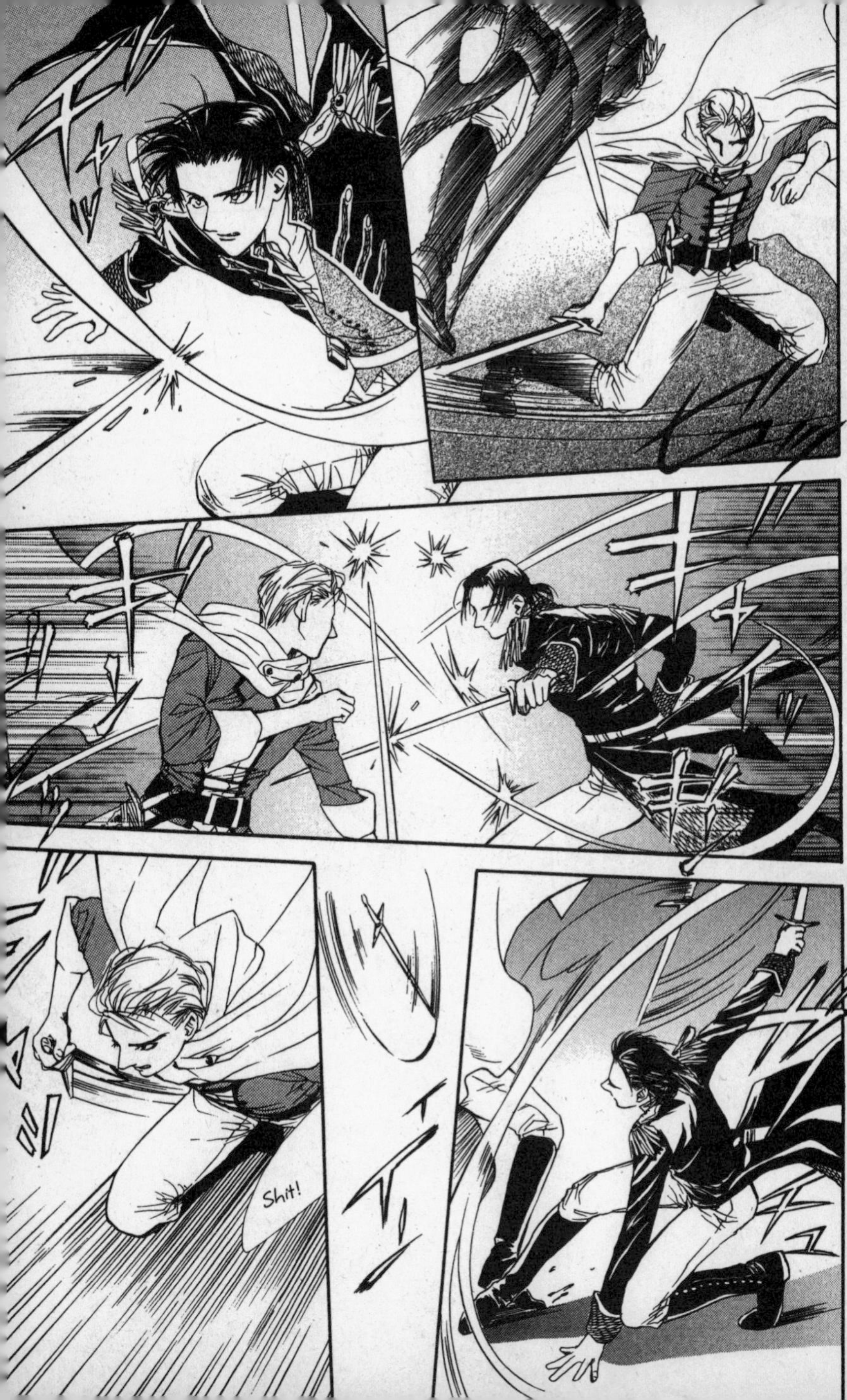
Shit!

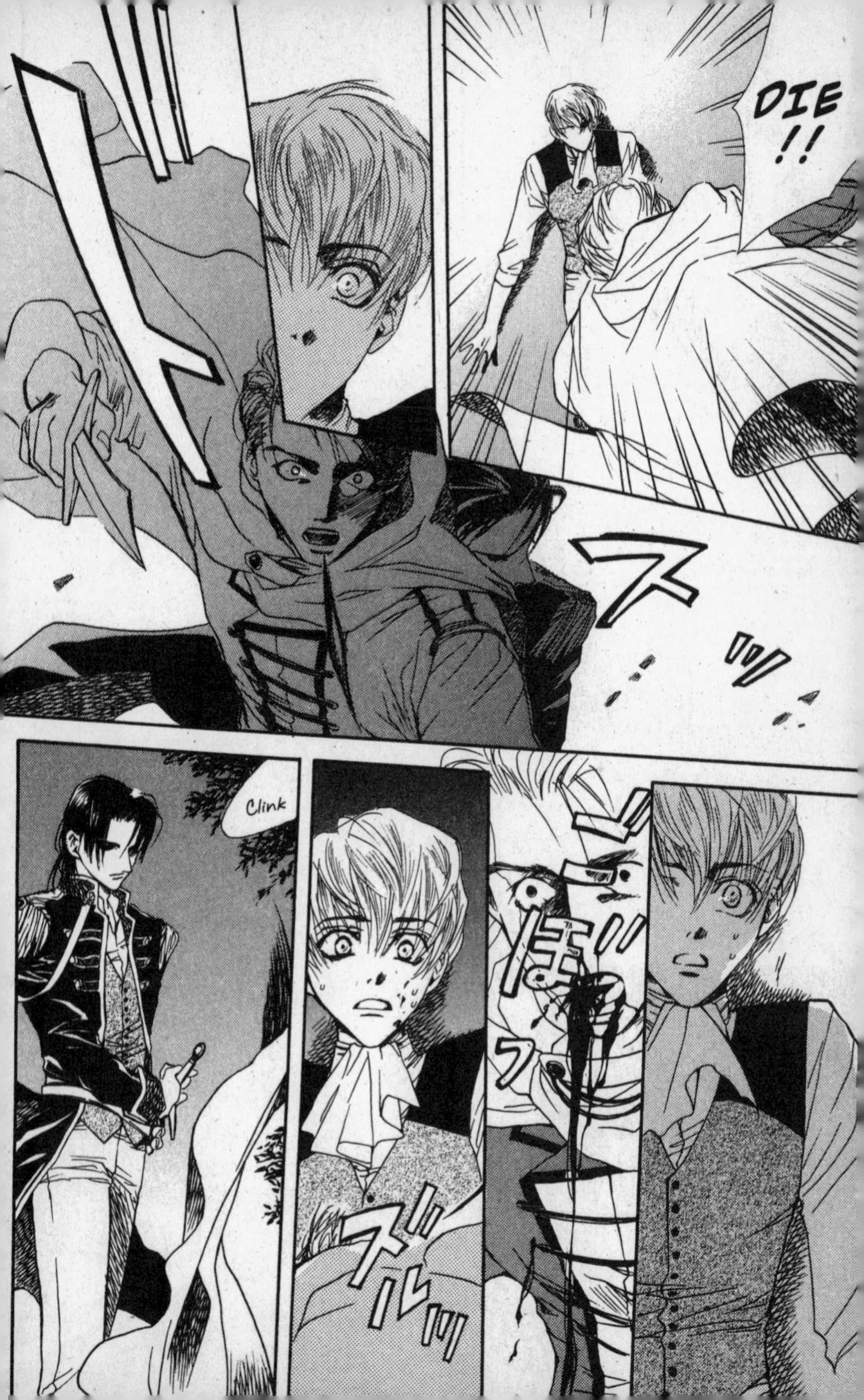
DIE !!
Clink

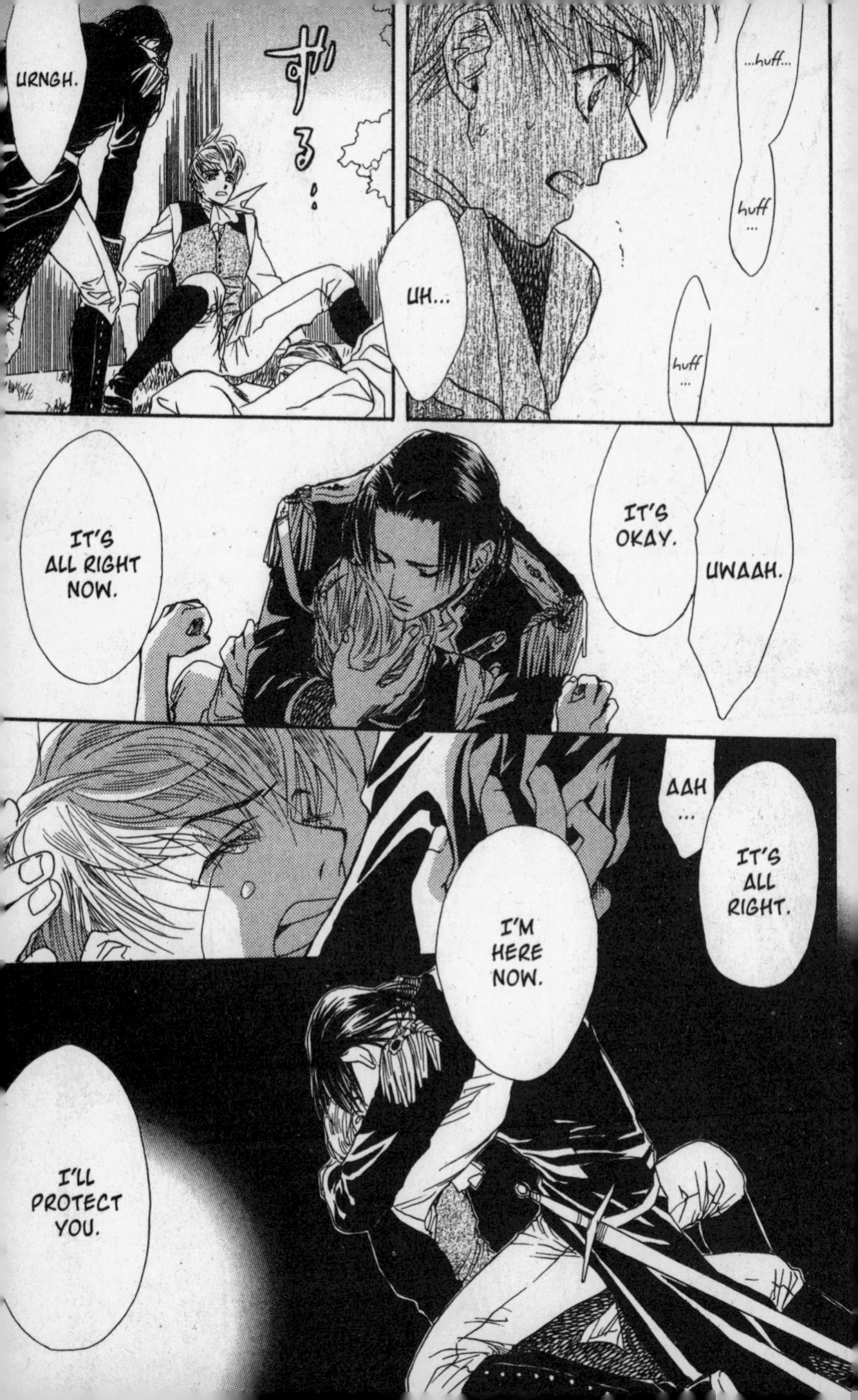
...huff...
huff ...
huff ...
UH...
ずる
URNGH.
UWAAH.
IT'S OKAY.
IT'S ALL RIGHT NOW.
AAH ...
IT'S ALL RIGHT.
I'M HERE NOW.
I'LL PROTECT YOU.

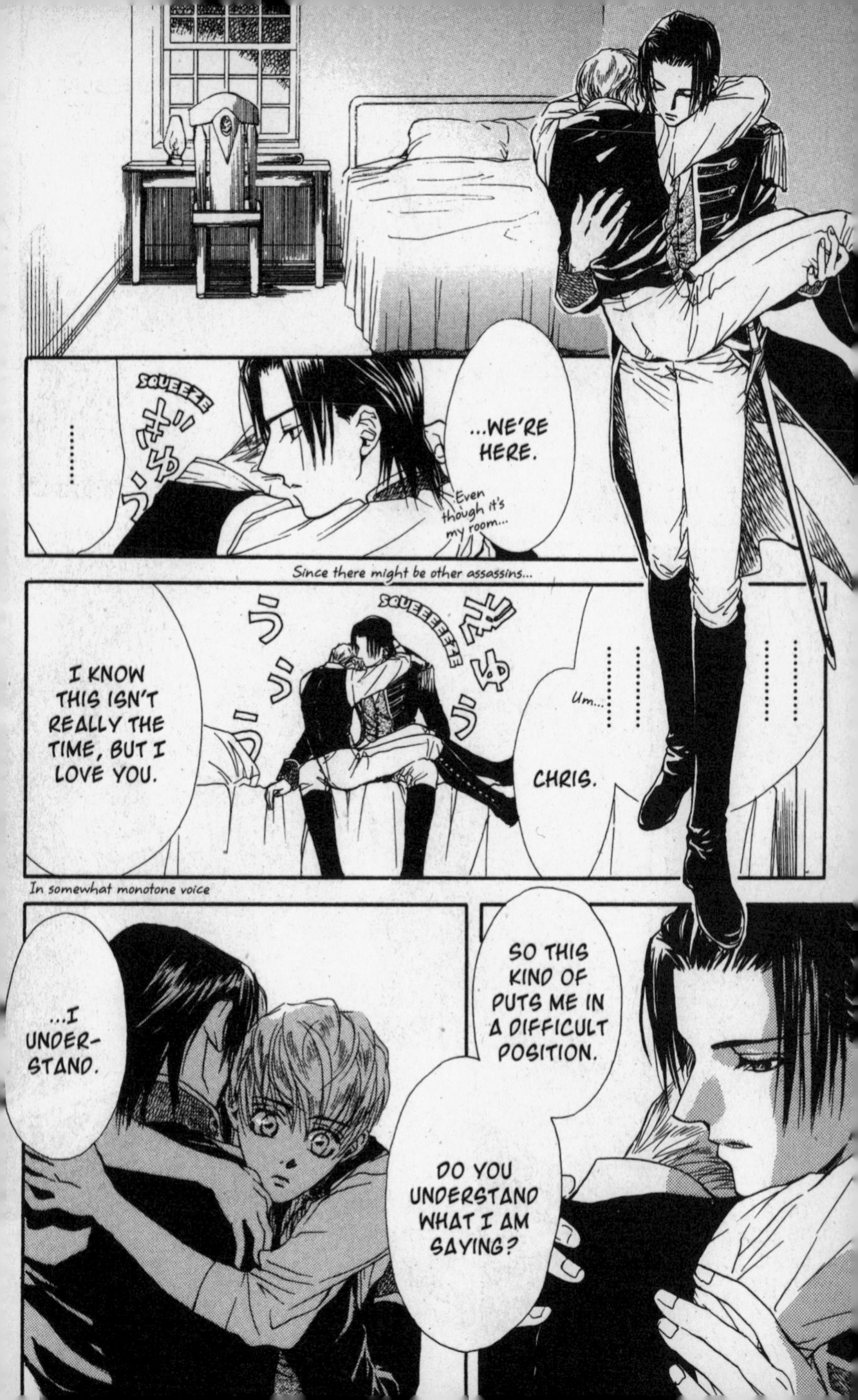
...WE'RE HERE.
Even though it's my room...
SQUEEZE ぎゅう
......
Since there might be other assassins...
......
Um...
......
CHRIS.
SQUEEEEEEZE ぎゅう
I KNOW THIS ISN'T REALLY THE TIME, BUT I LOVE YOU.
In somewhat monotone voice
SO THIS KIND OF PUTS ME IN A DIFFICULT POSITION.
DO YOU UNDERSTAND WHAT I AM SAYING?
...I UNDERSTAND.

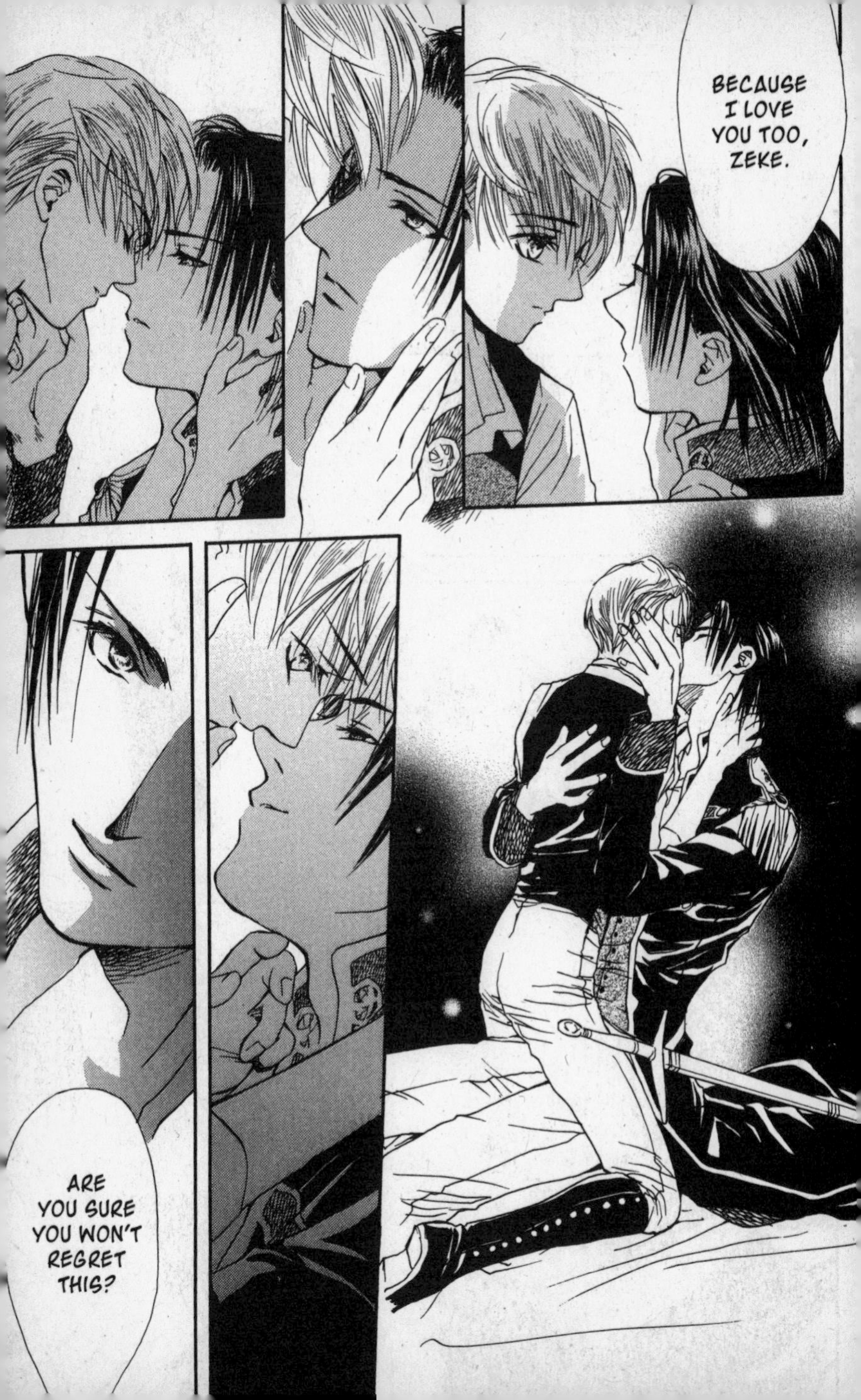
BECAUSE I LOVE YOU TOO, ZEKE.
ARE YOU SURE YOU WON'T REGRET THIS?

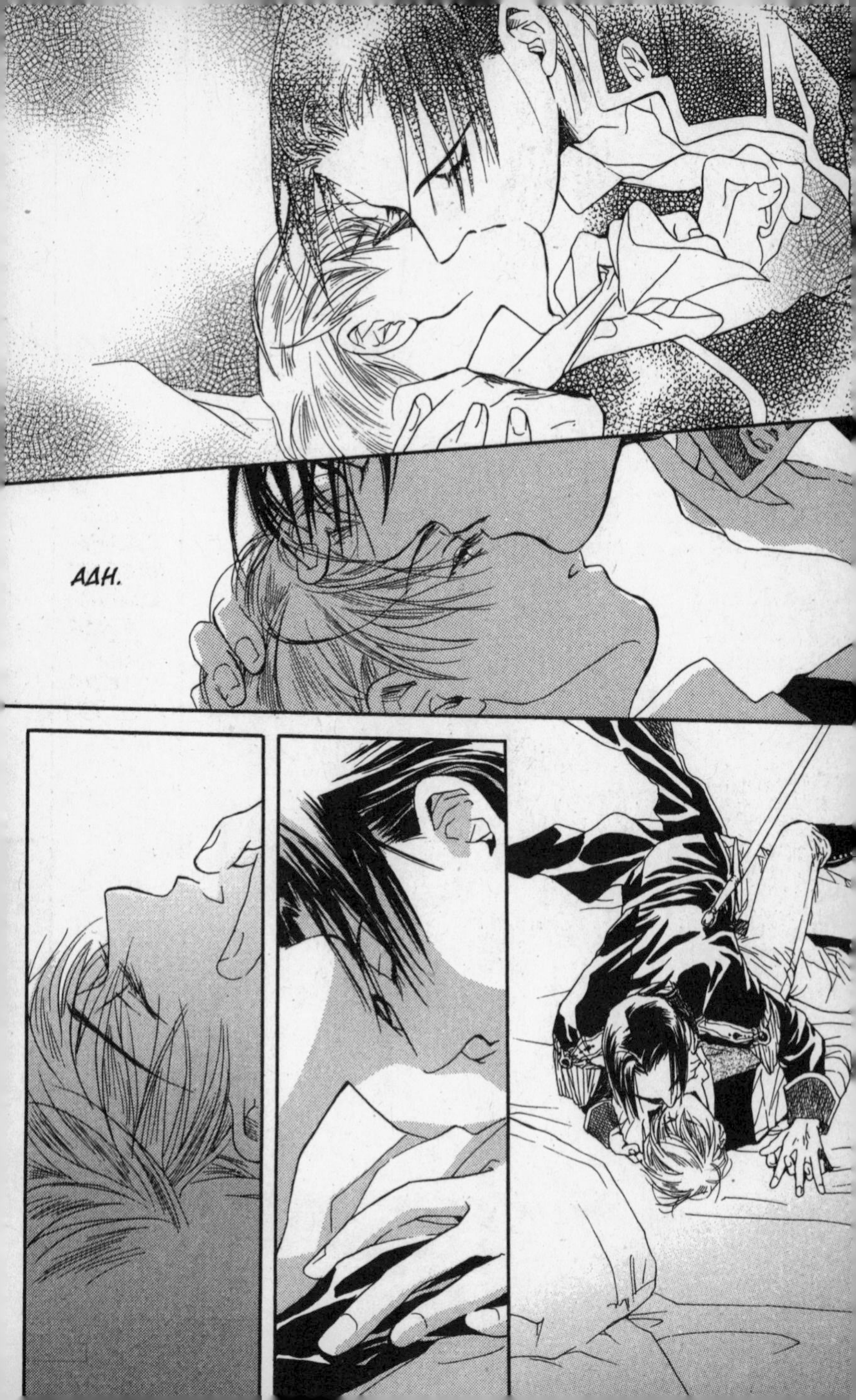
AAH.

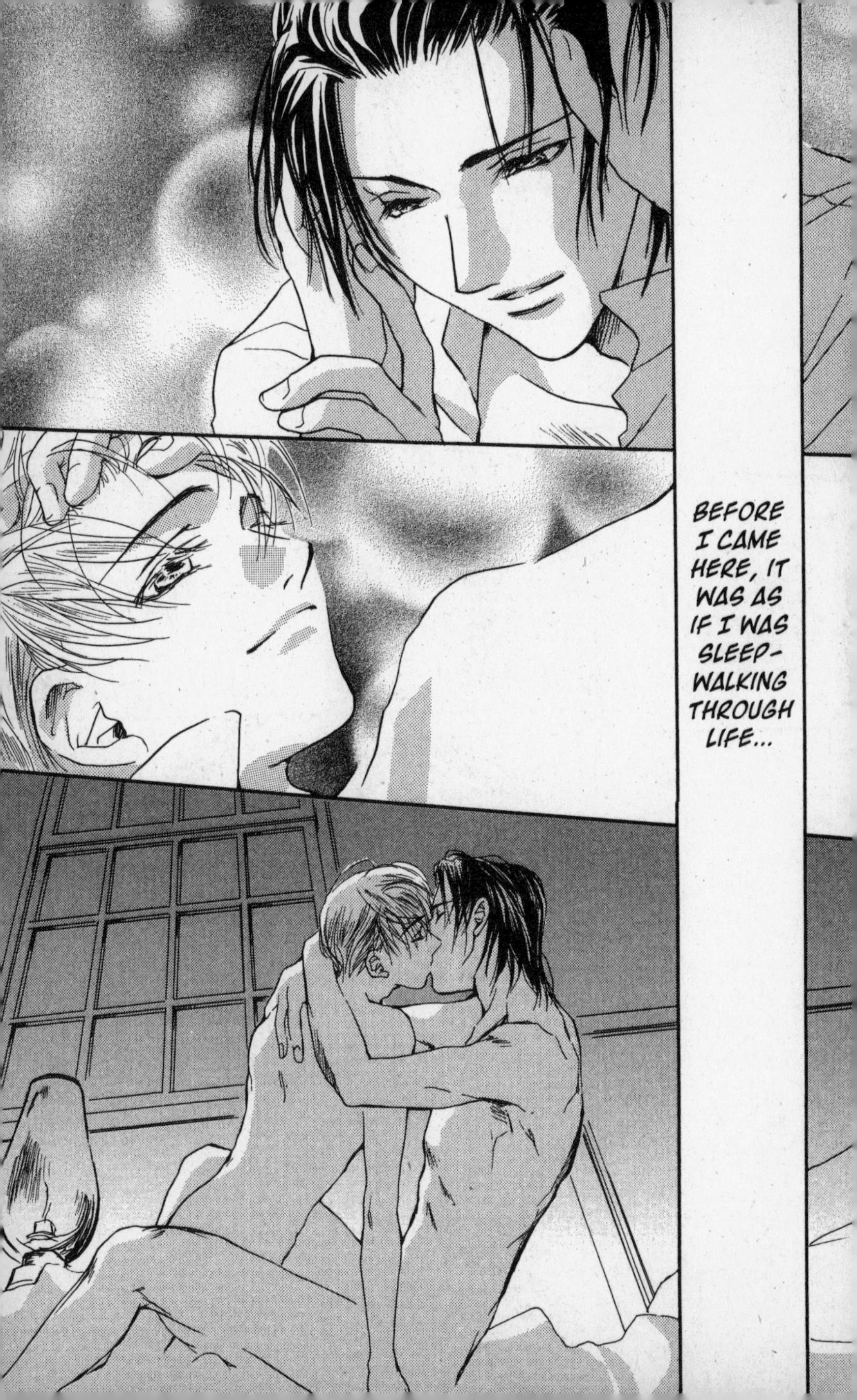
BEFORE I CAME HERE, IT WAS AS IF I WAS SLEEP-WALKING THROUGH LIFE...

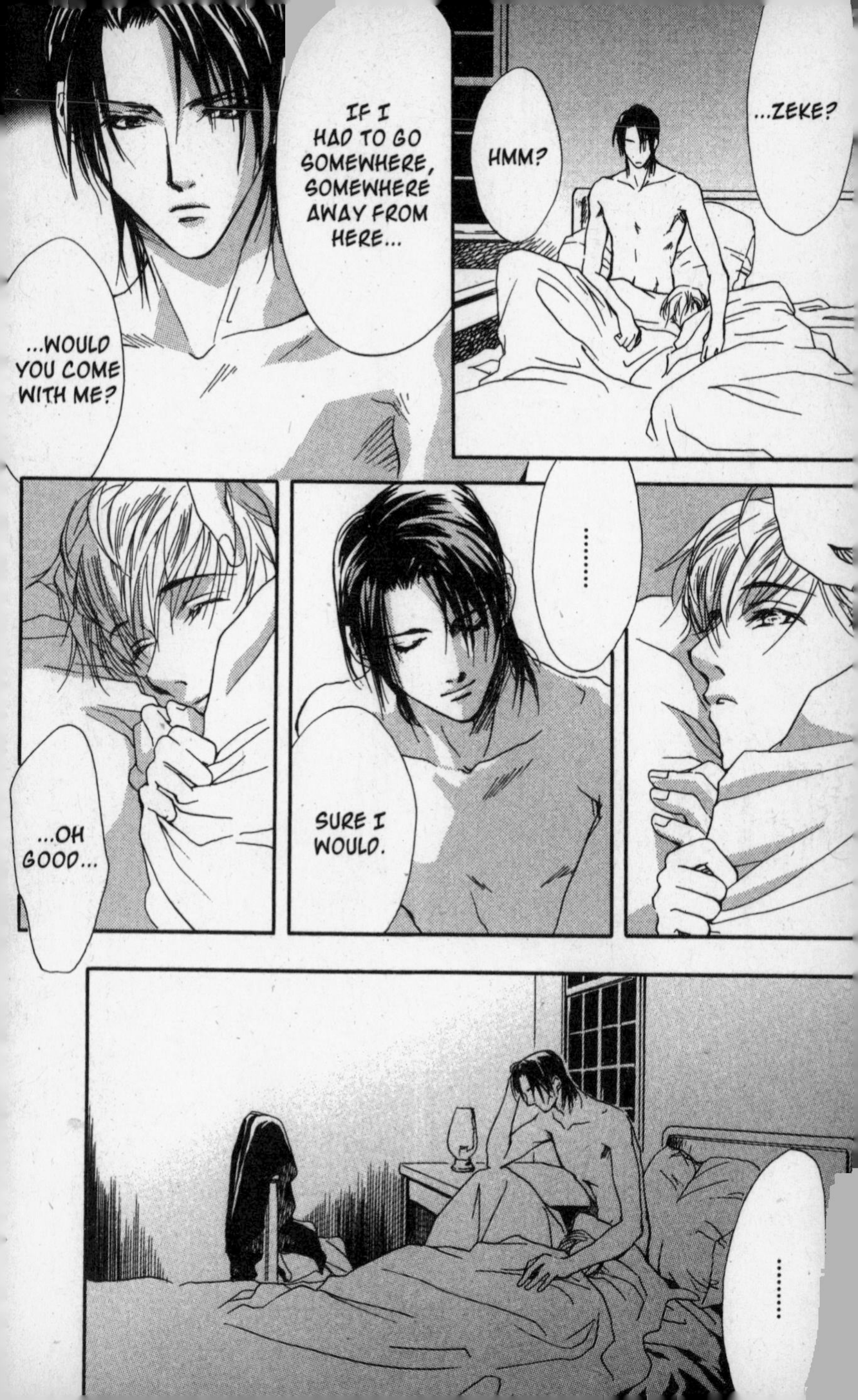
...ZEKE?
HMM?
IF I HAD TO GO SOMEWHERE, SOMEWHERE AWAY FROM HERE...
...WOULD YOU COME WITH ME?
......
SURE I WOULD.
...OH GOOD...
......

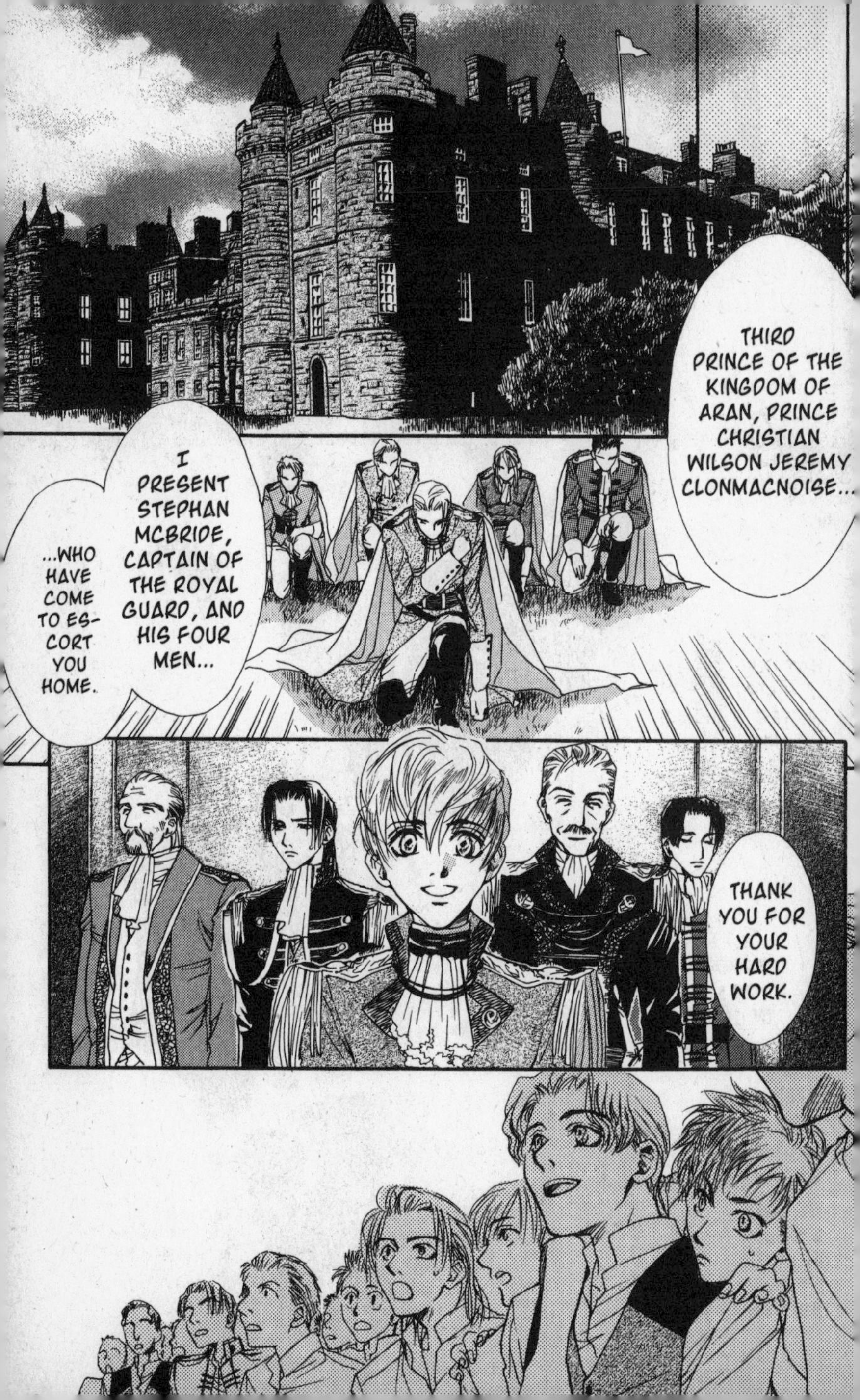

THIRD PRINCE OF THE KINGDOM OF ARAN, PRINCE CHRISTIAN WILSON JEREMY CLONMACNOISE...
I PRESENT STEPHAN MCBRIDE, CAPTAIN OF THE ROYAL GUARD, AND HIS FOUR MEN...
...WHO HAVE COME TO ES-CORT YOU HOME.
THANK YOU FOR YOUR HARD WORK.

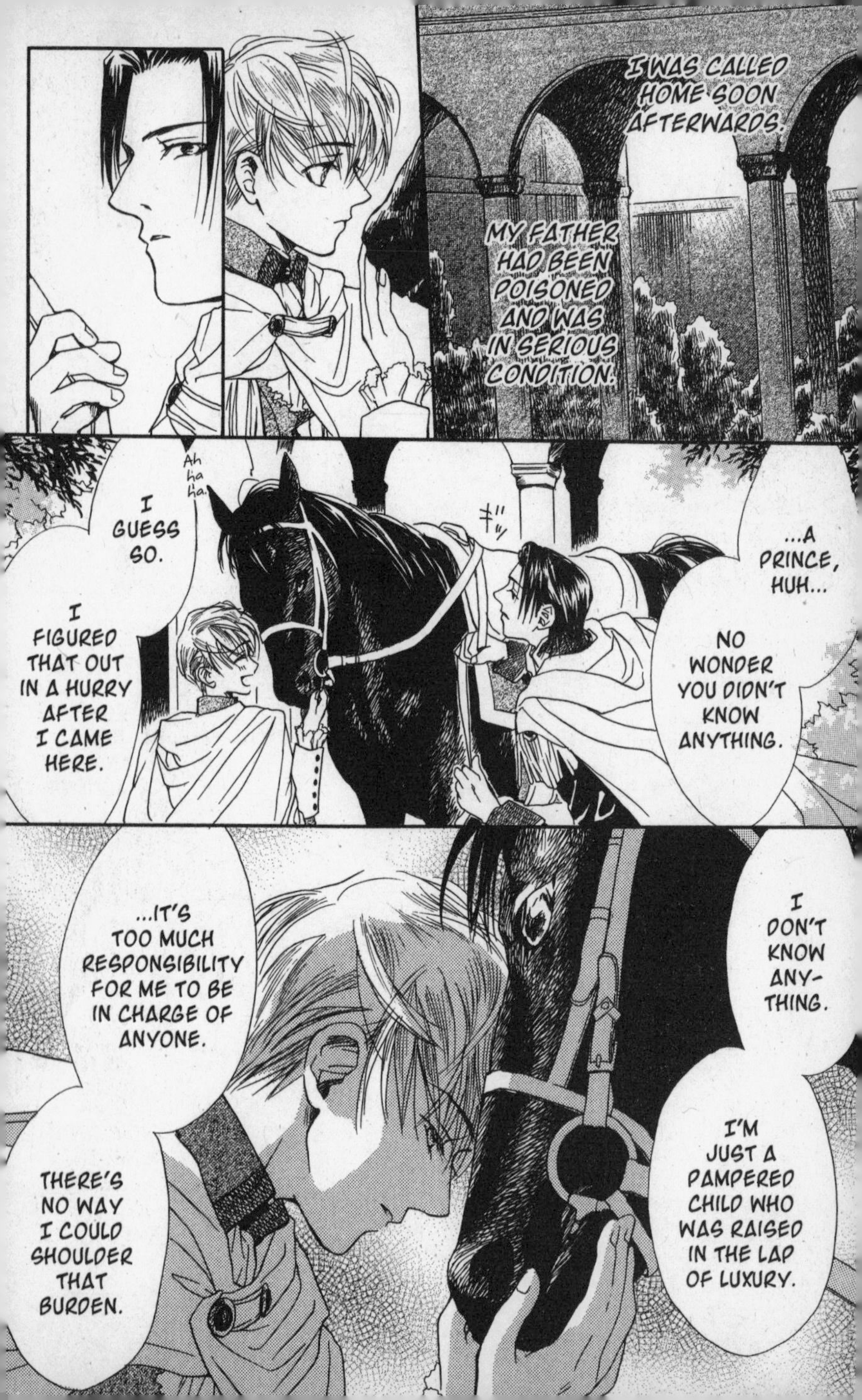
I WAS CALLED HOME SOON AFTERWARDS.
MY FATHER HAD BEEN POISONED AND WAS IN SERIOUS CONDITION.
...A PRINCE, HUH...
NO WONDER YOU DIDN'T KNOW ANYTHING.
ギッ
Ah ha ha.
I GUESS SO.
I FIGURED THAT OUT IN A HURRY AFTER I CAME HERE.
I DON'T KNOW ANY-THING.
I'M JUST A PAMPERED CHILD WHO WAS RAISED IN THE LAP OF LUXURY.
...IT'S TOO MUCH RESPONSIBILITY FOR ME TO BE IN CHARGE OF ANYONE.
THERE'S NO WAY I COULD SHOULDER THAT BURDEN.

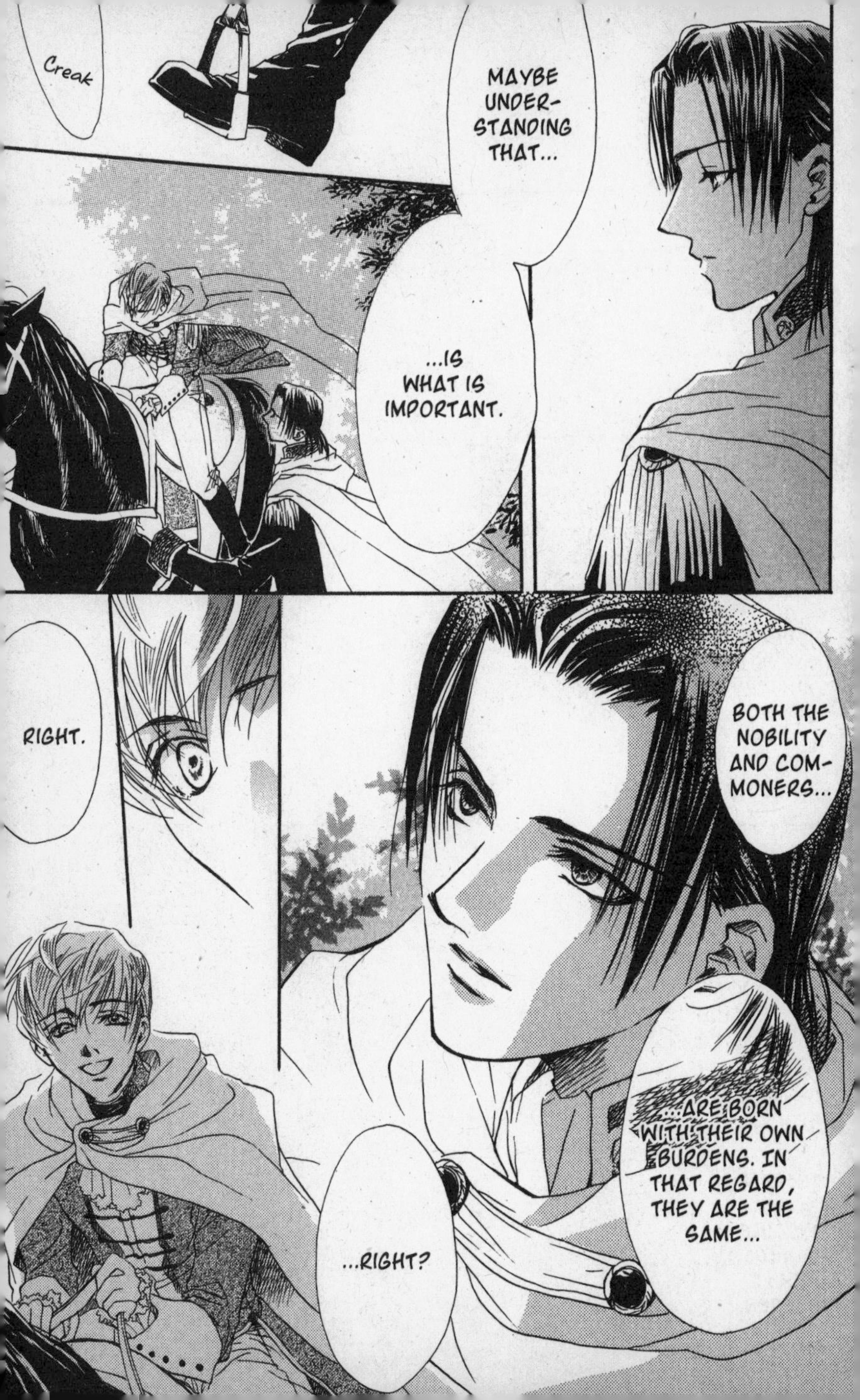
MAYBE UNDER-STANDING THAT...
...IS WHAT IS IMPORTANT.
Creak
BOTH THE NOBILITY AND COM-MONERS...
...ARE BORN WITH THEIR OWN BURDENS. IN THAT REGARD, THEY ARE THE SAME...
...RIGHT?
RIGHT.

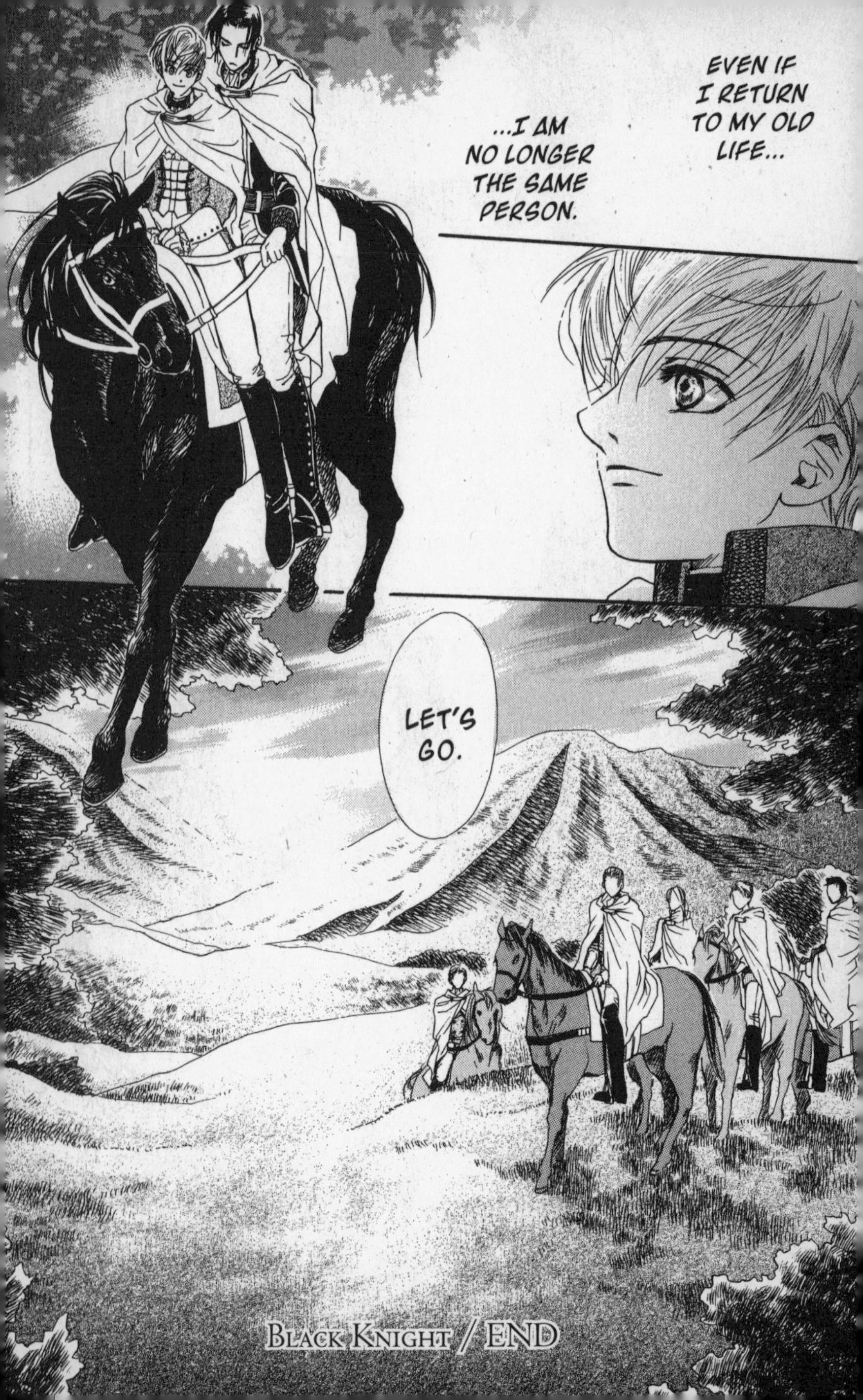
EVEN IF I RETURN TO MY OLD LIFE...
...I AM NO LONGER THE SAME PERSON.
LET'S GO.
BLACK KNIGHT / END

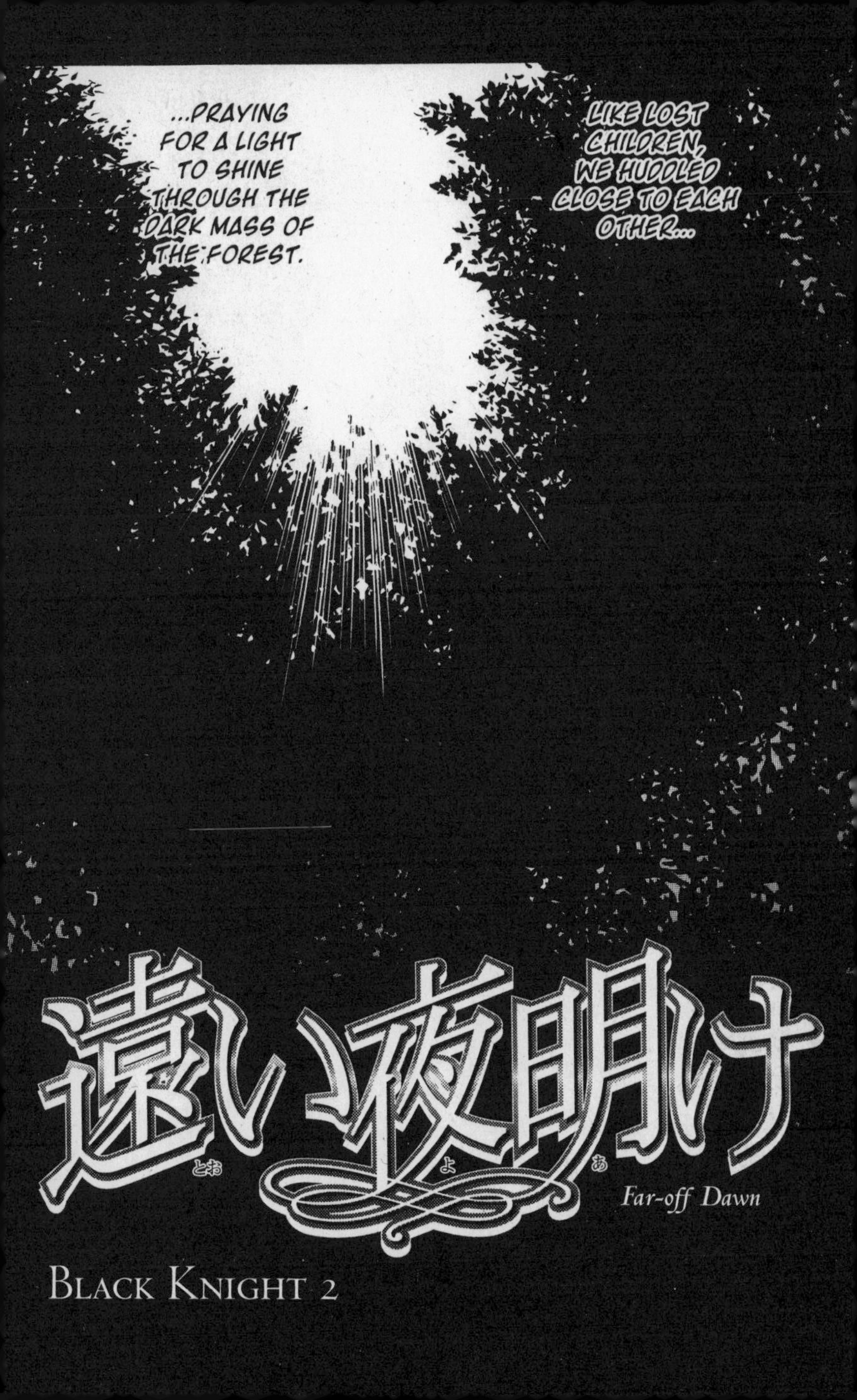
LIKE LOST CHILDREN, WE HUDDLED CLOSE TO EACH OTHER...
...PRAYING FOR A LIGHT TO SHINE THROUGH THE DARK MASS OF THE FOREST.
遠い夜明け
Far-off Dawn
BLACK KNIGHT 2

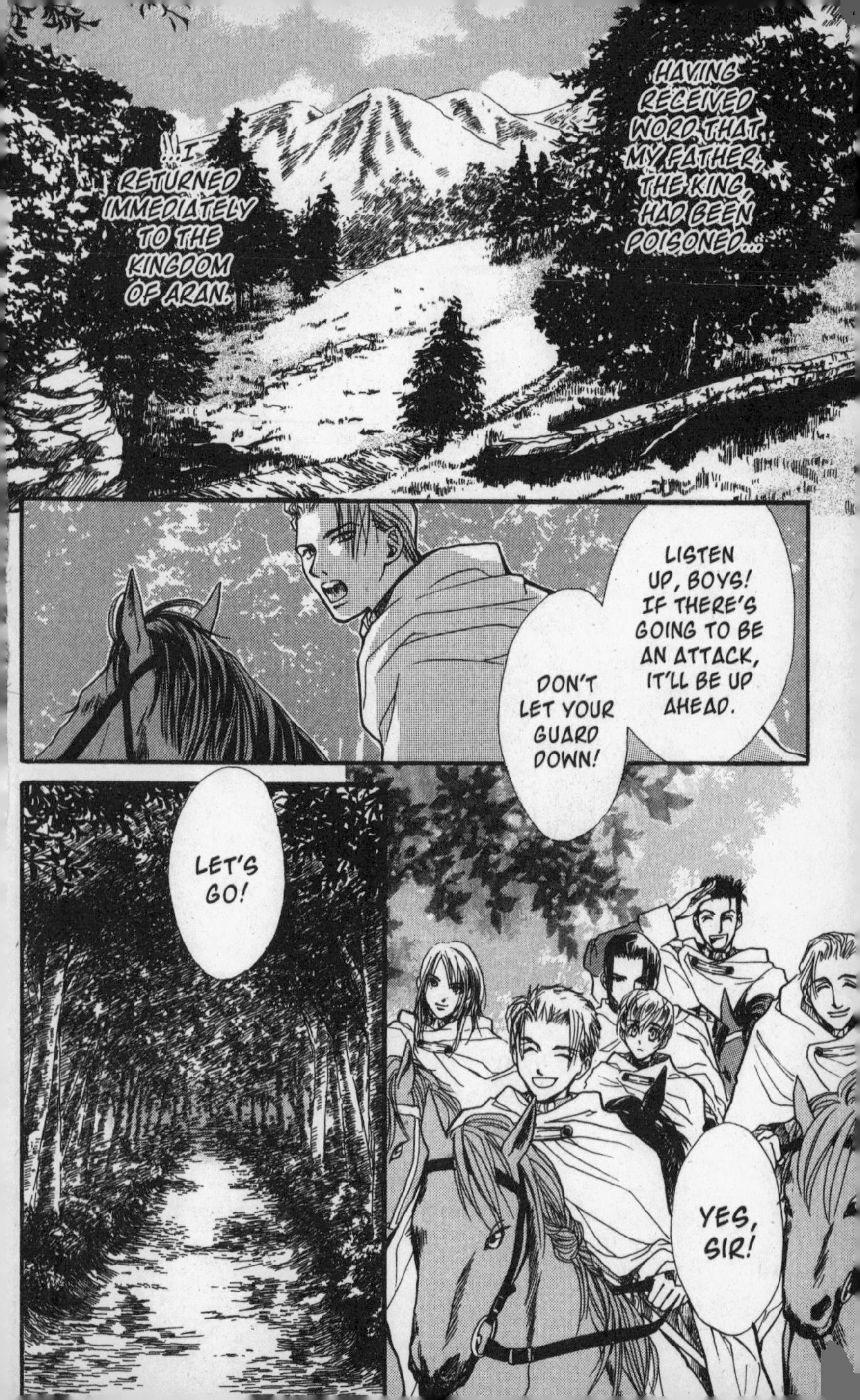
HAVING RECEIVED WORD THAT MY FATHER, THE KING, HAD BEEN POISONED...
...I RETURNED IMMEDIATELY TO THE KINGDOM OF ARAN.
LISTEN UP, BOYS! IF THERE'S GOING TO BE AN ATTACK, IT'LL BE UP AHEAD.
DON'T LET YOUR GUARD DOWN!
YES, SIR!
LET'S GO!

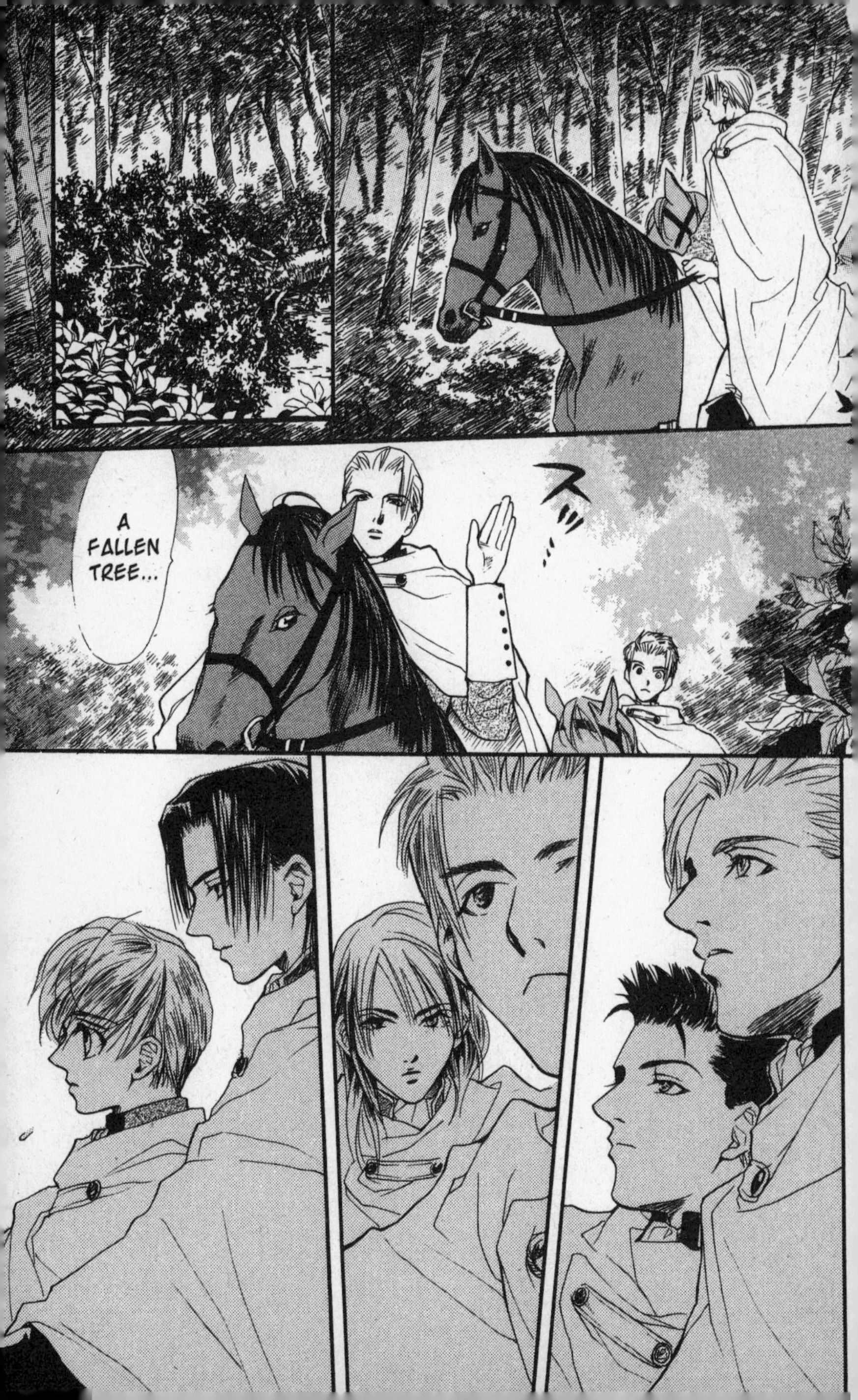
A FALLEN TREE...

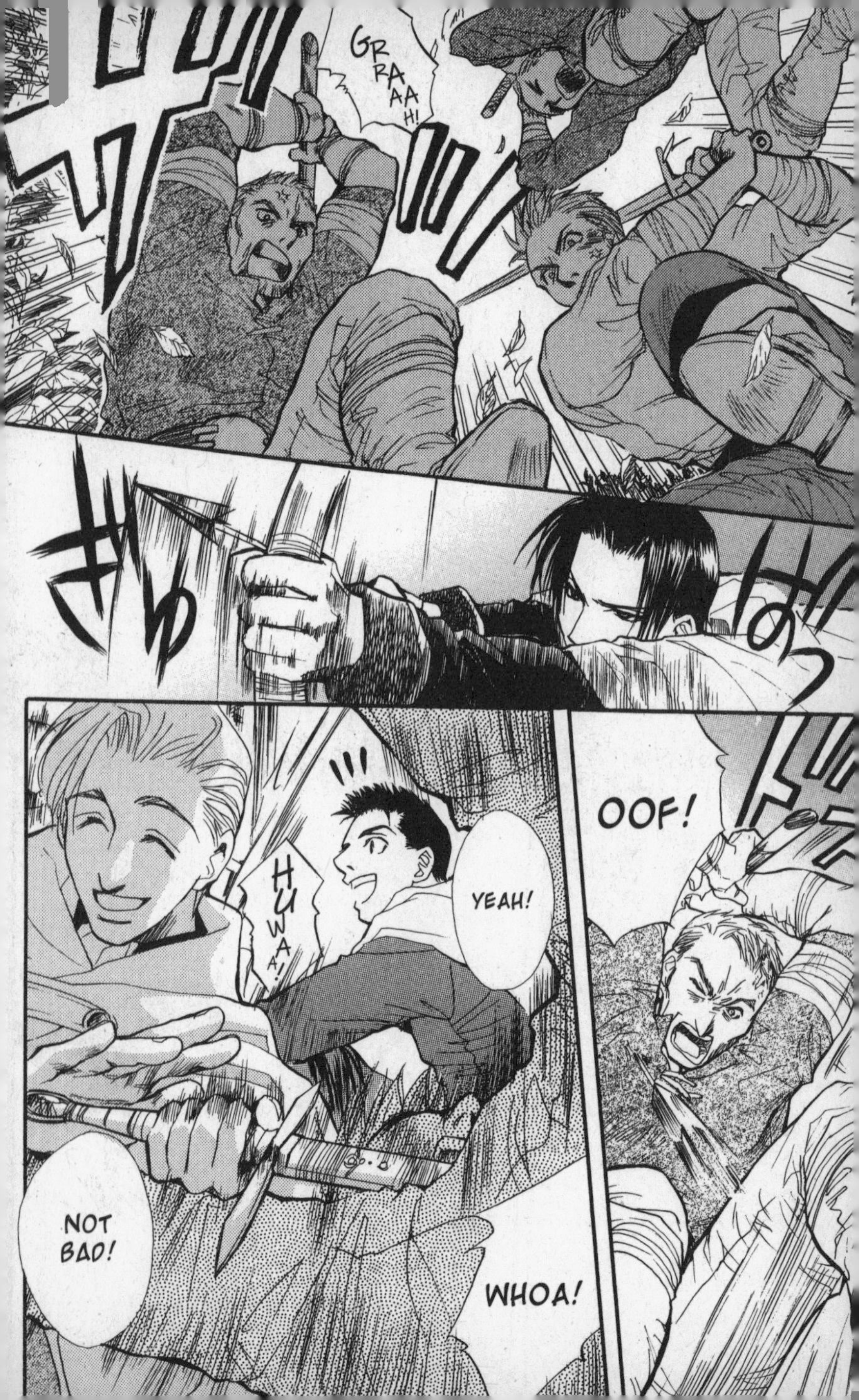
GRAAAH!
OOF!
YEAH!
HUWAA!
NOT BAD!
WHOA!

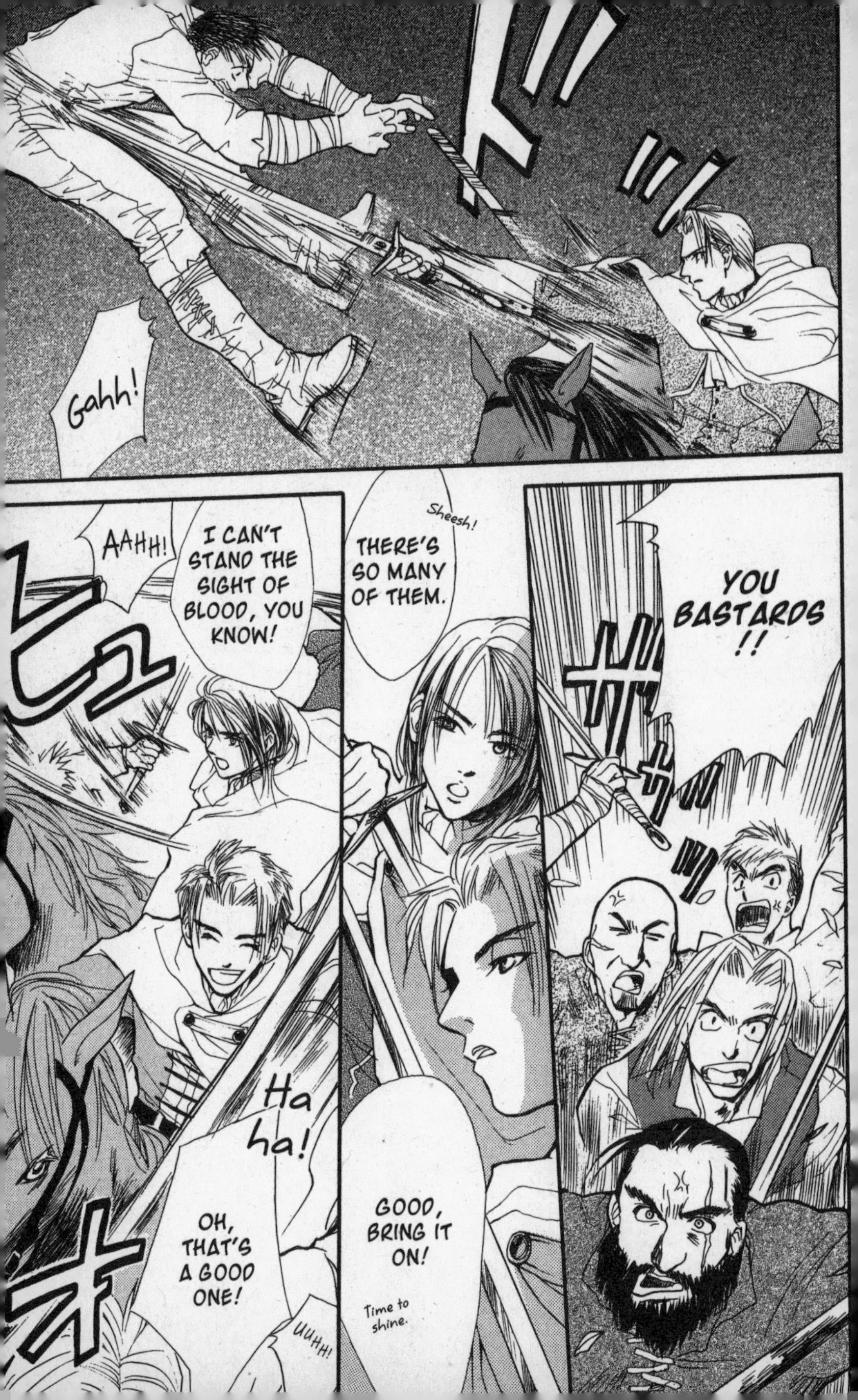
Gahh!
YOU BASTARDS !!
Sheesh!
THERE'S SO MANY OF THEM.
GOOD, BRING IT ON!
Time to shine.
AAHH!
I CAN'T STAND THE SIGHT OF BLOOD, YOU KNOW!
Ha ha!
OH, THAT'S A GOOD ONE!
UUHH!

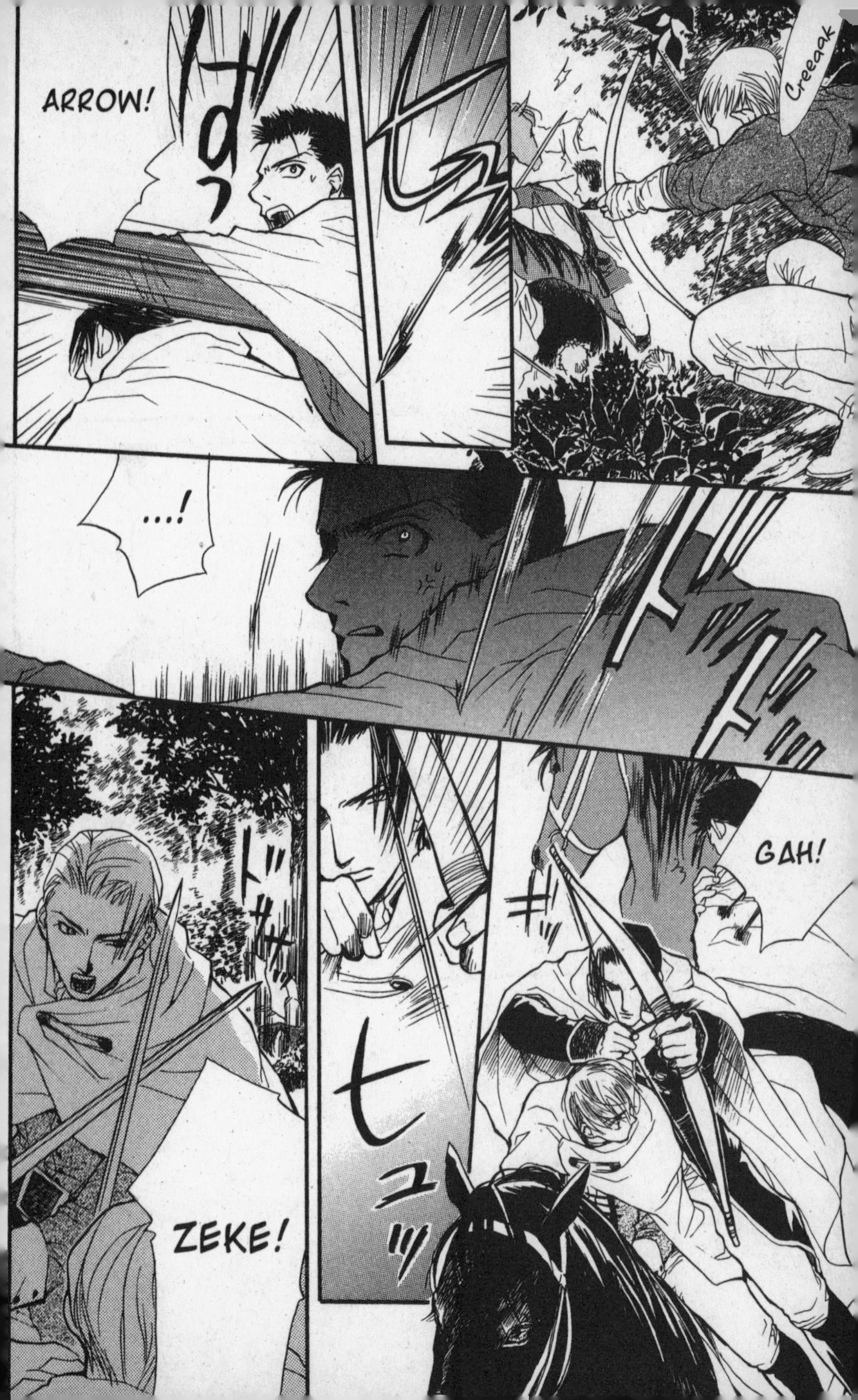
Creeaak
ARROW!
...!
GAH!
ZEKE!

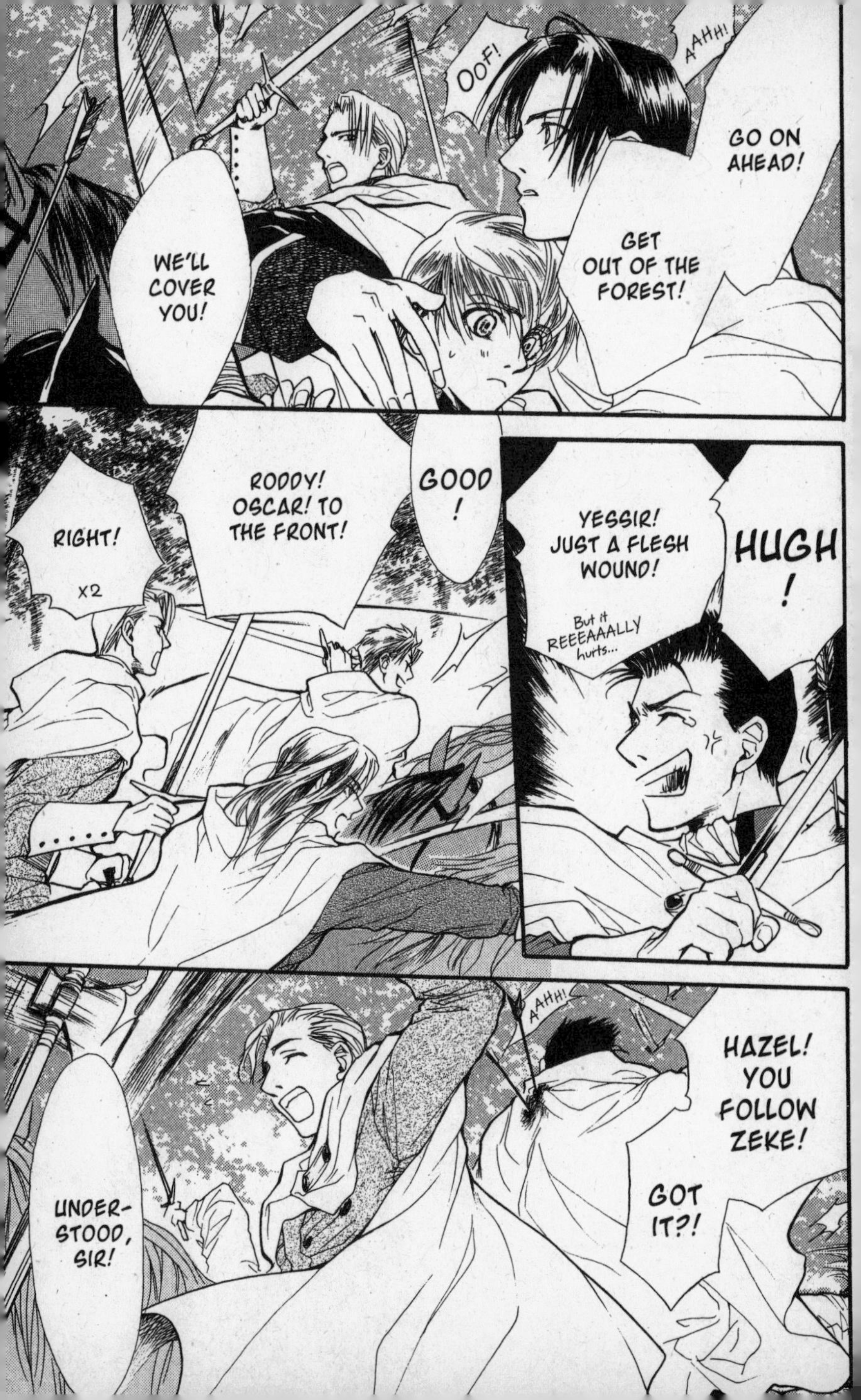
AAHH!
GO ON AHEAD!
OOF!
GET OUT OF THE FOREST!
WE'LL COVER YOU!
HUGH!
YESSIR! JUST A FLESH WOUND!
But it REEEAAALLY hurts...
GOOD!
RODDY! OSCAR! TO THE FRONT!
RIGHT!
X2
HAZEL! YOU FOLLOW ZEKE!
AAHH!
GOT IT?!
UNDER-STOOD, SIR!

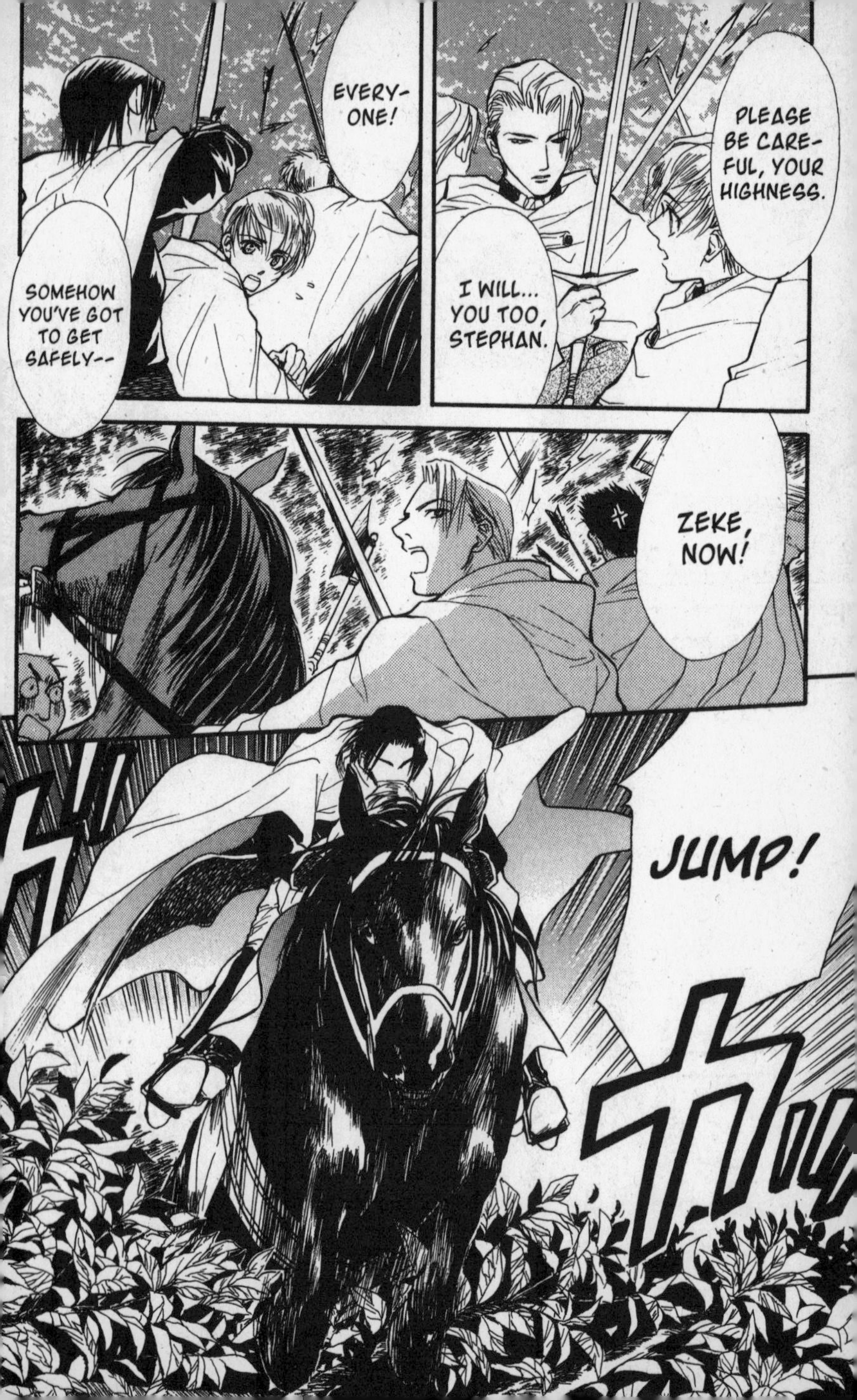
PLEASE BE CARE-FUL, YOUR HIGHNESS.
I WILL... YOU TOO, STEPHAN.
EVERY-ONE!
SOMEHOW YOU'VE GOT TO GET SAFELY--
ZEKE, NOW!
JUMP!

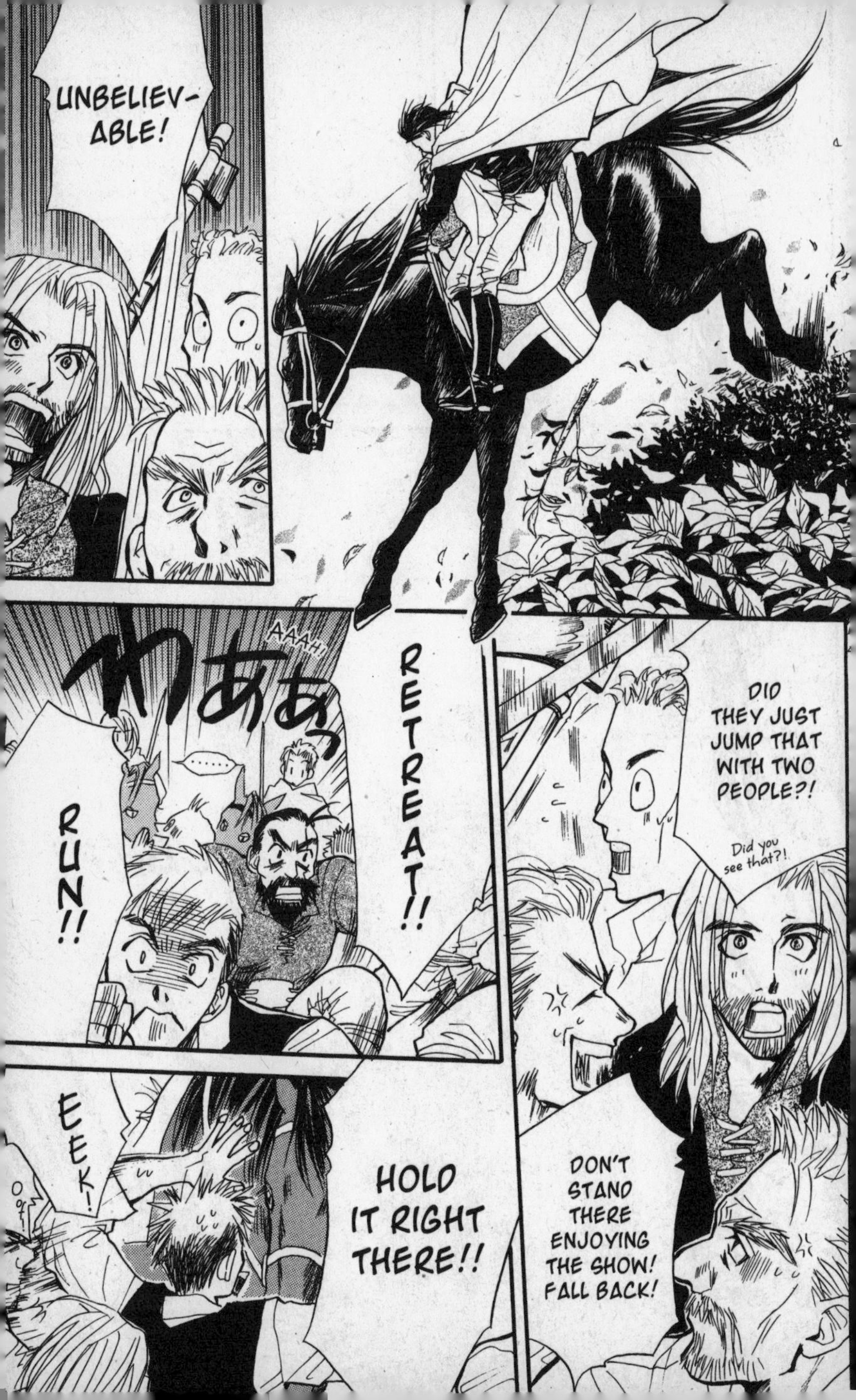
UNBELIEV-
ABLE!
DID THEY JUST JUMP THAT WITH TWO PEOPLE?!
Did you see that?!
DON'T STAND THERE ENJOYING THE SHOW! FALL BACK!
RETREAT!!
わあっ
AAAH!
......
RUN!!
HOLD IT RIGHT THERE!!
EEK!
Oof

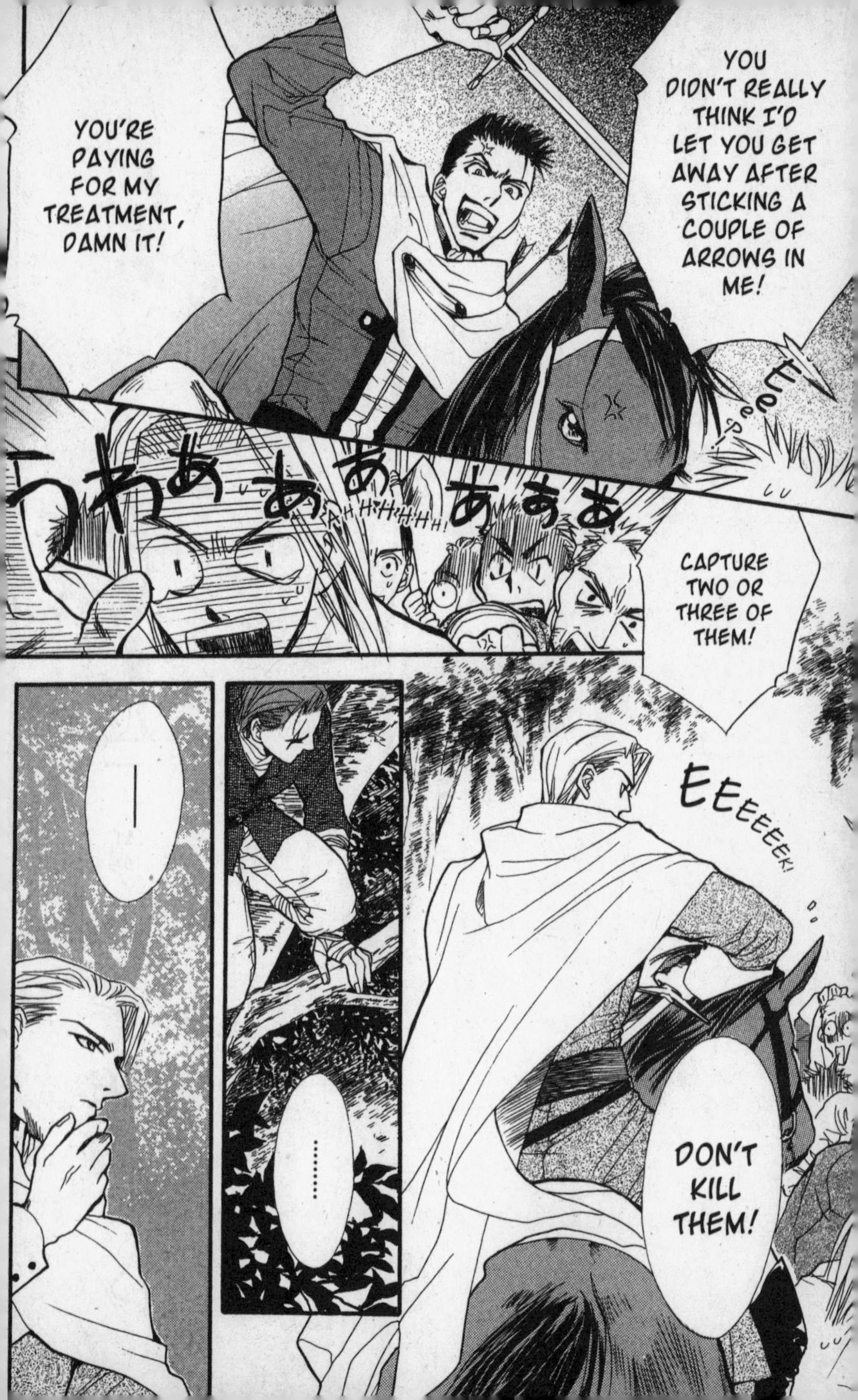
YOU DIDN'T REALLY THINK I'D LET YOU GET AWAY AFTER STICKING A COUPLE OF ARROWS IN ME!
YOU'RE PAYING FOR MY TREATMENT, DAMN IT!
Eeep!
うわあああああああ
AHHHHHHHHH!
CAPTURE TWO OR THREE OF THEM!
EEEEEEEK!
DON'T KILL THEM!
......
—

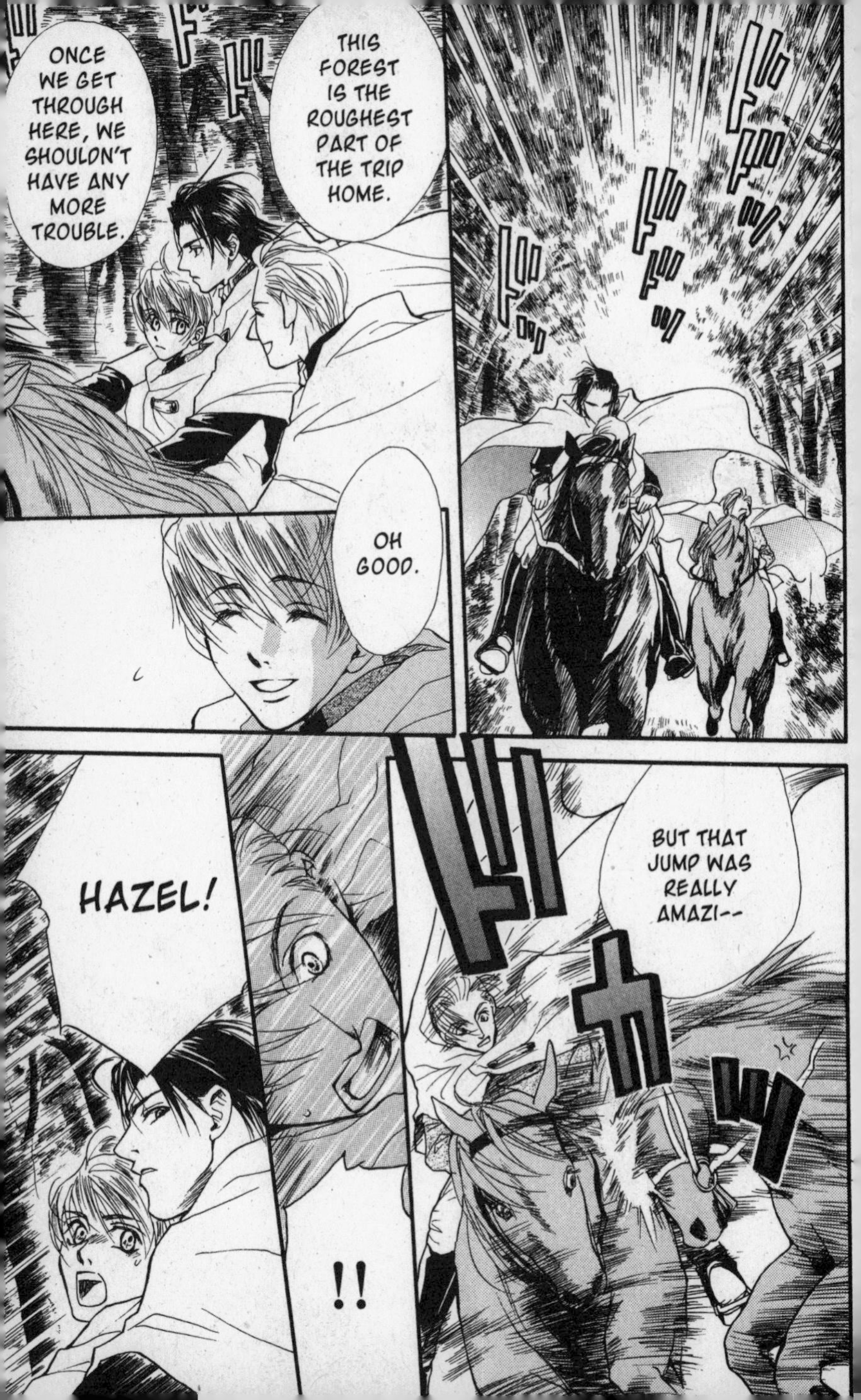
THIS FOREST IS THE ROUGHEST PART OF THE TRIP HOME.
ONCE WE GET THROUGH HERE, WE SHOULDN'T HAVE ANY MORE TROUBLE.
OH GOOD.
BUT THAT JUMP WAS REALLY AMAZI--
!!
HAZEL!

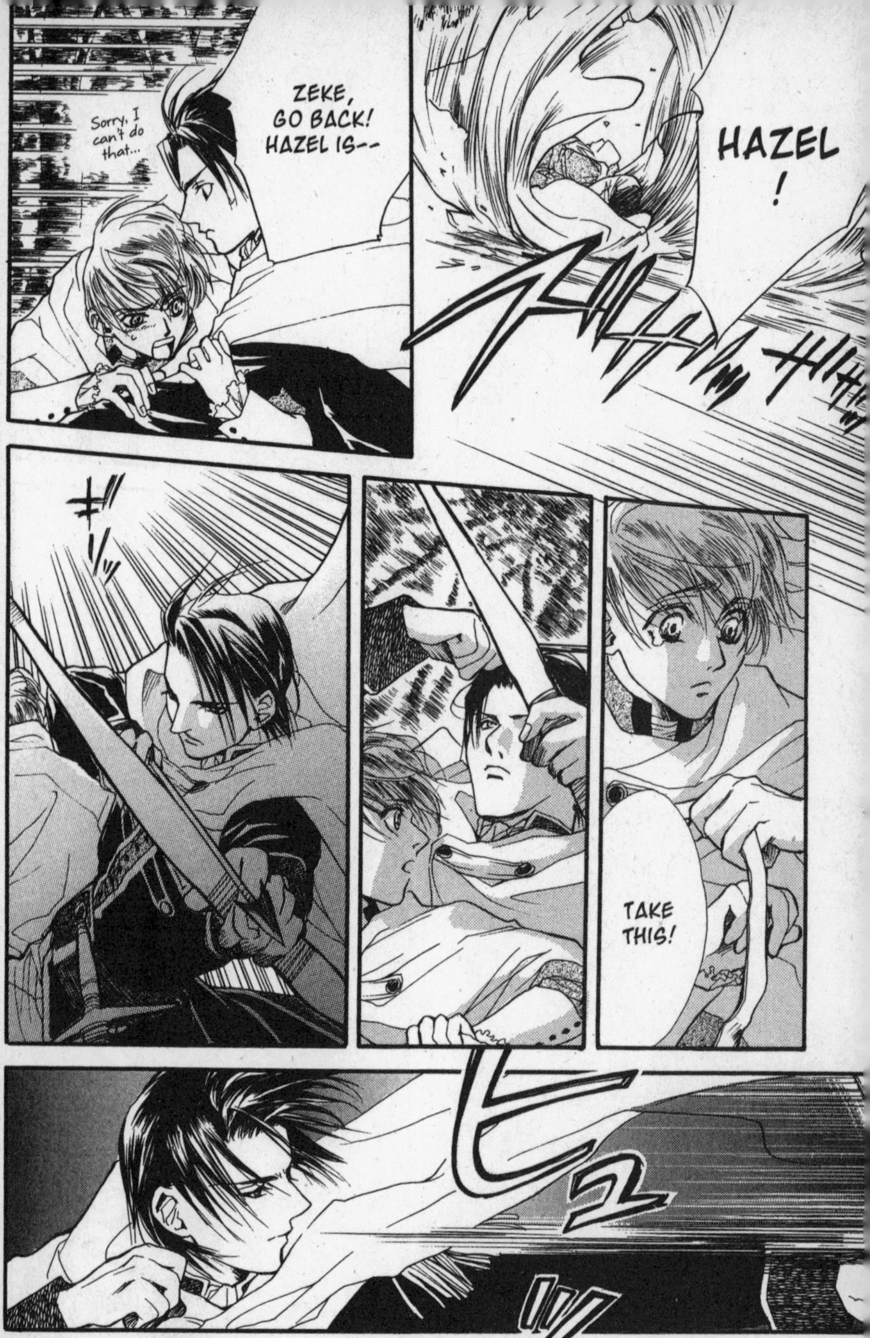
HAZEL
!
ZEKE, GO BACK! HAZEL IS--
Sorry, I can't do that...
TAKE THIS!

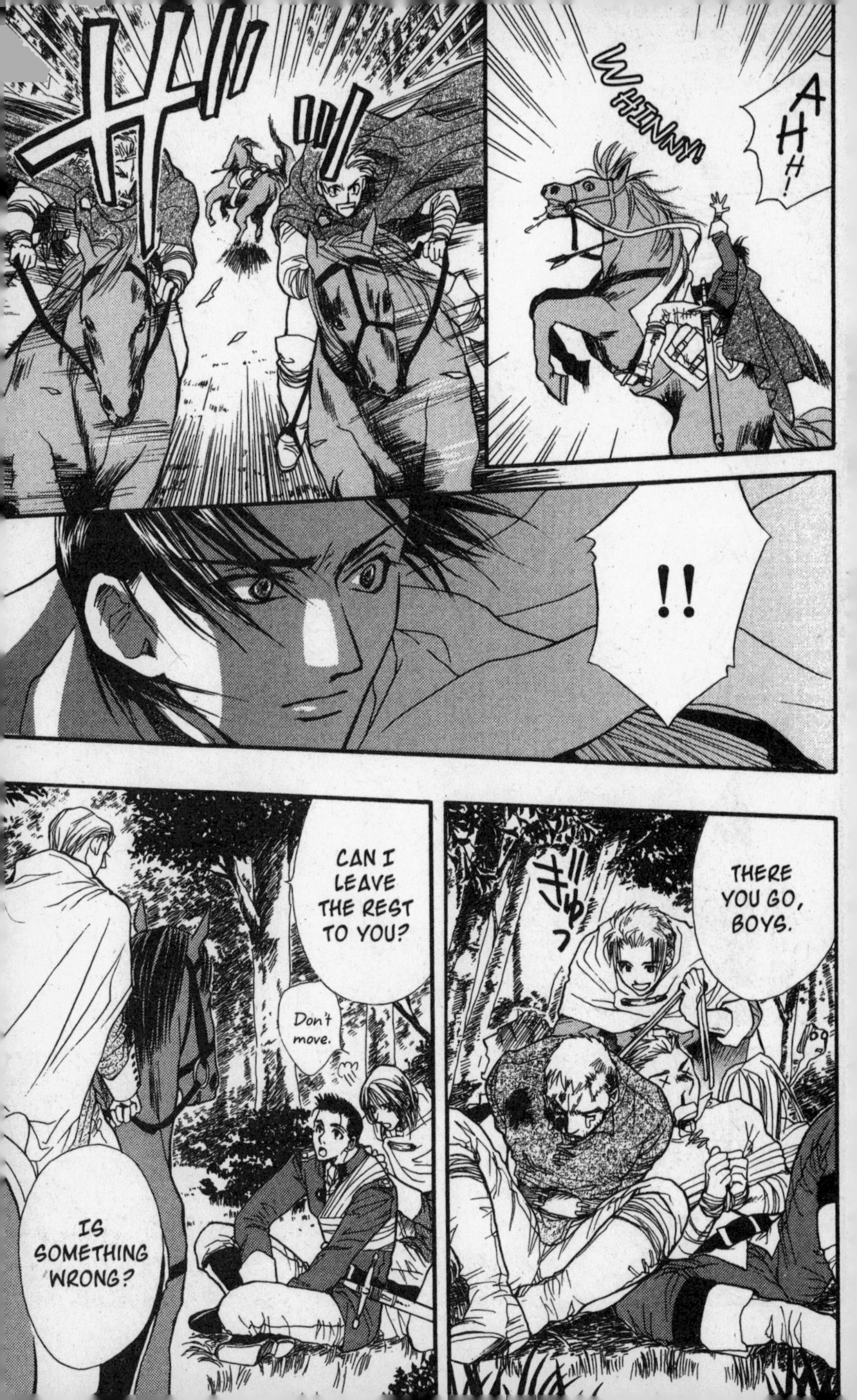
AHH!
WHINNY!
!!
THERE YOU GO, BOYS.
きゅっ
CAN I LEAVE THE REST TO YOU?
Don't move.
IS SOMETHING WRONG?

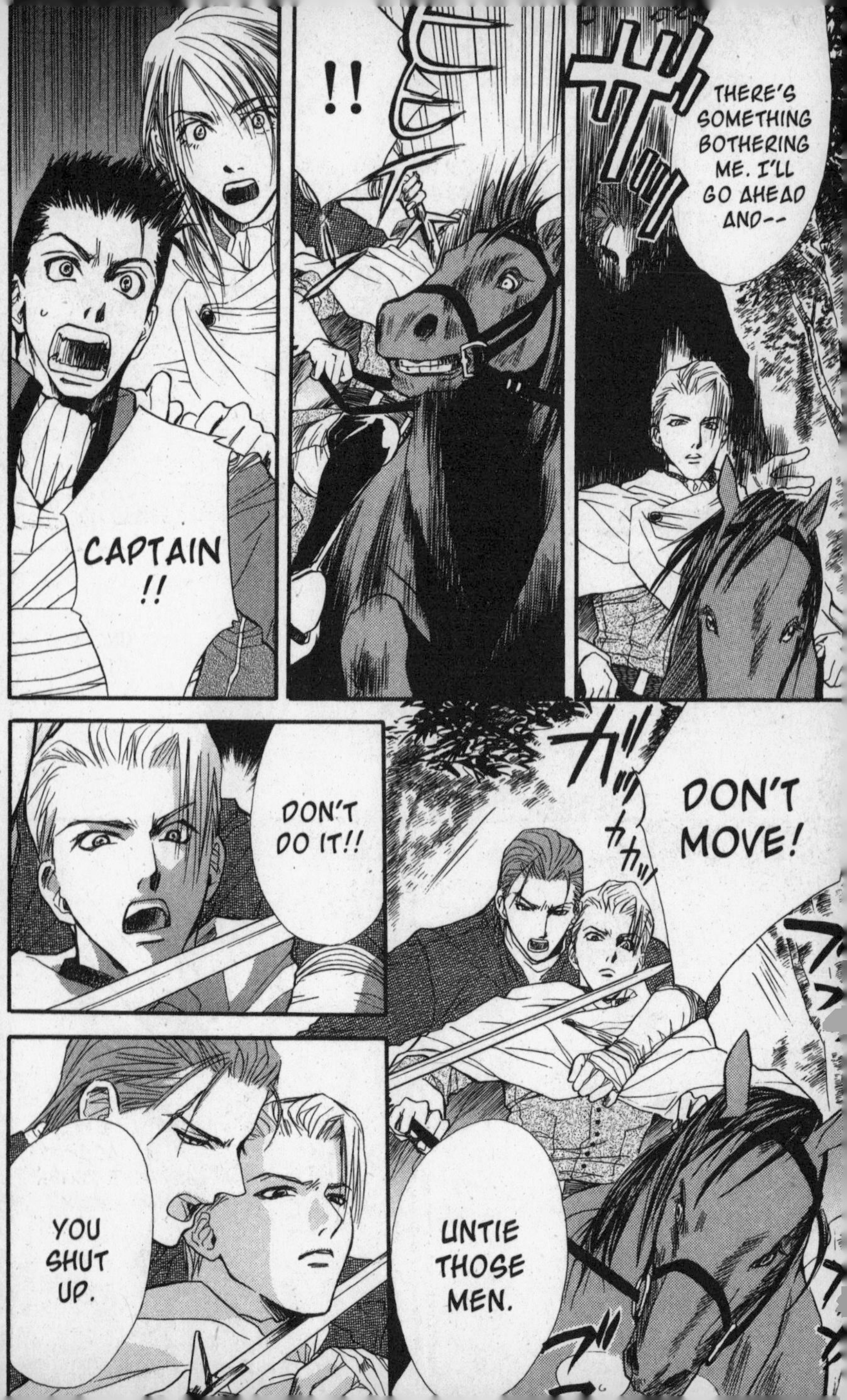
THERE'S SOMETHING BOTHERING ME. I'LL GO AHEAD AND--
!!
CAPTAIN !!
DON'T MOVE!
DON'T DO IT!!
UNTIE THOSE MEN.
YOU SHUT UP.

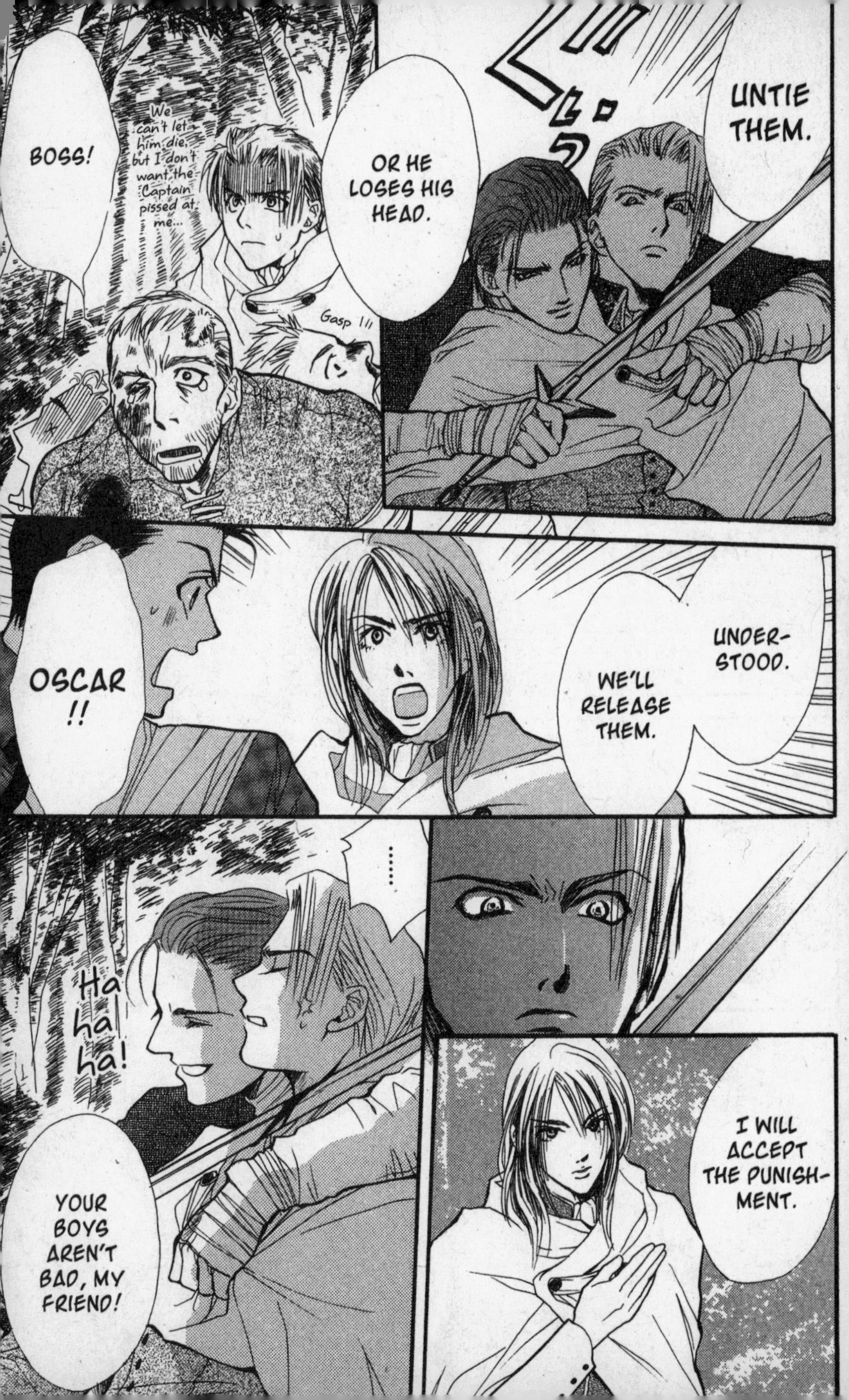
UNTIE THEM.
OR HE LOSES HIS HEAD.
We can't let him die, but I don't want the Captain pissed at me...
BOSS!
Gasp !!!
UNDER-STOOD.
WE'LL RELEASE THEM.
OSCAR !!
I WILL ACCEPT THE PUNISH-MENT.
......
Ha ha ha!
YOUR BOYS AREN'T BAD, MY FRIEND!

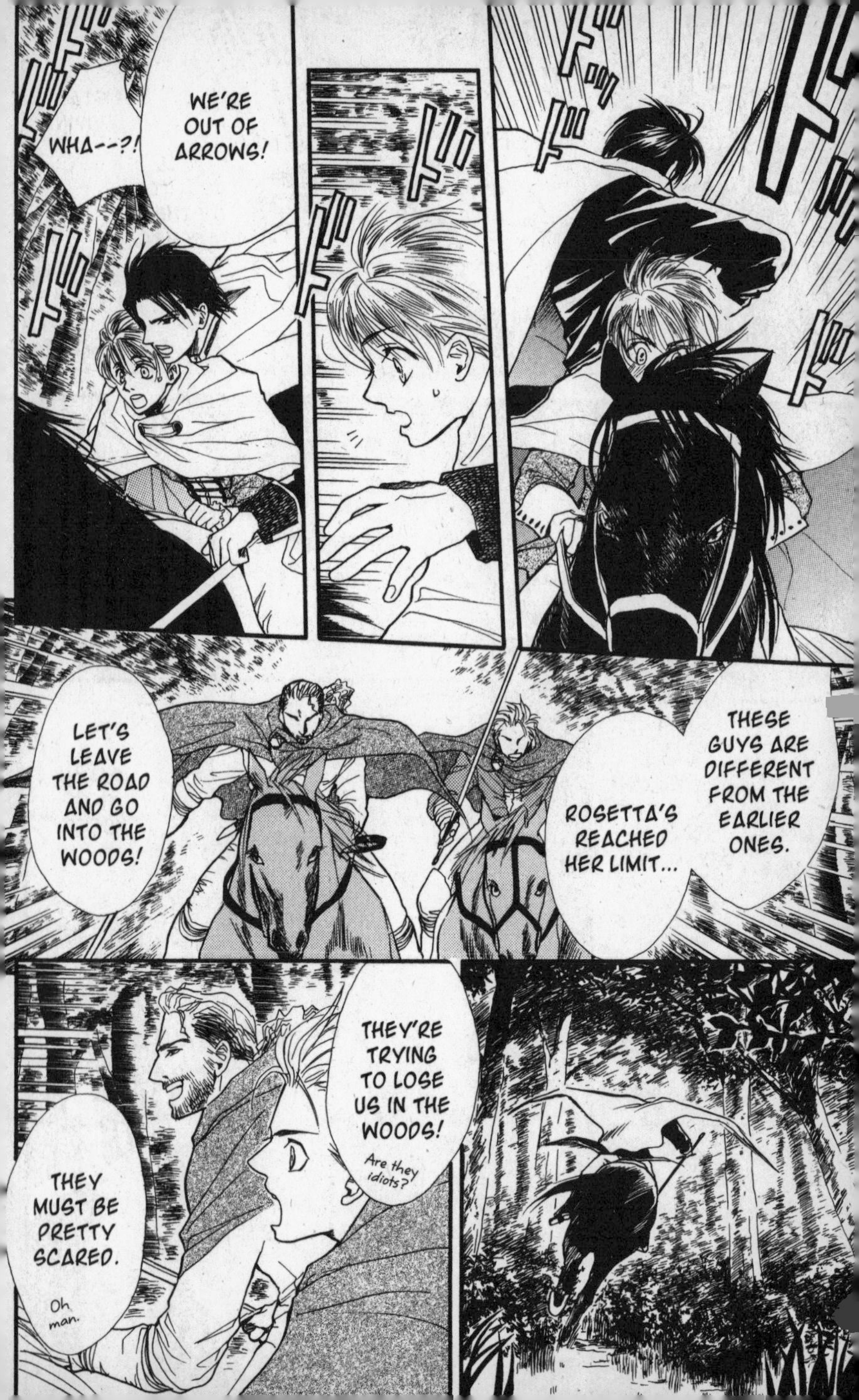
WE'RE OUT OF ARROWS!
WHA--?!
THESE GUYS ARE DIFFERENT FROM THE EARLIER ONES.
ROSETTA'S REACHED HER LIMIT...
LET'S LEAVE THE ROAD AND GO INTO THE WOODS!
THEY'RE TRYING TO LOSE US IN THE WOODS!
Are they idiots?
THEY MUST BE PRETTY SCARED.
Oh man.

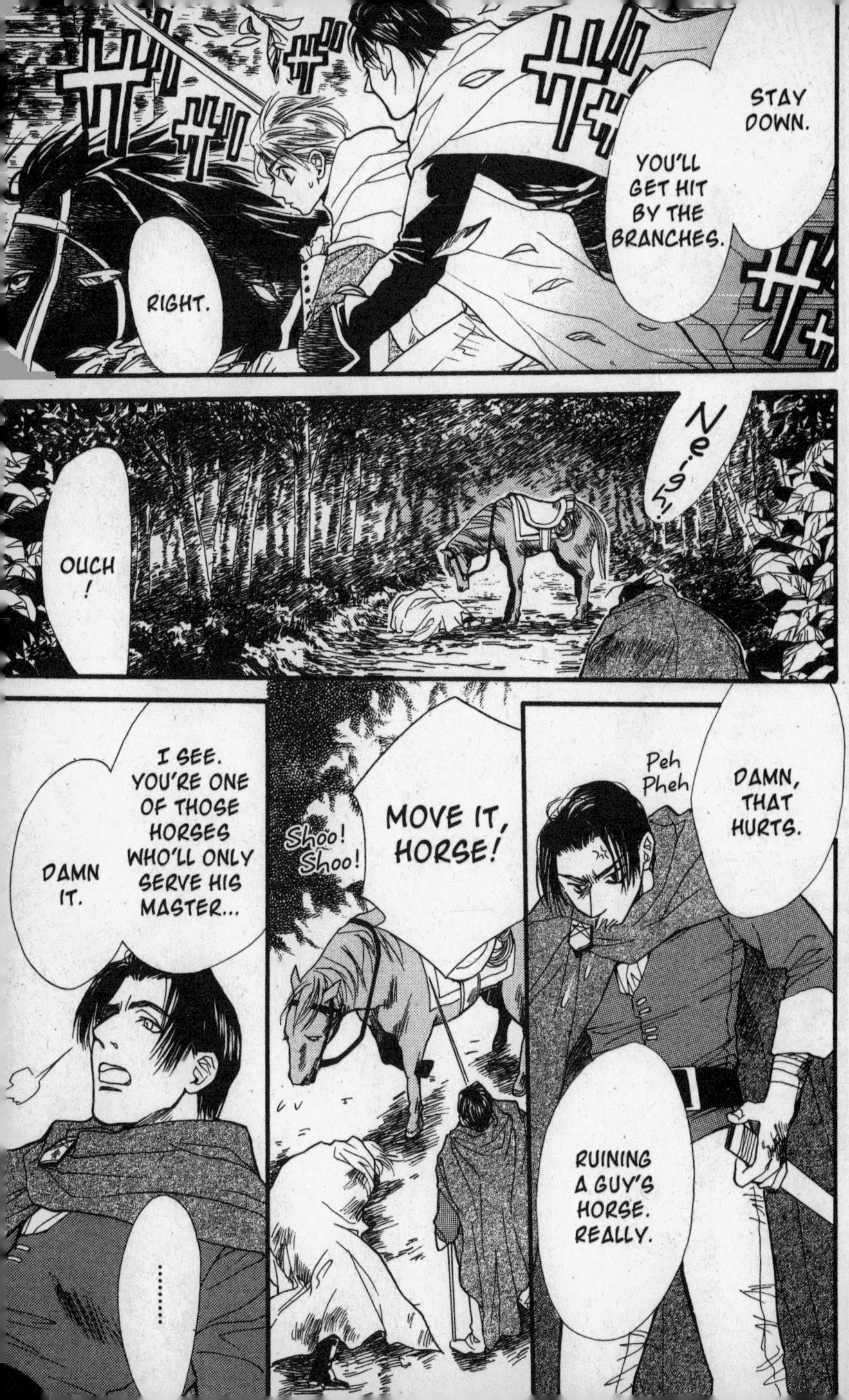
STAY DOWN.
YOU'LL GET HIT BY THE BRANCHES.
RIGHT.
Ne-gh!
OUCH!
Peh Pheh
DAMN, THAT HURTS.
RUINING A GUY'S HORSE. REALLY.
MOVE IT, HORSE!
Shoo! Shoo!
I SEE. YOU'RE ONE OF THOSE HORSES WHO'LL ONLY SERVE HIS MASTER...
DAMN IT.
......

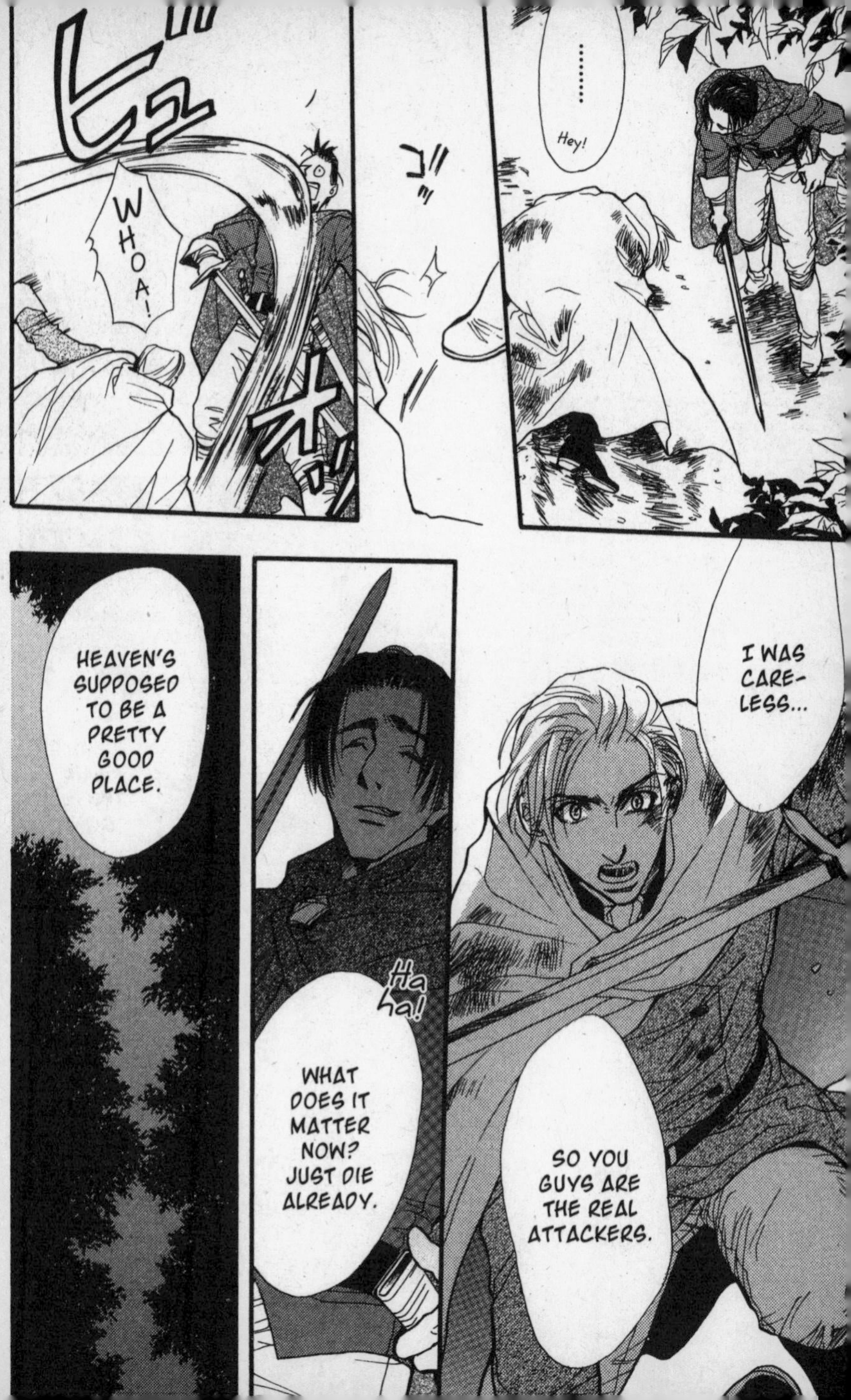
……
Hey!
WHOA!
I WAS CARELESS...
SO YOU GUYS ARE THE REAL ATTACKERS.
Ha ha!
WHAT DOES IT MATTER NOW? JUST DIE ALREADY.
HEAVEN'S SUPPOSED TO BE A PRETTY GOOD PLACE.

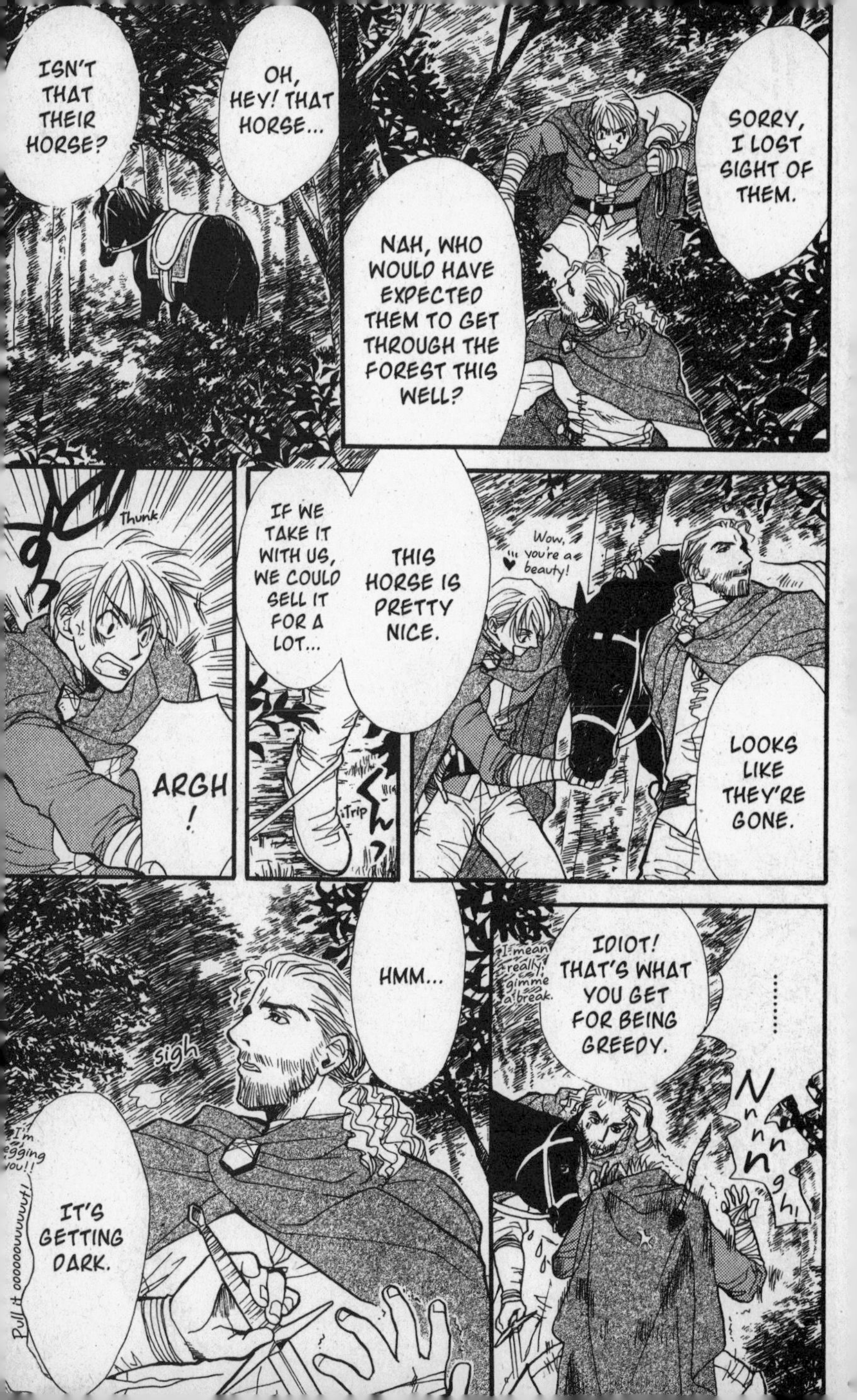
SORRY, I LOST SIGHT OF THEM.
NAH, WHO WOULD HAVE EXPECTED THEM TO GET THROUGH THE FOREST THIS WELL?
OH, HEY! THAT HORSE...
ISN'T THAT THEIR HORSE?
LOOKS LIKE THEY'RE GONE.
Wow, you're a beauty!
THIS HORSE IS PRETTY NICE.
IF WE TAKE IT WITH US, WE COULD SELL IT FOR A LOT...
Trip
Thunk
ARGH!
......
Nnnnngh!
IDIOT! THAT'S WHAT YOU GET FOR BEING GREEDY.
I mean really, gimme a break.
HMM...
sigh
IT'S GETTING DARK.
I'm egging you!!
Pull it ooooooouuuuut!

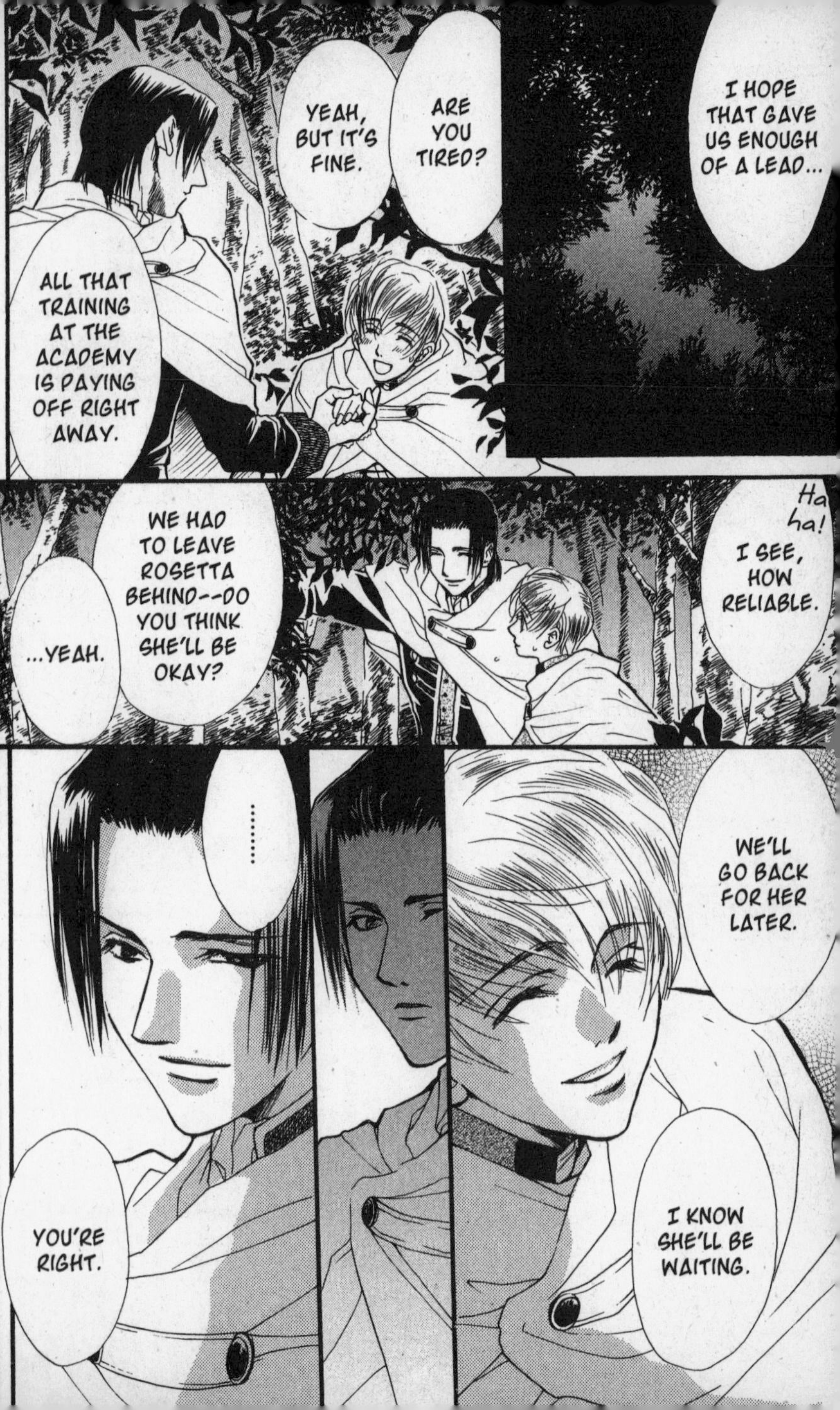
I HOPE THAT GAVE US ENOUGH OF A LEAD...
ARE YOU TIRED?
YEAH, BUT IT'S FINE.
ALL THAT TRAINING AT THE ACADEMY IS PAYING OFF RIGHT AWAY.
Ha ha!
I SEE, HOW RELIABLE.
WE HAD TO LEAVE ROSETTA BEHIND--DO YOU THINK SHE'LL BE OKAY?
...YEAH.
WE'LL GO BACK FOR HER LATER.
I KNOW SHE'LL BE WAITING.
....
YOU'RE RIGHT.

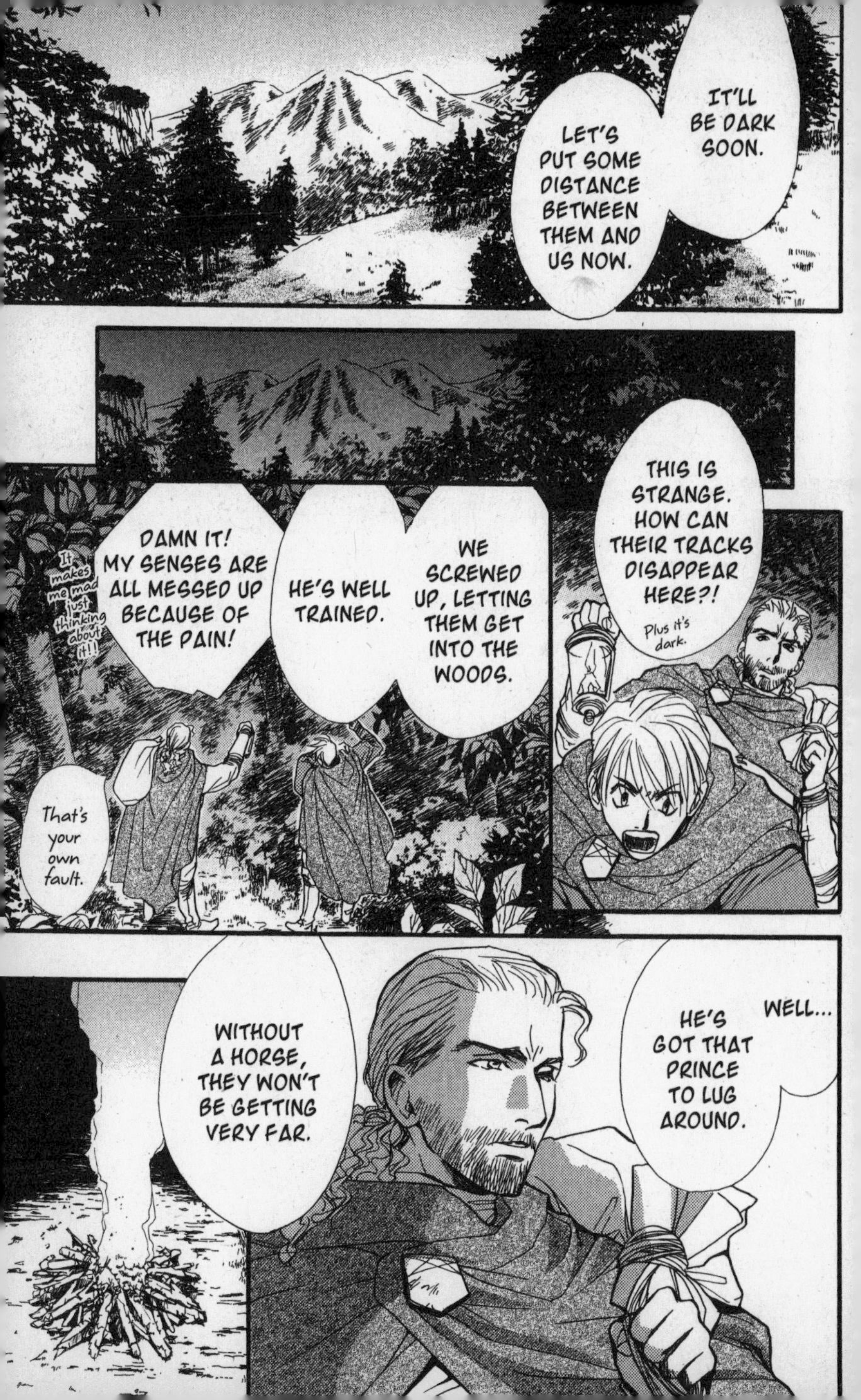
IT'LL BE DARK SOON.
LET'S PUT SOME DISTANCE BETWEEN THEM AND US NOW.
THIS IS STRANGE. HOW CAN THEIR TRACKS DISAPPEAR HERE?!
Plus it's dark.
WE SCREWED UP, LETTING THEM GET INTO THE WOODS.
HE'S WELL TRAINED.
DAMN IT! MY SENSES ARE ALL MESSED UP BECAUSE OF THE PAIN!
It makes me mad just thinking about it!!
That's your own fault.
WELL...
HE'S GOT THAT PRINCE TO LUG AROUND.
WITHOUT A HORSE, THEY WON'T BE GETTING VERY FAR.

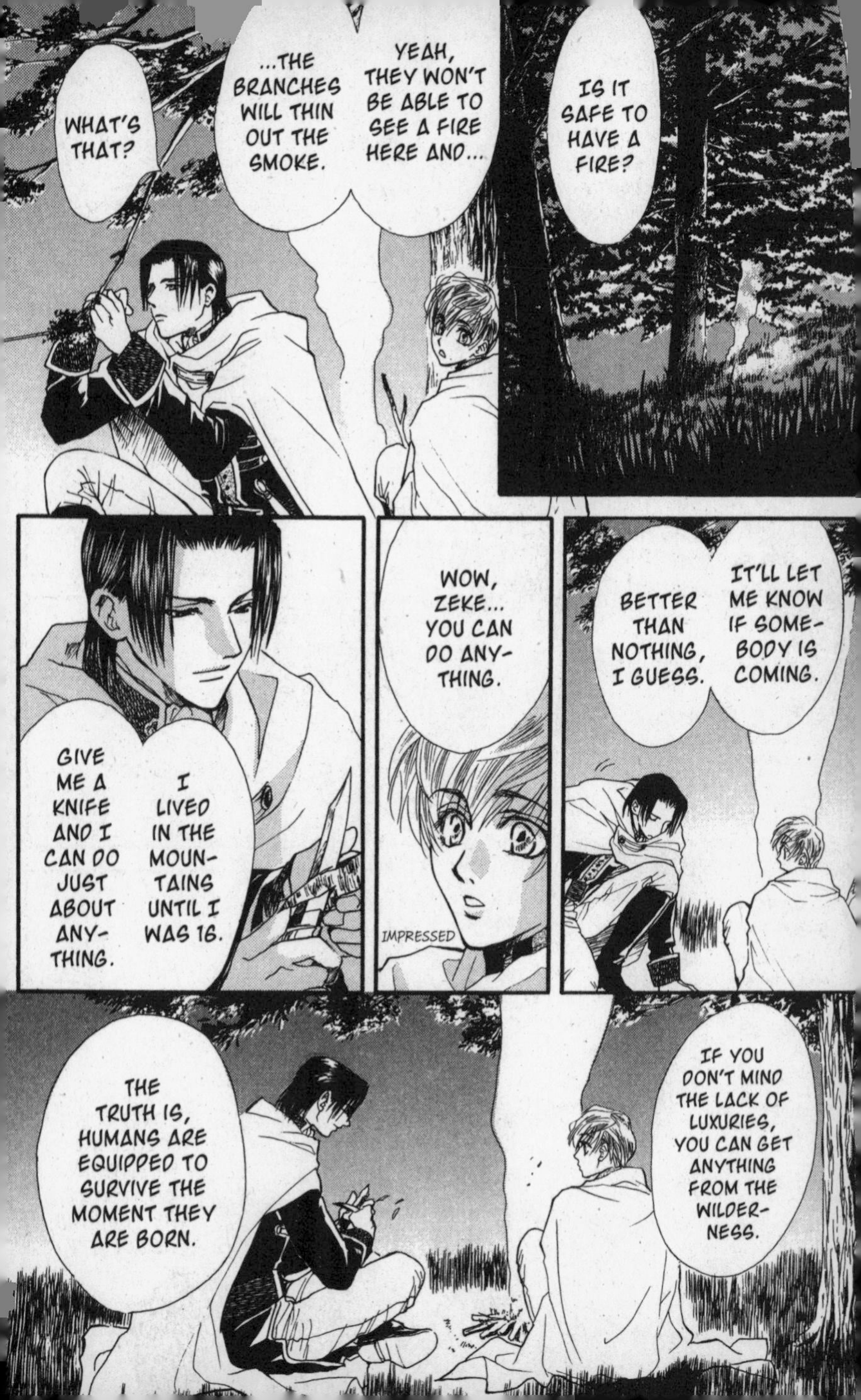
IS IT SAFE TO HAVE A FIRE?
YEAH, THEY WON'T BE ABLE TO SEE A FIRE HERE AND...
...THE BRANCHES WILL THIN OUT THE SMOKE.
WHAT'S THAT?
IT'LL LET ME KNOW IF SOMEBODY IS COMING.
BETTER THAN NOTHING, I GUESS.
WOW, ZEKE... YOU CAN DO ANYTHING.
IMPRESSED
I LIVED IN THE MOUNTAINS UNTIL I WAS 16.
GIVE ME A KNIFE AND I CAN DO JUST ABOUT ANYTHING.
IF YOU DON'T MIND THE LACK OF LUXURIES, YOU CAN GET ANYTHING FROM THE WILDERNESS.
THE TRUTH IS, HUMANS ARE EQUIPPED TO SURVIVE THE MOMENT THEY ARE BORN.

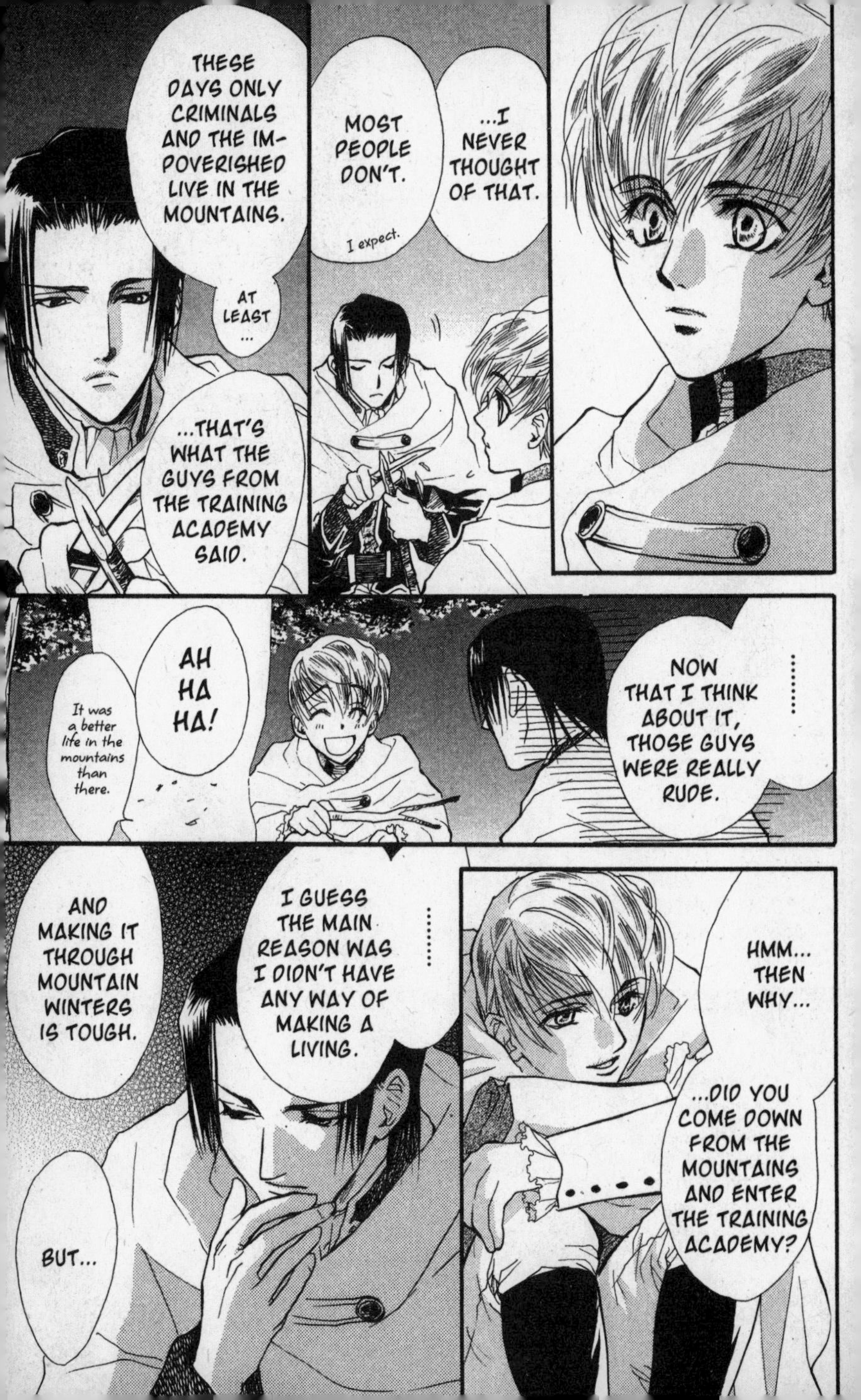
...I NEVER THOUGHT OF THAT.
MOST PEOPLE DON'T.
I expect.
THESE DAYS ONLY CRIMINALS AND THE IM-POVERISHED LIVE IN THE MOUNTAINS.
AT LEAST ...
...THAT'S WHAT THE GUYS FROM THE TRAINING ACADEMY SAID.
......
NOW THAT I THINK ABOUT IT, THOSE GUYS WERE REALLY RUDE.
AH HA HA!
It was a better life in the mountains than there.
HMM... THEN WHY...
...DID YOU COME DOWN FROM THE MOUNTAINS AND ENTER THE TRAINING ACADEMY?
......
I GUESS THE MAIN REASON WAS I DIDN'T HAVE ANY WAY OF MAKING A LIVING.
AND MAKING IT THROUGH MOUNTAIN WINTERS IS TOUGH.
BUT...

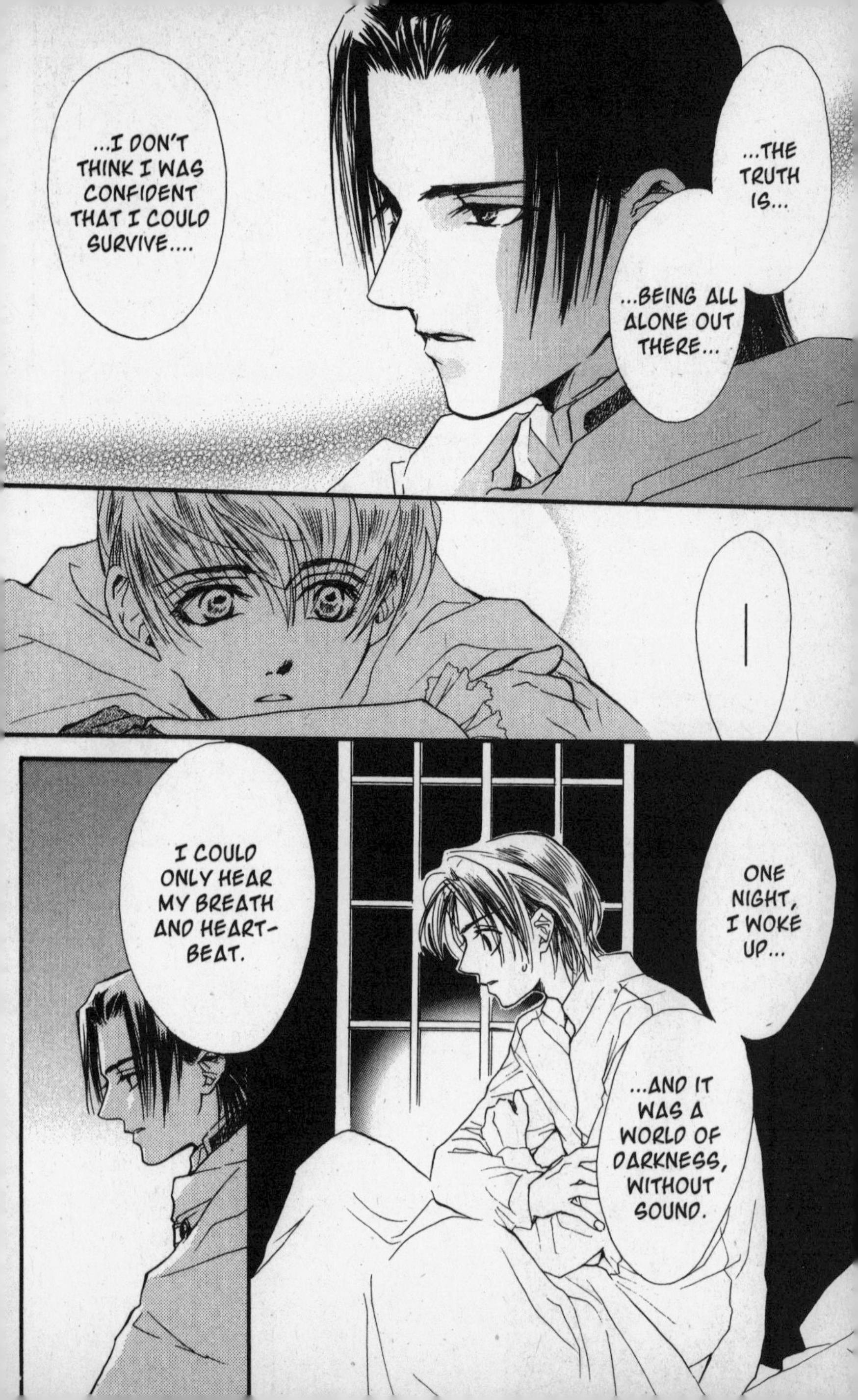
...THE TRUTH IS...
...BEING ALL ALONE OUT THERE...
...I DON'T THINK I WAS CONFIDENT THAT I COULD SURVIVE....
—
ONE NIGHT, I WOKE UP...
...AND IT WAS A WORLD OF DARKNESS, WITHOUT SOUND.
I COULD ONLY HEAR MY BREATH AND HEART-BEAT.

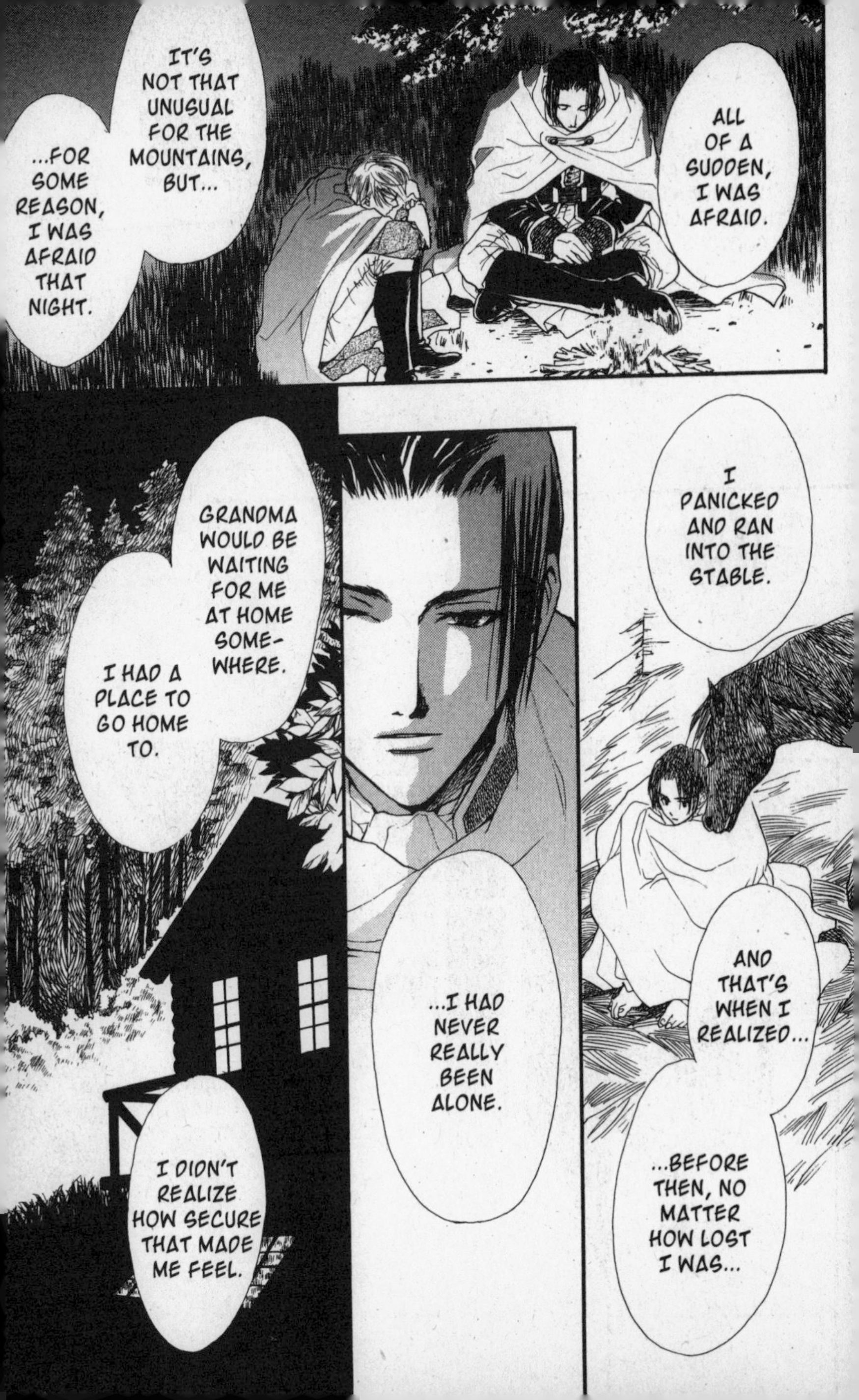
ALL OF A SUDDEN, I WAS AFRAID.
IT'S NOT THAT UNUSUAL FOR THE MOUNTAINS, BUT...
...FOR SOME REASON, I WAS AFRAID THAT NIGHT.
I PANICKED AND RAN INTO THE STABLE.
AND THAT'S WHEN I REALIZED...
...BEFORE THEN, NO MATTER HOW LOST I WAS...
...I HAD NEVER REALLY BEEN ALONE.
GRANDMA WOULD BE WAITING FOR ME AT HOME SOME-WHERE.
I HAD A PLACE TO GO HOME TO.
I DIDN'T REALIZE HOW SECURE THAT MADE ME FEEL.

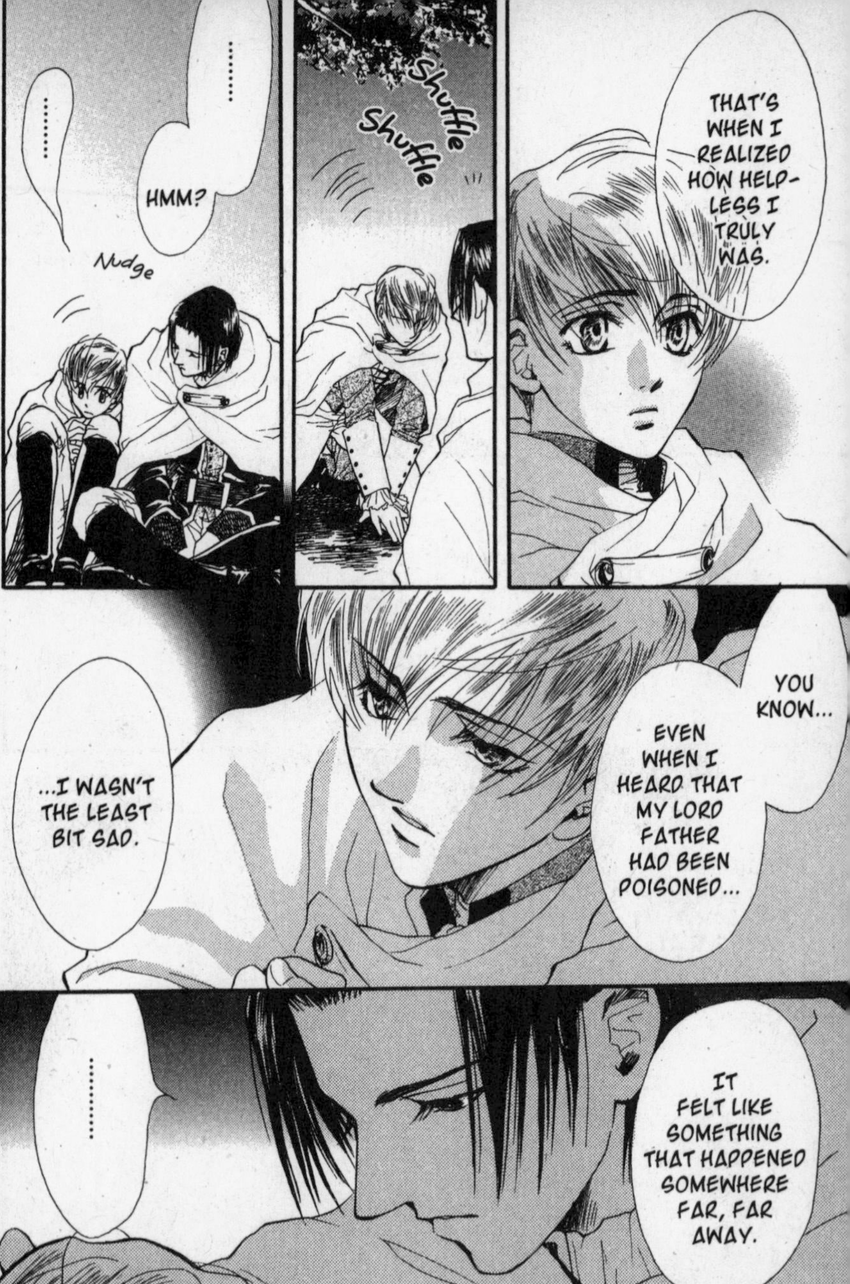
THAT'S WHEN I REALIZED HOW HELP-LESS I TRULY WAS.
Shuffle
Shuffle
......
HMM?
......
Nudge
YOU KNOW...
EVEN WHEN I HEARD THAT MY LORD FATHER HAD BEEN POISONED...
...I WASN'T THE LEAST BIT SAD.
IT FELT LIKE SOMETHING THAT HAPPENED SOMEWHERE FAR, FAR AWAY.
......

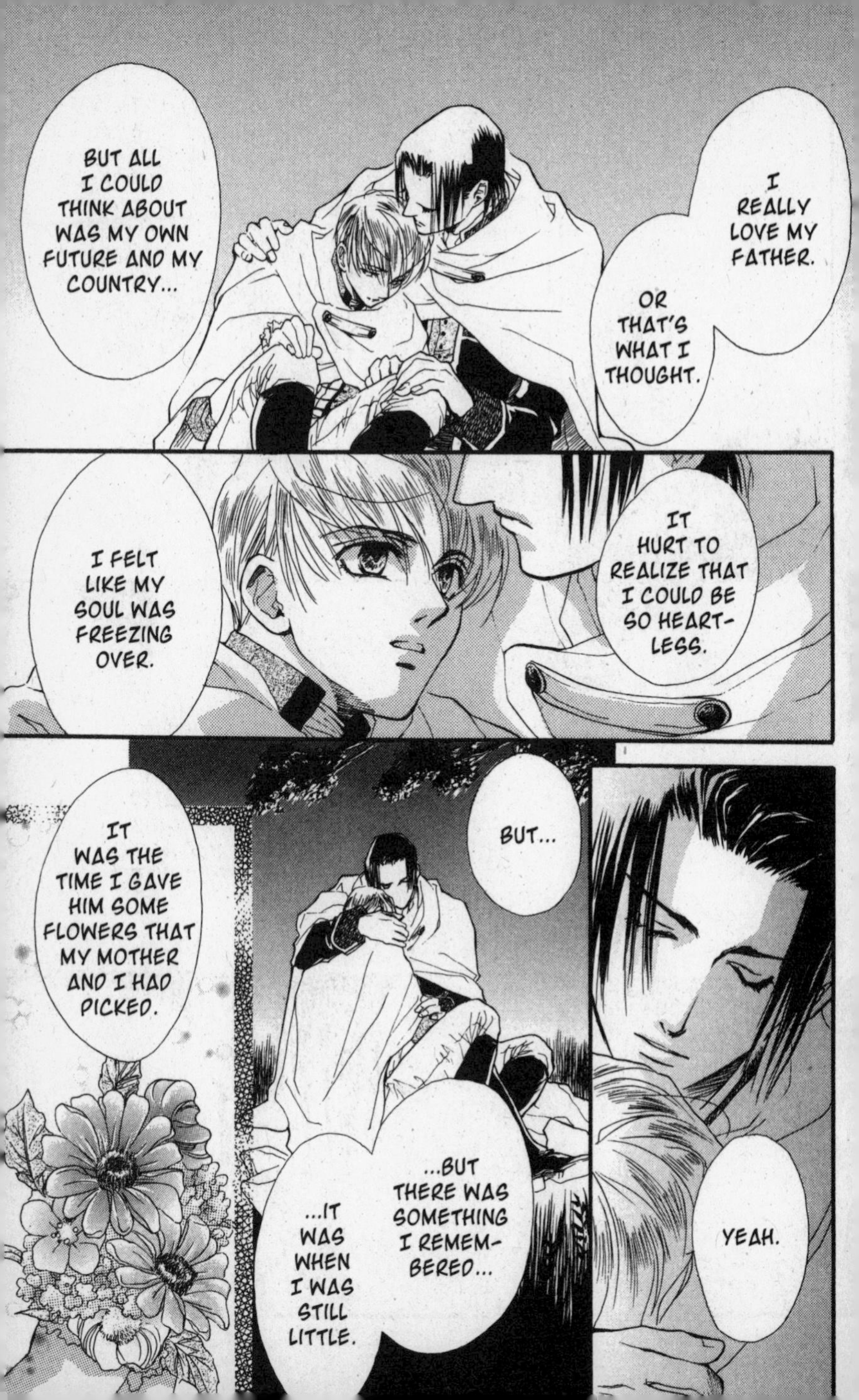
I REALLY LOVE MY FATHER.
OR THAT'S WHAT I THOUGHT.
BUT ALL I COULD THINK ABOUT WAS MY OWN FUTURE AND MY COUNTRY...
IT HURT TO REALIZE THAT I COULD BE SO HEART-LESS.
I FELT LIKE MY SOUL WAS FREEZING OVER.
YEAH.
BUT...
...BUT THERE WAS SOMETHING I REMEM-BERED...
...IT WAS WHEN I WAS STILL LITTLE.
IT WAS THE TIME I GAVE HIM SOME FLOWERS THAT MY MOTHER AND I HAD PICKED.

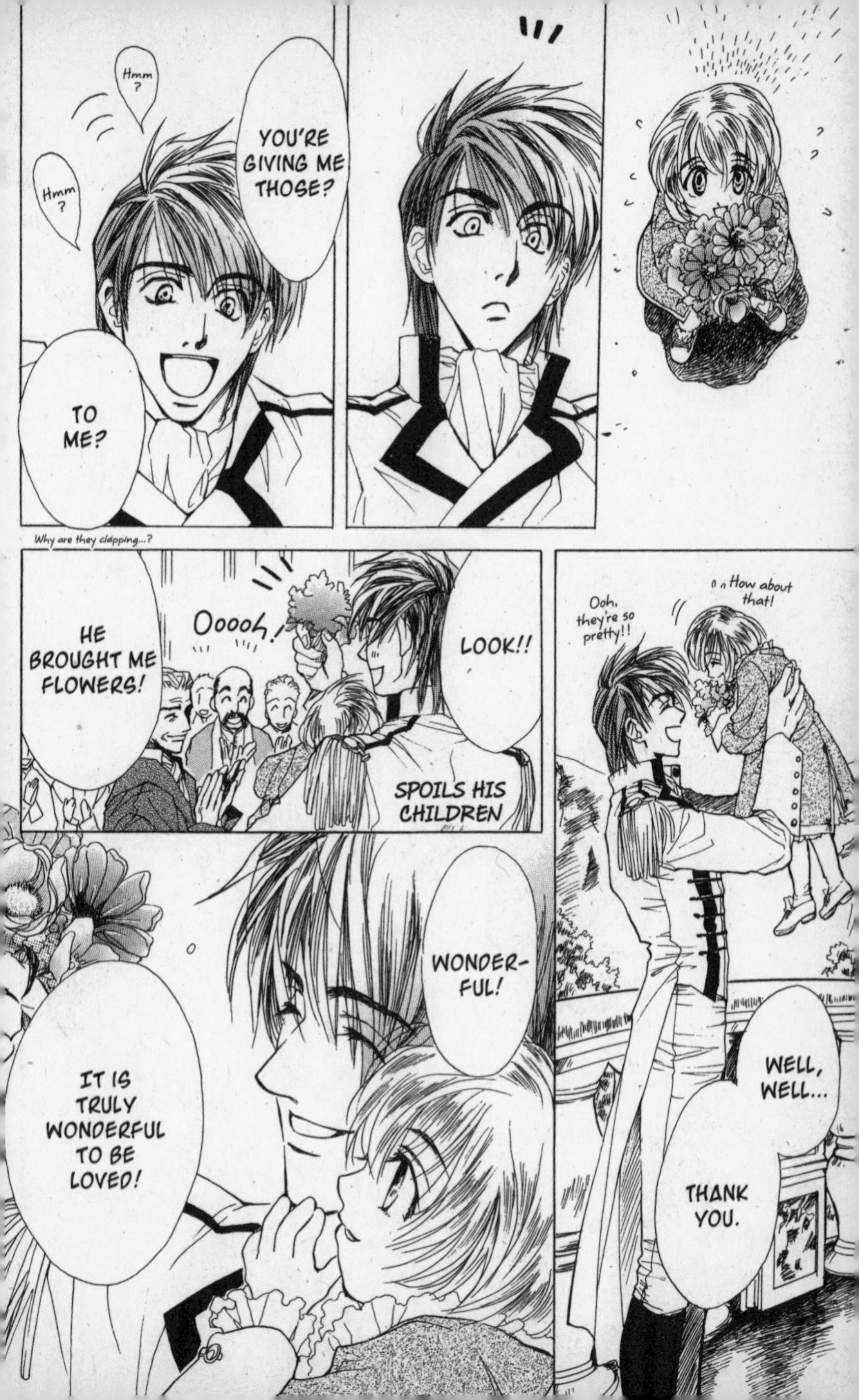
YOU'RE GIVING ME THOSE?
Hmm ?
Hmm ?
TO ME?
How about that!
Ooh, they're so pretty!!
WELL, WELL...
THANK YOU.
Why are they clapping...?
LOOK!!
SPOILS HIS CHILDREN
Ooooh!
HE BROUGHT ME FLOWERS!
WONDERFUL!
IT IS TRULY WONDERFUL TO BE LOVED!

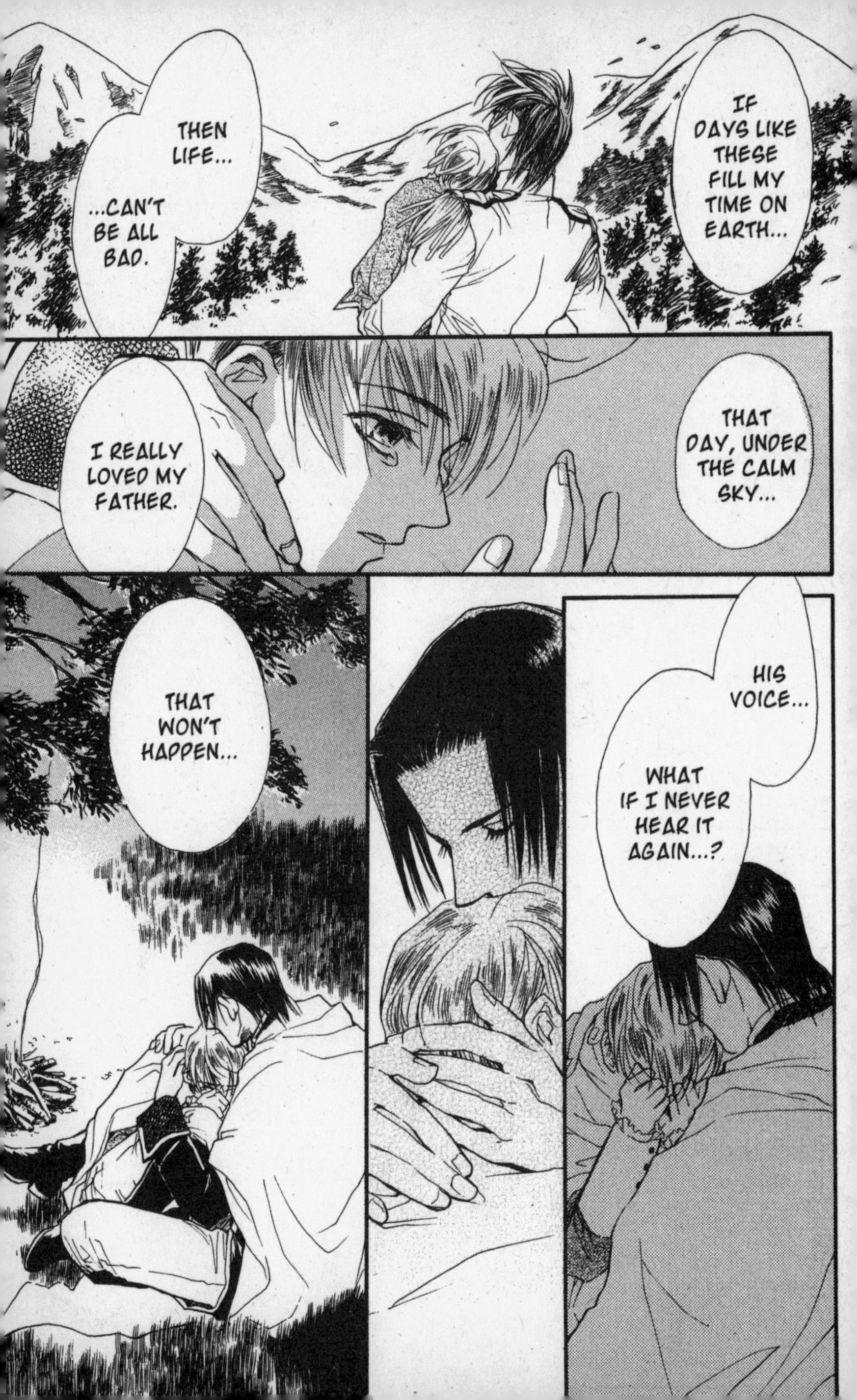
IF DAYS LIKE THESE FILL MY TIME ON EARTH...
THEN LIFE...
...CAN'T BE ALL BAD.
THAT DAY, UNDER THE CALM SKY...
I REALLY LOVED MY FATHER.
HIS VOICE...
WHAT IF I NEVER HEAR IT AGAIN...?
THAT WON'T HAPPEN...

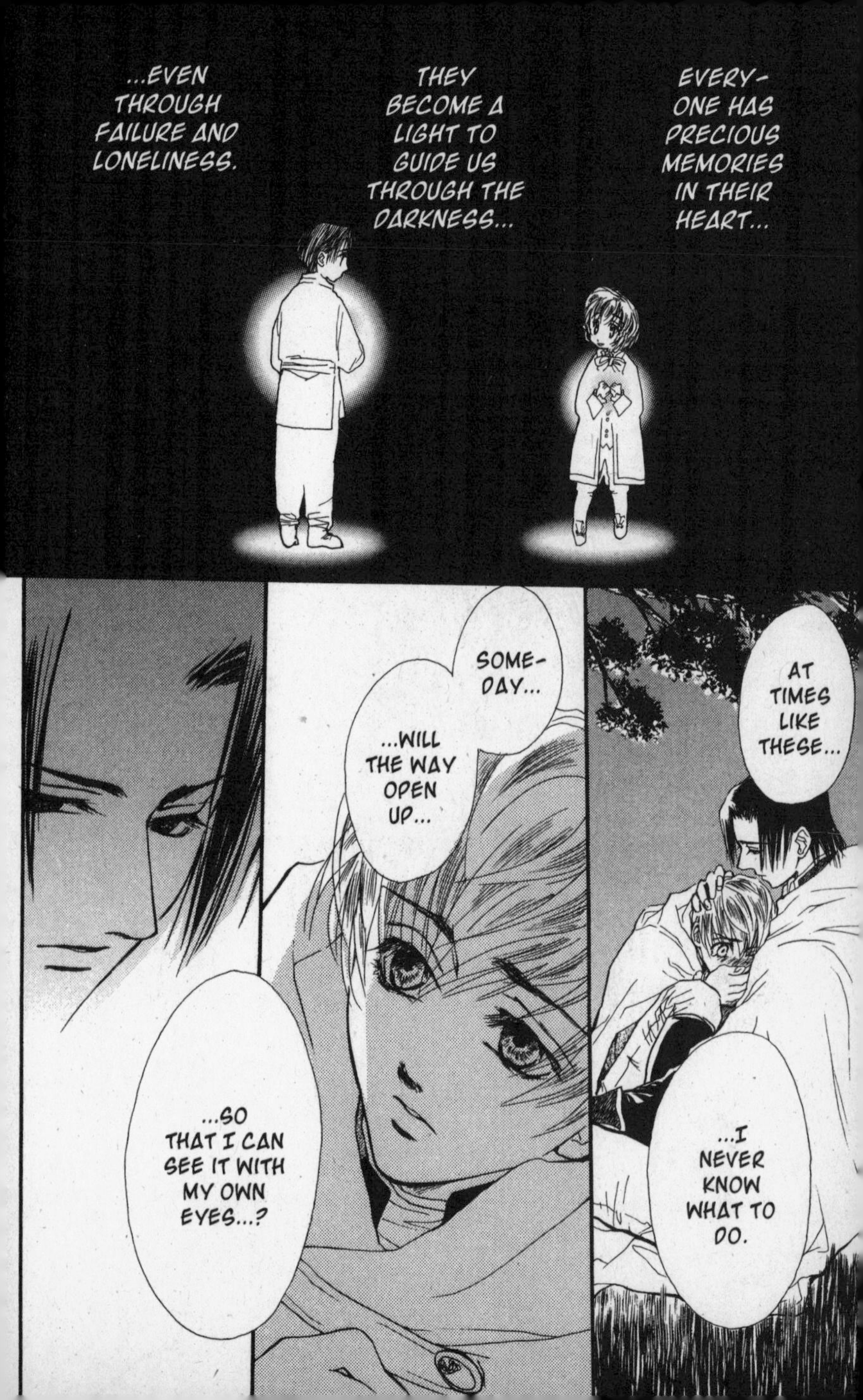
EVERY-ONE HAS PRECIOUS MEMORIES IN THEIR HEART...
THEY BECOME A LIGHT TO GUIDE US THROUGH THE DARKNESS...
...EVEN THROUGH FAILURE AND LONELINESS.
AT TIMES LIKE THESE...
...I NEVER KNOW WHAT TO DO.
SOME-DAY...
...WILL THE WAY OPEN UP...
...SO THAT I CAN SEE IT WITH MY OWN EYES...?

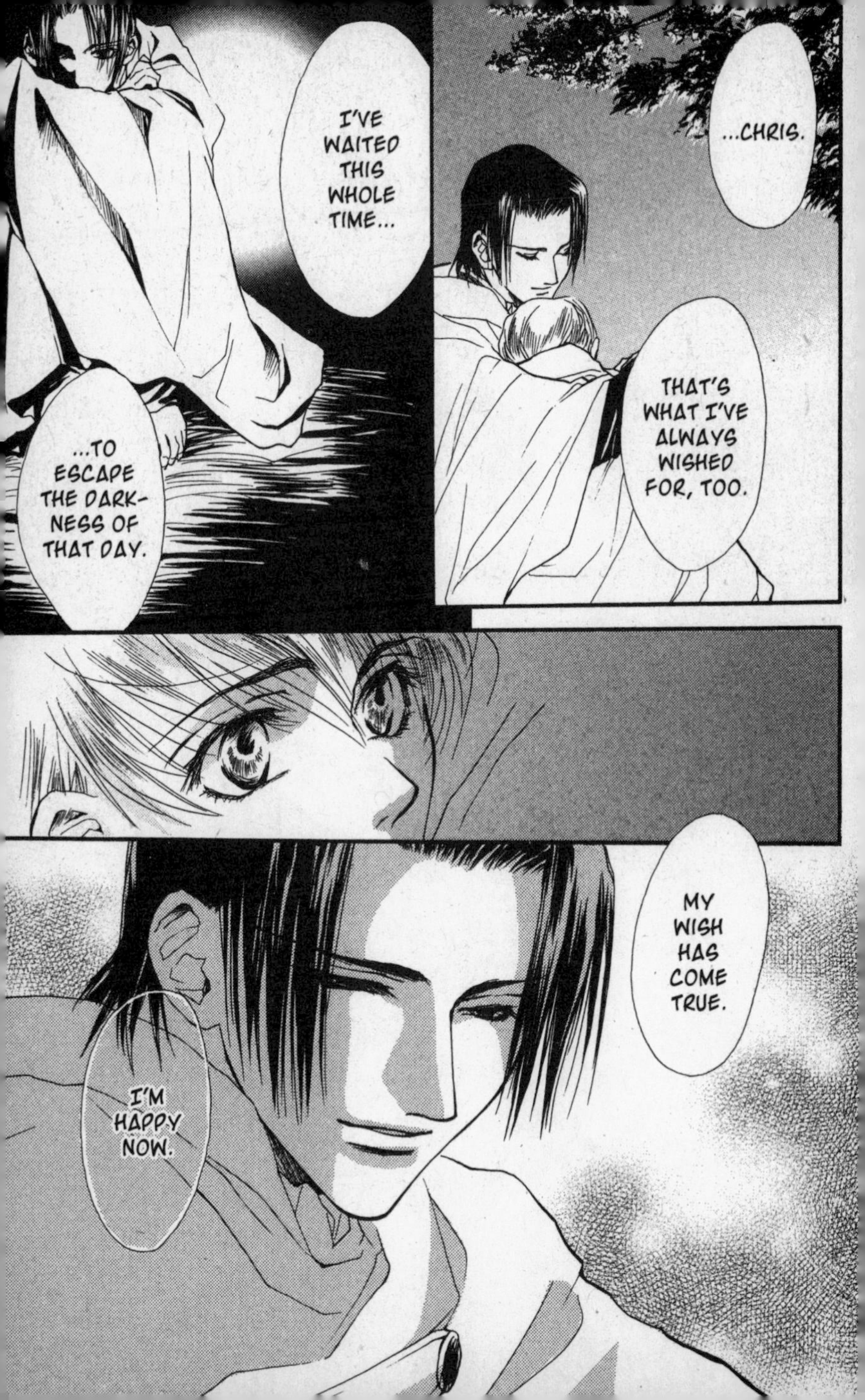
...CHRIS.
THAT'S WHAT I'VE ALWAYS WISHED FOR, TOO.
I'VE WAITED THIS WHOLE TIME...
...TO ESCAPE THE DARK-NESS OF THAT DAY.
MY WISH HAS COME TRUE.
I'M HAPPY NOW.

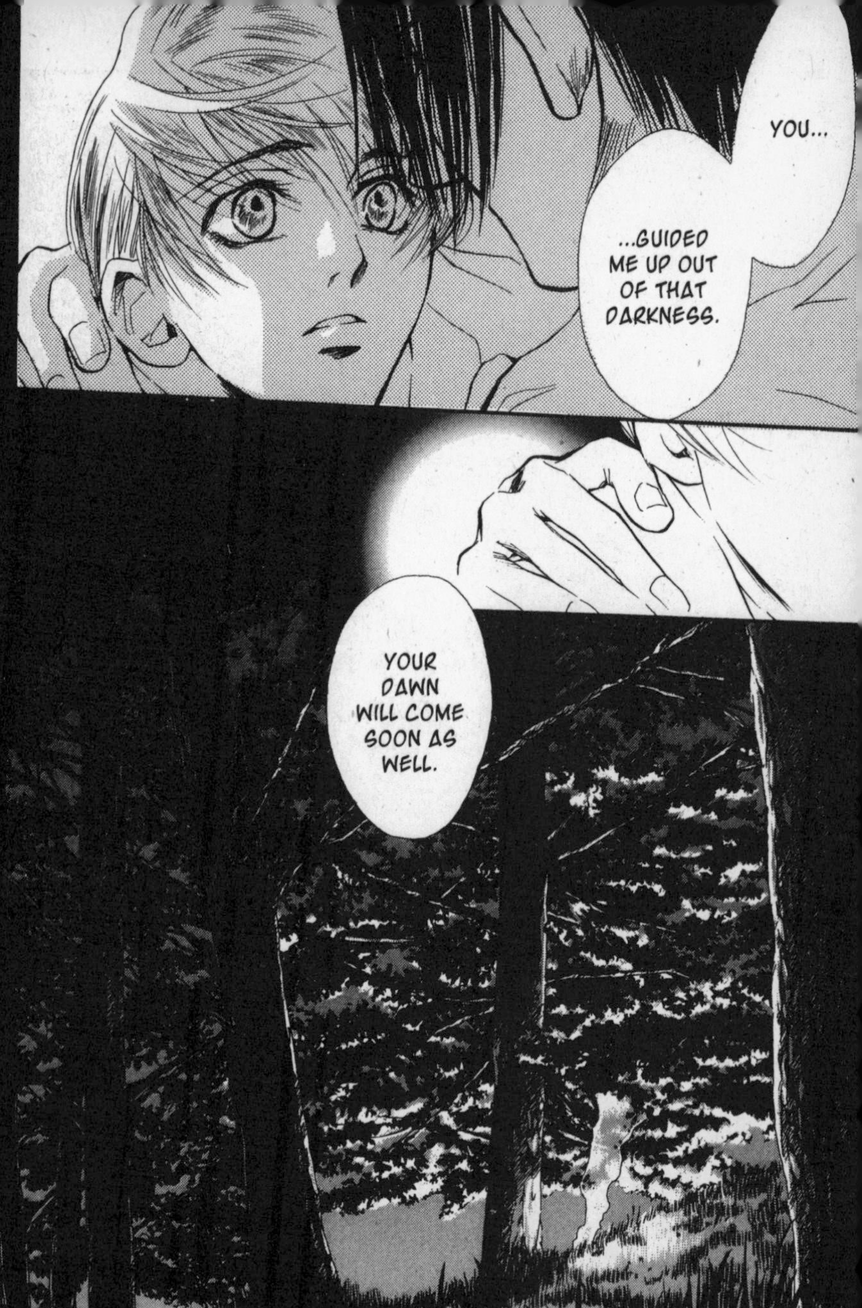
YOU...
...GUIDED ME UP OUT OF THAT DARKNESS.
YOUR DAWN WILL COME SOON AS WELL.
BLACK KNIGHT 2. A Far-off Dawn / END

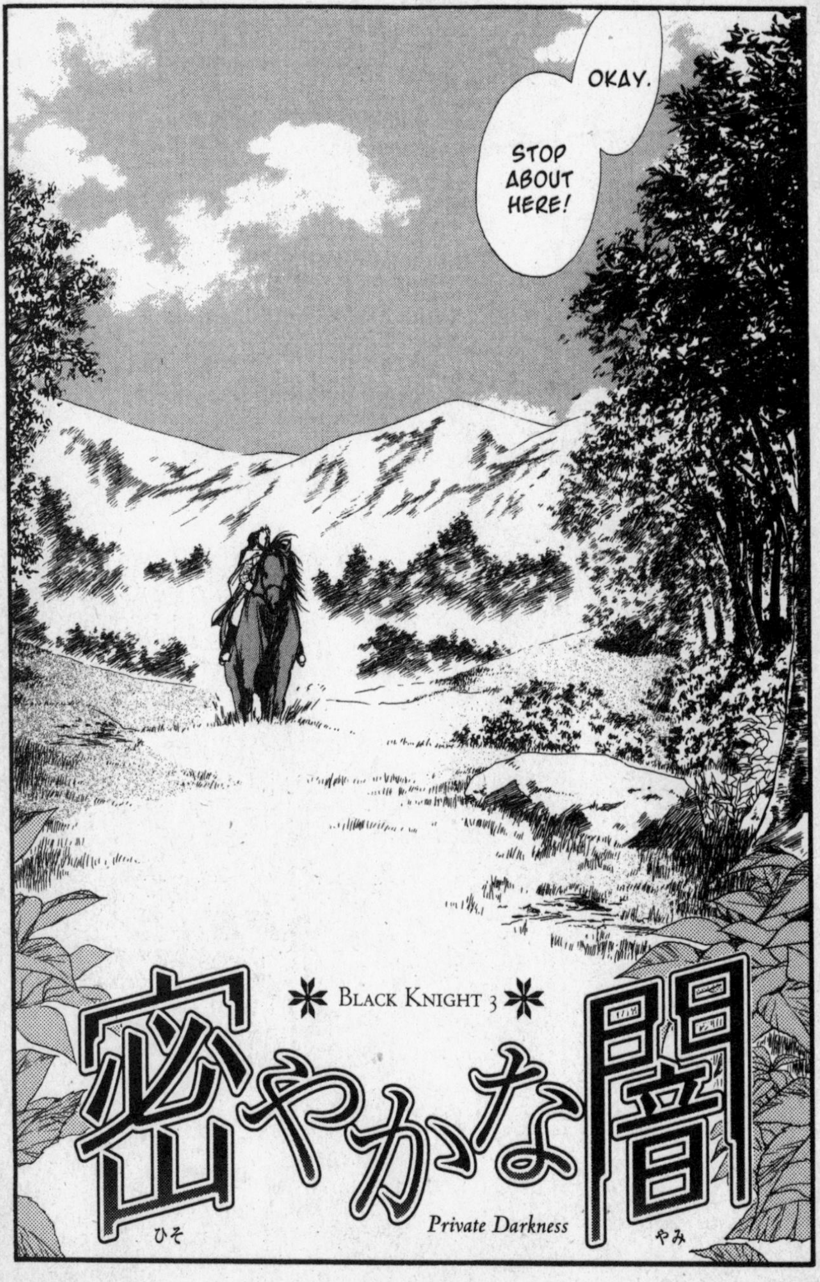
OKAY.
STOP ABOUT HERE!
BLACK KNIGHT 3
密やかな闇
Private Darkness

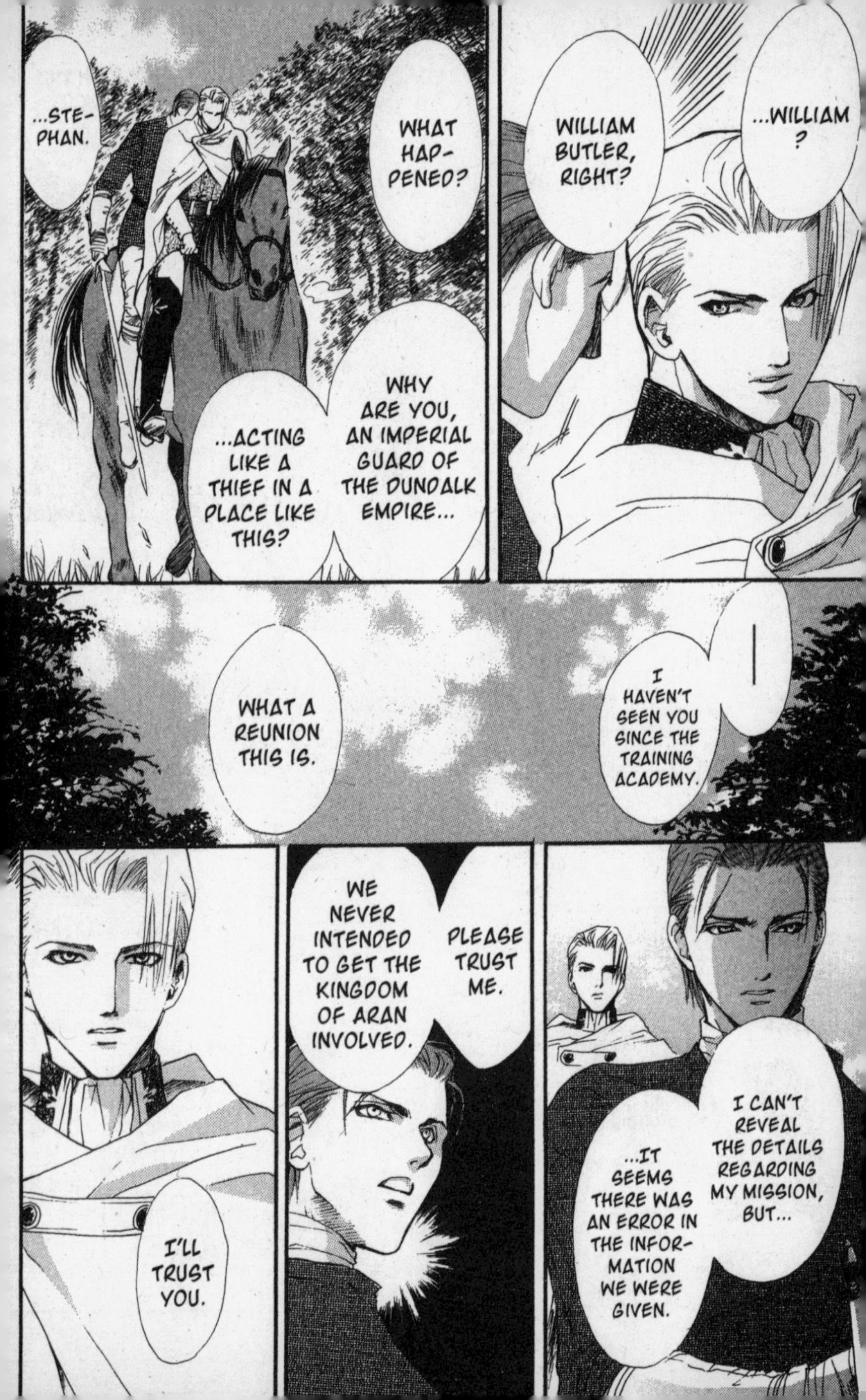
...WILLIAM ?
WILLIAM BUTLER, RIGHT?
WHAT HAP-PENED?
WHY ARE YOU, AN IMPERIAL GUARD OF THE DUNDALK EMPIRE...
...ACTING LIKE A THIEF IN A PLACE LIKE THIS?
...STE-PHAN.
I HAVEN'T SEEN YOU SINCE THE TRAINING ACADEMY.
WHAT A REUNION THIS IS.
I CAN'T REVEAL THE DETAILS REGARDING MY MISSION, BUT...
...IT SEEMS THERE WAS AN ERROR IN THE INFOR-MATION WE WERE GIVEN.
PLEASE TRUST ME.
WE NEVER INTENDED TO GET THE KINGDOM OF ARAN INVOLVED.
I'LL TRUST YOU.

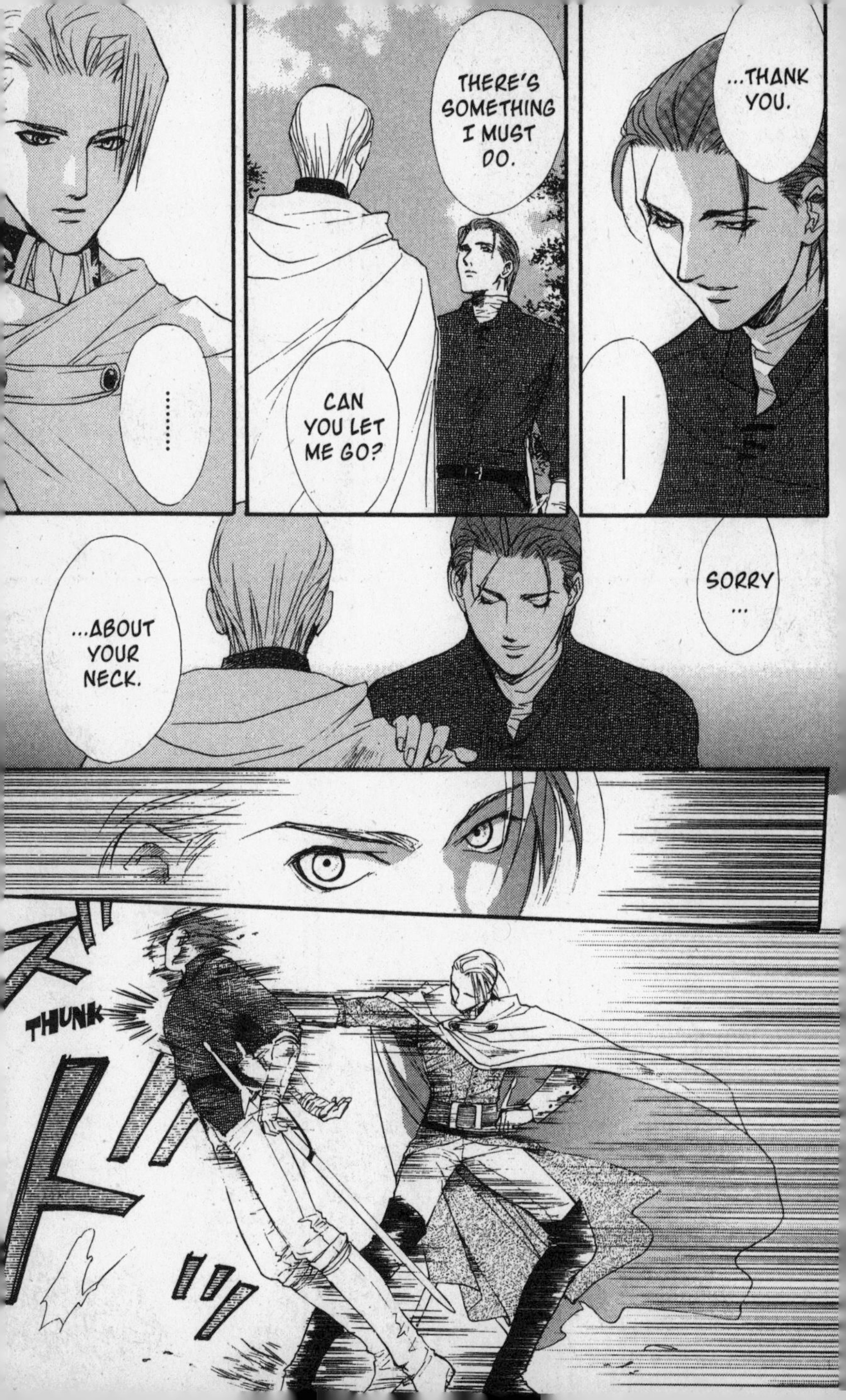
...THANK YOU.
—
THERE'S SOMETHING I MUST DO.
CAN YOU LET ME GO?
......
SORRY...
...ABOUT YOUR NECK.
THUNK

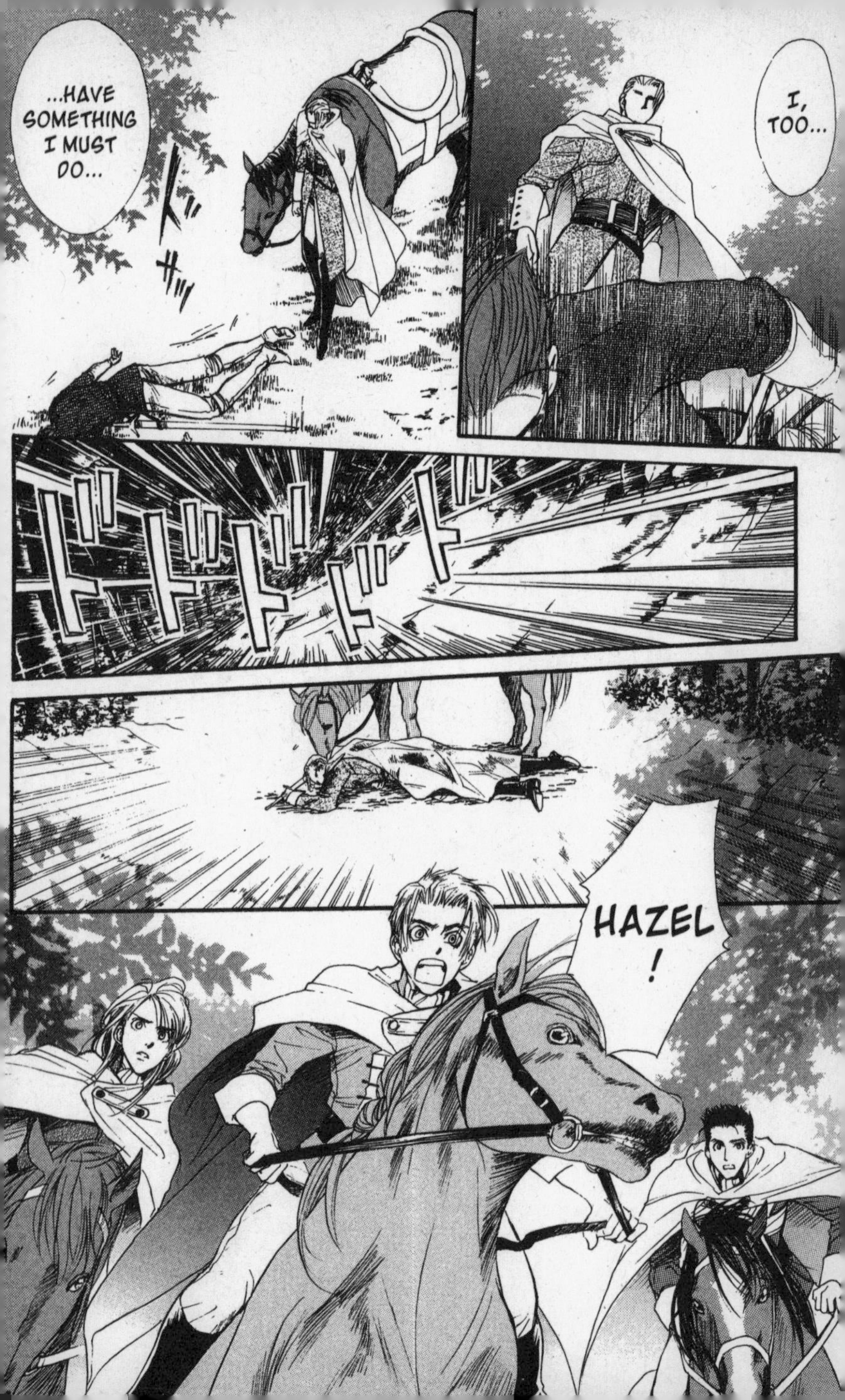
I, TOO...
...HAVE SOMETHING I MUST DO...
ドッ
ザッ
ドドドドドッ
HAZEL!

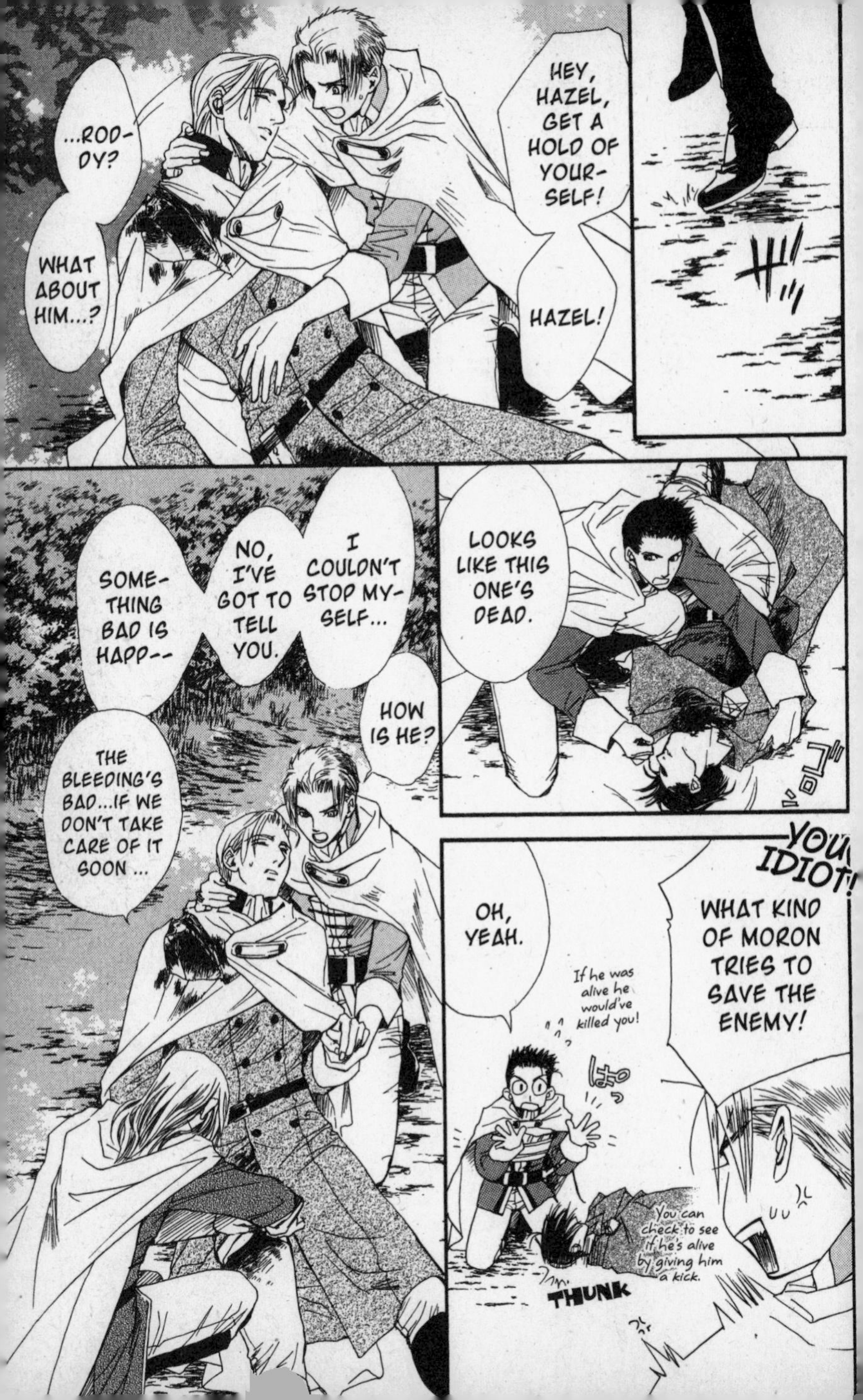
HEY, HAZEL, GET A HOLD OF YOURSELF!
...ROD-DY?
WHAT ABOUT HIM...?
HAZEL!
LOOKS LIKE THIS ONE'S DEAD.
YOU IDIOT!
WHAT KIND OF MORON TRIES TO SAVE THE ENEMY!
OH, YEAH.
If he was alive he would've killed you!
You can check to see if he's alive by giving him a kick.
THUNK
I COULDN'T STOP MYSELF...
NO, I'VE GOT TO TELL YOU.
SOME-THING BAD IS HAPP--
HOW IS HE?
THE BLEEDING'S BAD...IF WE DON'T TAKE CARE OF IT SOON ...

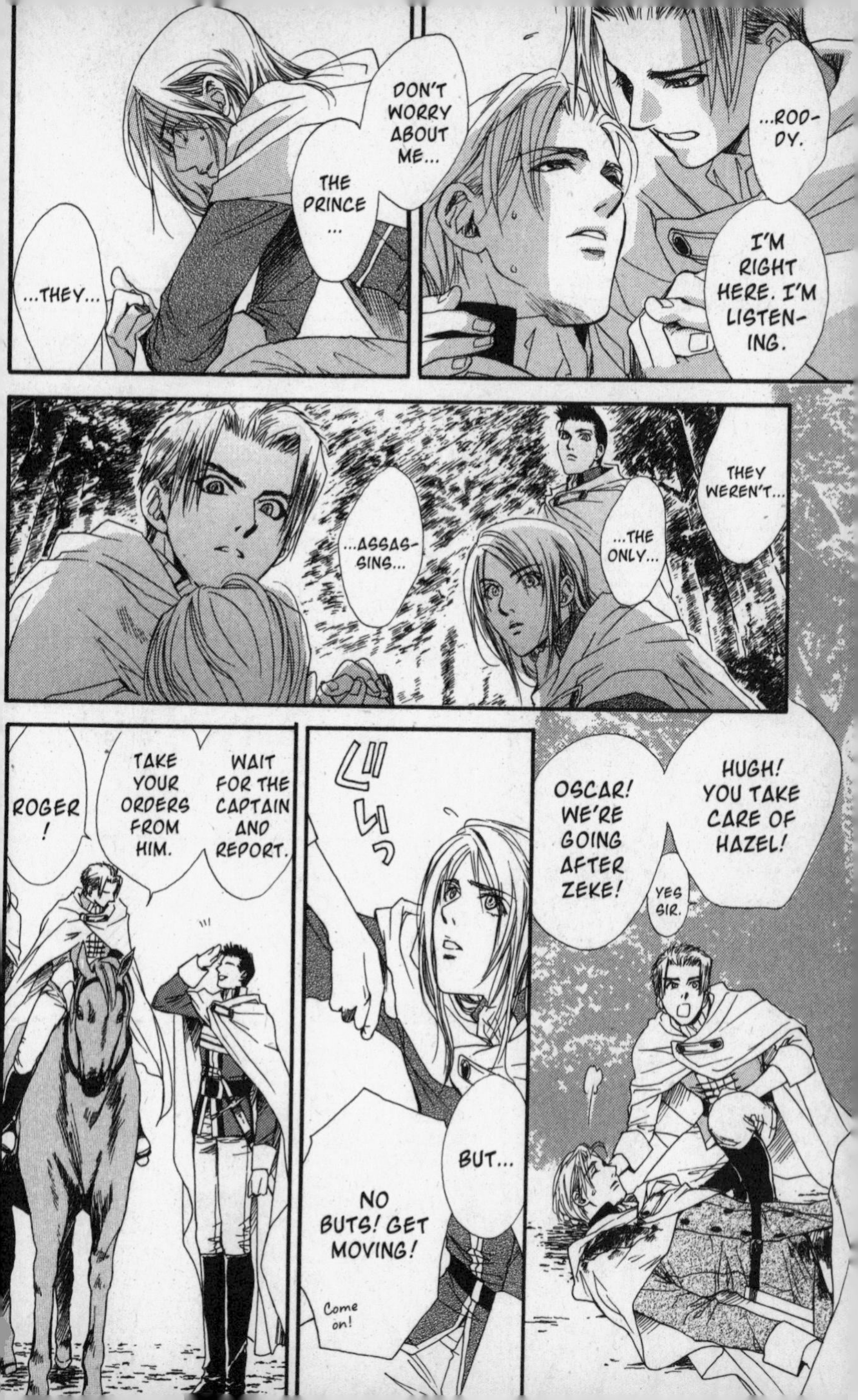
...ROD-DY.
I'M RIGHT HERE. I'M LISTEN-ING.
DON'T WORRY ABOUT ME...
THE PRINCE ...
...THEY...
THEY WEREN'T...
...THE ONLY...
...ASSAS-SINS...
HUGH! YOU TAKE CARE OF HAZEL!
OSCAR! WE'RE GOING AFTER ZEKE!
YES SIR.
ぐいっ
BUT...
NO BUTS! GET MOVING!
Come on!
WAIT FOR THE CAPTAIN AND REPORT.
TAKE YOUR ORDERS FROM HIM.
ROGER!

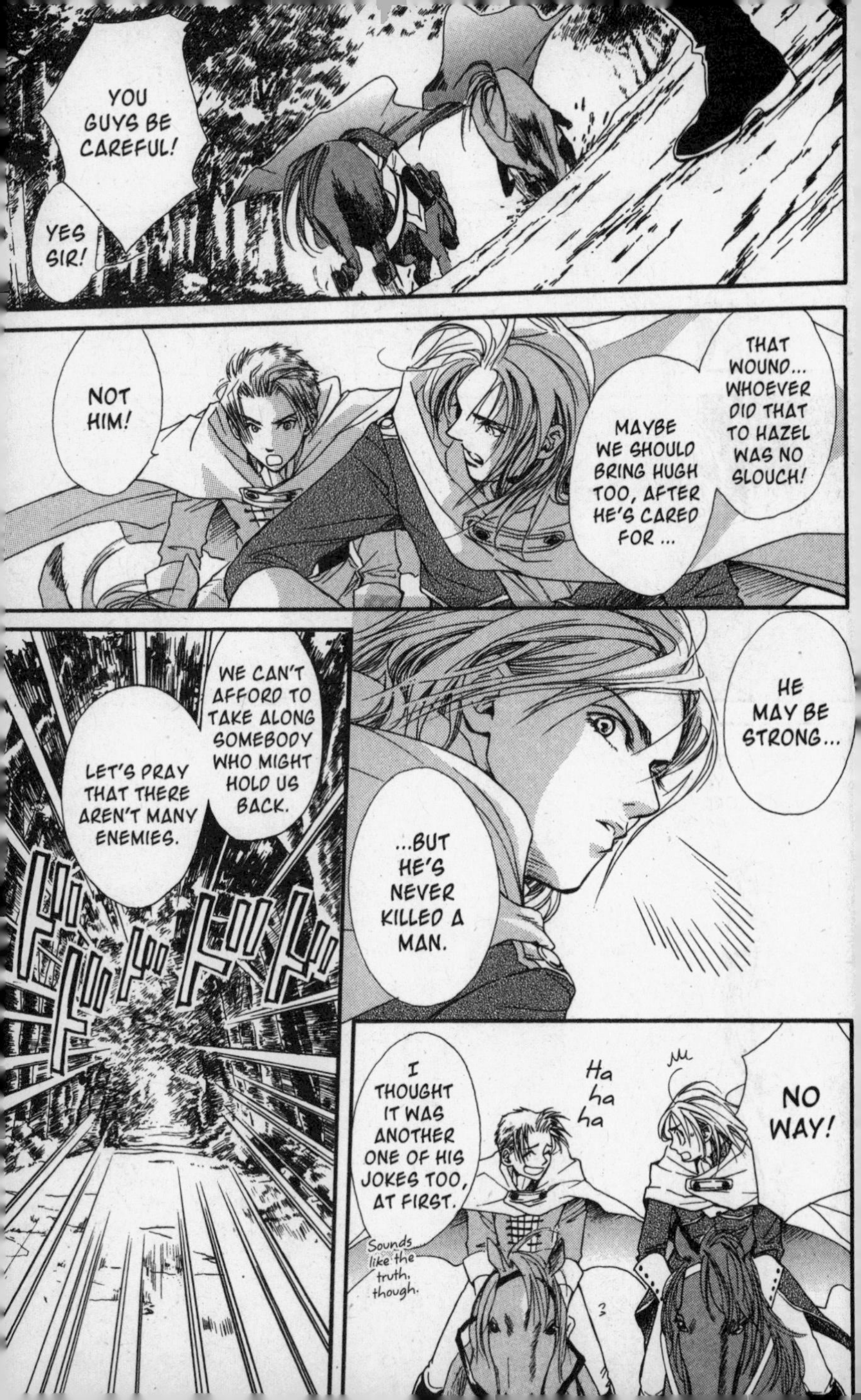
YOU GUYS BE CAREFUL!
YES SIR!
THAT WOUND... WHOEVER DID THAT TO HAZEL WAS NO SLOUCH!
MAYBE WE SHOULD BRING HUGH TOO, AFTER HE'S CARED FOR ...
NOT HIM!
HE MAY BE STRONG...
...BUT HE'S NEVER KILLED A MAN.
NO WAY!
Ha ha ha
I THOUGHT IT WAS ANOTHER ONE OF HIS JOKES TOO, AT FIRST.
Sounds like the truth, though.
WE CAN'T AFFORD TO TAKE ALONG SOMEBODY WHO MIGHT HOLD US BACK.
LET'S PRAY THAT THERE AREN'T MANY ENEMIES.

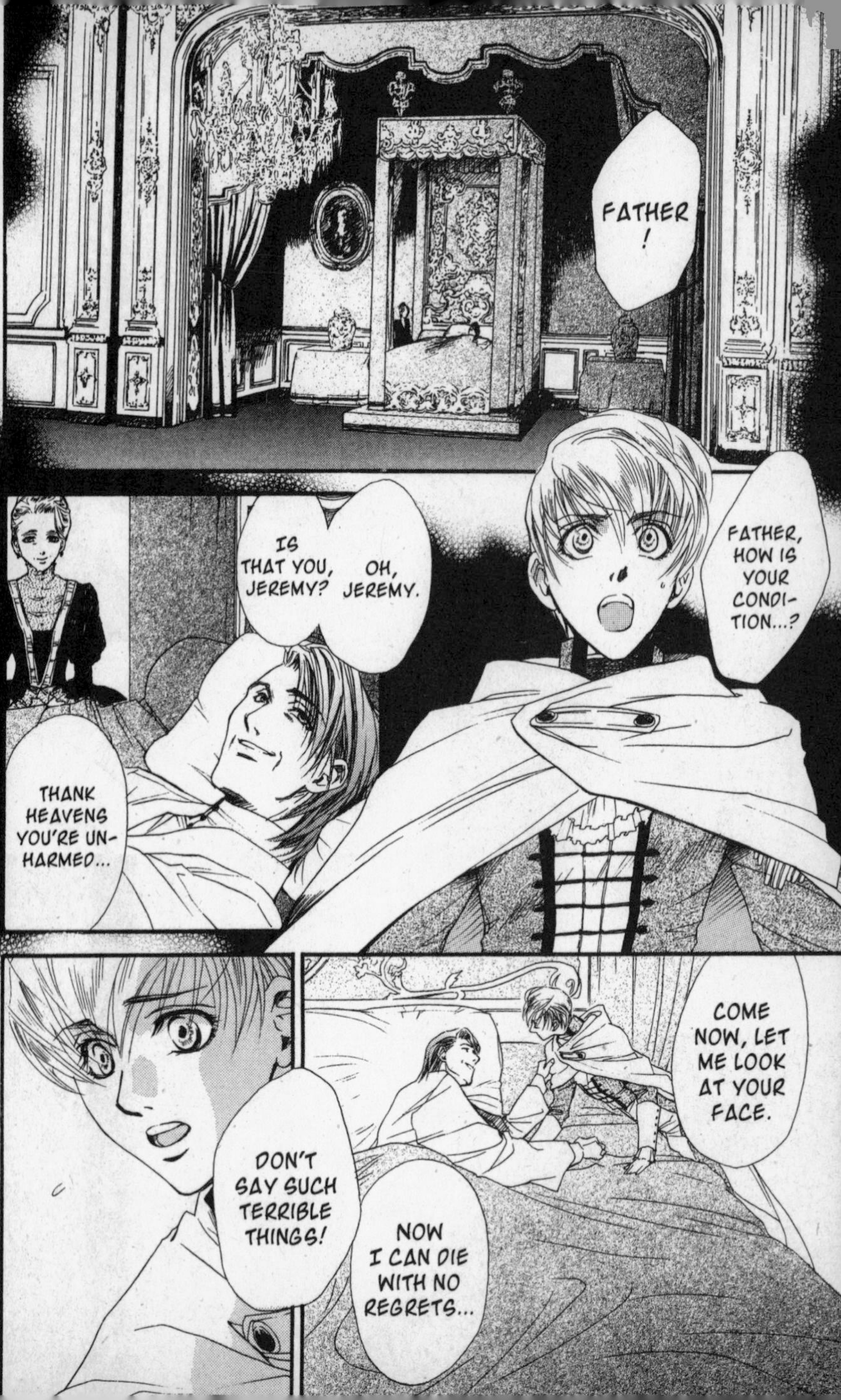
FATHER!
FATHER, HOW IS YOUR CONDITION...?
OH, JEREMY.
IS THAT YOU, JEREMY?
THANK HEAVENS YOU'RE UNHARMED...
COME NOW, LET ME LOOK AT YOUR FACE.
NOW I CAN DIE WITH NO REGRETS...
DON'T SAY SUCH TERRIBLE THINGS!

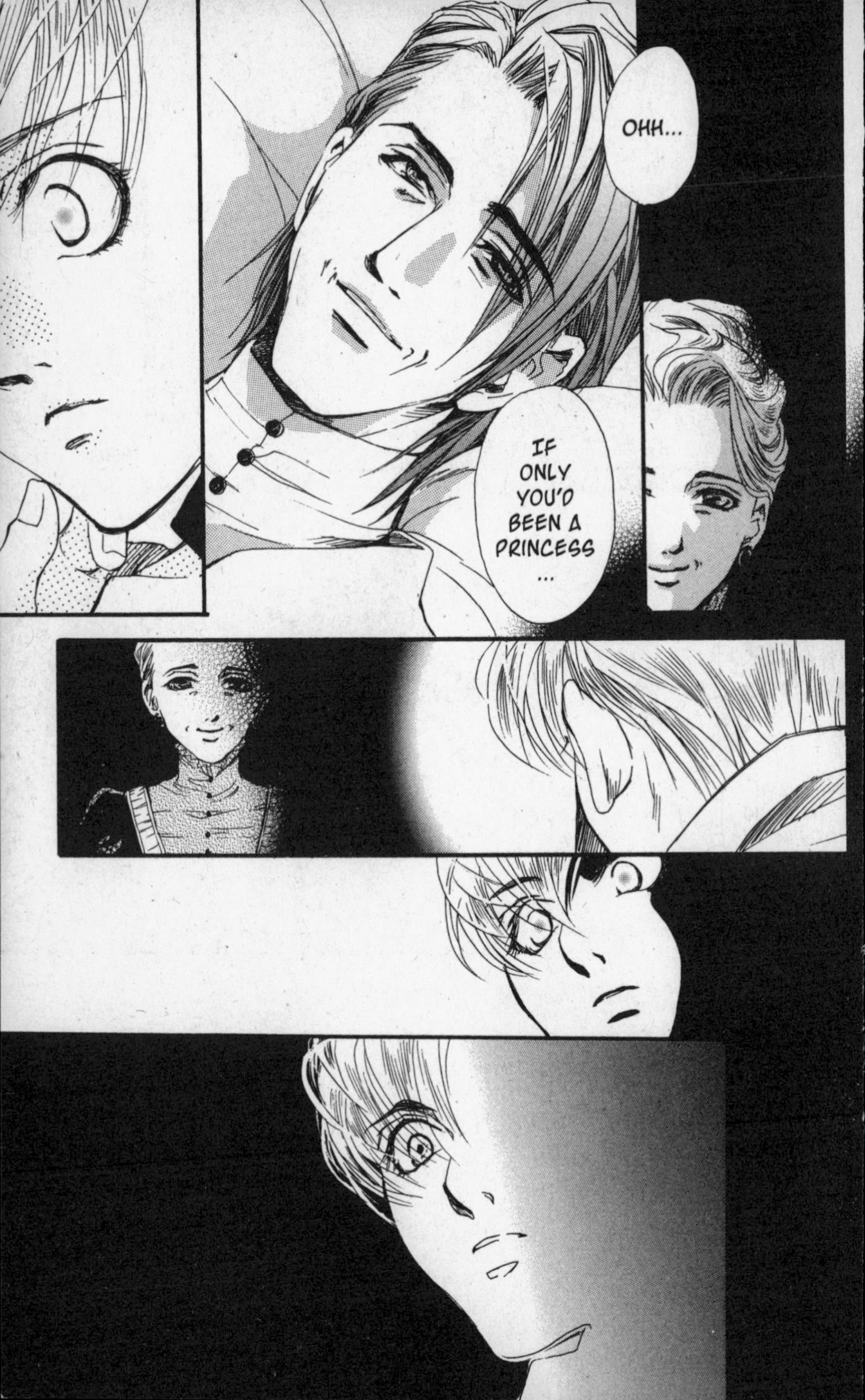
OHH...
IF ONLY YOU'D BEEN A PRINCESS ...

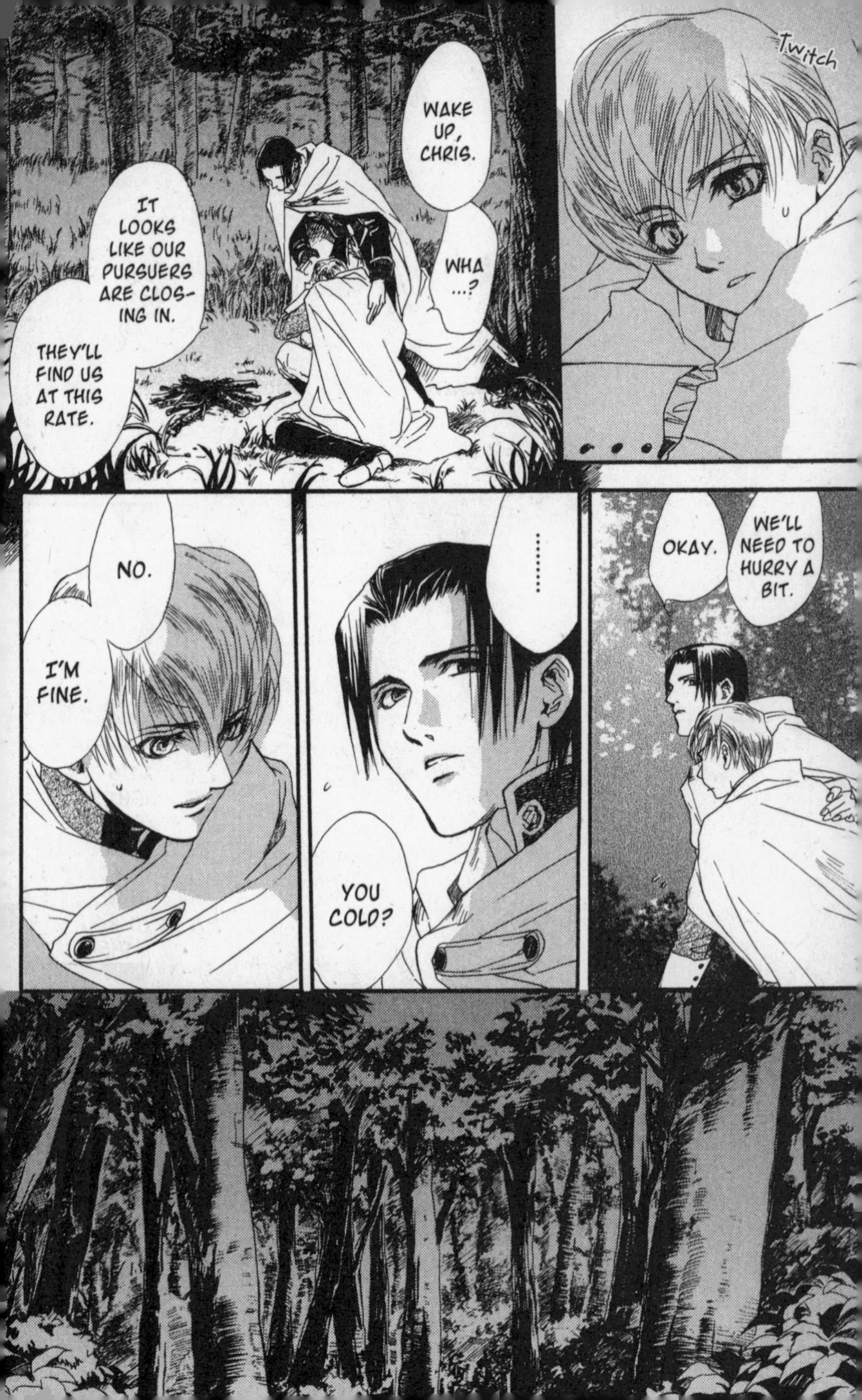
Twitch
...
WAKE UP, CHRIS.
WHA ...?
IT LOOKS LIKE OUR PURSUERS ARE CLOSING IN.
THEY'LL FIND US AT THIS RATE.
WE'LL NEED TO HURRY A BIT.
OKAY.
......
YOU COLD?
NO.
I'M FINE.

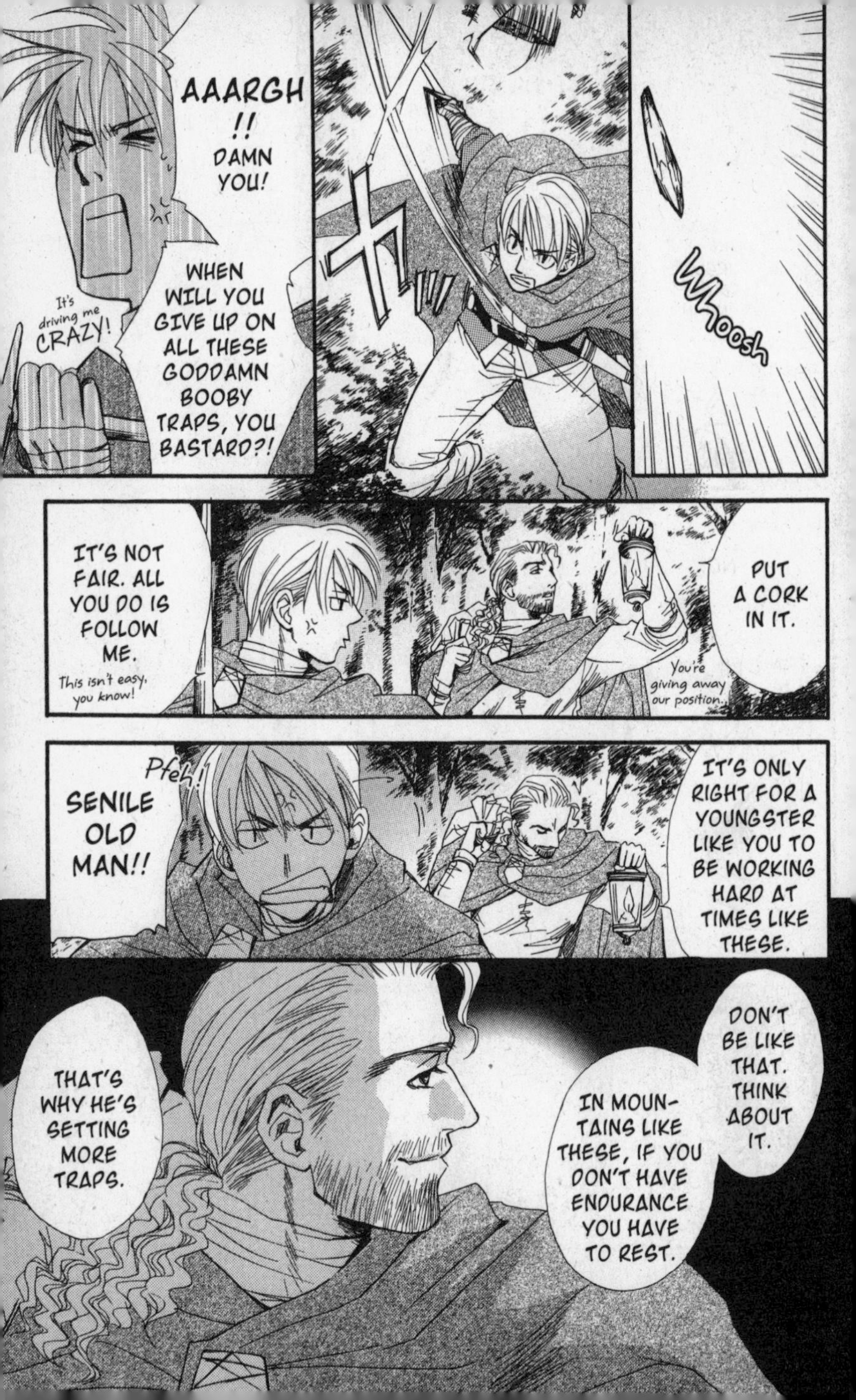
Whoosh
AAARGH!! DAMN YOU!
WHEN WILL YOU GIVE UP ON ALL THESE GODDAMN BOOBY TRAPS, YOU BASTARD?!
It's driving me CRAZY!
PUT A CORK IN IT.
You're giving away our position...
IT'S NOT FAIR. ALL YOU DO IS FOLLOW ME.
This isn't easy, you know!
IT'S ONLY RIGHT FOR A YOUNGSTER LIKE YOU TO BE WORKING HARD AT TIMES LIKE THESE.
Pfeh!
SENILE OLD MAN!!
DON'T BE LIKE THAT. THINK ABOUT IT.
IN MOUNTAINS LIKE THESE, IF YOU DON'T HAVE ENDURANCE YOU HAVE TO REST.
THAT'S WHY HE'S SETTING MORE TRAPS.

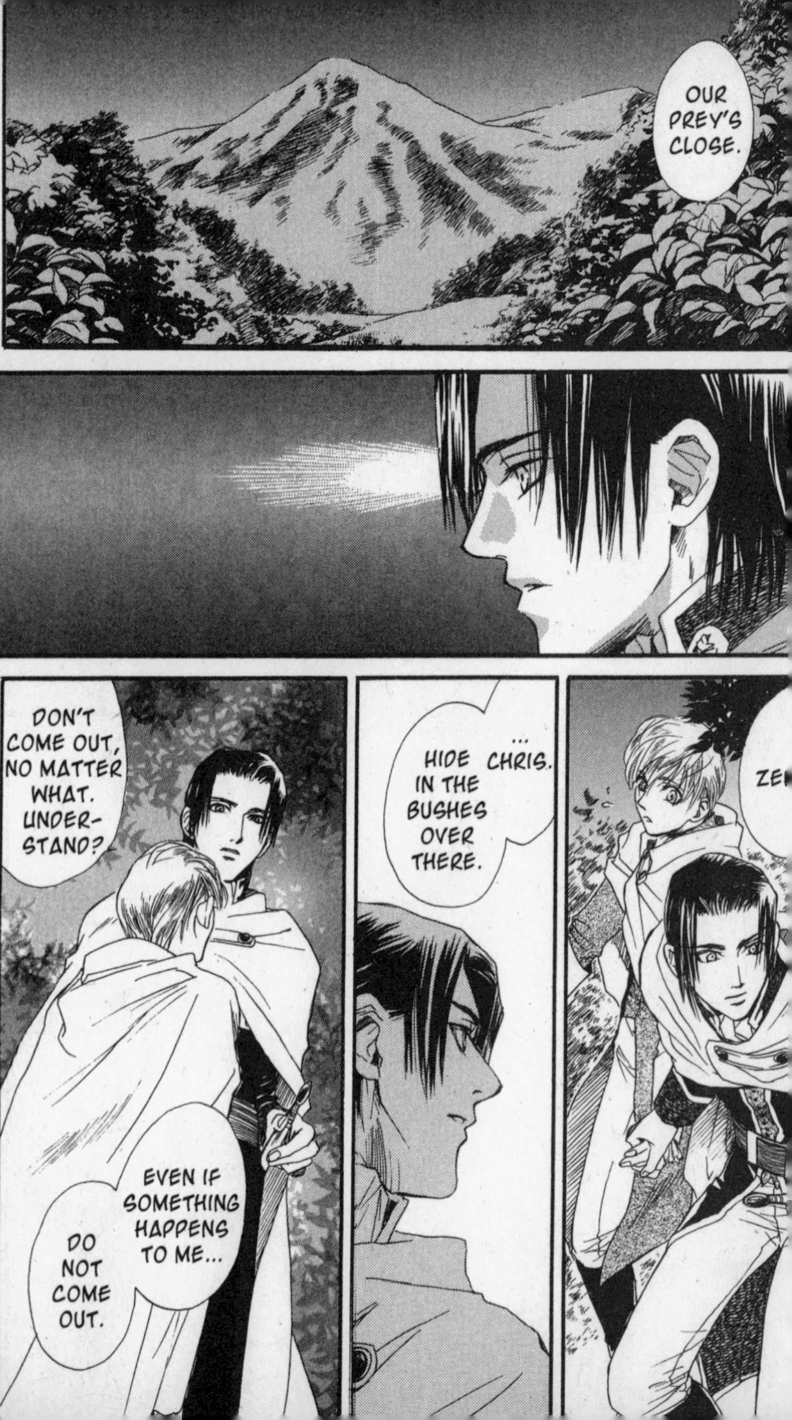
OUR PREY'S CLOSE.
ZE
... CHRIS.
HIDE IN THE BUSHES OVER THERE.
DON'T COME OUT, NO MATTER WHAT. UNDER-STAND?
EVEN IF SOMETHING HAPPENS TO ME...
DO NOT COME OUT.

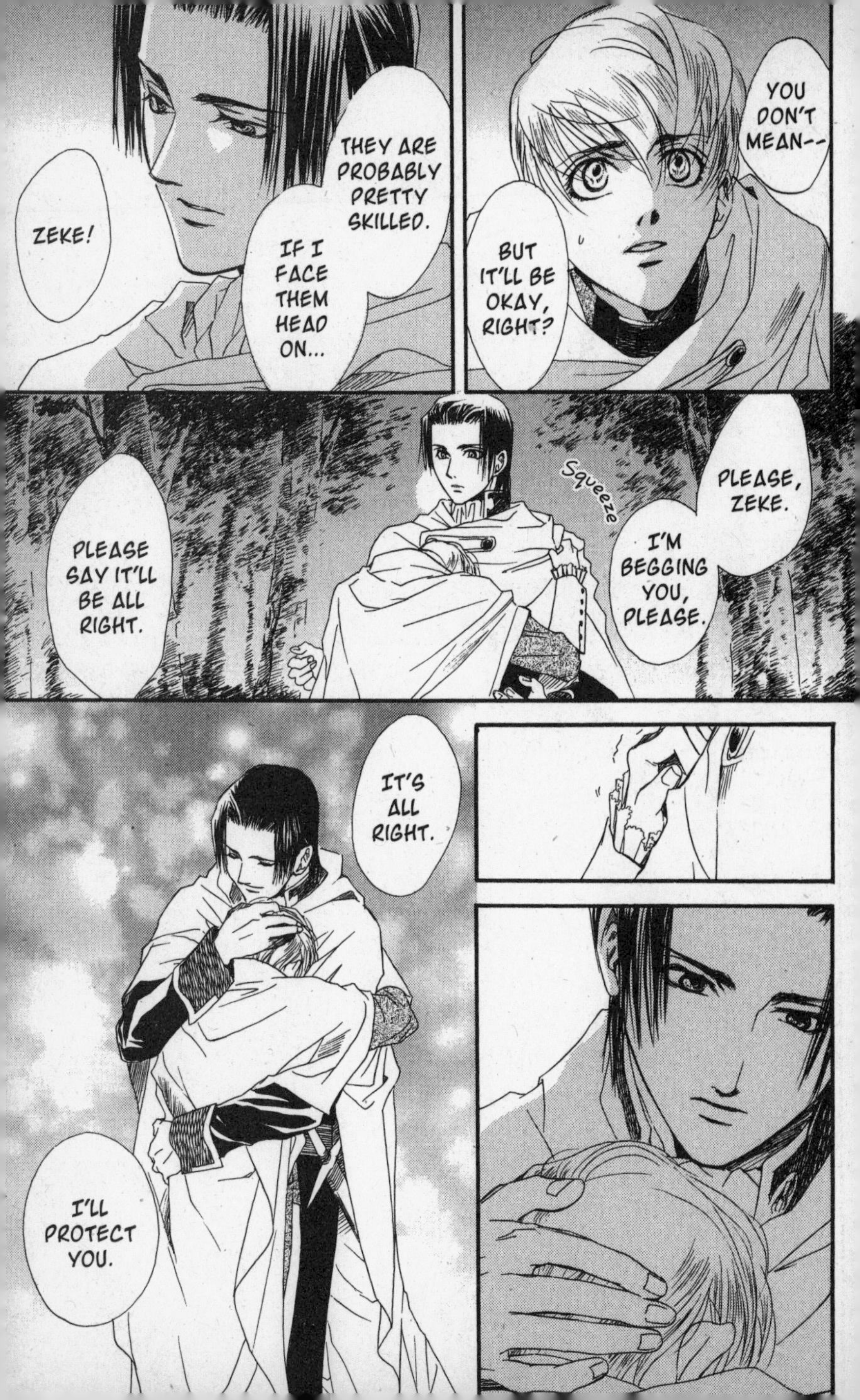

YOU DON'T MEAN--
BUT IT'LL BE OKAY, RIGHT?
THEY ARE PROBABLY PRETTY SKILLED.
IF I FACE THEM HEAD ON...
ZEKE!
PLEASE, ZEKE.
I'M BEGGING YOU, PLEASE.
Squeeze
PLEASE SAY IT'LL BE ALL RIGHT.
IT'S ALL RIGHT.
I'LL PROTECT YOU.

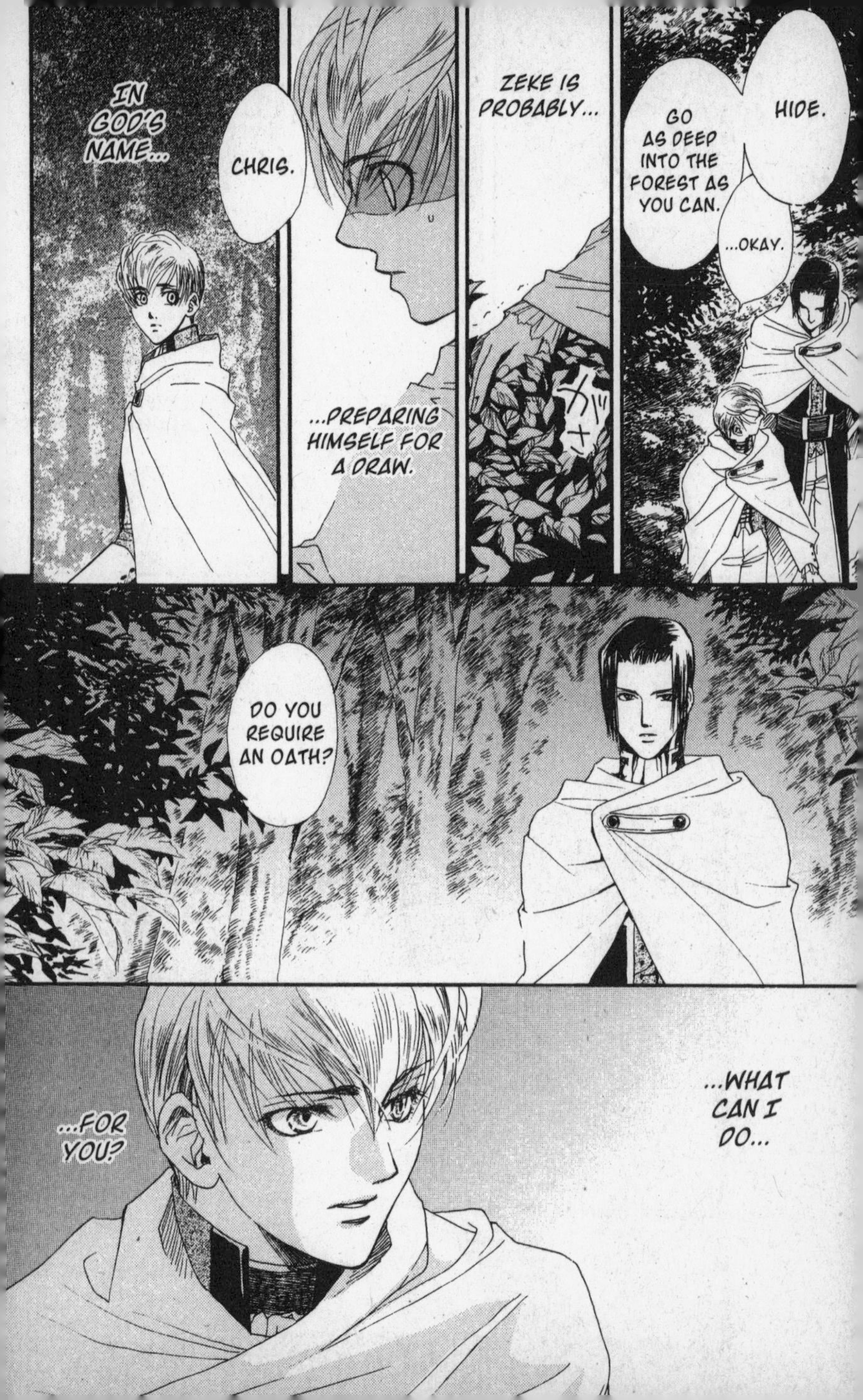
HIDE.
GO AS DEEP INTO THE FOREST AS YOU CAN.
...OKAY.
ZEKE IS PROBABLY...
...PREPARING HIMSELF FOR A DRAW.
CHRIS.
IN GOD'S NAME...
DO YOU REQUIRE AN OATH?
...WHAT CAN I DO...
...FOR YOU?

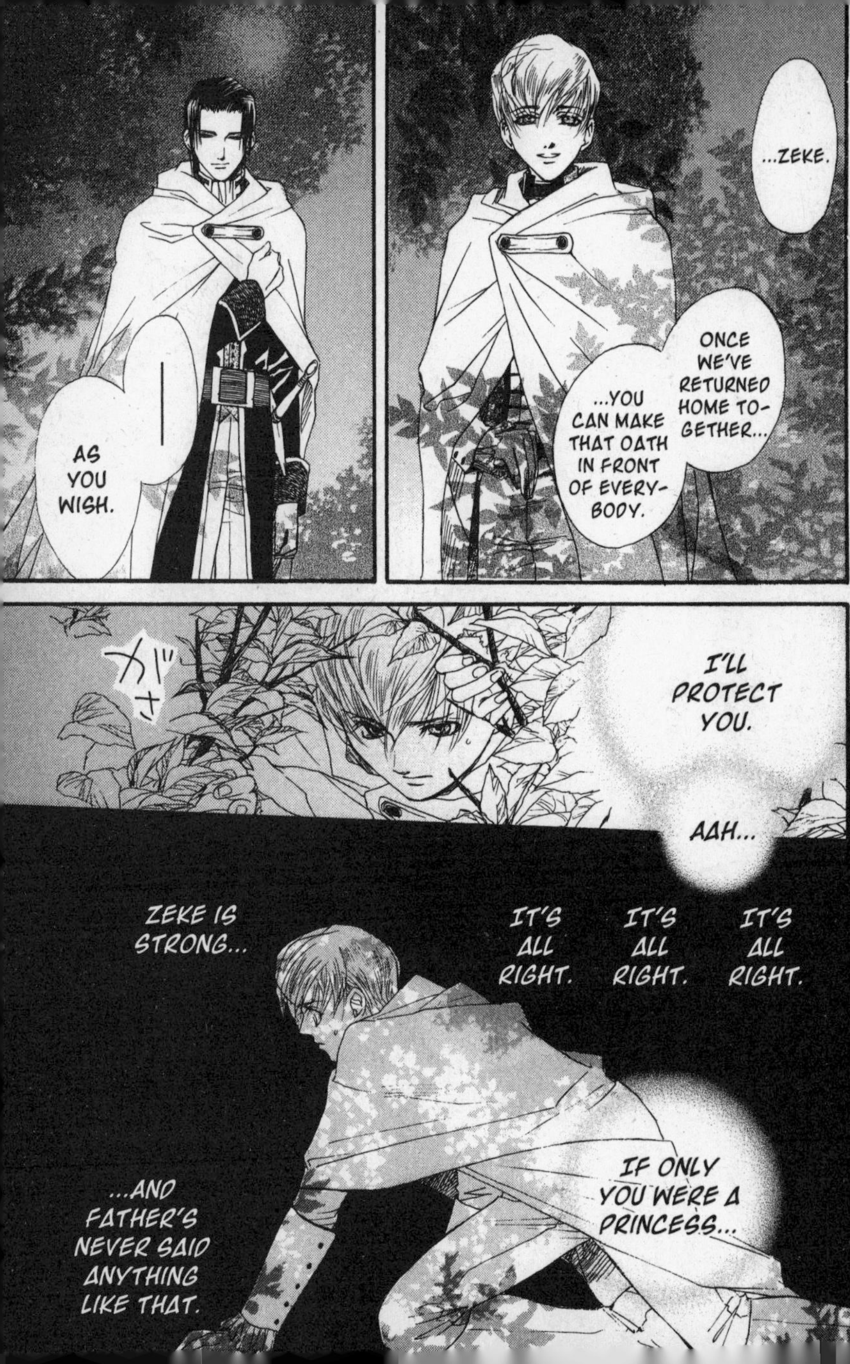
...ZEKE.
ONCE WE'VE RETURNED HOME TO-GETHER...
...YOU CAN MAKE THAT OATH IN FRONT OF EVERY-BODY.
AS YOU WISH.
がさ
I'LL PROTECT YOU.
AAH...
IT'S ALL RIGHT.
IT'S ALL RIGHT.
IT'S ALL RIGHT.
ZEKE IS STRONG...
IF ONLY YOU WERE A PRINCESS...
...AND FATHER'S NEVER SAID ANYTHING LIKE THAT.

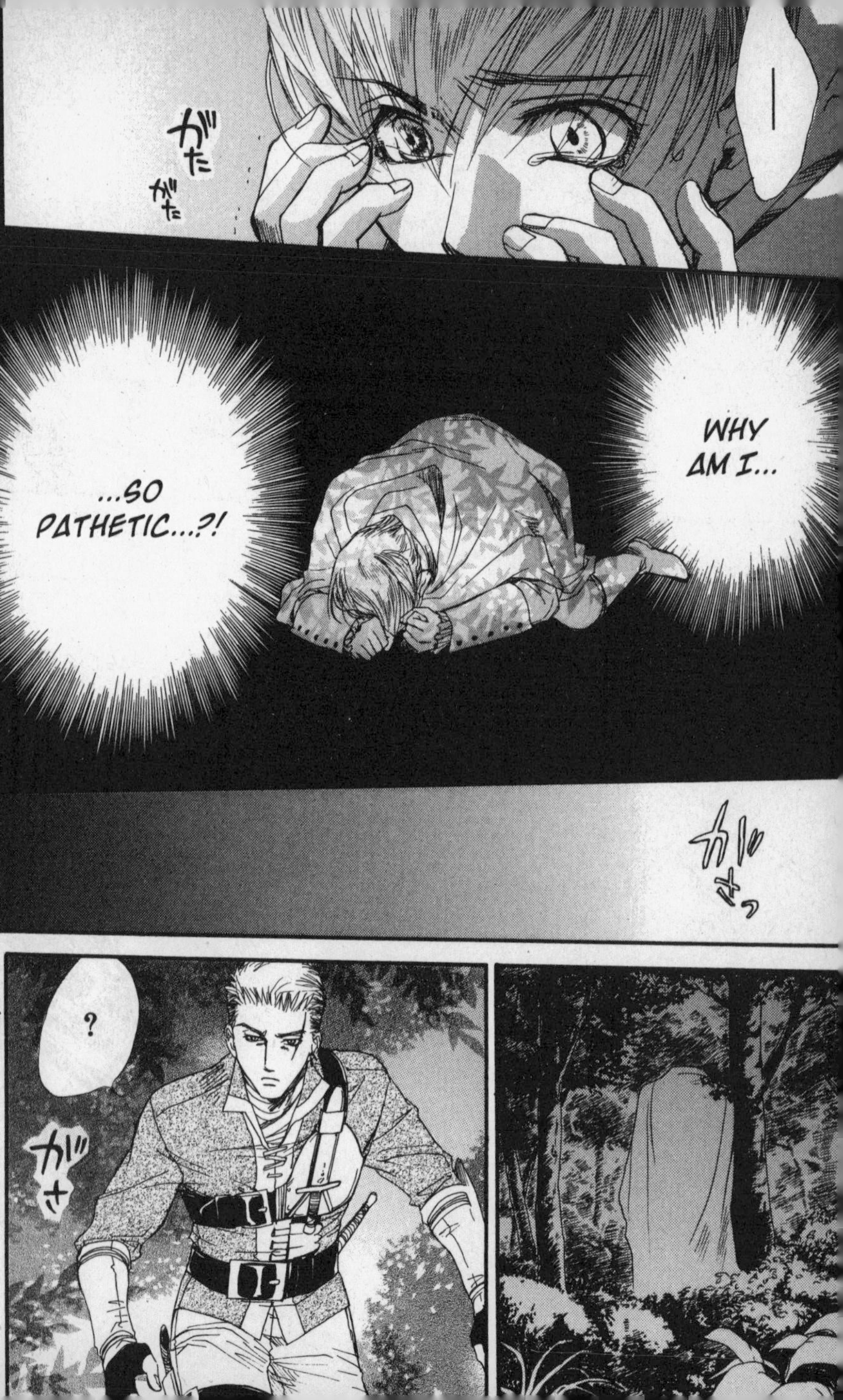
—
がた
がた
WHY AM I...
...SO PATHETIC...?!
がさっ
?
がさ

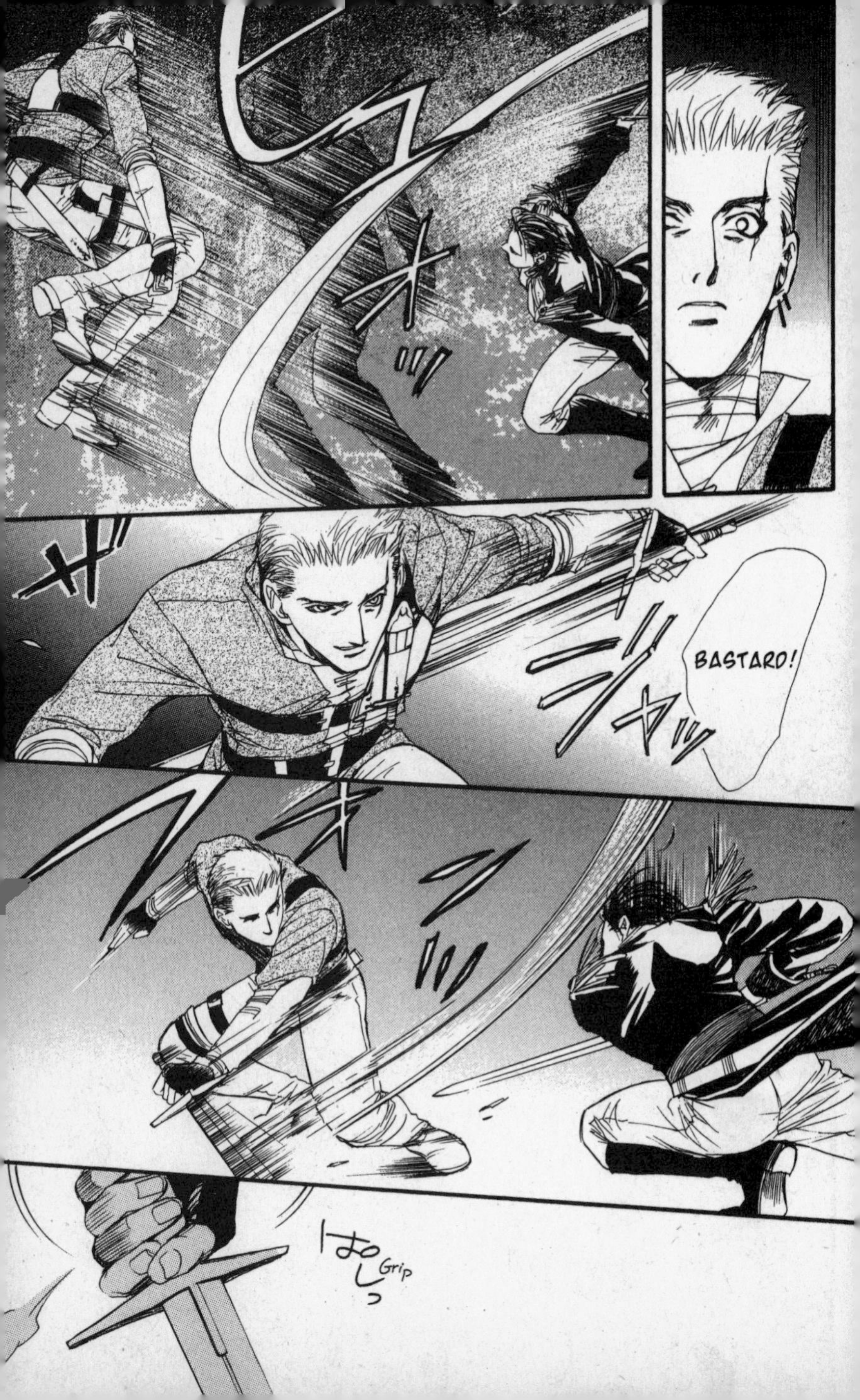
BASTARD!
Grip

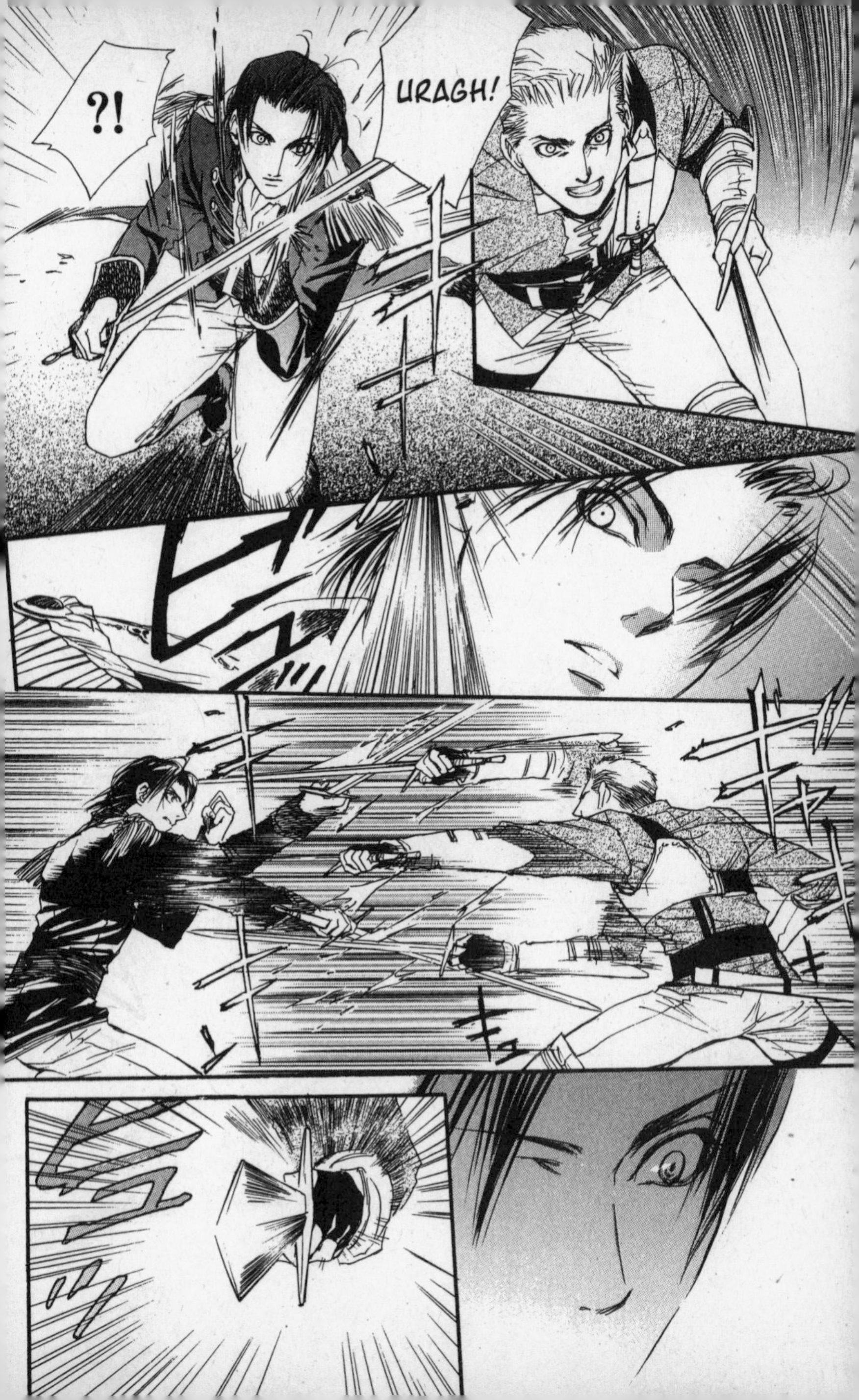
URAGH!
?!

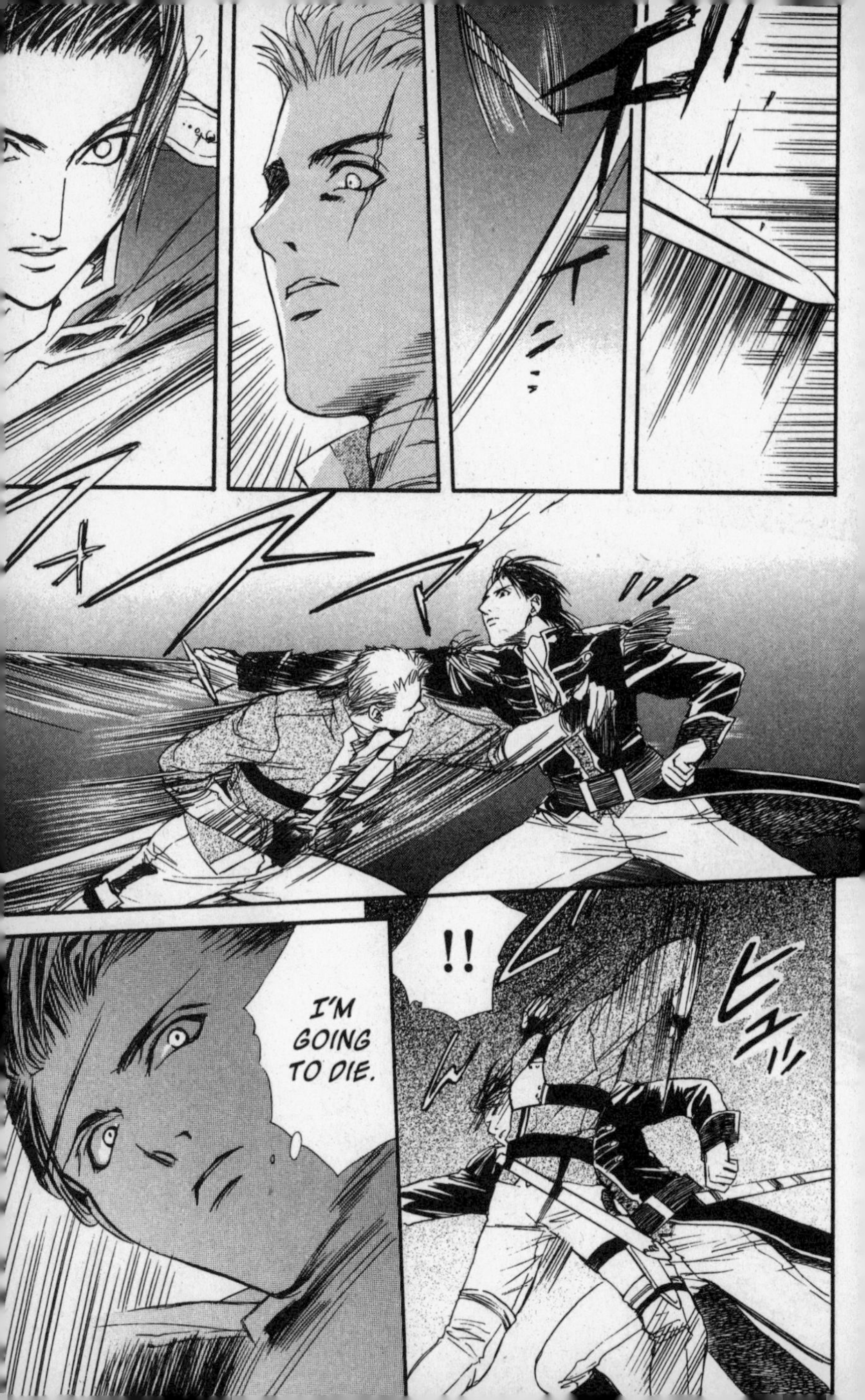
!!
I'M GOING TO DIE.

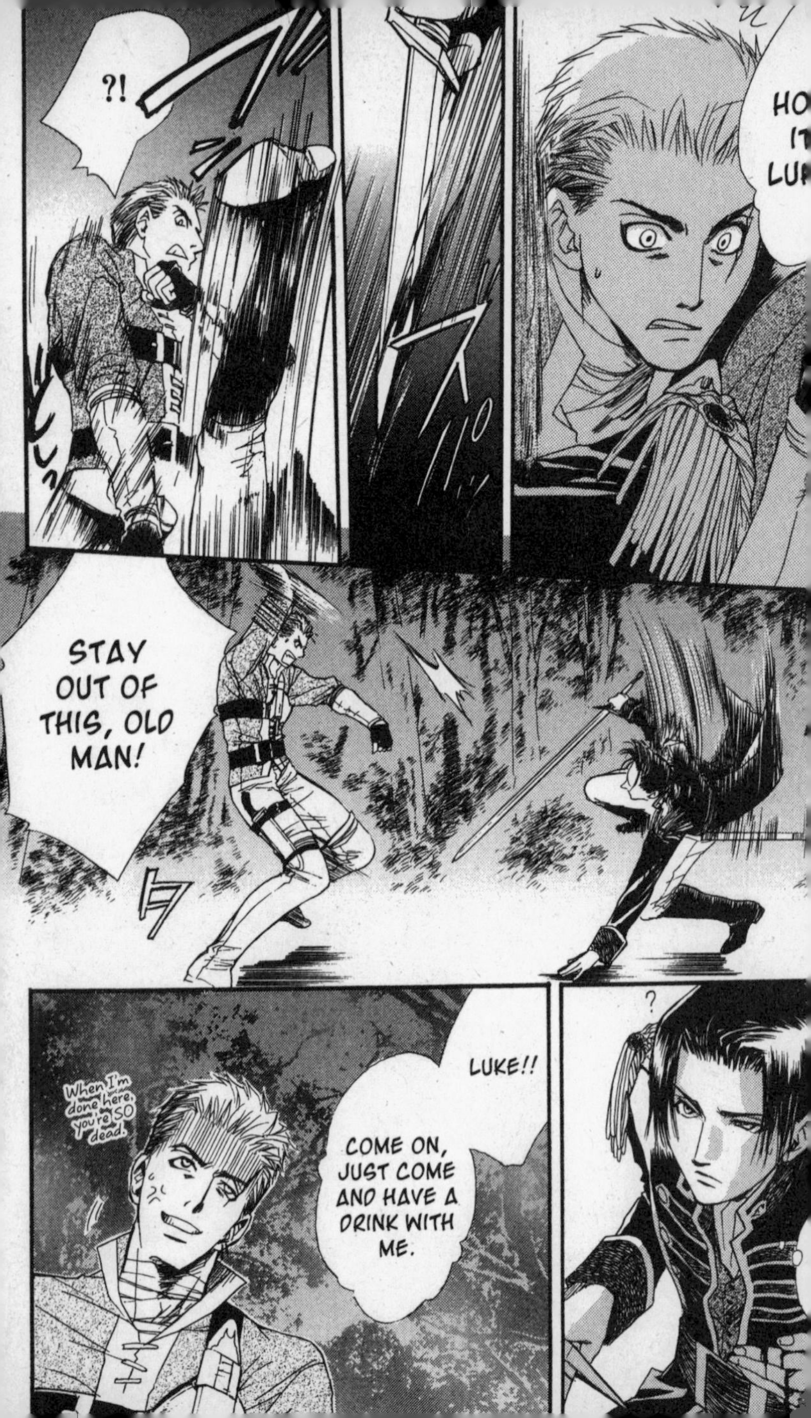
HO IT LU
?!
STAY OUT OF THIS, OLD MAN!
?
LUKE!!
COME ON, JUST COME AND HAVE A DRINK WITH ME.
When I'm done here, you're SO dead.

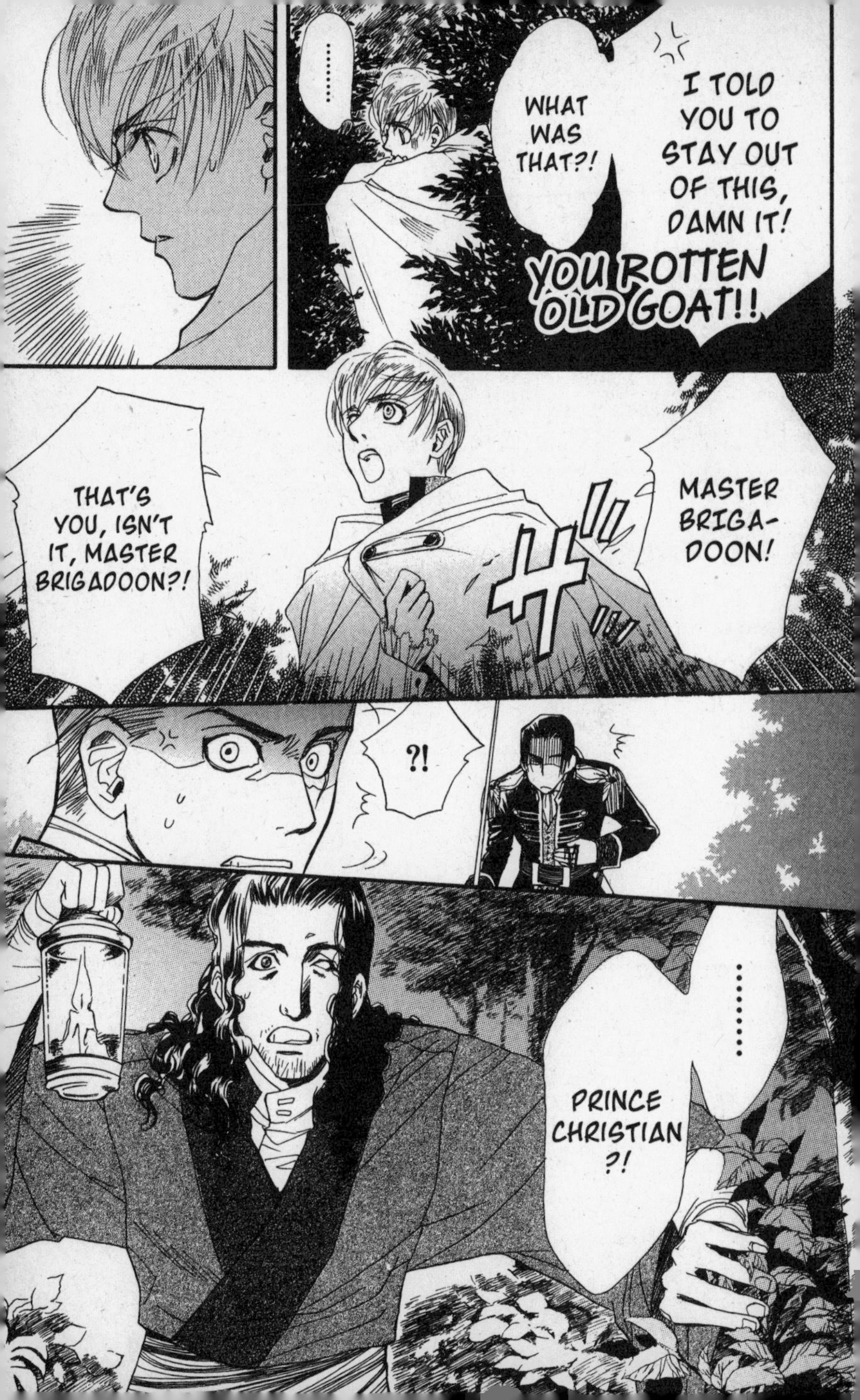
I TOLD YOU TO STAY OUT OF THIS, DAMN IT!
YOU ROTTEN OLD GOAT!!
WHAT WAS THAT?!
......
MASTER BRIGADOON!
THAT'S YOU, ISN'T IT, MASTER BRIGADOON?!
?!
......
PRINCE CHRISTIAN ?!

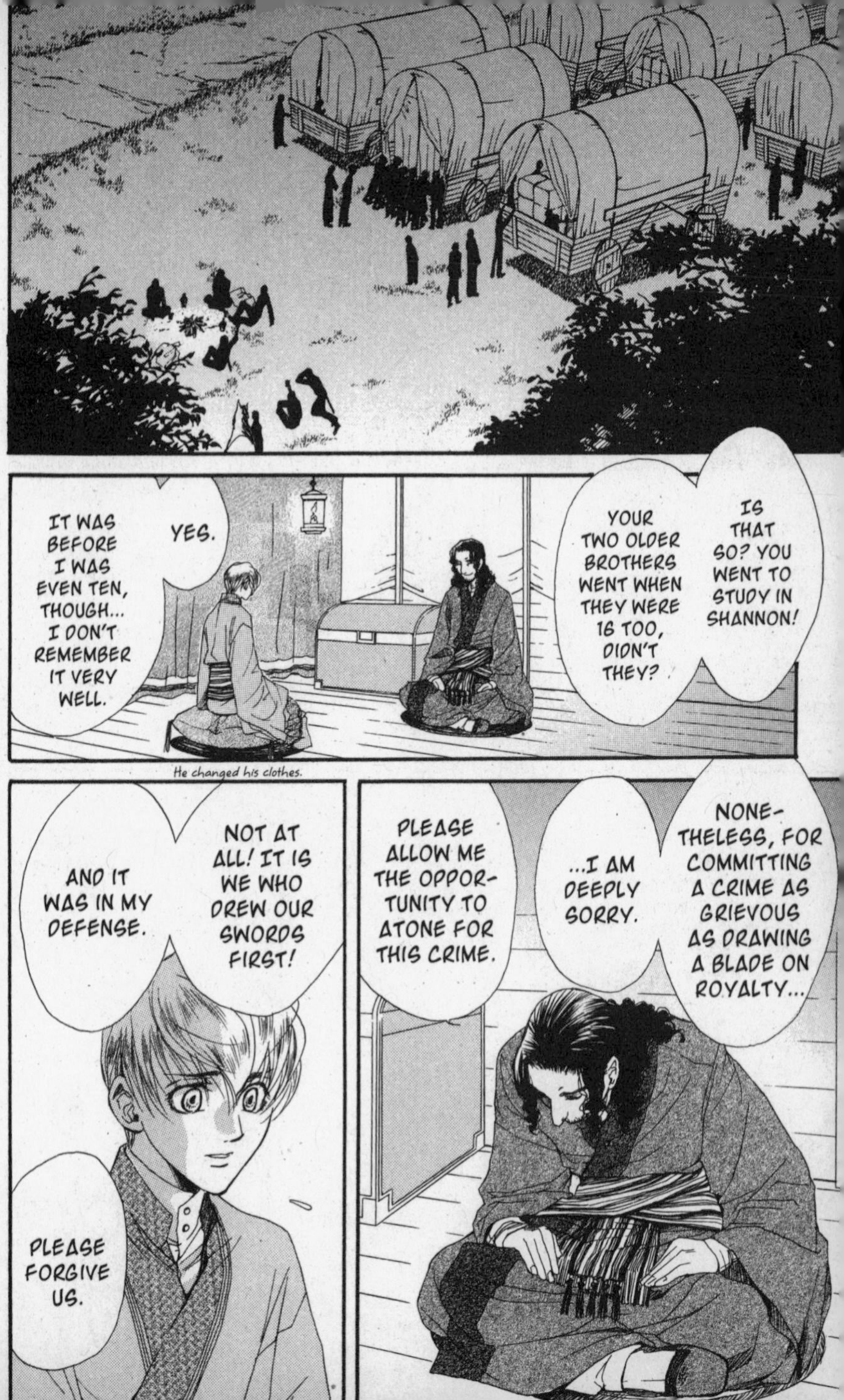
IS THAT SO? YOU WENT TO STUDY IN SHANNON!
YOUR TWO OLDER BROTHERS WENT WHEN THEY WERE 16 TOO, DIDN'T THEY?
YES.
IT WAS BEFORE I WAS EVEN TEN, THOUGH... I DON'T REMEMBER IT VERY WELL.
He changed his clothes.
NONE-THELESS, FOR COMMITTING A CRIME AS GRIEVOUS AS DRAWING A BLADE ON ROYALTY...
...I AM DEEPLY SORRY.
PLEASE ALLOW ME THE OPPOR-TUNITY TO ATONE FOR THIS CRIME.
NOT AT ALL! IT IS WE WHO DREW OUR SWORDS FIRST!
AND IT WAS IN MY DEFENSE.
PLEASE FORGIVE US.

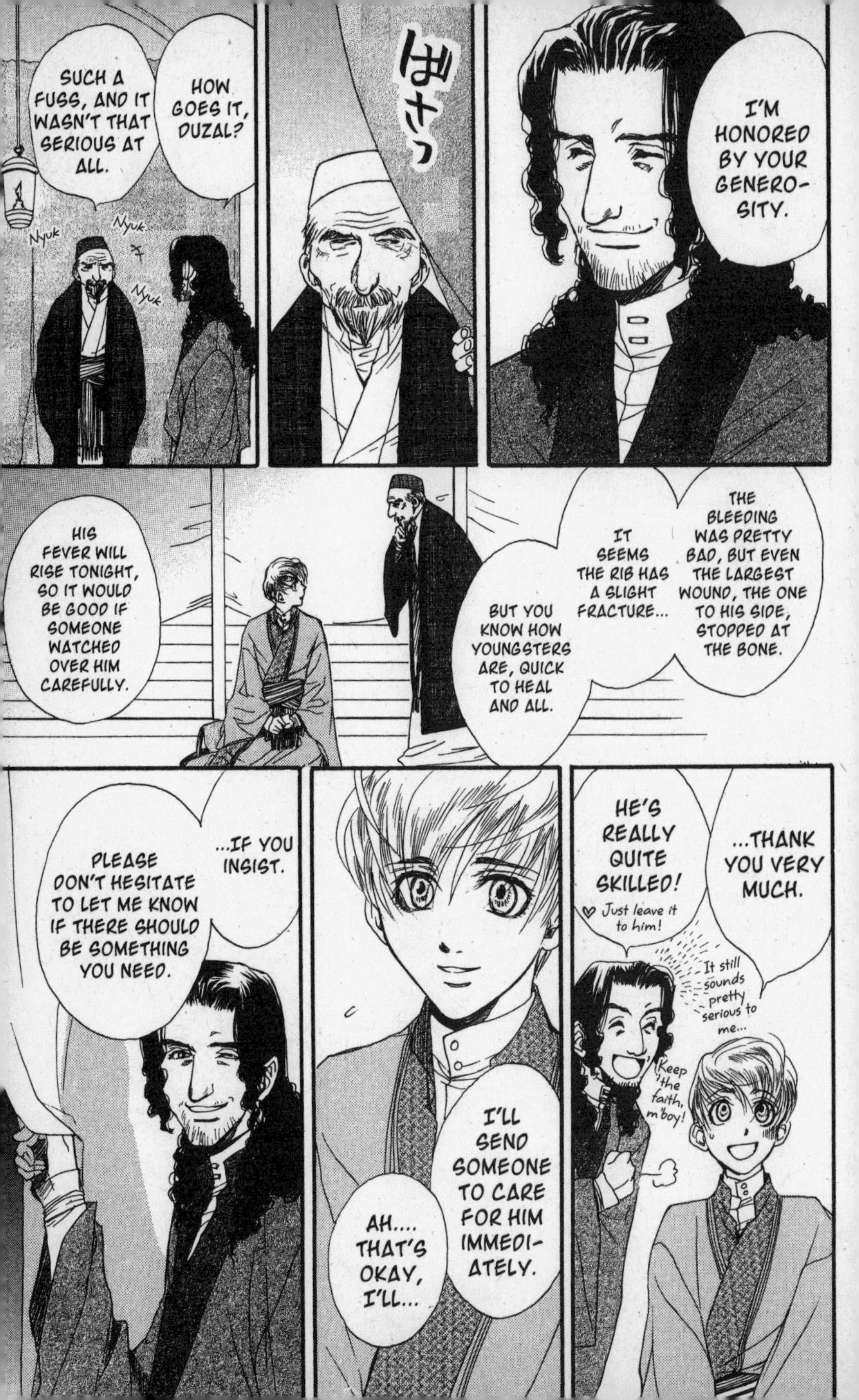
I'M HONORED BY YOUR GENEROSITY.
ばさっ
HOW GOES IT, DUZAL?
SUCH A FUSS, AND IT WASN'T THAT SERIOUS AT ALL.
Nyuk
Nyuk
Nyuk
THE BLEEDING WAS PRETTY BAD, BUT EVEN THE LARGEST WOUND, THE ONE TO HIS SIDE, STOPPED AT THE BONE.
IT SEEMS THE RIB HAS A SLIGHT FRACTURE...
BUT YOU KNOW HOW YOUNGSTERS ARE, QUICK TO HEAL AND ALL.
HIS FEVER WILL RISE TONIGHT, SO IT WOULD BE GOOD IF SOMEONE WATCHED OVER HIM CAREFULLY.
...THANK YOU VERY MUCH.
HE'S REALLY QUITE SKILLED!
Just leave it to him!
It still sounds pretty serious to me...
Keep the faith, m'boy!
I'LL SEND SOMEONE TO CARE FOR HIM IMMEDIATELY.
AH.... THAT'S OKAY, I'LL...
...IF YOU INSIST.
PLEASE DON'T HESITATE TO LET ME KNOW IF THERE SHOULD BE SOMETHING YOU NEED.

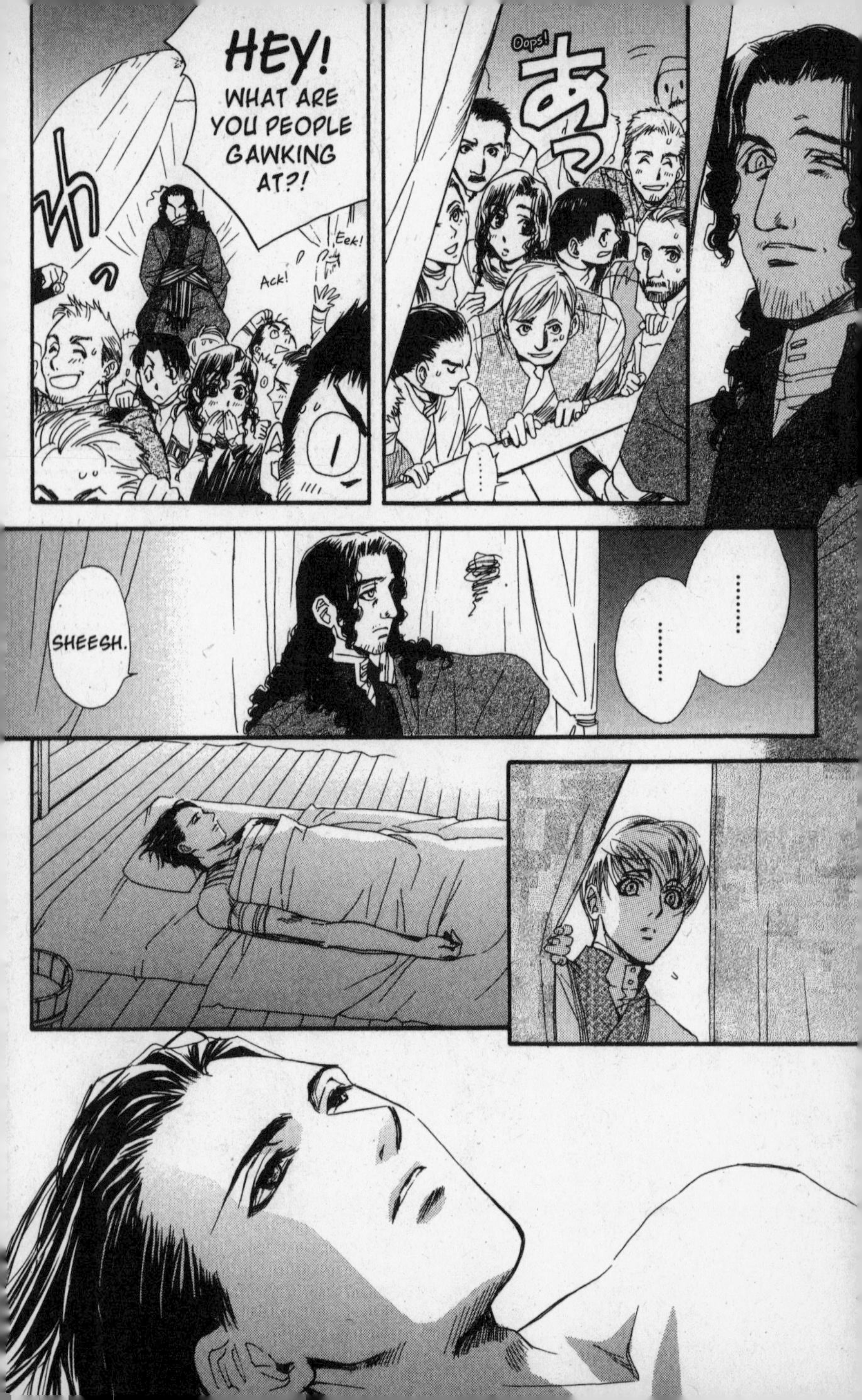
Oops!
あっ
......
HEY! WHAT ARE YOU PEOPLE GAWKING AT?!
Eek!
Ack!
わっ
......
......
SHEESH.

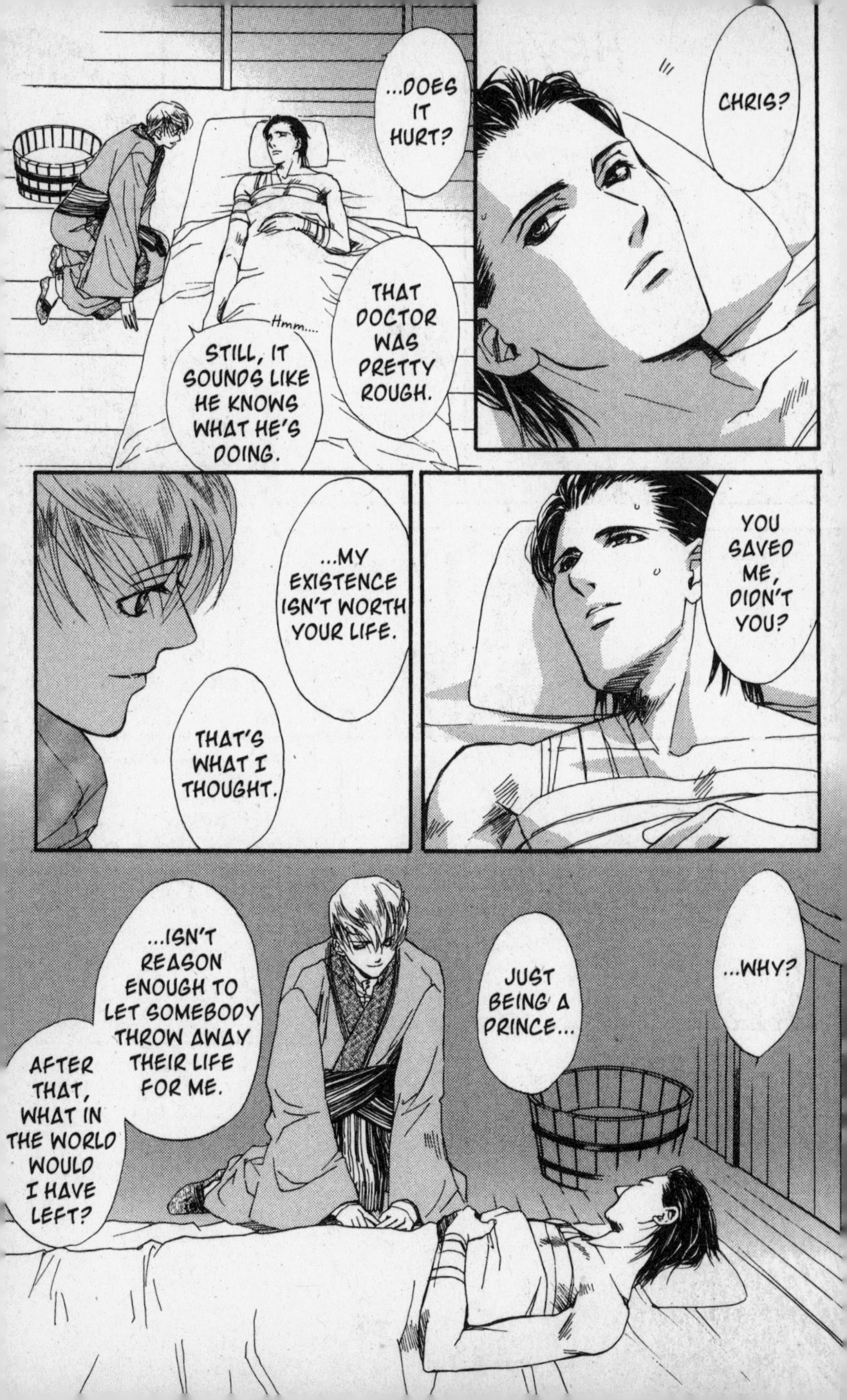
CHRIS?
...DOES IT HURT?
THAT DOCTOR WAS PRETTY ROUGH.
Hmm....
STILL, IT SOUNDS LIKE HE KNOWS WHAT HE'S DOING.
YOU SAVED ME, DIDN'T YOU?
...MY EXISTENCE ISN'T WORTH YOUR LIFE.
THAT'S WHAT I THOUGHT.
...WHY?
JUST BEING A PRINCE...
...ISN'T REASON ENOUGH TO LET SOMEBODY THROW AWAY THEIR LIFE FOR ME.
AFTER THAT, WHAT IN THE WORLD WOULD I HAVE LEFT?

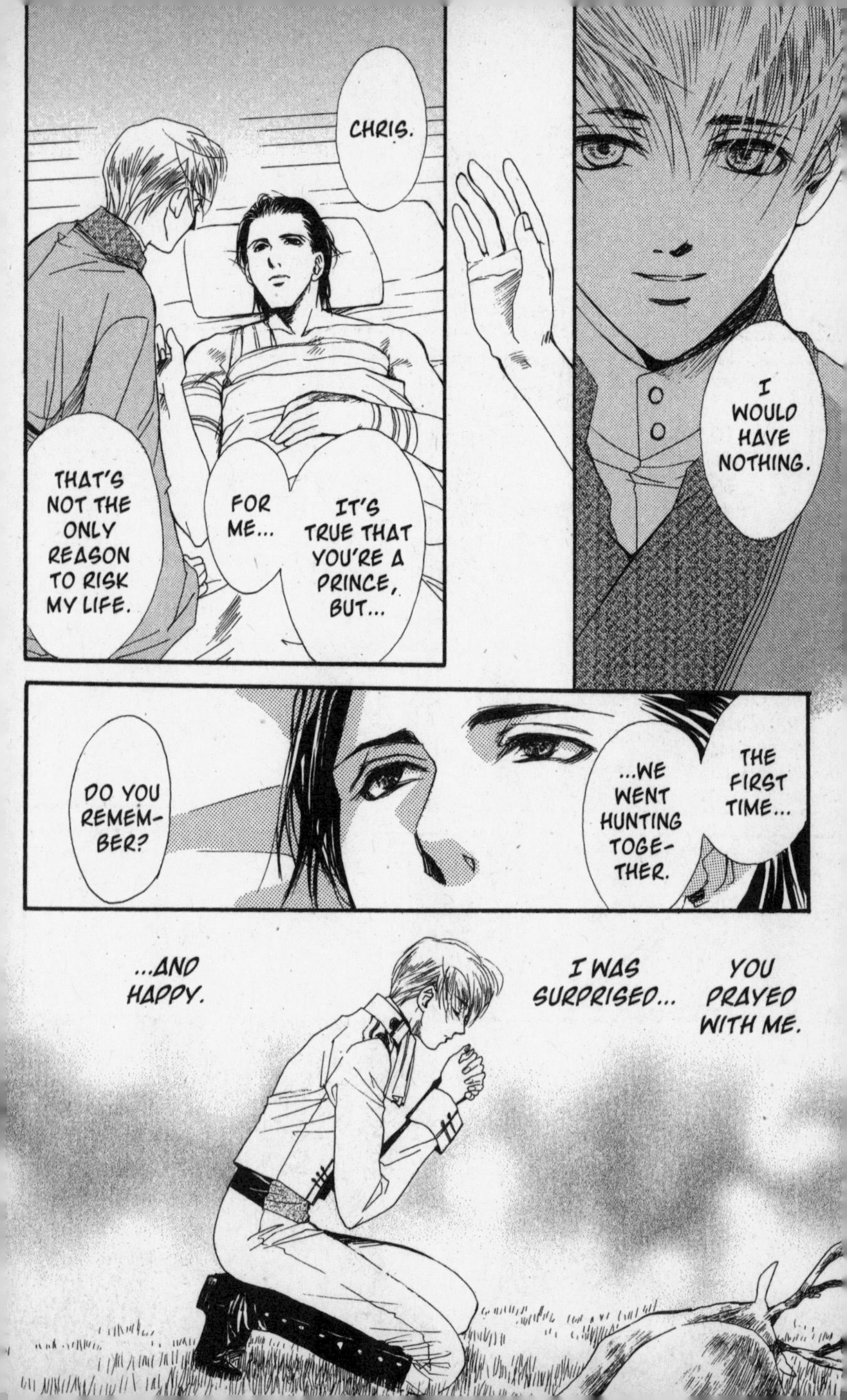
I WOULD HAVE NOTHING.
CHRIS.
IT'S TRUE THAT YOU'RE A PRINCE, BUT...
FOR ME...
THAT'S NOT THE ONLY REASON TO RISK MY LIFE.
THE FIRST TIME...
...WE WENT HUNTING TOGE-THER.
DO YOU REMEM-BER?
YOU PRAYED WITH ME.
I WAS SURPRISED...
...AND HAPPY.

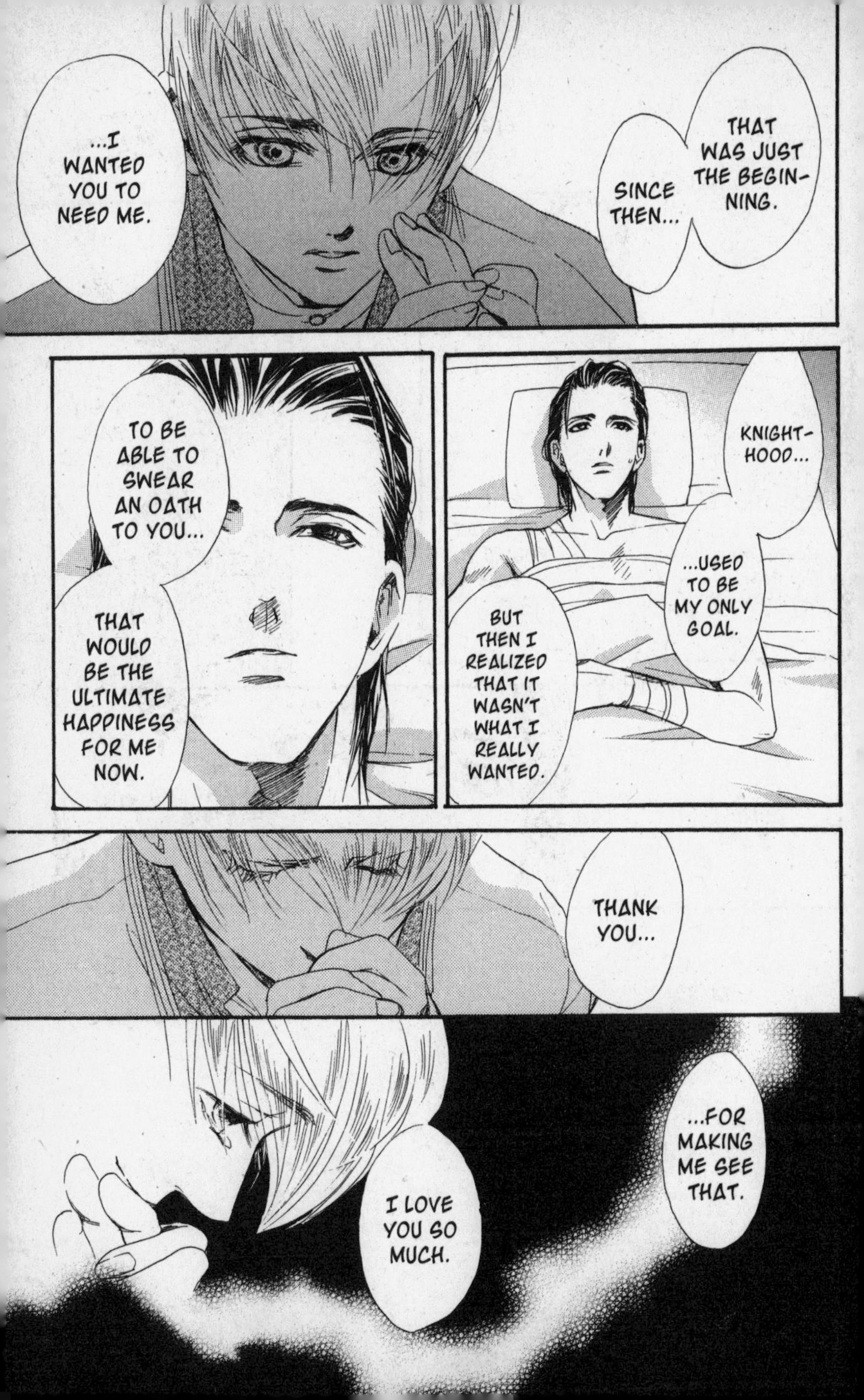
THAT WAS JUST THE BEGINNING.
SINCE THEN...
...I WANTED YOU TO NEED ME.
KNIGHTHOOD...
...USED TO BE MY ONLY GOAL.
BUT THEN I REALIZED THAT IT WASN'T WHAT I REALLY WANTED.
TO BE ABLE TO SWEAR AN OATH TO YOU...
THAT WOULD BE THE ULTIMATE HAPPINESS FOR ME NOW.
THANK YOU...
...FOR MAKING ME SEE THAT.
I LOVE YOU SO MUCH.

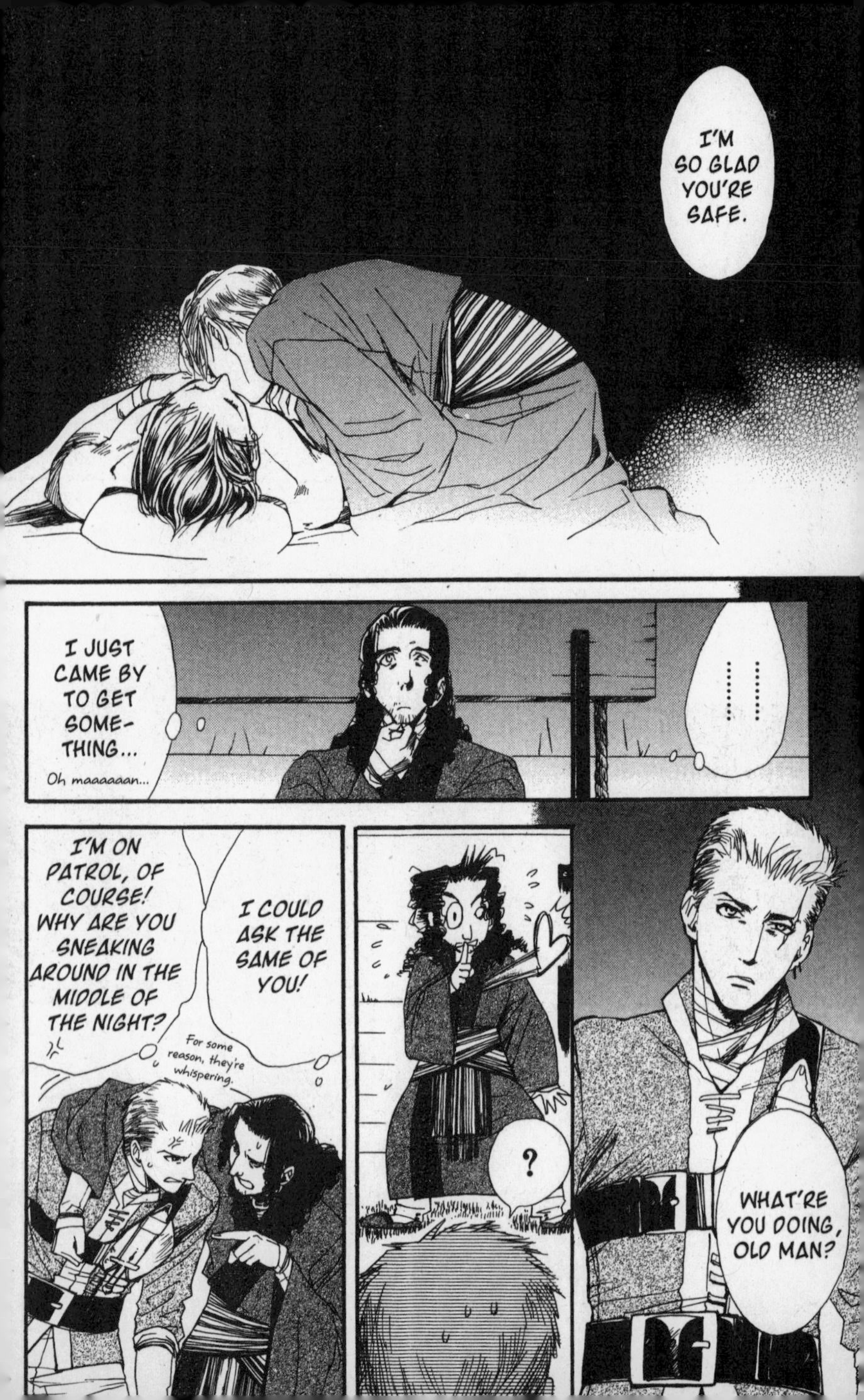
I'M SO GLAD YOU'RE SAFE.
......
I JUST CAME BY TO GET SOME-THING...
Oh maaaaaan...
WHAT'RE YOU DOING, OLD MAN?
?
I COULD ASK THE SAME OF YOU!
I'M ON PATROL, OF COURSE! WHY ARE YOU SNEAKING AROUND IN THE MIDDLE OF THE NIGHT?
For some reason, they're whispering.

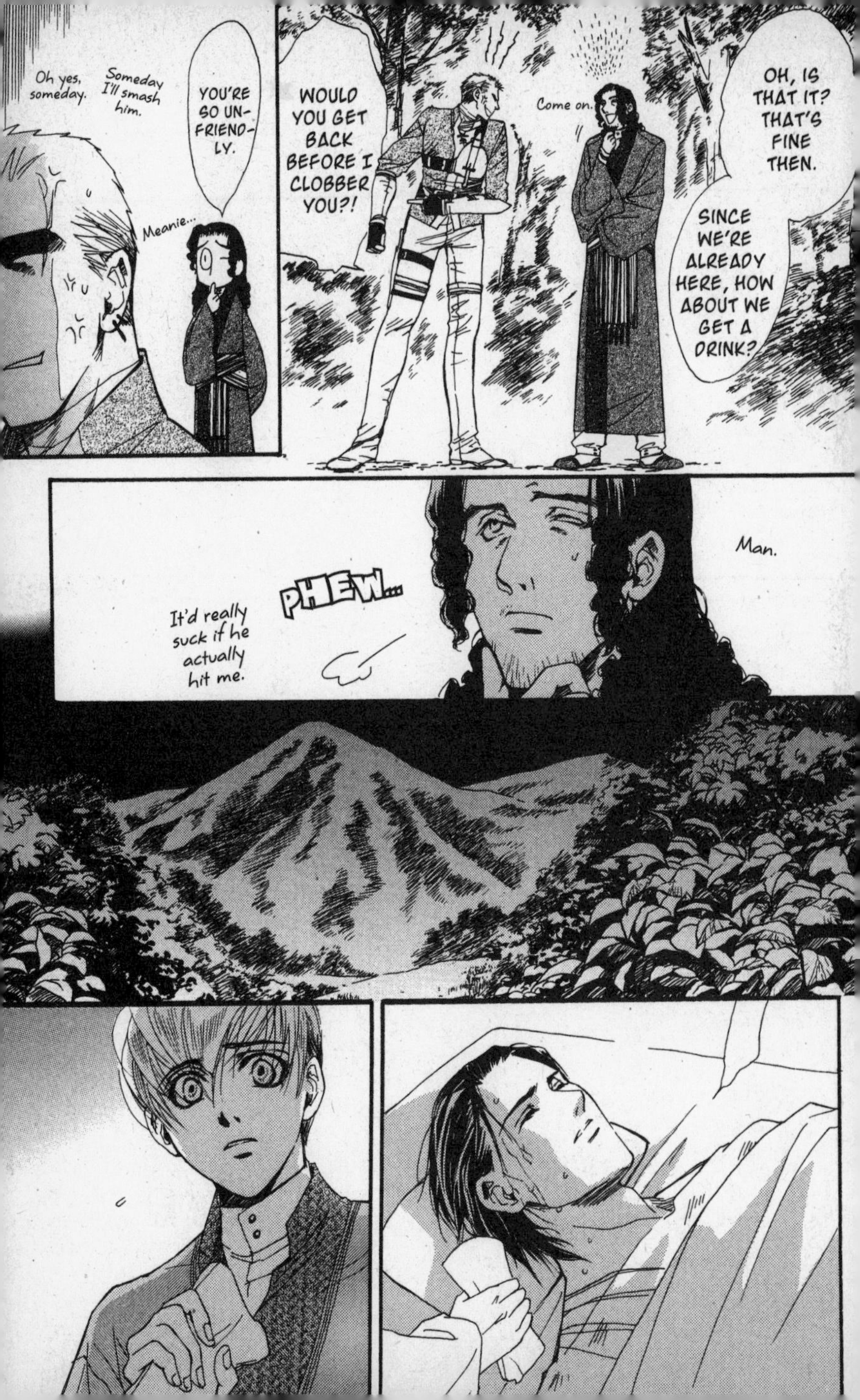
OH, IS THAT IT? THAT'S FINE THEN.
SINCE WE'RE ALREADY HERE, HOW ABOUT WE GET A DRINK?
Come on.
WOULD YOU GET BACK BEFORE I CLOBBER YOU?!
YOU'RE SO UN-FRIEND-LY.
Meanie...
Someday I'll smash him.
Oh yes, someday.
Man.
PHEW...
It'd really suck if he actually hit me.

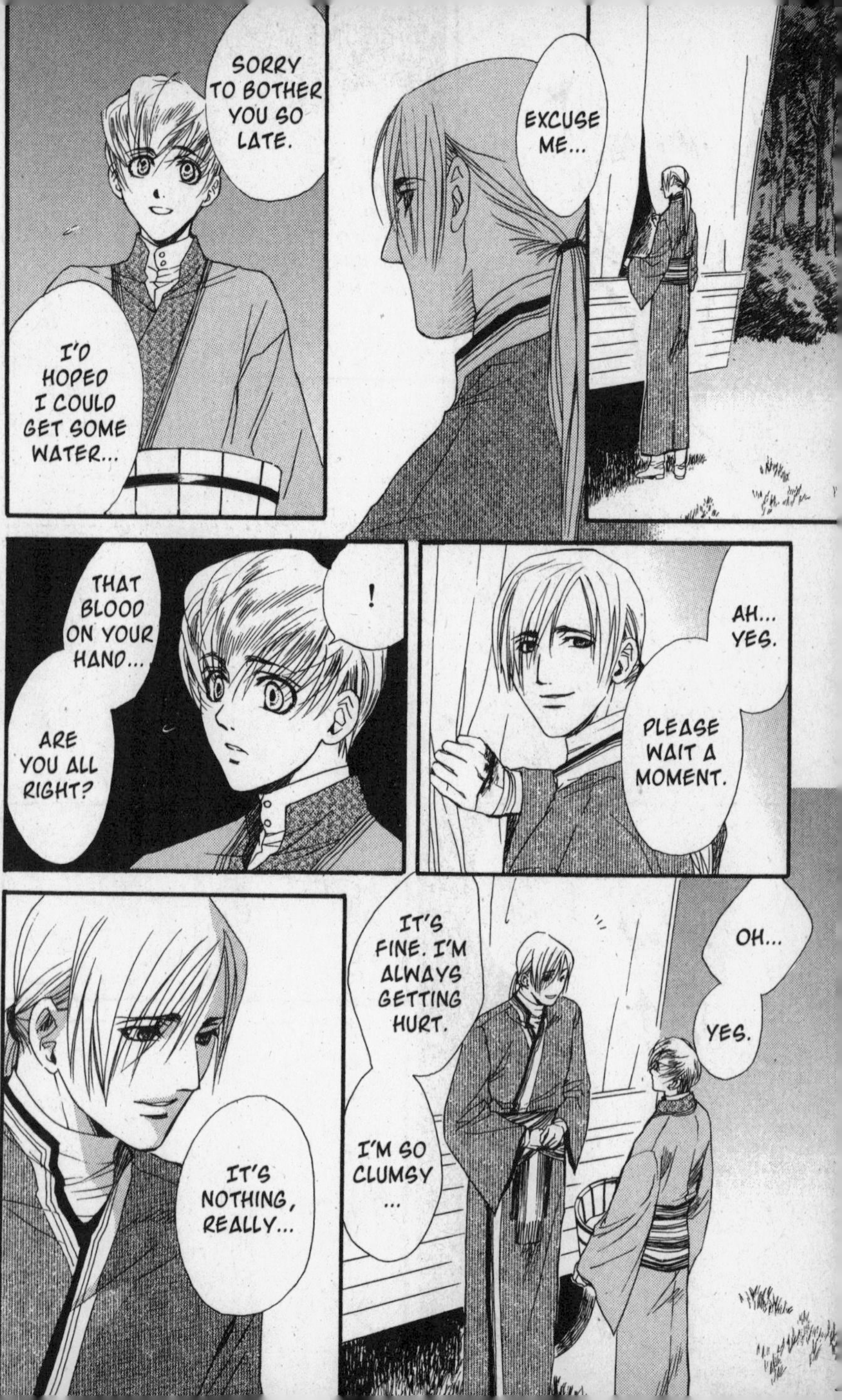
EXCUSE ME...
SORRY TO BOTHER YOU SO LATE.
I'D HOPED I COULD GET SOME WATER...
AH... YES.
PLEASE WAIT A MOMENT.
!
THAT BLOOD ON YOUR HAND...
ARE YOU ALL RIGHT?
OH...
YES.
IT'S FINE. I'M ALWAYS GETTING HURT.
I'M SO CLUMSY ...
IT'S NOTHING, REALLY...

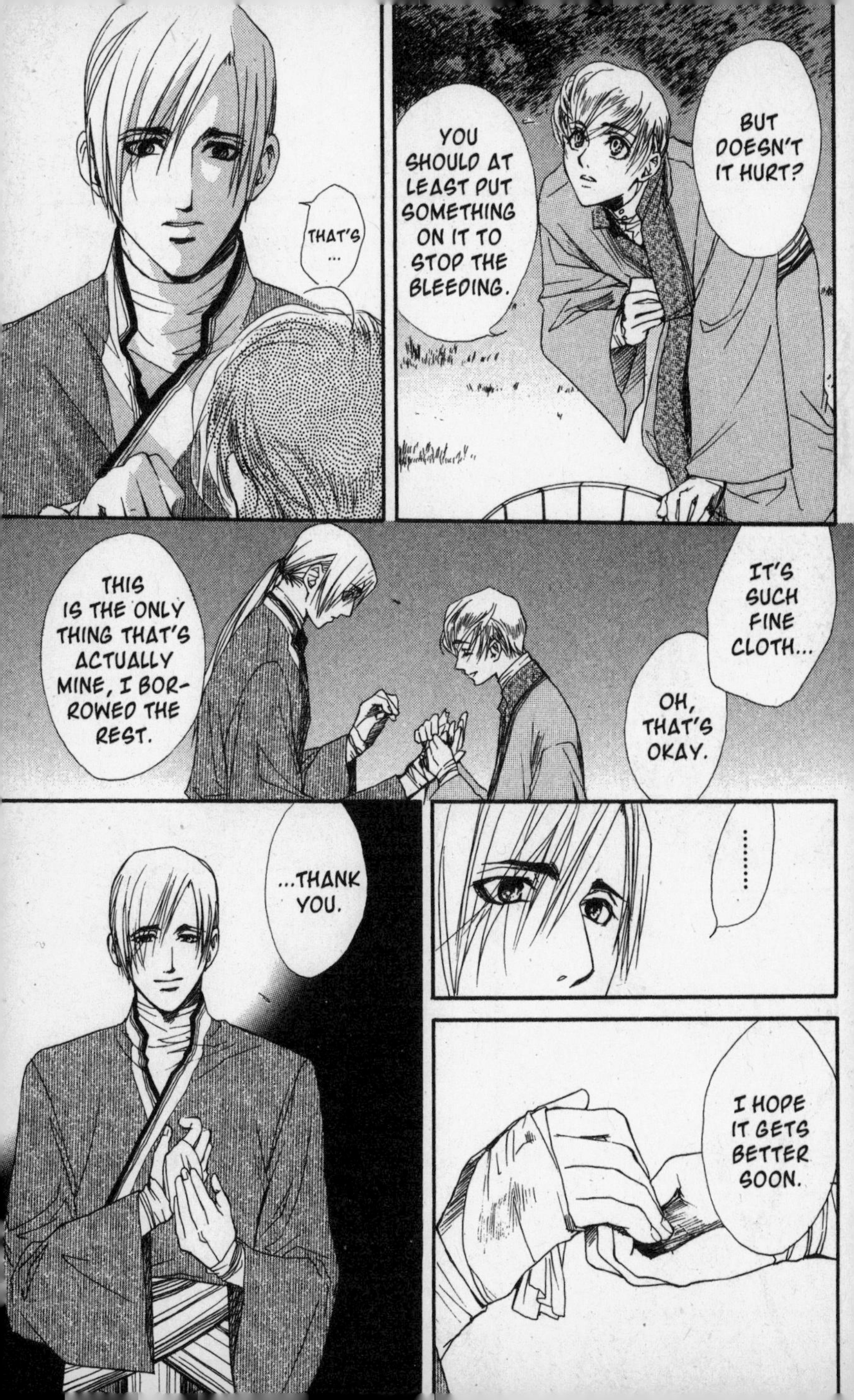
BUT DOESN'T IT HURT?
YOU SHOULD AT LEAST PUT SOMETHING ON IT TO STOP THE BLEEDING.
THAT'S ...
IT'S SUCH FINE CLOTH...
OH, THAT'S OKAY.
THIS IS THE ONLY THING THAT'S ACTUALLY MINE, I BOR-ROWED THE REST.
......
I HOPE IT GETS BETTER SOON.
...THANK YOU.

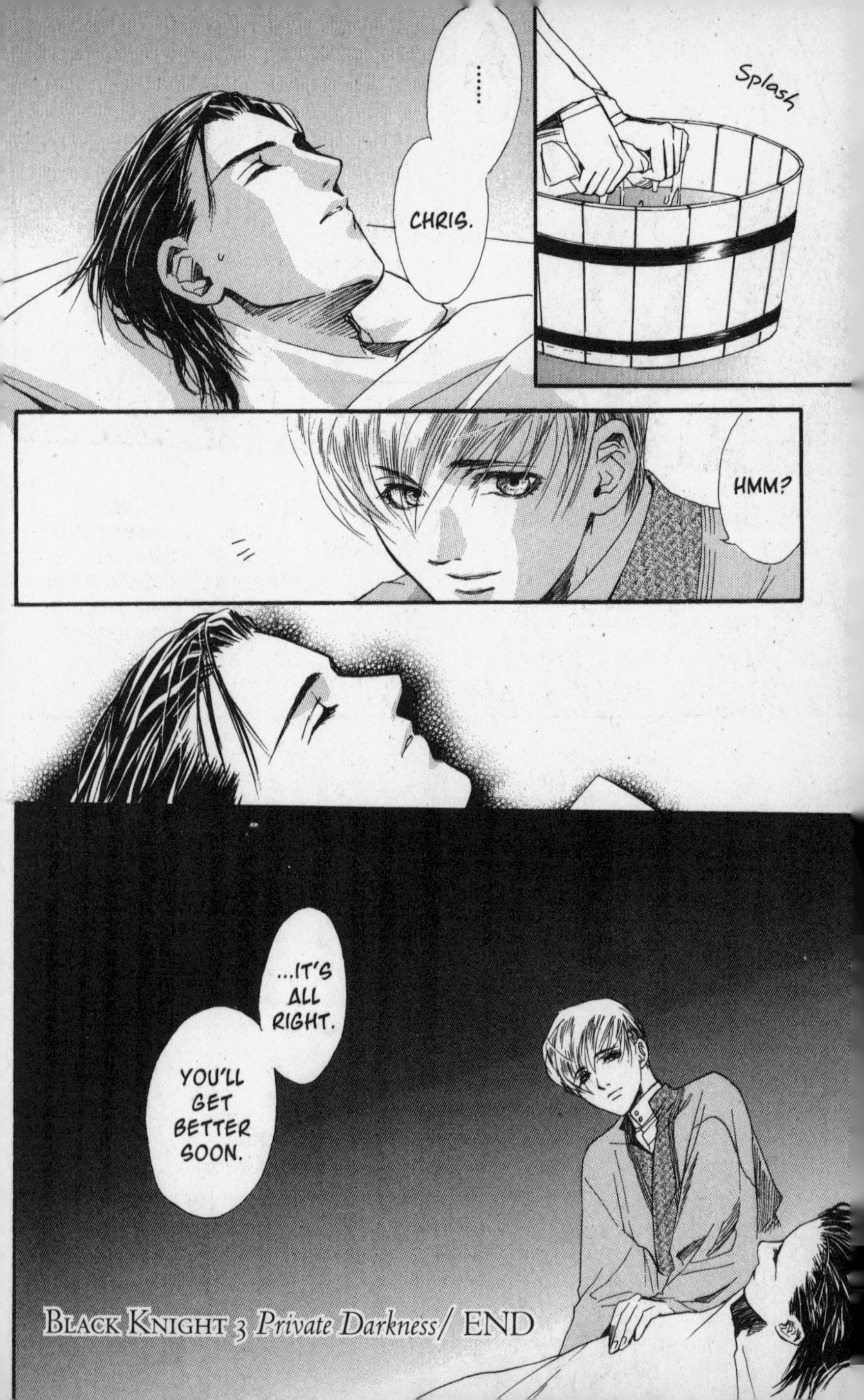
Splash
......
CHRIS.
HMM?
...IT'S ALL RIGHT.
YOU'LL GET BETTER SOON.
BLACK KNIGHT 3 Private Darkness/ END

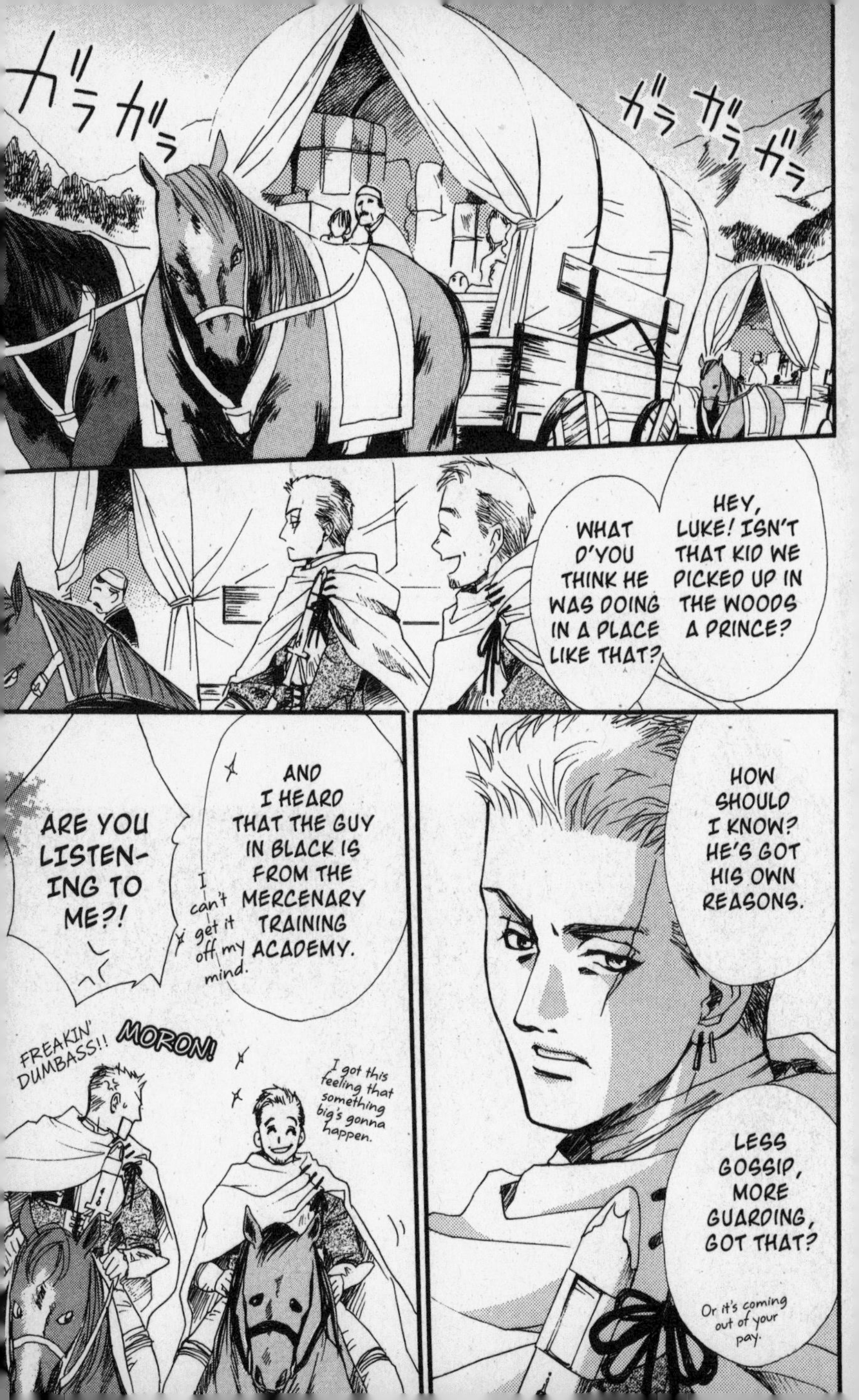
ガラ ガラ ガラ
ガラ ガラ
HEY, LUKE! ISN'T THAT KID WE PICKED UP IN THE WOODS A PRINCE?
WHAT D'YOU THINK HE WAS DOING IN A PLACE LIKE THAT?
HOW SHOULD I KNOW? HE'S GOT HIS OWN REASONS.
LESS GOSSIP, MORE GUARDING, GOT THAT?
Or it's coming out of your pay.
AND I HEARD THAT THE GUY IN BLACK IS FROM THE MERCENARY TRAINING ACADEMY.
I can't get it off my mind.
ARE YOU LISTENING TO ME?!
I got this feeling that something big's gonna happen.
MORON!
FREAKIN' DUMBASS!!

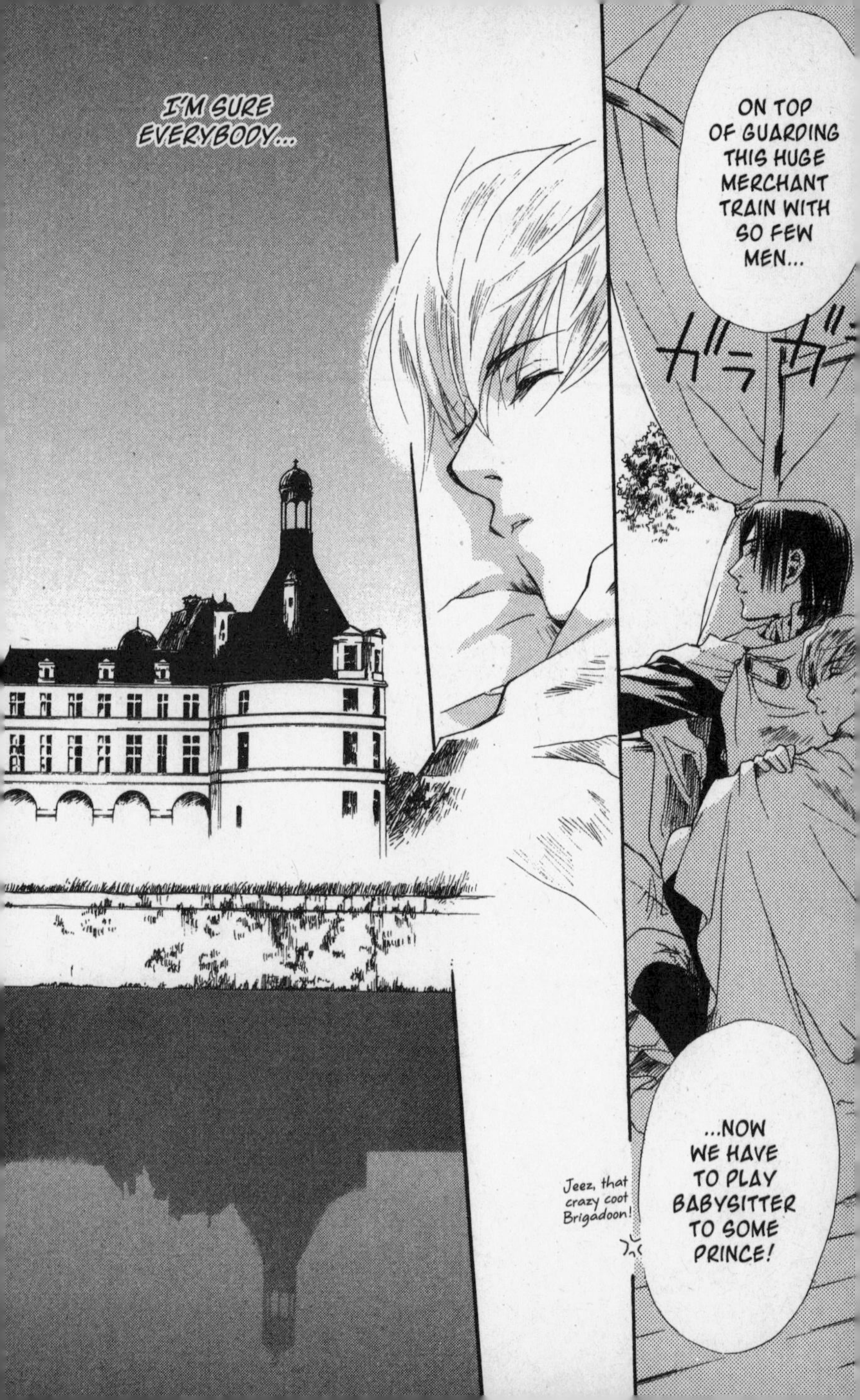
ON TOP OF GUARDING THIS HUGE MERCHANT TRAIN WITH SO FEW MEN...
ガラガ
...NOW WE HAVE TO PLAY BABYSITTER TO SOME PRINCE!
Jeez, that crazy coot Brigadoon!
I'M SURE EVERYBODY...

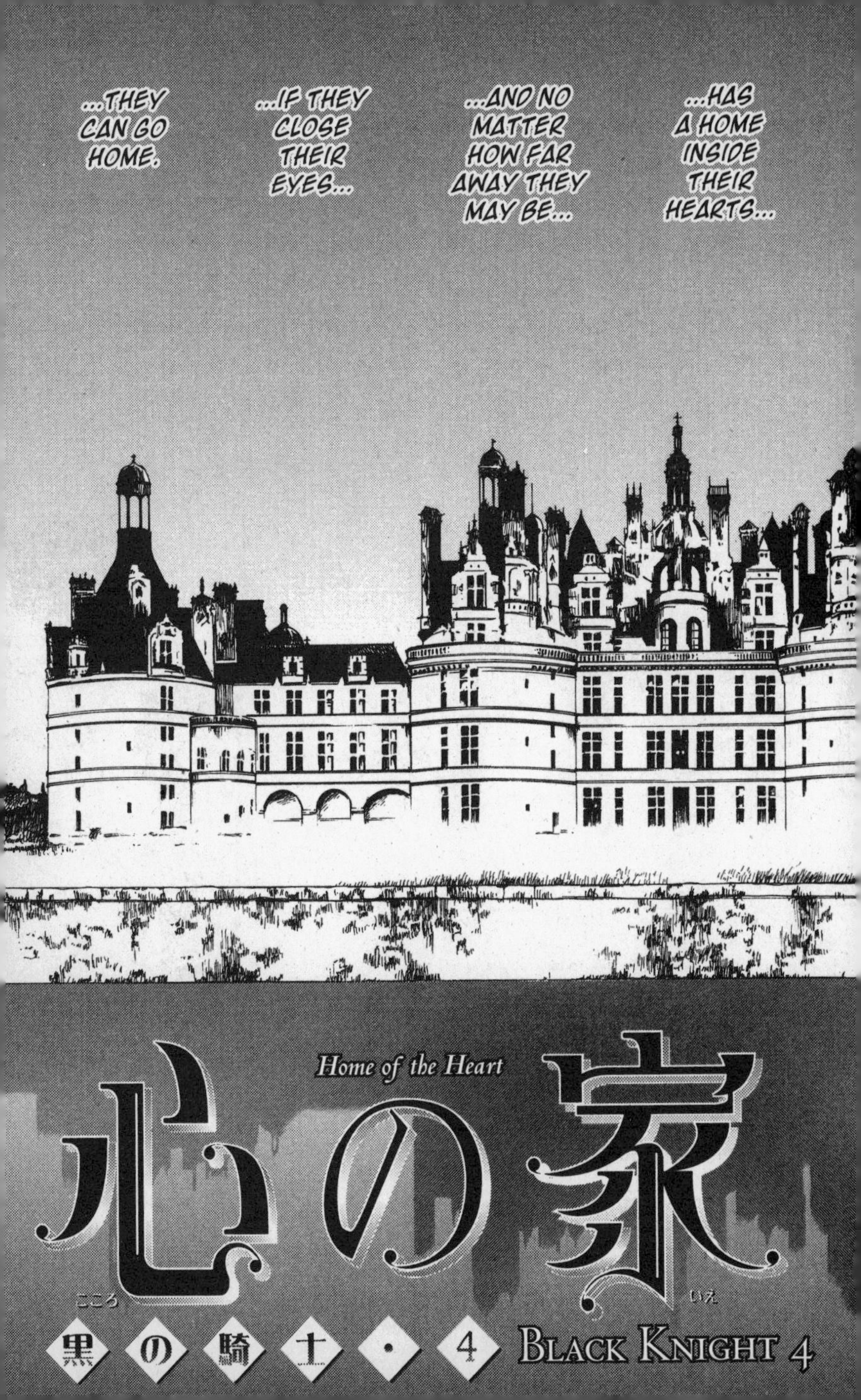
...HAS A HOME INSIDE THEIR HEARTS...
...AND NO MATTER HOW FAR AWAY THEY MAY BE...
...IF THEY CLOSE THEIR EYES...
...THEY CAN GO HOME.
Home of the Heart
心の家
こころ
いえ
黒の騎士・4
BLACK KNIGHT 4

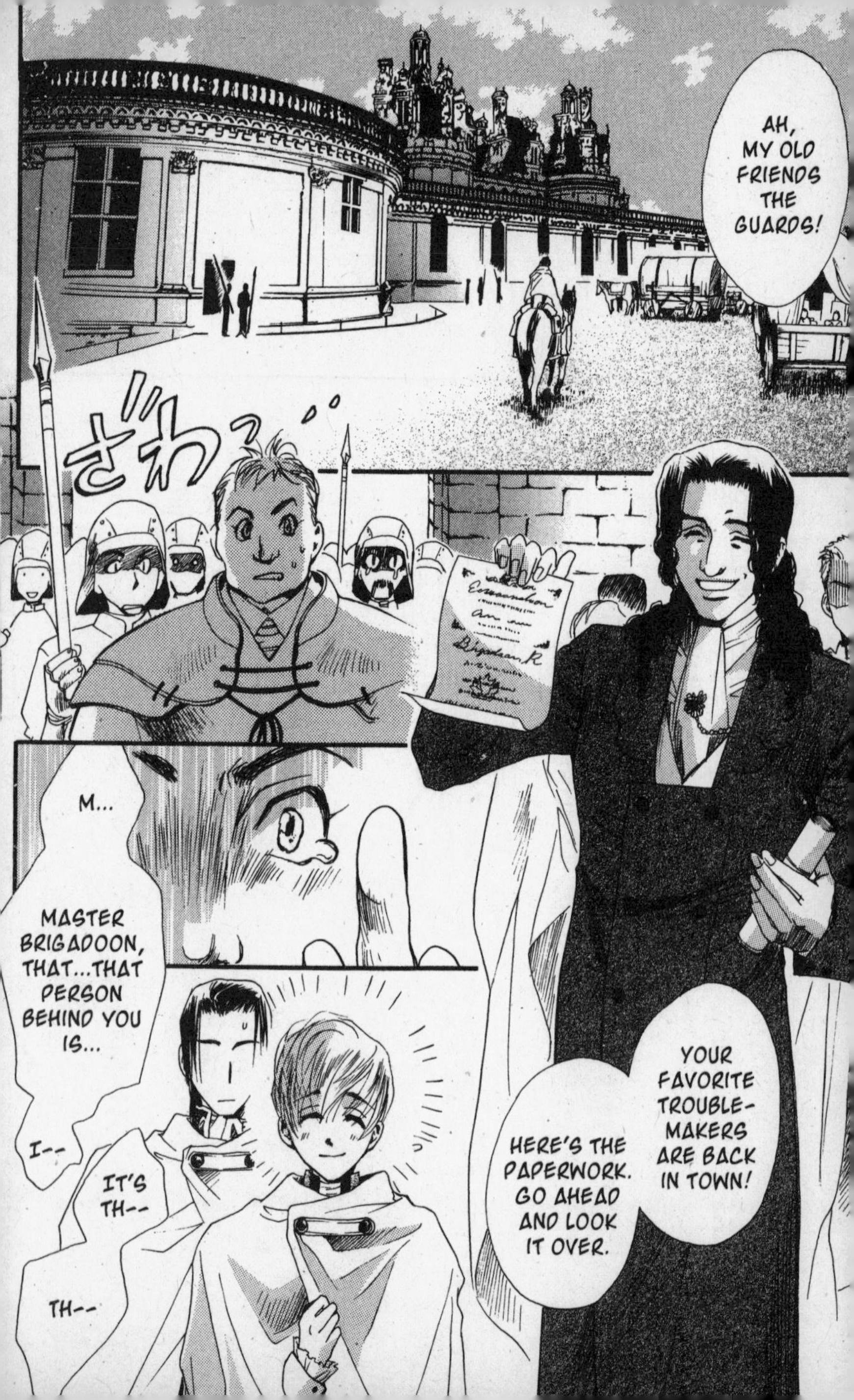
AH, MY OLD FRIENDS THE GUARDS!
YOUR FAVORITE TROUBLE-MAKERS ARE BACK IN TOWN!
HERE'S THE PAPERWORK. GO AHEAD AND LOOK IT OVER.
ざわっ
M...
MASTER BRIGADOON, THAT...THAT PERSON BEHIND YOU IS...
I--
IT'S TH--
TH--

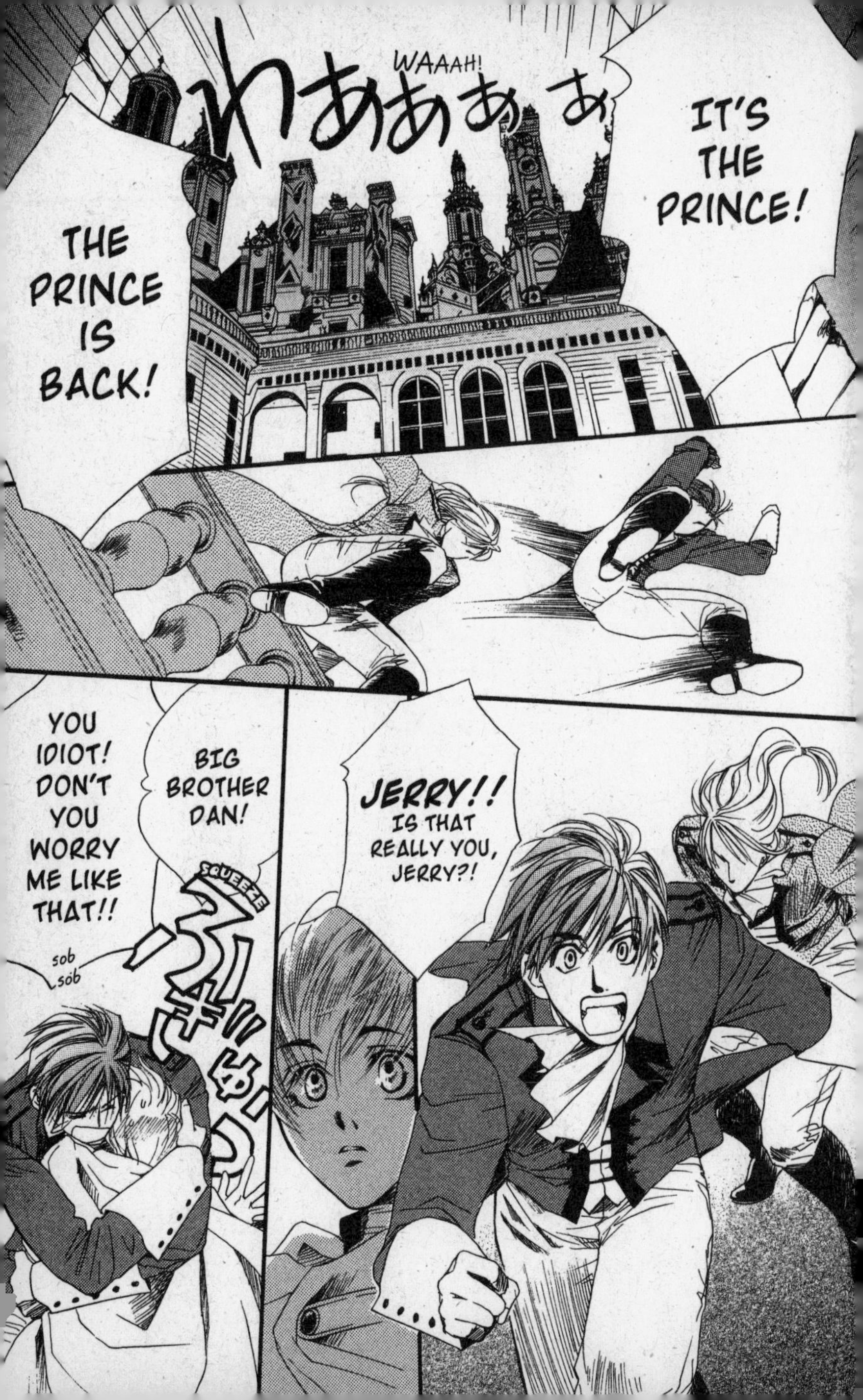
わあああぁ
WAAAH!
IT'S THE PRINCE!
THE PRINCE IS BACK!
JERRY!! IS THAT REALLY YOU, JERRY?!
BIG BROTHER DAN!
YOU IDIOT! DON'T YOU WORRY ME LIKE THAT!!
SQUEEZE
sob sob

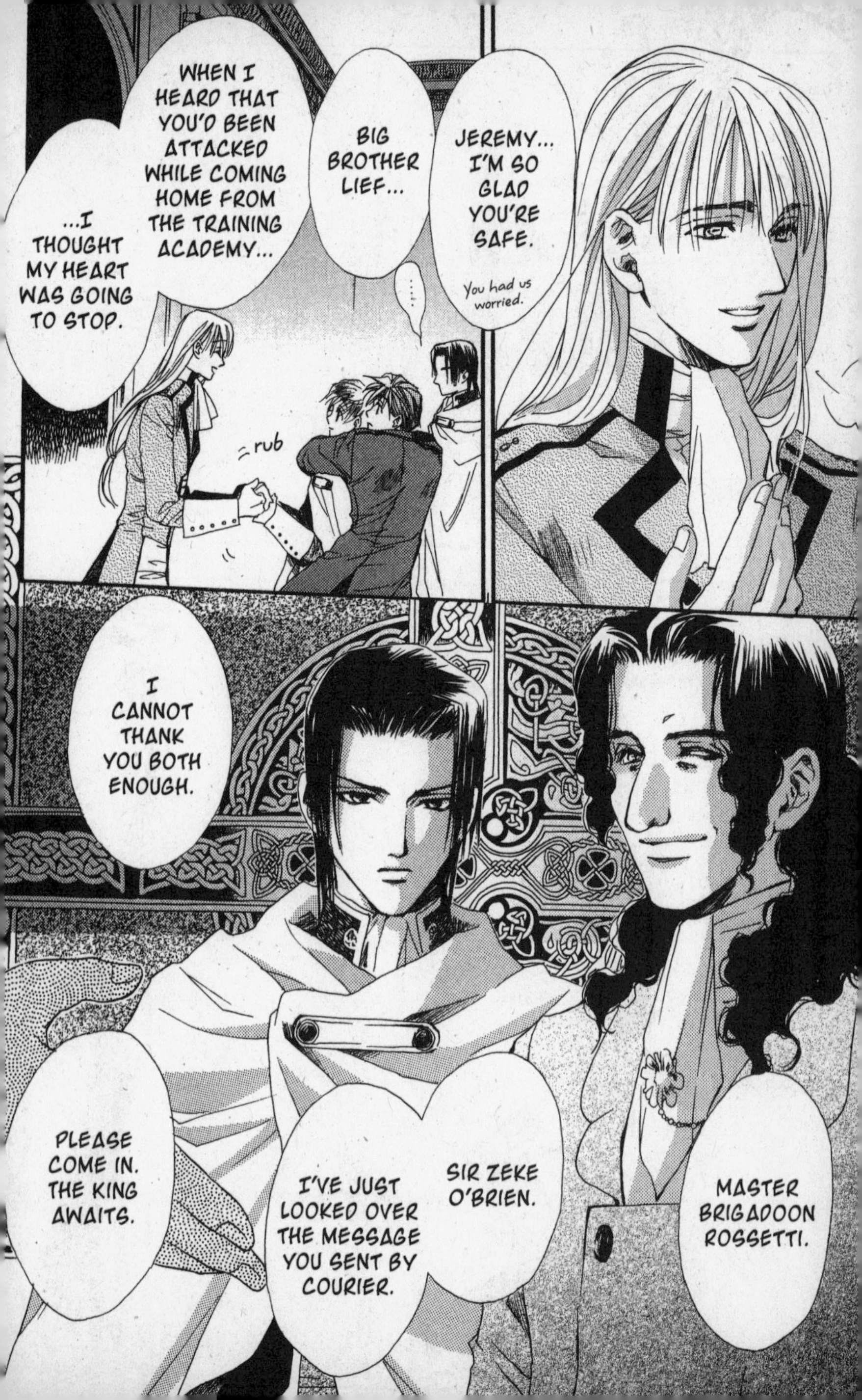
JEREMY... I'M SO GLAD YOU'RE SAFE.
You had us worried.
BIG BROTHER LIEF...
...
WHEN I HEARD THAT YOU'D BEEN ATTACKED WHILE COMING HOME FROM THE TRAINING ACADEMY...
...I THOUGHT MY HEART WAS GOING TO STOP.
rub
MASTER BRIGADOON ROSSETTI.
SIR ZEKE O'BRIEN.
I'VE JUST LOOKED OVER THE MESSAGE YOU SENT BY COURIER.
I CANNOT THANK YOU BOTH ENOUGH.
PLEASE COME IN. THE KING AWAITS.

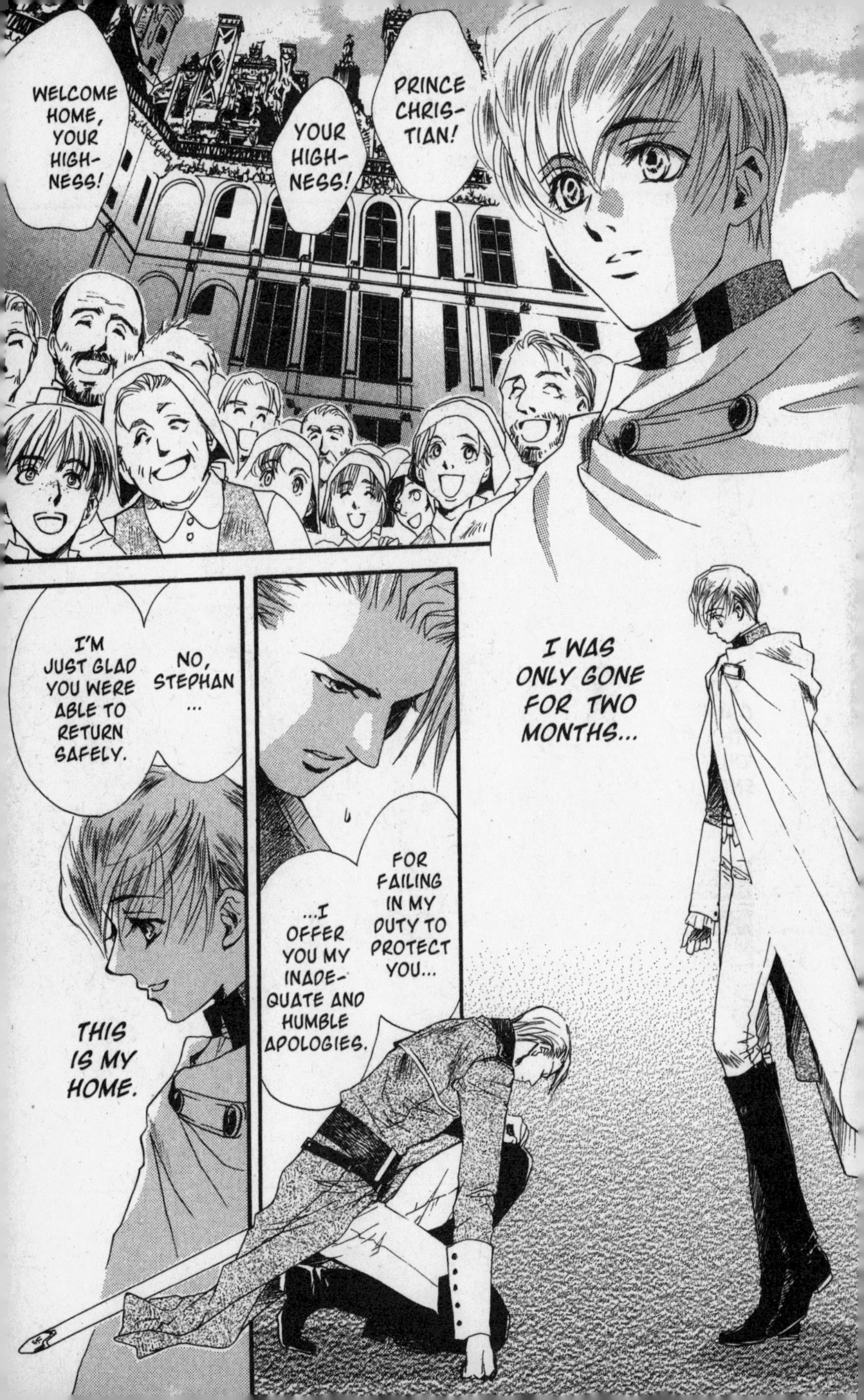
PRINCE CHRISTIAN!
YOUR HIGHNESS!
WELCOME HOME, YOUR HIGHNESS!
I WAS ONLY GONE FOR TWO MONTHS...
FOR FAILING IN MY DUTY TO PROTECT YOU...
...I OFFER YOU MY INADEQUATE AND HUMBLE APOLOGIES.
NO, STEPHAN...
I'M JUST GLAD YOU WERE ABLE TO RETURN SAFELY.
THIS IS MY HOME.

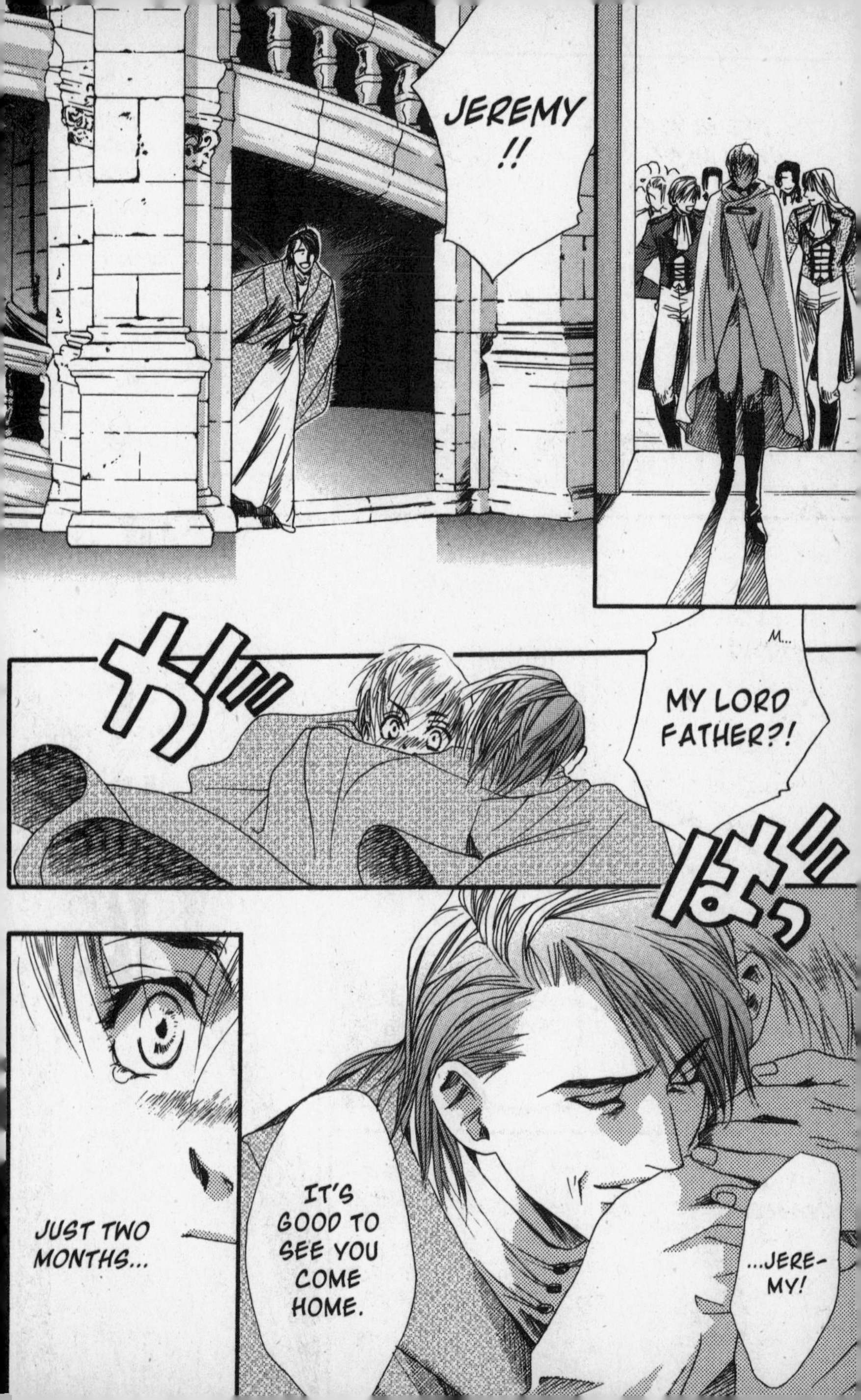
JEREMY !!
M... MY LORD FATHER?!
ガッ
はっ
...JERE-MY!
IT'S GOOD TO SEE YOU COME HOME.
JUST TWO MONTHS...

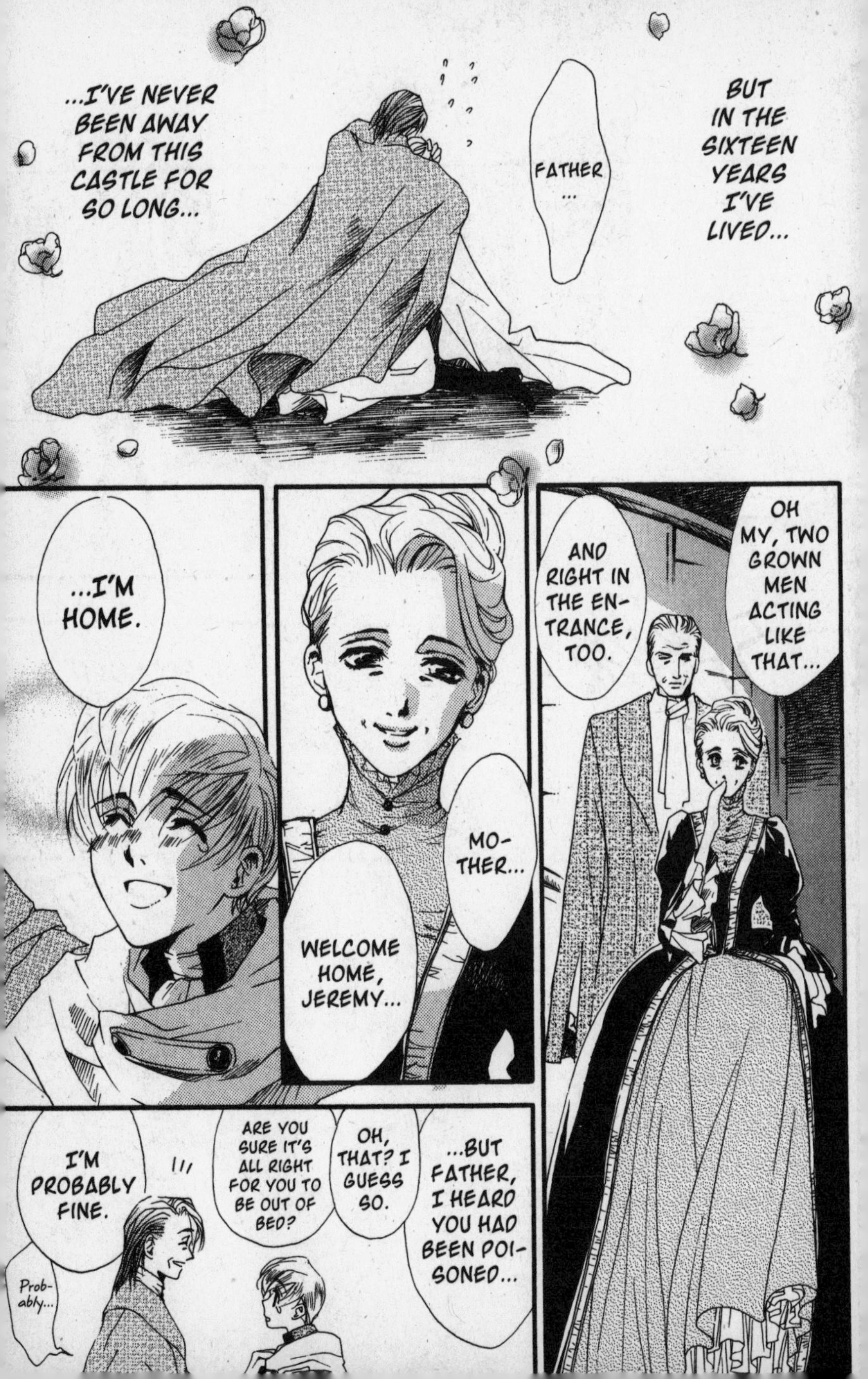
BUT IN THE SIXTEEN YEARS I'VE LIVED...
FATHER...
...I'VE NEVER BEEN AWAY FROM THIS CASTLE FOR SO LONG...
OH MY, TWO GROWN MEN ACTING LIKE THAT...
AND RIGHT IN THE EN-TRANCE, TOO.
MO-THER...
WELCOME HOME, JEREMY...
...I'M HOME.
...BUT FATHER, I HEARD YOU HAD BEEN POI-SONED...
OH, THAT? I GUESS SO.
ARE YOU SURE IT'S ALL RIGHT FOR YOU TO BE OUT OF BED?
I'M PROBABLY FINE.
Prob-ably...

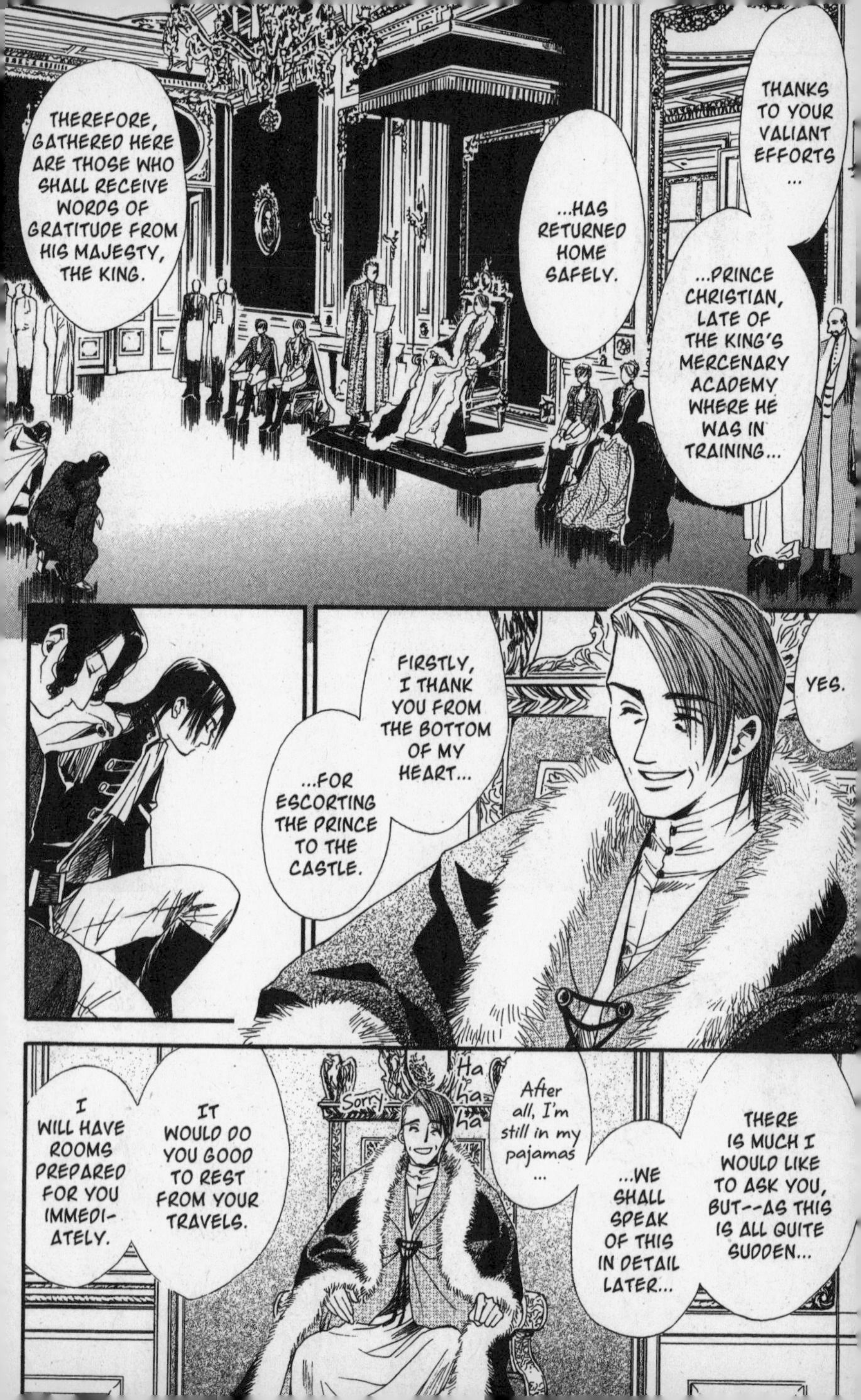
THANKS TO YOUR VALIANT EFFORTS ...
...PRINCE CHRISTIAN, LATE OF THE KING'S MERCENARY ACADEMY WHERE HE WAS IN TRAINING...
...HAS RETURNED HOME SAFELY.
THEREFORE, GATHERED HERE ARE THOSE WHO SHALL RECEIVE WORDS OF GRATITUDE FROM HIS MAJESTY, THE KING.
YES.
FIRSTLY, I THANK YOU FROM THE BOTTOM OF MY HEART...
...FOR ESCORTING THE PRINCE TO THE CASTLE.
THERE IS MUCH I WOULD LIKE TO ASK YOU, BUT--AS THIS IS ALL QUITE SUDDEN...
...WE SHALL SPEAK OF THIS IN DETAIL LATER...
After all, I'm still in my pajamas ...
Ha ha ha
Sorry
IT WOULD DO YOU GOOD TO REST FROM YOUR TRAVELS.
I WILL HAVE ROOMS PREPARED FOR YOU IMMEDIATELY.

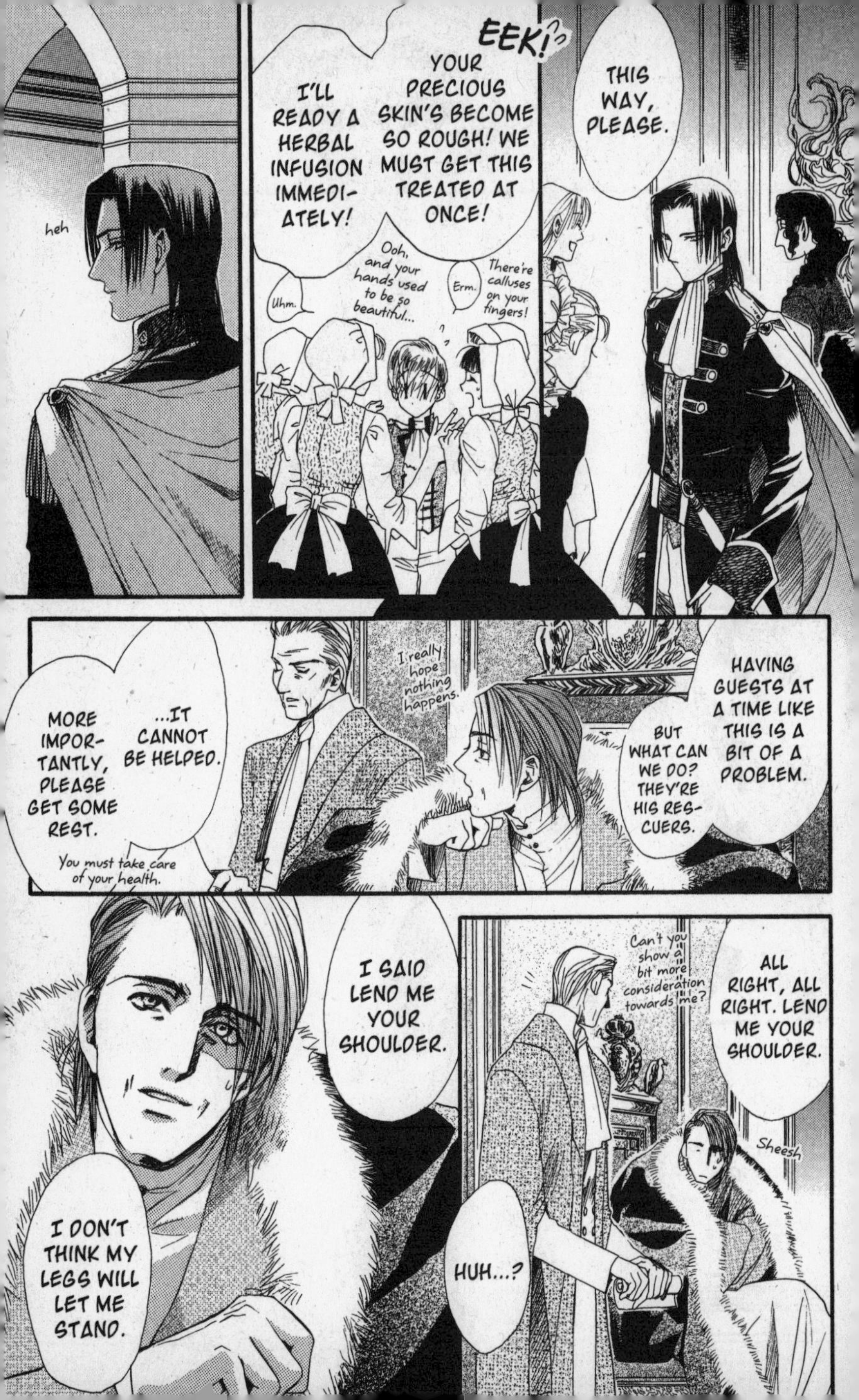
EEK!
THIS WAY, PLEASE.
YOUR PRECIOUS SKIN'S BECOME SO ROUGH! WE MUST GET THIS TREATED AT ONCE!
I'LL READY A HERBAL INFUSION IMMEDIATELY!
There're calluses on your fingers!
Erm.
Ooh, and your hands used to be so beautiful...
Uhm.
heh
HAVING GUESTS AT A TIME LIKE THIS IS A BIT OF A PROBLEM.
BUT WHAT CAN WE DO? THEY'RE HIS RESCUERS.
I really hope nothing happens.
...IT CANNOT BE HELPED.
MORE IMPORTANTLY, PLEASE GET SOME REST.
You must take care of your health.
ALL RIGHT, ALL RIGHT. LEND ME YOUR SHOULDER.
Can't you show a bit more consideration towards me?
Sheesh
I SAID LEND ME YOUR SHOULDER.
HUH...?
I DON'T THINK MY LEGS WILL LET ME STAND.

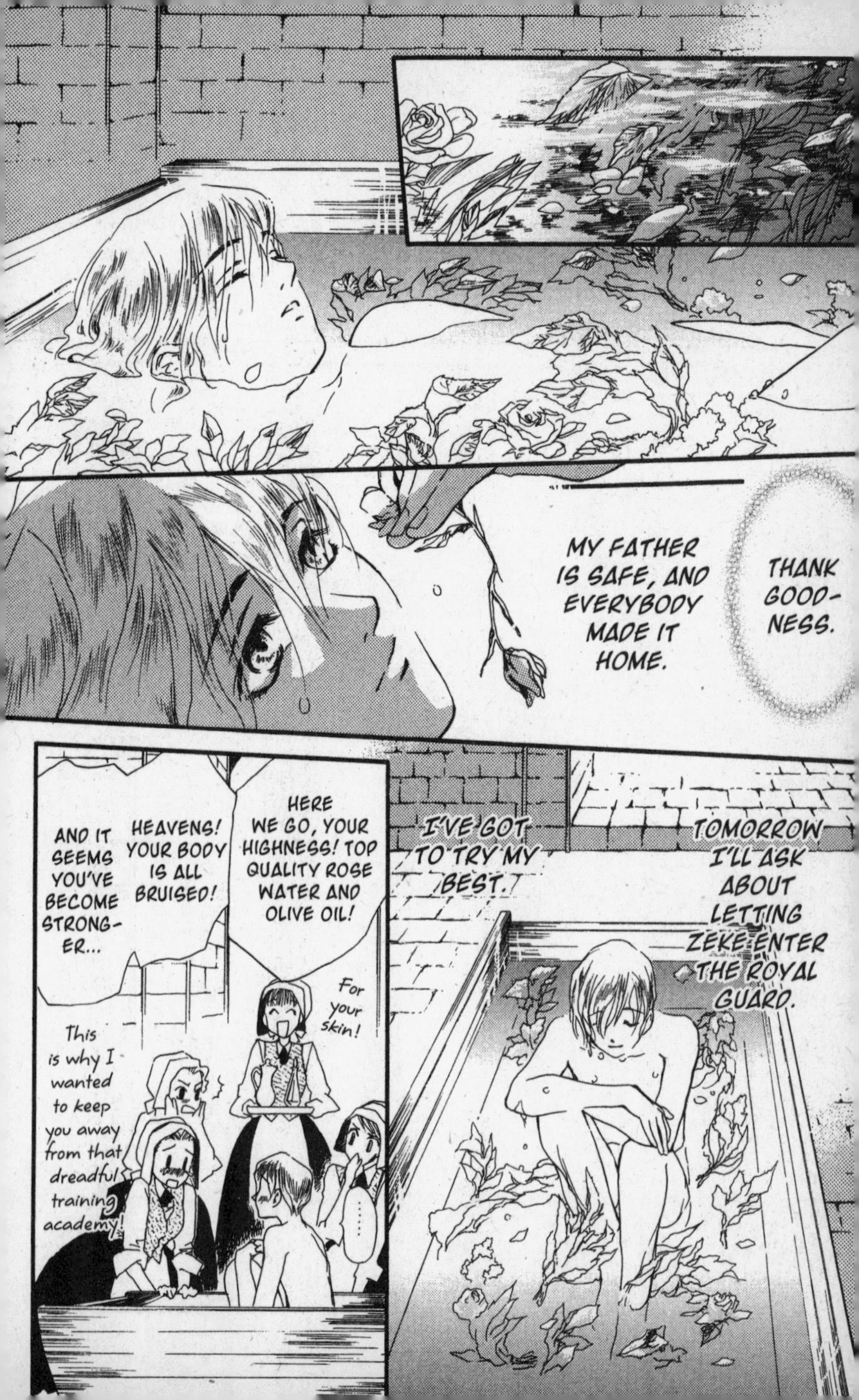
THANK GOOD-NESS.
MY FATHER IS SAFE, AND EVERYBODY MADE IT HOME.
TOMORROW I'LL ASK ABOUT LETTING ZEKE ENTER THE ROYAL GUARD.
I'VE GOT TO TRY MY BEST.
HERE WE GO, YOUR HIGHNESS! TOP QUALITY ROSE WATER AND OLIVE OIL!
HEAVENS! YOUR BODY IS ALL BRUISED!
AND IT SEEMS YOU'VE BECOME STRONG-ER...
For your skin!
This is why I wanted to keep you away from that dreadful training academy!
......

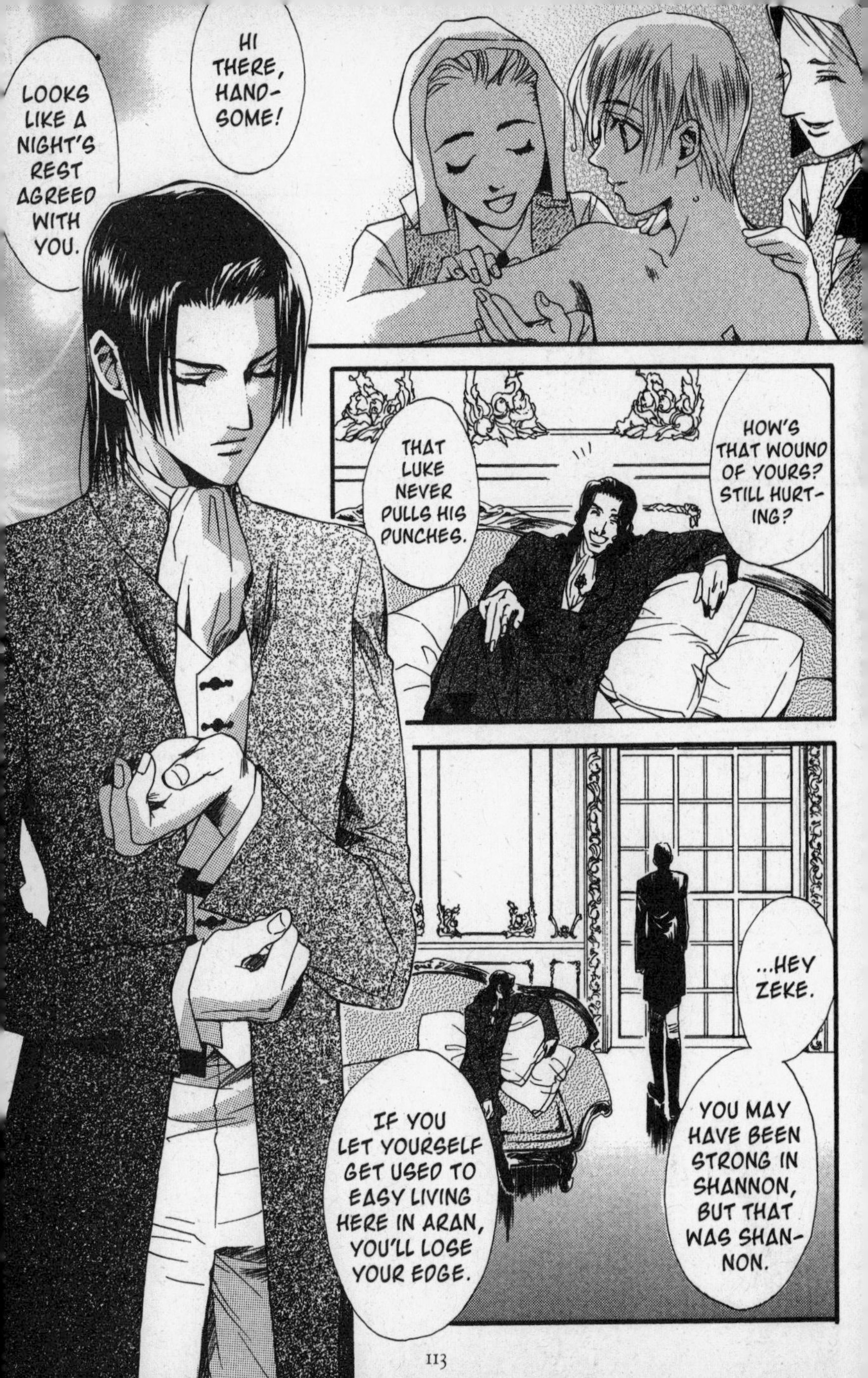
HI THERE, HANDSOME!
LOOKS LIKE A NIGHT'S REST AGREED WITH YOU.
HOW'S THAT WOUND OF YOURS? STILL HURTING?
THAT LUKE NEVER PULLS HIS PUNCHES.
...HEY ZEKE.
YOU MAY HAVE BEEN STRONG IN SHANNON, BUT THAT WAS SHANNON.
IF YOU LET YOURSELF GET USED TO EASY LIVING HERE IN ARAN, YOU'LL LOSE YOUR EDGE.

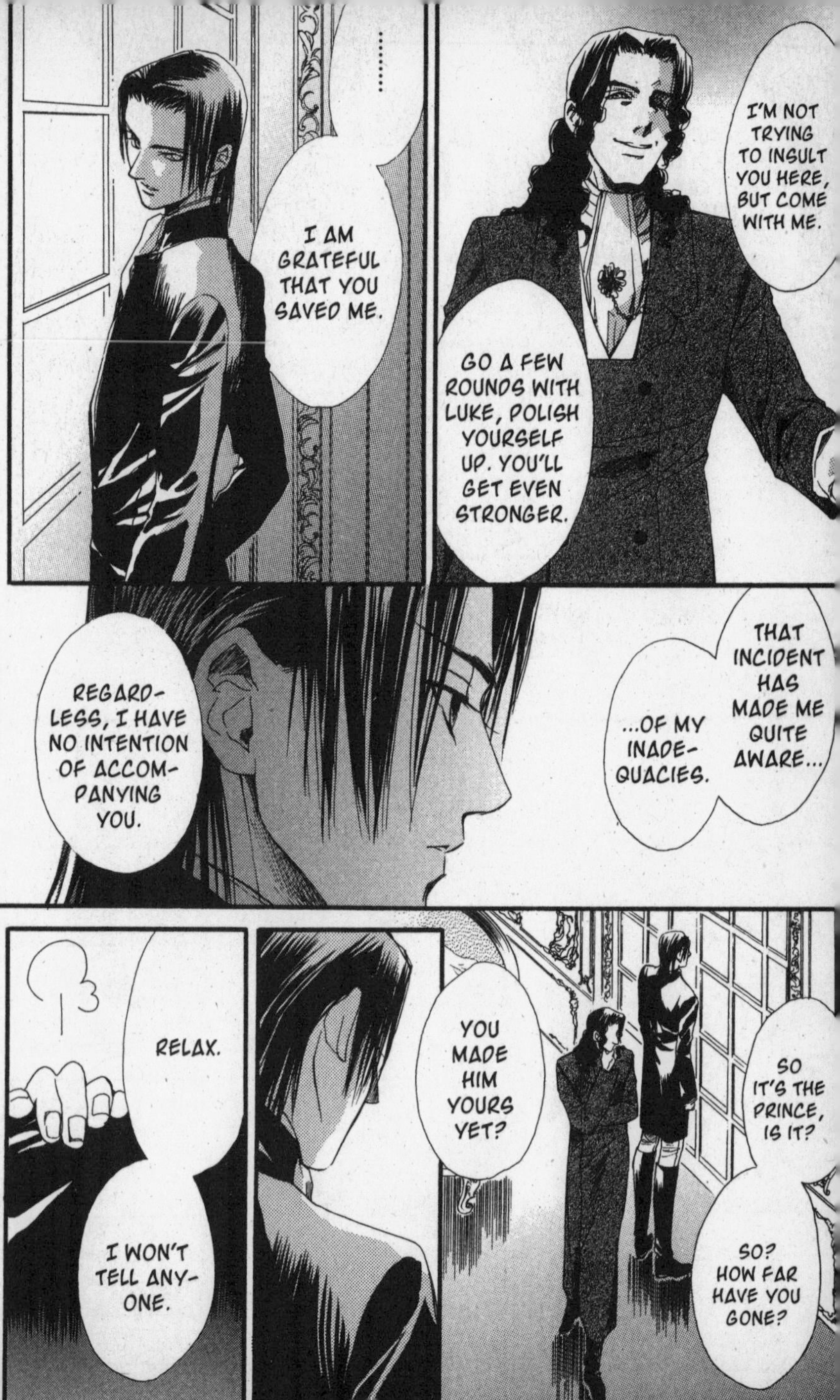
I'M NOT TRYING TO INSULT YOU HERE, BUT COME WITH ME.
GO A FEW ROUNDS WITH LUKE, POLISH YOURSELF UP. YOU'LL GET EVEN STRONGER.
......
I AM GRATEFUL THAT YOU SAVED ME.
THAT INCIDENT HAS MADE ME QUITE AWARE...
...OF MY INADE-QUACIES.
REGARD-LESS, I HAVE NO INTENTION OF ACCOM-PANYING YOU.
SO IT'S THE PRINCE, IS IT?
SO? HOW FAR HAVE YOU GONE?
YOU MADE HIM YOURS YET?
RELAX.
I WON'T TELL ANY-ONE.

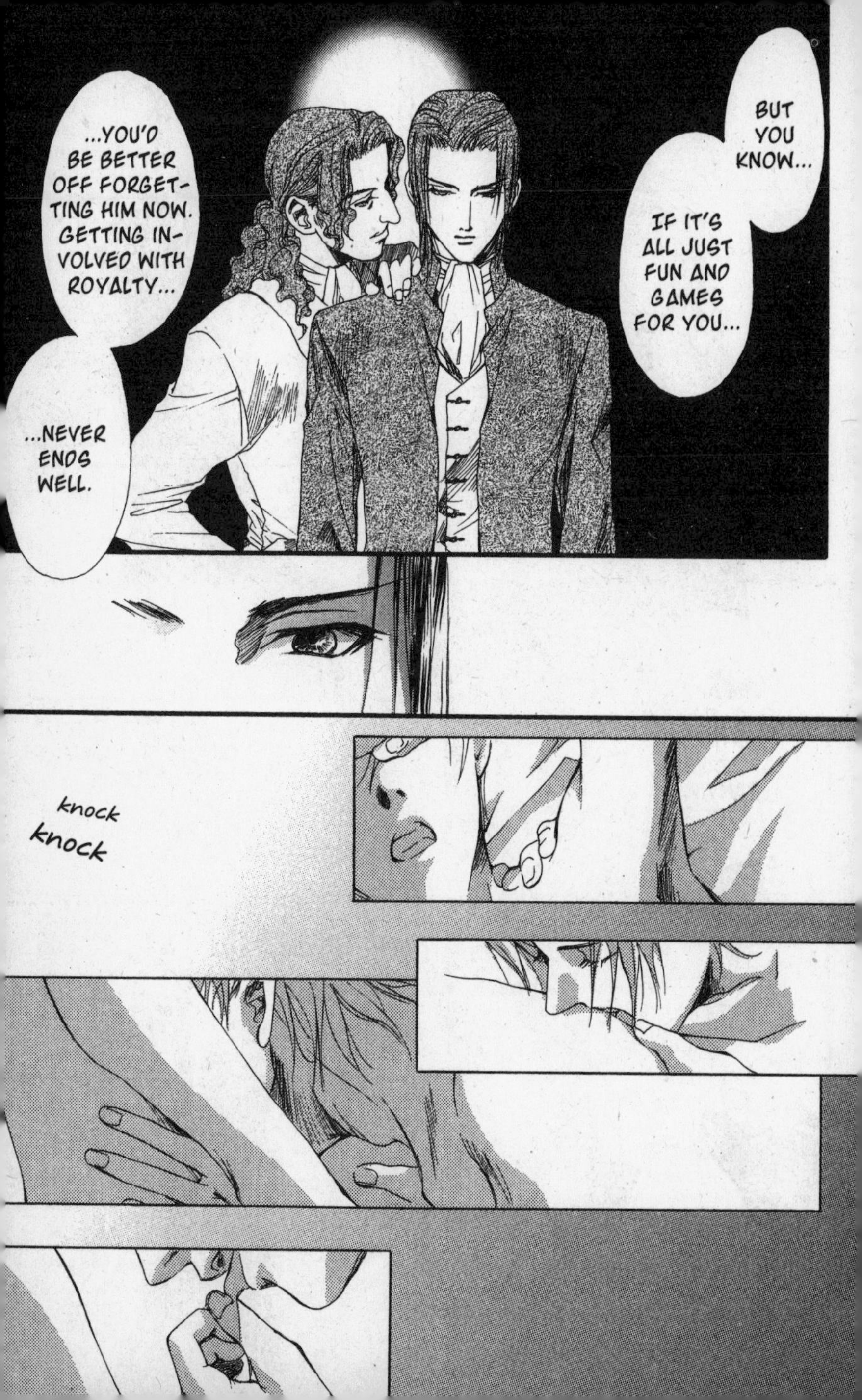
BUT YOU KNOW...
IF IT'S ALL JUST FUN AND GAMES FOR YOU...
...YOU'D BE BETTER OFF FORGET-TING HIM NOW. GETTING IN-VOLVED WITH ROYALTY...
...NEVER ENDS WELL.
knock knock

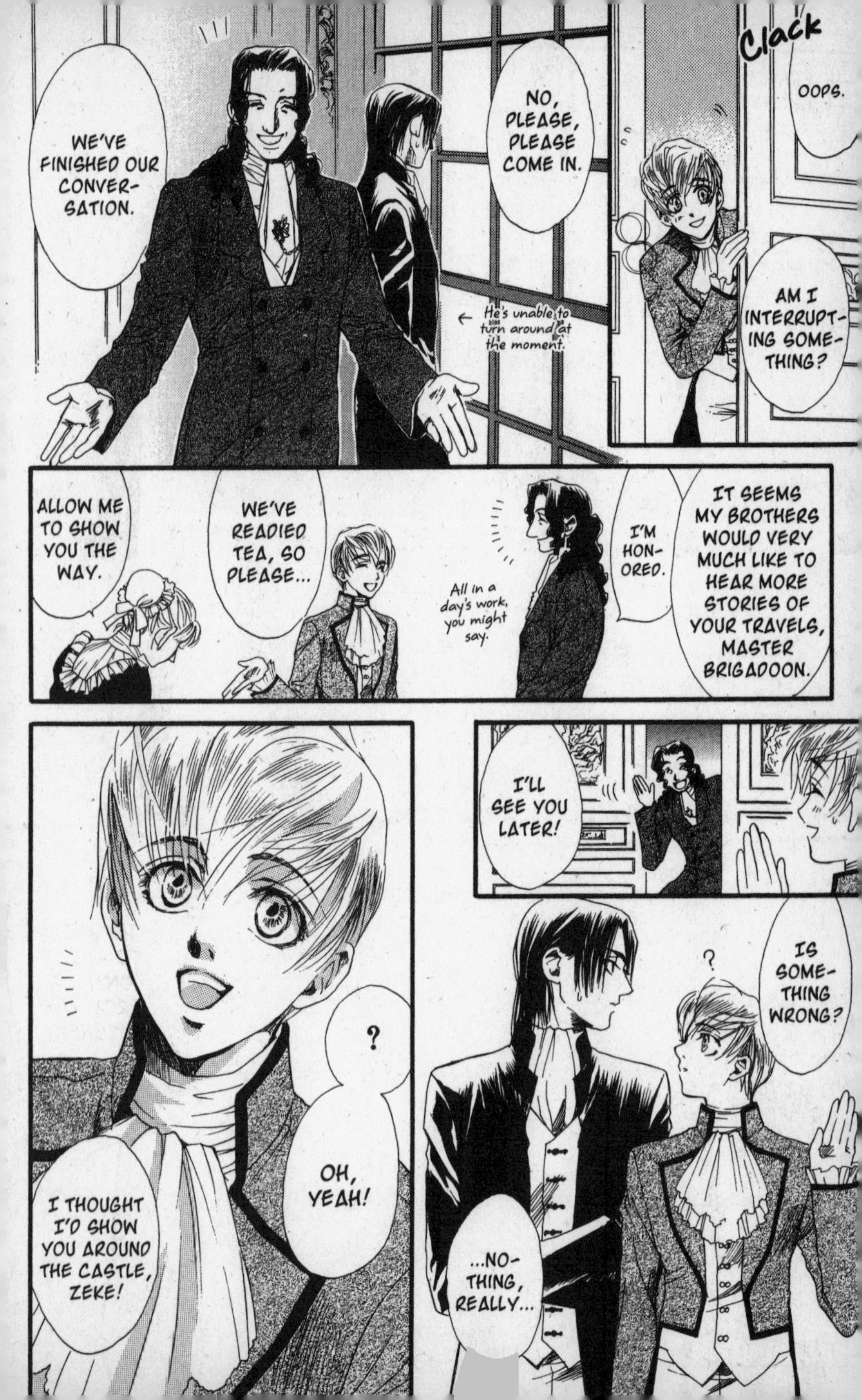
Clack
OOPS.
AM I INTERRUPTING SOMETHING?
NO, PLEASE, PLEASE COME IN.
WE'VE FINISHED OUR CONVERSATION.
← He's unable to turn around at the moment.
IT SEEMS MY BROTHERS WOULD VERY MUCH LIKE TO HEAR MORE STORIES OF YOUR TRAVELS, MASTER BRIGADOON.
I'M HONORED.
All in a day's work, you might say.
WE'VE READIED TEA, SO PLEASE...
ALLOW ME TO SHOW YOU THE WAY.
I'LL SEE YOU LATER!
IS SOMETHING WRONG?
...NOTHING, REALLY...
?
OH, YEAH!
I THOUGHT I'D SHOW YOU AROUND THE CASTLE, ZEKE!

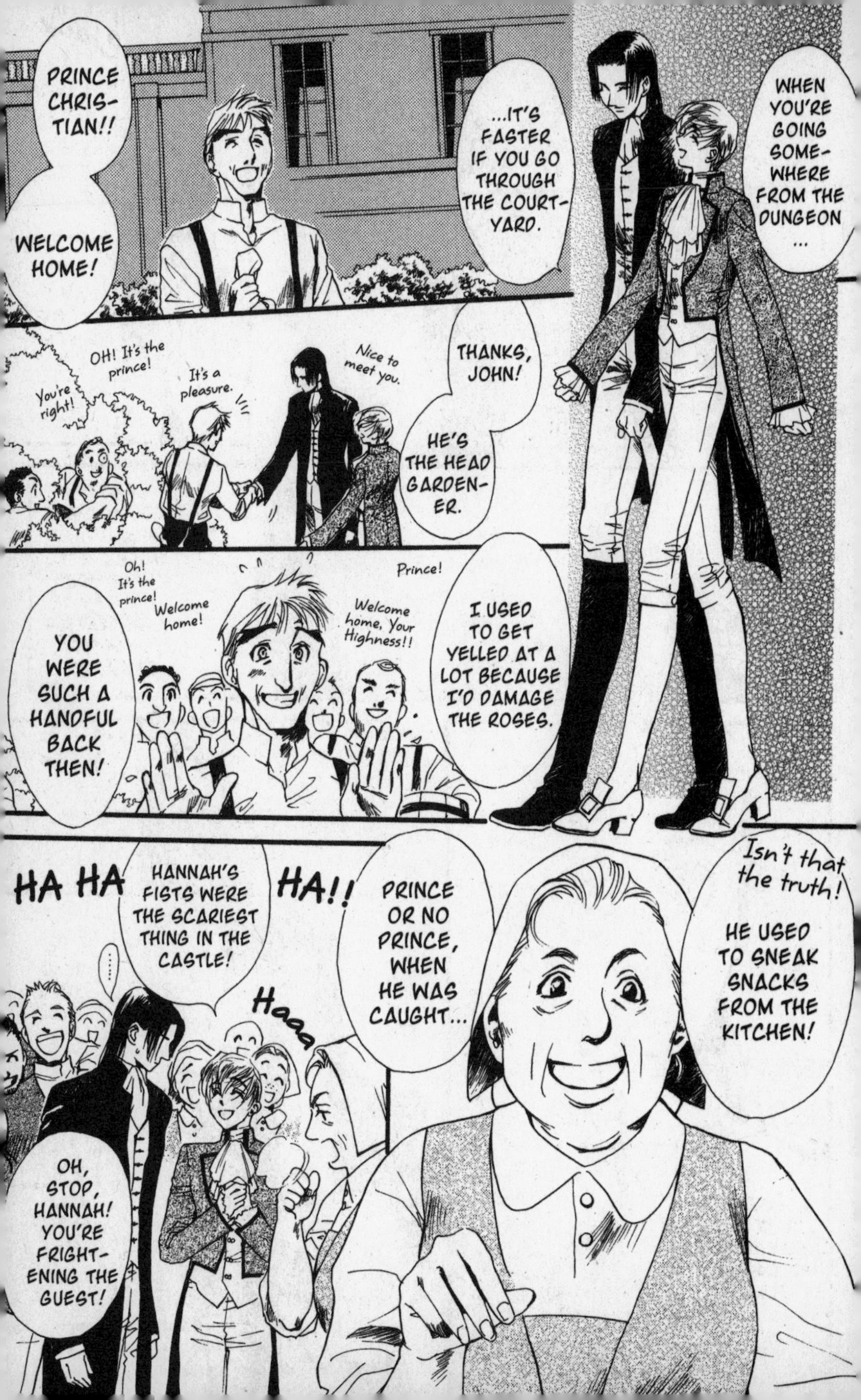
WHEN YOU'RE GOING SOMEWHERE FROM THE DUNGEON ...
...IT'S FASTER IF YOU GO THROUGH THE COURTYARD.
PRINCE CHRISTIAN!!
WELCOME HOME!
THANKS, JOHN!
HE'S THE HEAD GARDENER.
Nice to meet you.
It's a pleasure.
OH! It's the prince!
You're right!
I USED TO GET YELLED AT A LOT BECAUSE I'D DAMAGE THE ROSES.
Prince!
Welcome home, Your Highness!!
Oh! It's the prince!
Welcome home!
YOU WERE SUCH A HANDFUL BACK THEN!
Isn't that the truth!
HE USED TO SNEAK SNACKS FROM THE KITCHEN!
PRINCE OR NO PRINCE, WHEN HE WAS CAUGHT...
HA!!
HA HA
HANNAH'S FISTS WERE THE SCARIEST THING IN THE CASTLE!
Haaa
......
OH, STOP, HANNAH! YOU'RE FRIGHTENING THE GUEST!

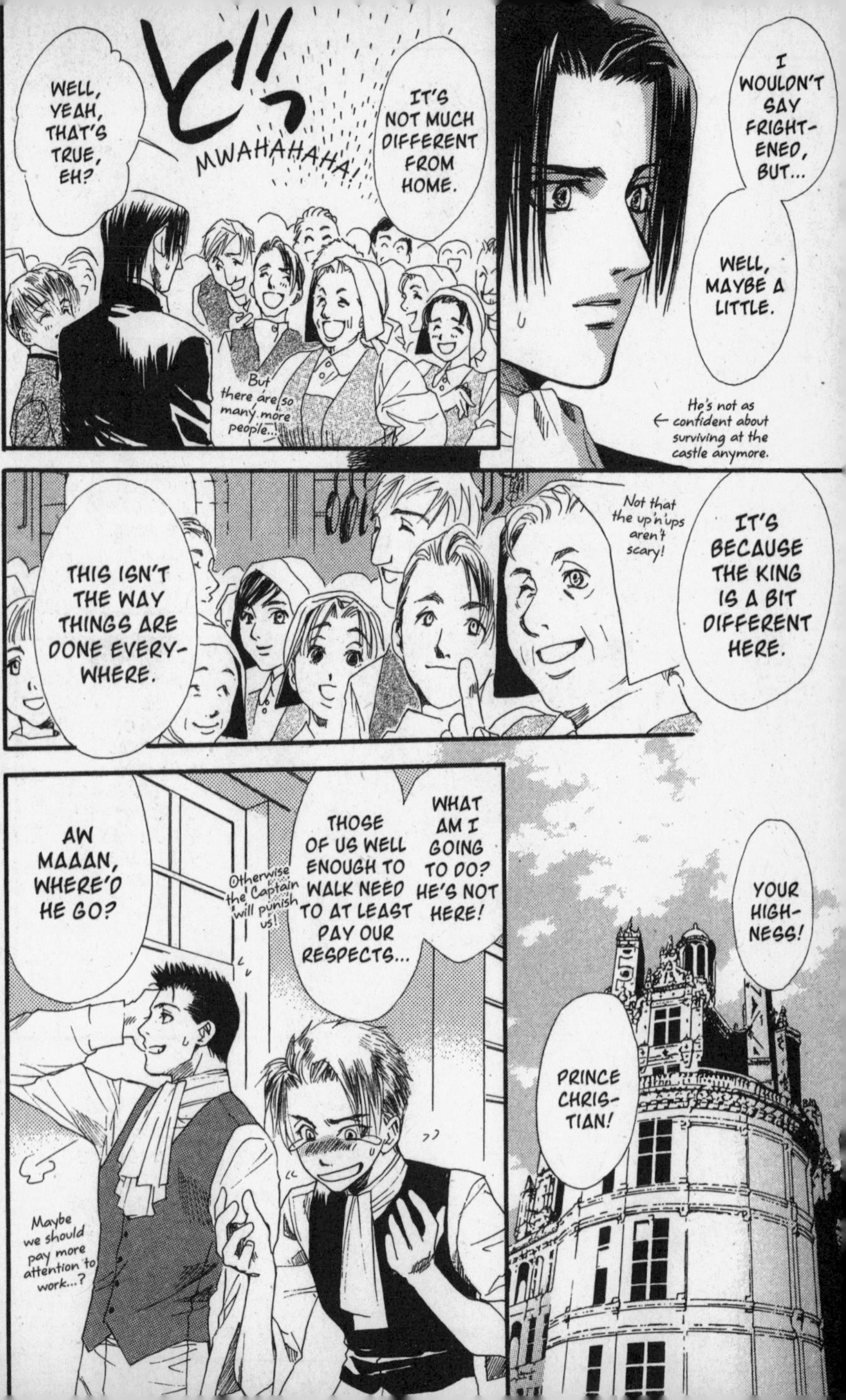
I WOULDN'T SAY FRIGHT-ENED, BUT...
WELL, MAYBE A LITTLE.
← He's not as confident about surviving at the castle anymore.
IT'S NOT MUCH DIFFERENT FROM HOME.
MWAHAHAHA!
WELL, YEAH, THAT'S TRUE, EH?
But there are so many more people...
Not that the up'n'ups aren't scary!
IT'S BECAUSE THE KING IS A BIT DIFFERENT HERE.
THIS ISN'T THE WAY THINGS ARE DONE EVERY-WHERE.
YOUR HIGH-NESS!
PRINCE CHRIS-TIAN!
WHAT AM I GOING TO DO? HE'S NOT HERE!
THOSE OF US WELL ENOUGH TO WALK NEED TO AT LEAST PAY OUR RESPECTS...
Otherwise the Captain will punish us!
AW MAAAN, WHERE'D HE GO?
Maybe we should pay more attention to work...?

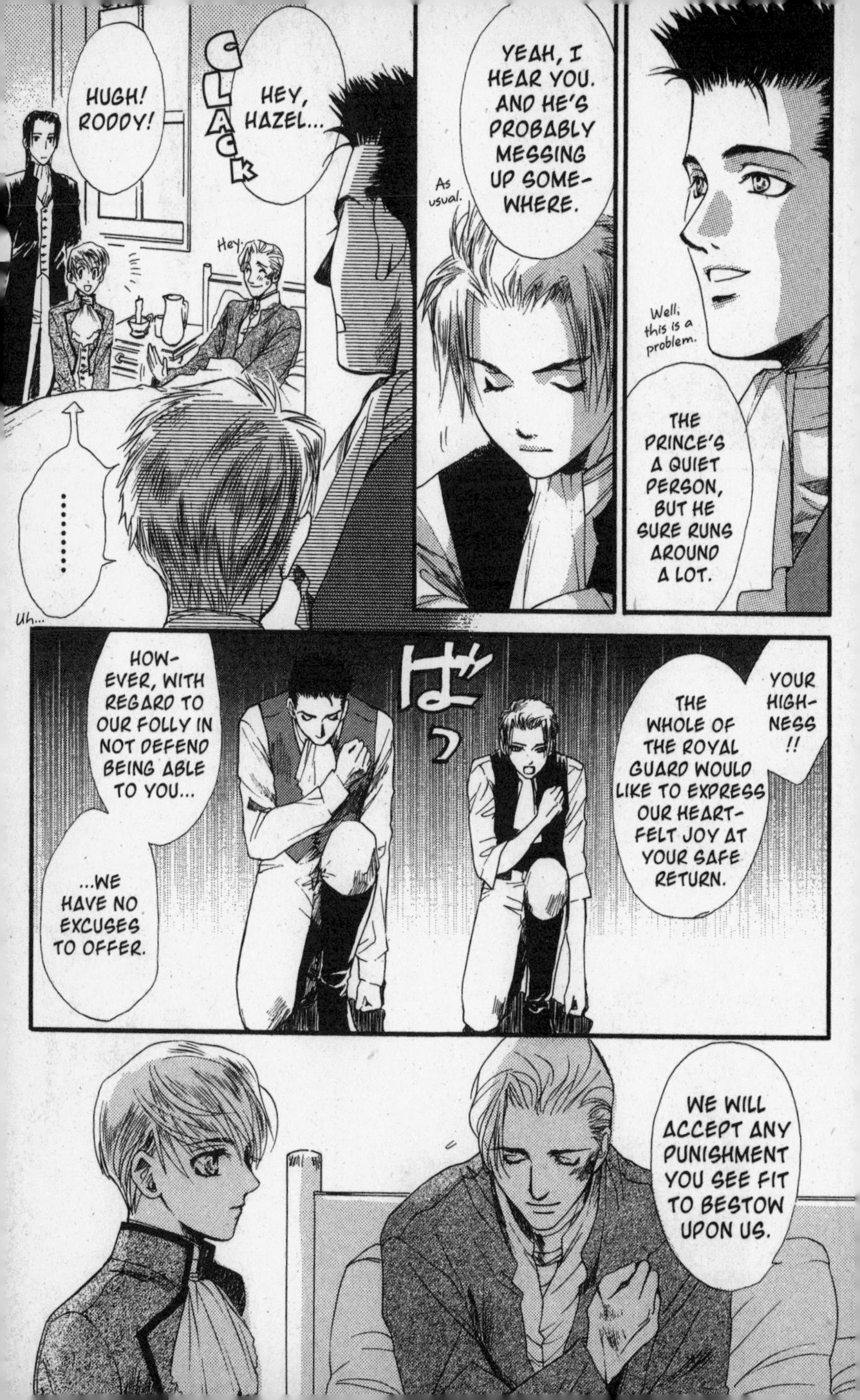
Well, this is a problem.
THE PRINCE'S A QUIET PERSON, BUT HE SURE RUNS AROUND A LOT.
YEAH, I HEAR YOU. AND HE'S PROBABLY MESSING UP SOME-WHERE.
As usual.
HEY, HAZEL...
CLACK
HUGH! RODDY!
Hey.
......
Uh...
YOUR HIGH-NESS!!
THE WHOLE OF THE ROYAL GUARD WOULD LIKE TO EXPRESS OUR HEART-FELT JOY AT YOUR SAFE RETURN.
ばっ
HOW-EVER, WITH REGARD TO OUR FOLLY IN NOT DEFEND BEING ABLE TO YOU...
...WE HAVE NO EXCUSES TO OFFER.
WE WILL ACCEPT ANY PUNISHMENT YOU SEE FIT TO BESTOW UPON US.

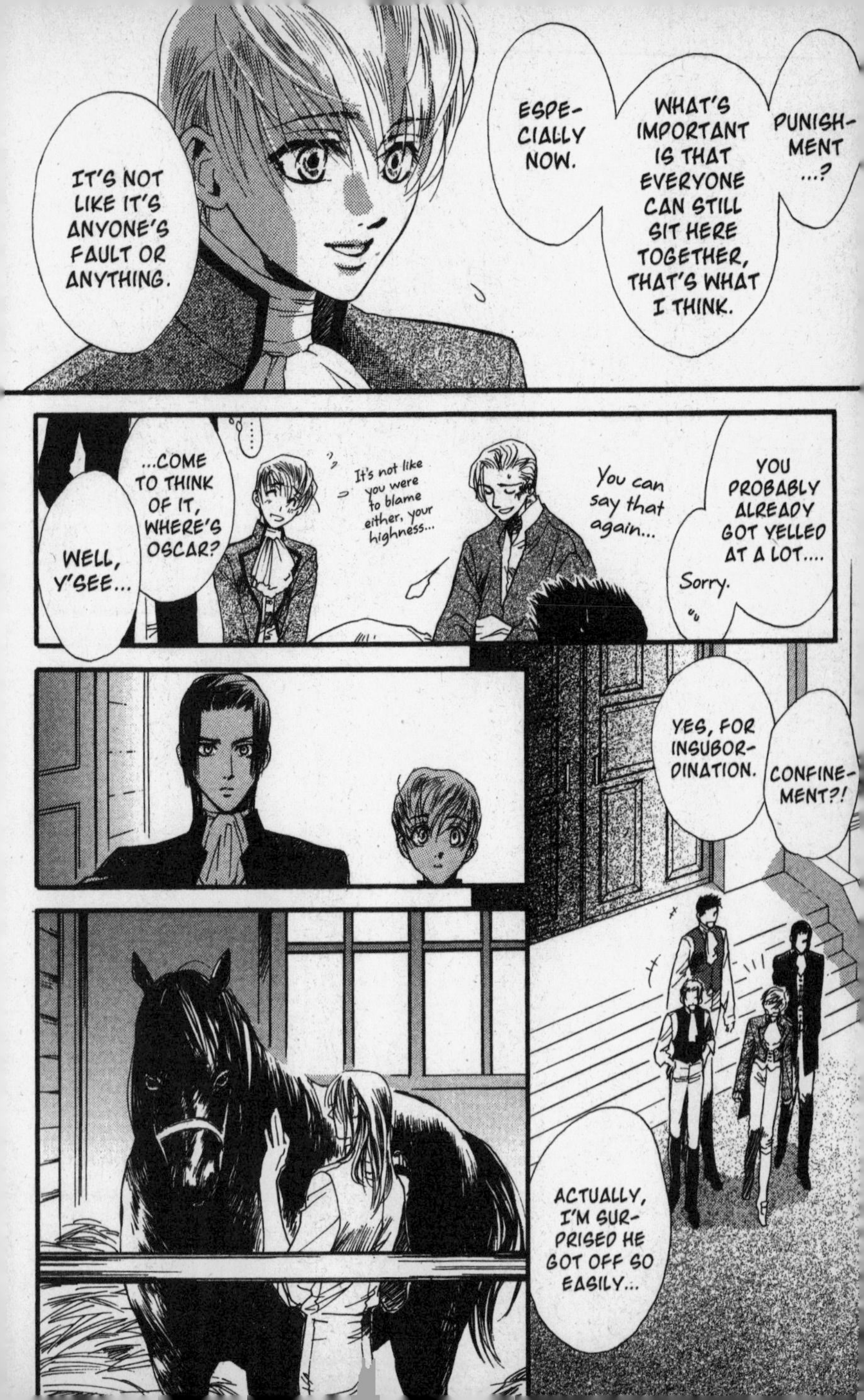
PUNISHMENT...?
WHAT'S IMPORTANT IS THAT EVERYONE CAN STILL SIT HERE TOGETHER, THAT'S WHAT I THINK.
ESPECIALLY NOW.
IT'S NOT LIKE IT'S ANYONE'S FAULT OR ANYTHING.
YOU PROBABLY ALREADY GOT YELLED AT A LOT....
Sorry.
You can say that again...
It's not like you were to blame either, your highness...
...COME TO THINK OF IT, WHERE'S OSCAR?
WELL, Y'SEE...
CONFINEMENT?!
YES, FOR INSUBORDINATION.
ACTUALLY, I'M SURPRISED HE GOT OFF SO EASILY...

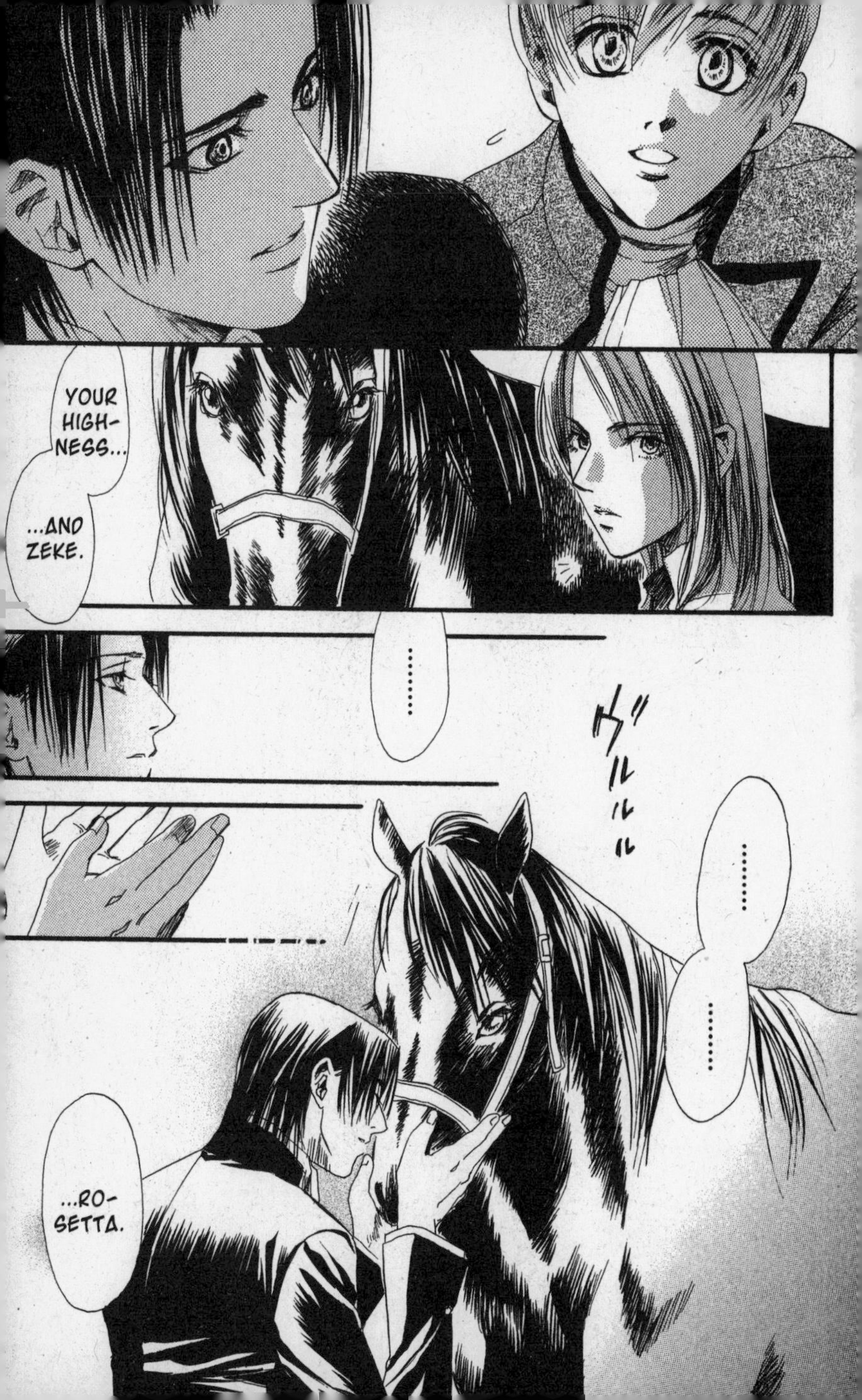
YOUR HIGH-NESS...
...AND ZEKE.
ヴルルル
......
......
......
...RO-SETTA.

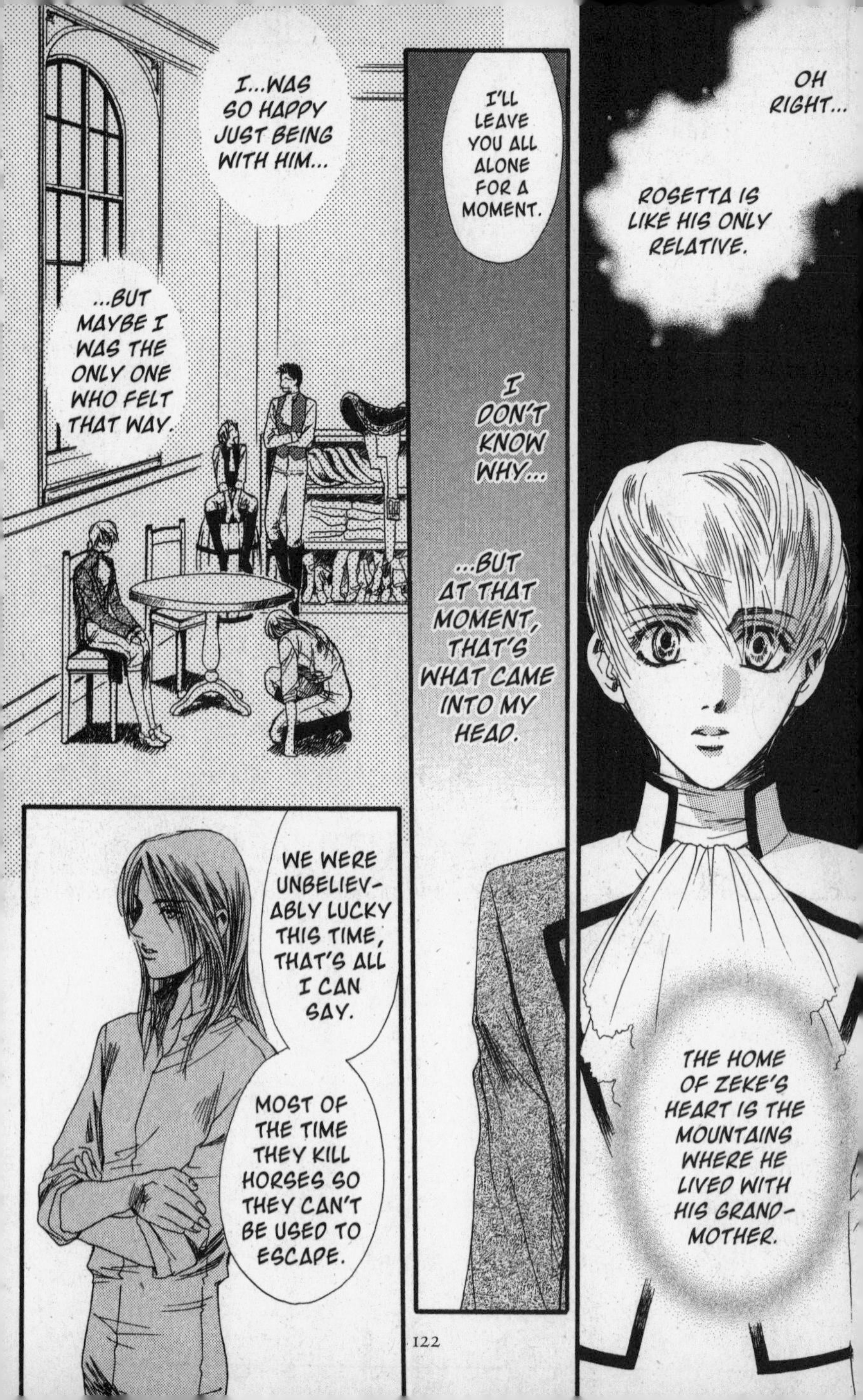
OH RIGHT...
ROSETTA IS LIKE HIS ONLY RELATIVE.
THE HOME OF ZEKE'S HEART IS THE MOUNTAINS WHERE HE LIVED WITH HIS GRAND-MOTHER.
I'LL LEAVE YOU ALL ALONE FOR A MOMENT.
I DON'T KNOW WHY...
...BUT AT THAT MOMENT, THAT'S WHAT CAME INTO MY HEAD.
I...WAS SO HAPPY JUST BEING WITH HIM...
...BUT MAYBE I WAS THE ONLY ONE WHO FELT THAT WAY.
WE WERE UNBELIEV-ABLY LUCKY THIS TIME, THAT'S ALL I CAN SAY.
MOST OF THE TIME THEY KILL HORSES SO THEY CAN'T BE USED TO ESCAPE.

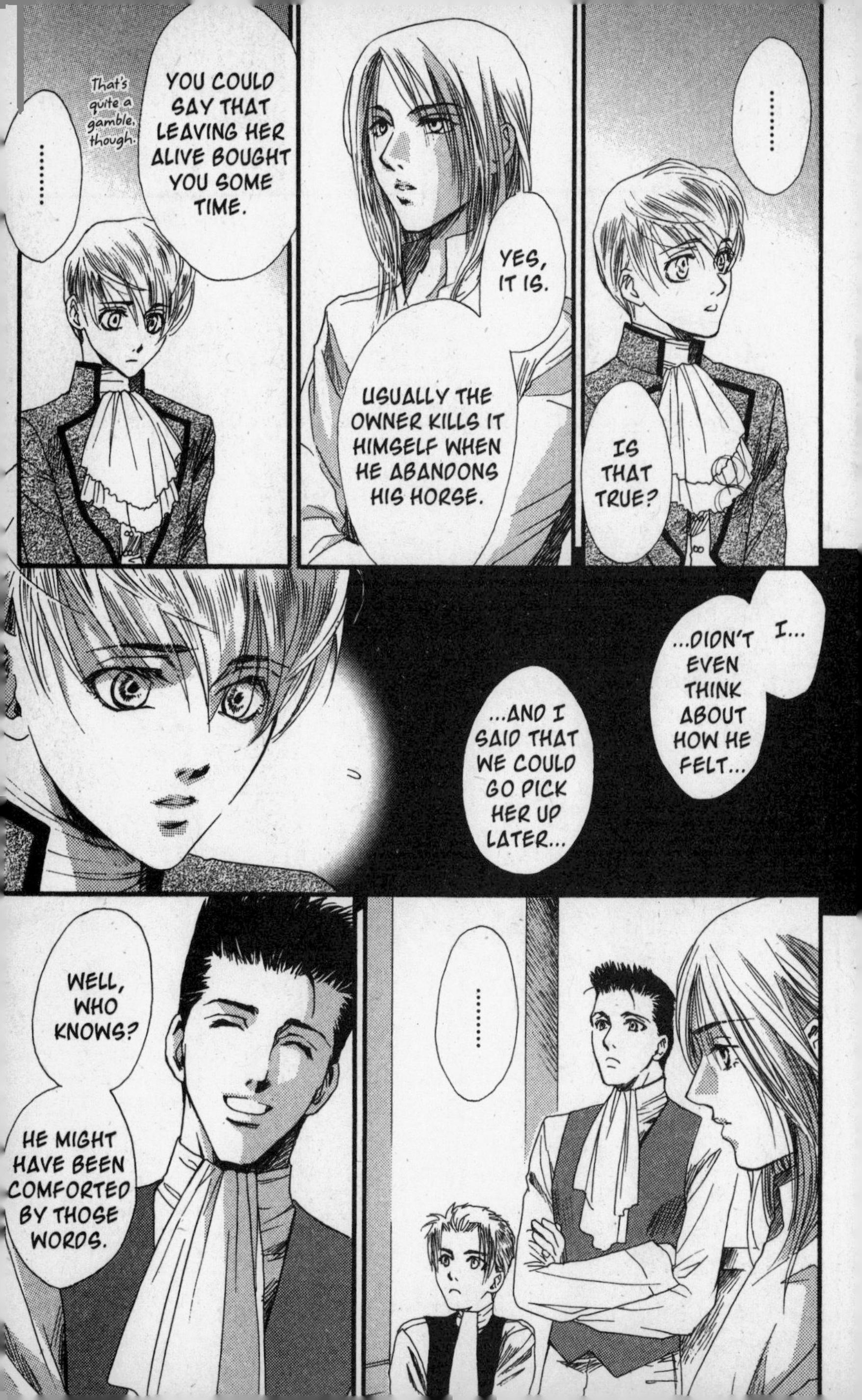
……
IS THAT TRUE?
YES, IT IS.
USUALLY THE OWNER KILLS IT HIMSELF WHEN HE ABANDONS HIS HORSE.
YOU COULD SAY THAT LEAVING HER ALIVE BOUGHT YOU SOME TIME.
That's quite a gamble, though.
……
I...
...DIDN'T EVEN THINK ABOUT HOW HE FELT...
...AND I SAID THAT WE COULD GO PICK HER UP LATER...
……
WELL, WHO KNOWS?
HE MIGHT HAVE BEEN COMFORTED BY THOSE WORDS.

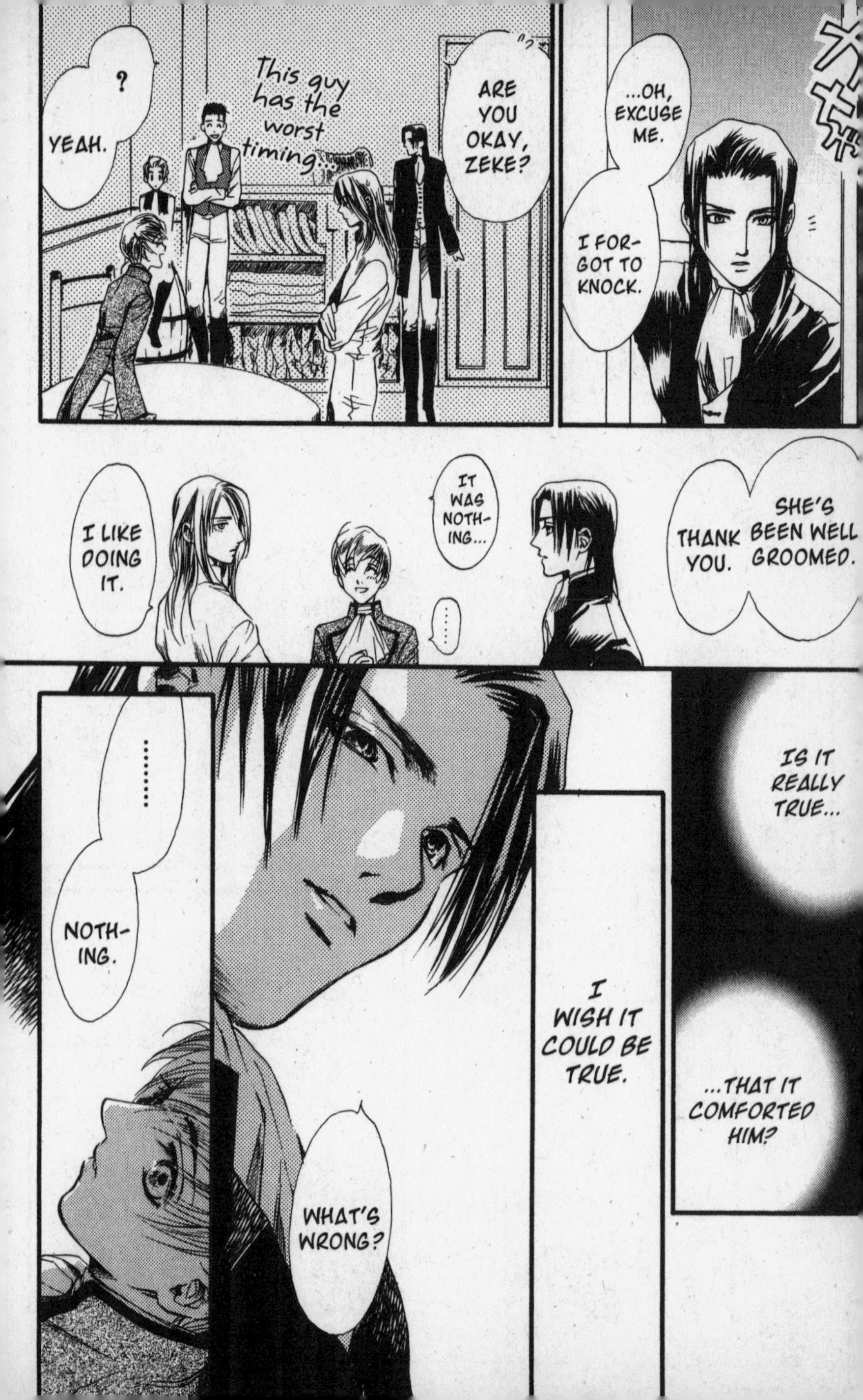
...OH, EXCUSE ME.
I FORGOT TO KNOCK.
ARE YOU OKAY, ZEKE?
This guy has the worst timing...
?
YEAH.
SHE'S BEEN WELL GROOMED.
THANK YOU.
IT WAS NOTHING...
......
I LIKE DOING IT.
IS IT REALLY TRUE...
...THAT IT COMFORTED HIM?
I WISH IT COULD BE TRUE.
WHAT'S WRONG?
....
NOTHING.

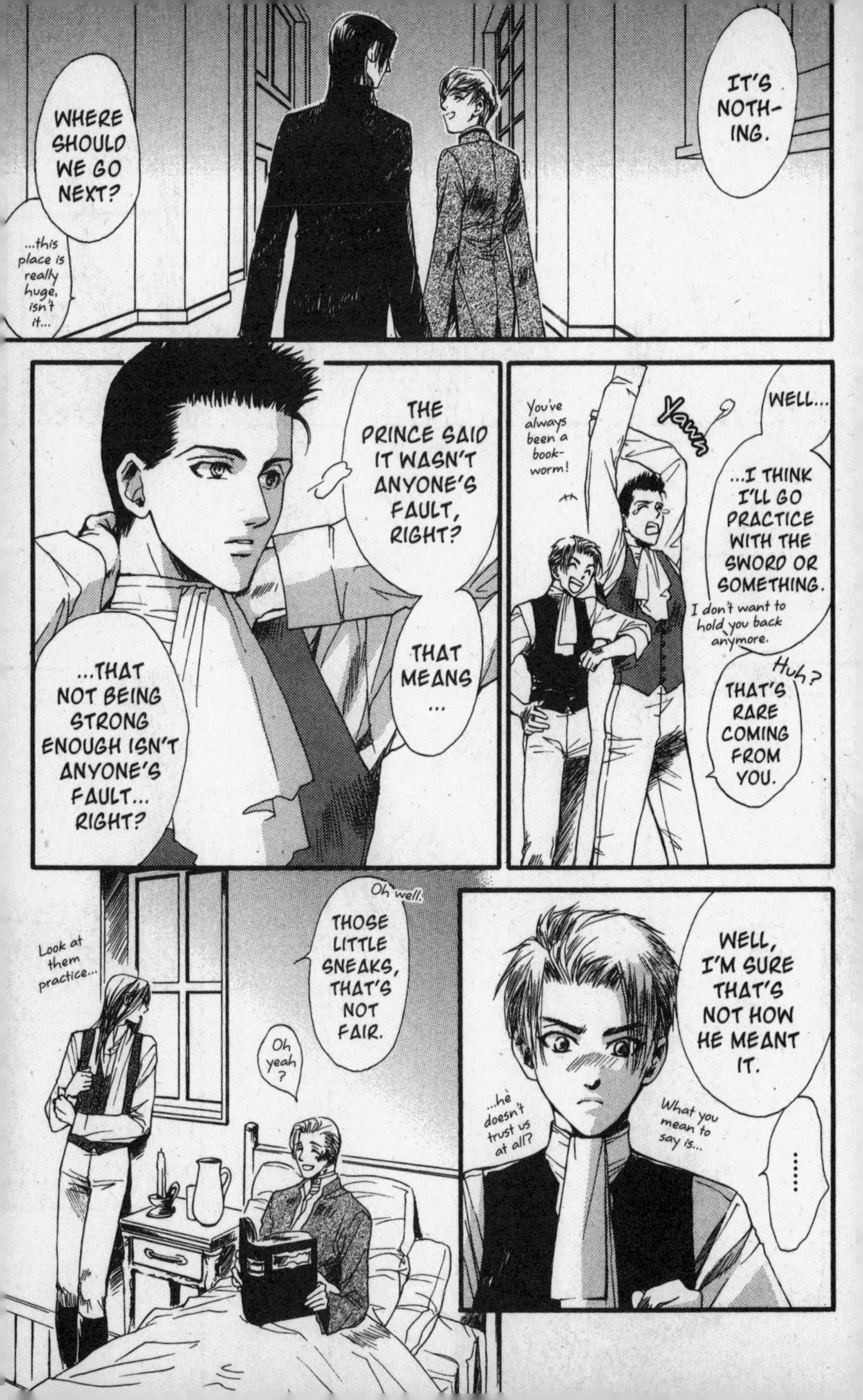
IT'S NOTHING.
WHERE SHOULD WE GO NEXT?
...this place is really huge, isn't it...
WELL...
...I THINK I'LL GO PRACTICE WITH THE SWORD OR SOMETHING.
Yawn
You've always been a book-worm!
I don't want to hold you back anymore.
Huh?
THAT'S RARE COMING FROM YOU.
THE PRINCE SAID IT WASN'T ANYONE'S FAULT, RIGHT?
THAT MEANS...
...THAT NOT BEING STRONG ENOUGH ISN'T ANYONE'S FAULT... RIGHT?
WELL, I'M SURE THAT'S NOT HOW HE MEANT IT.
What you mean to say is...
......
...he doesn't trust us at all?
Oh well.
THOSE LITTLE SNEAKS, THAT'S NOT FAIR.
Look at them practice...
Oh yeah?

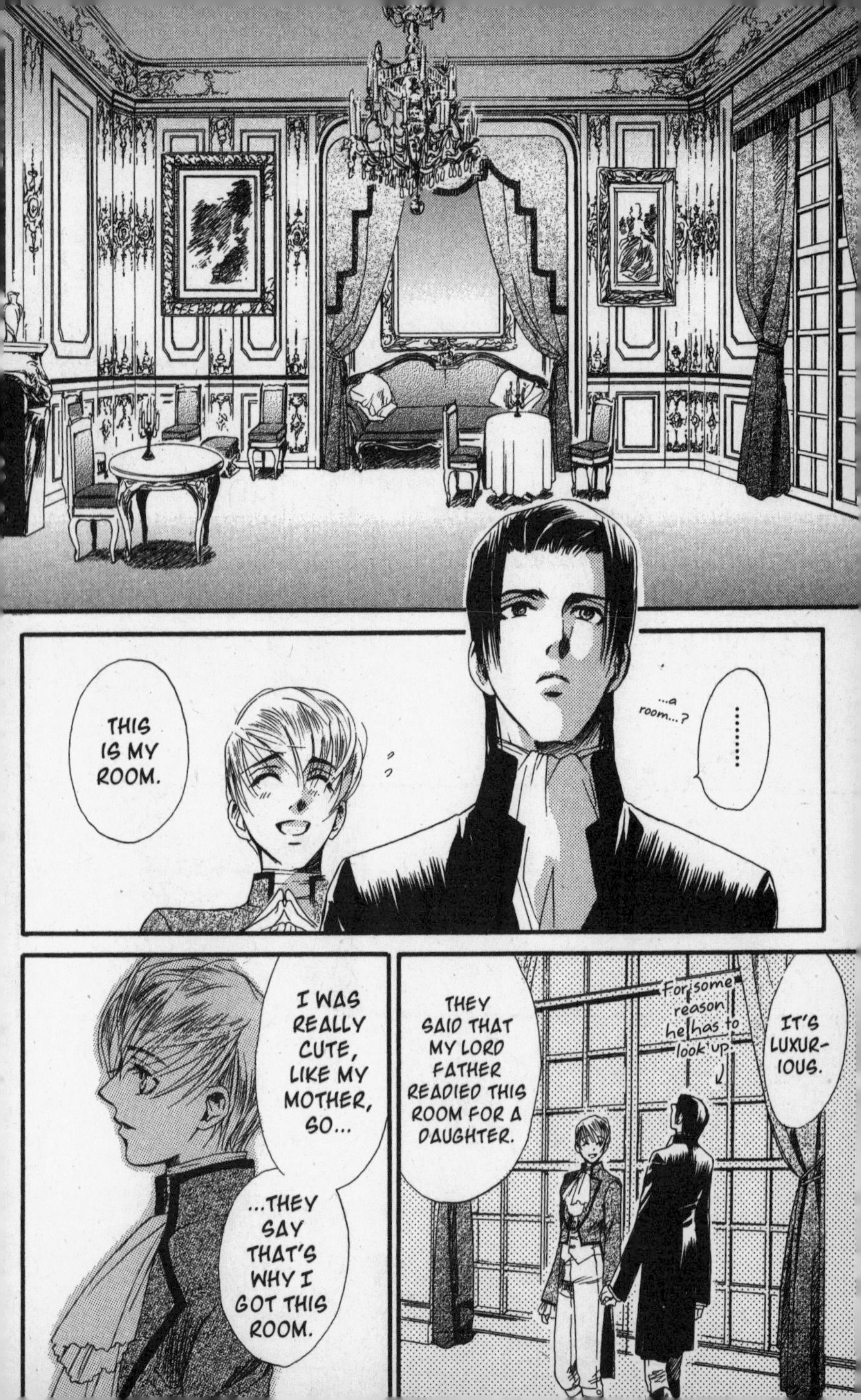

....
...a room...?
THIS IS MY ROOM.
IT'S LUXUR-IOUS.
For some reason he has to look up.
THEY SAID THAT MY LORD FATHER READIED THIS ROOM FOR A DAUGHTER.
I WAS REALLY CUTE, LIKE MY MOTHER, SO...
...THEY SAY THAT'S WHY I GOT THIS ROOM.

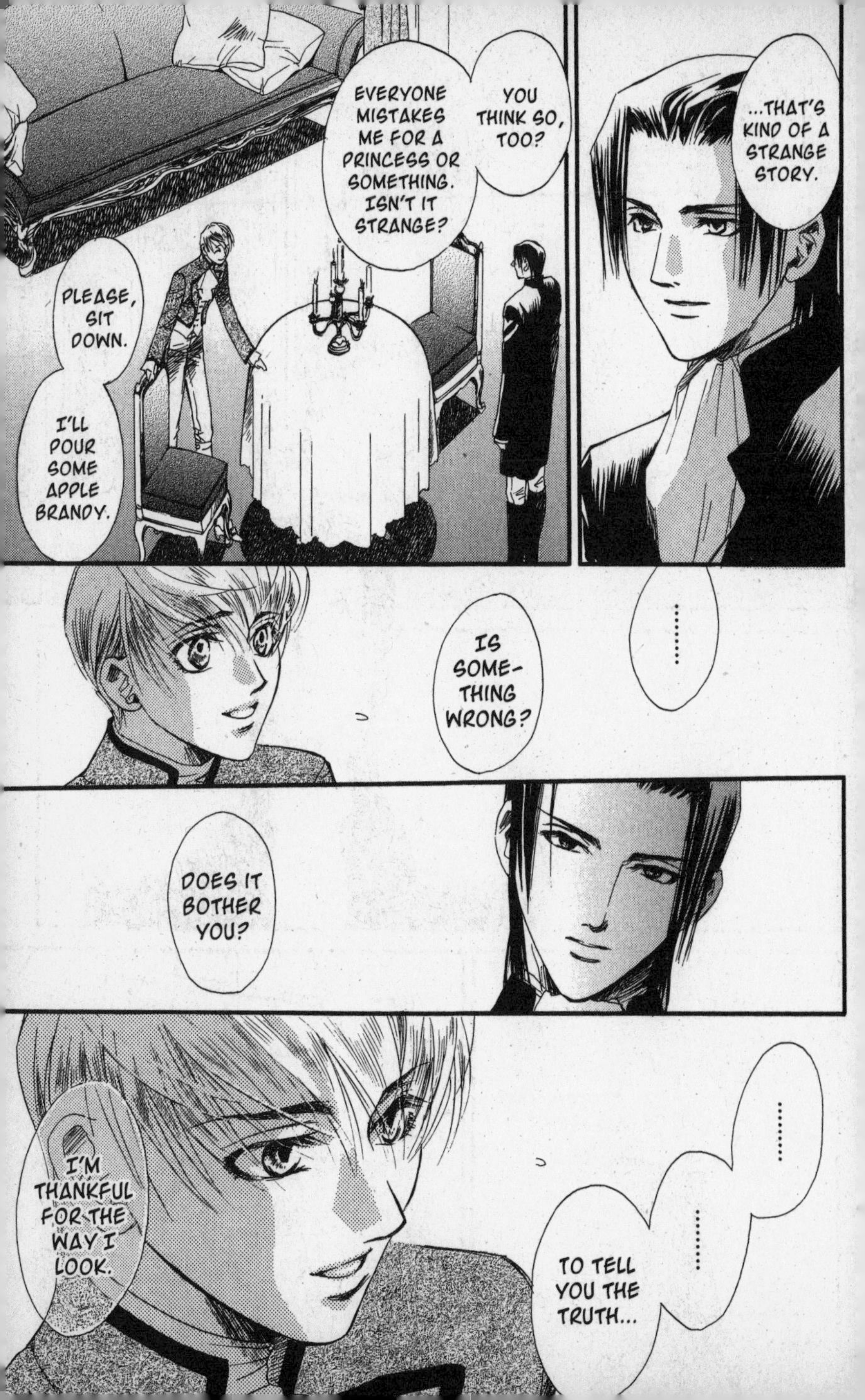
...THAT'S KIND OF A STRANGE STORY.
YOU THINK SO, TOO?
EVERYONE MISTAKES ME FOR A PRINCESS OR SOMETHING. ISN'T IT STRANGE?
PLEASE, SIT DOWN.
I'LL POUR SOME APPLE BRANDY.
......
IS SOME-THING WRONG?
DOES IT BOTHER YOU?
......
......
TO TELL YOU THE TRUTH...
I'M THANKFUL FOR THE WAY I LOOK.

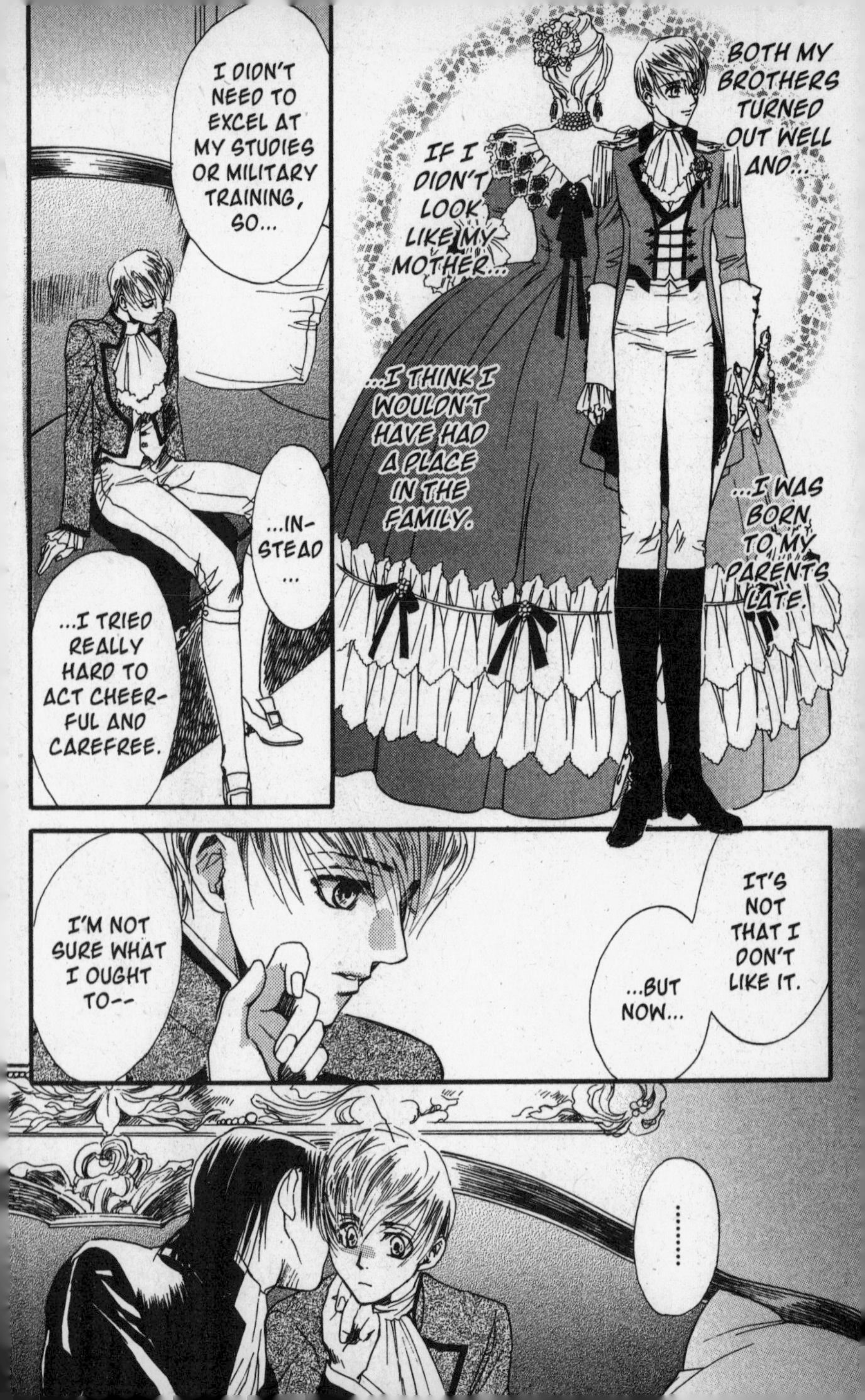

BOTH MY BROTHERS TURNED OUT WELL AND...
...I WAS BORN TO MY PARENTS LATE.
IF I DIDN'T LOOK LIKE MY MOTHER...
...I THINK I WOULDN'T HAVE HAD A PLACE IN THE FAMILY.
I DIDN'T NEED TO EXCEL AT MY STUDIES OR MILITARY TRAINING, SO...
...IN-STEAD...
...I TRIED REALLY HARD TO ACT CHEER-FUL AND CAREFREE.
IT'S NOT THAT I DON'T LIKE IT.
...BUT NOW...
I'M NOT SURE WHAT I OUGHT TO--
......

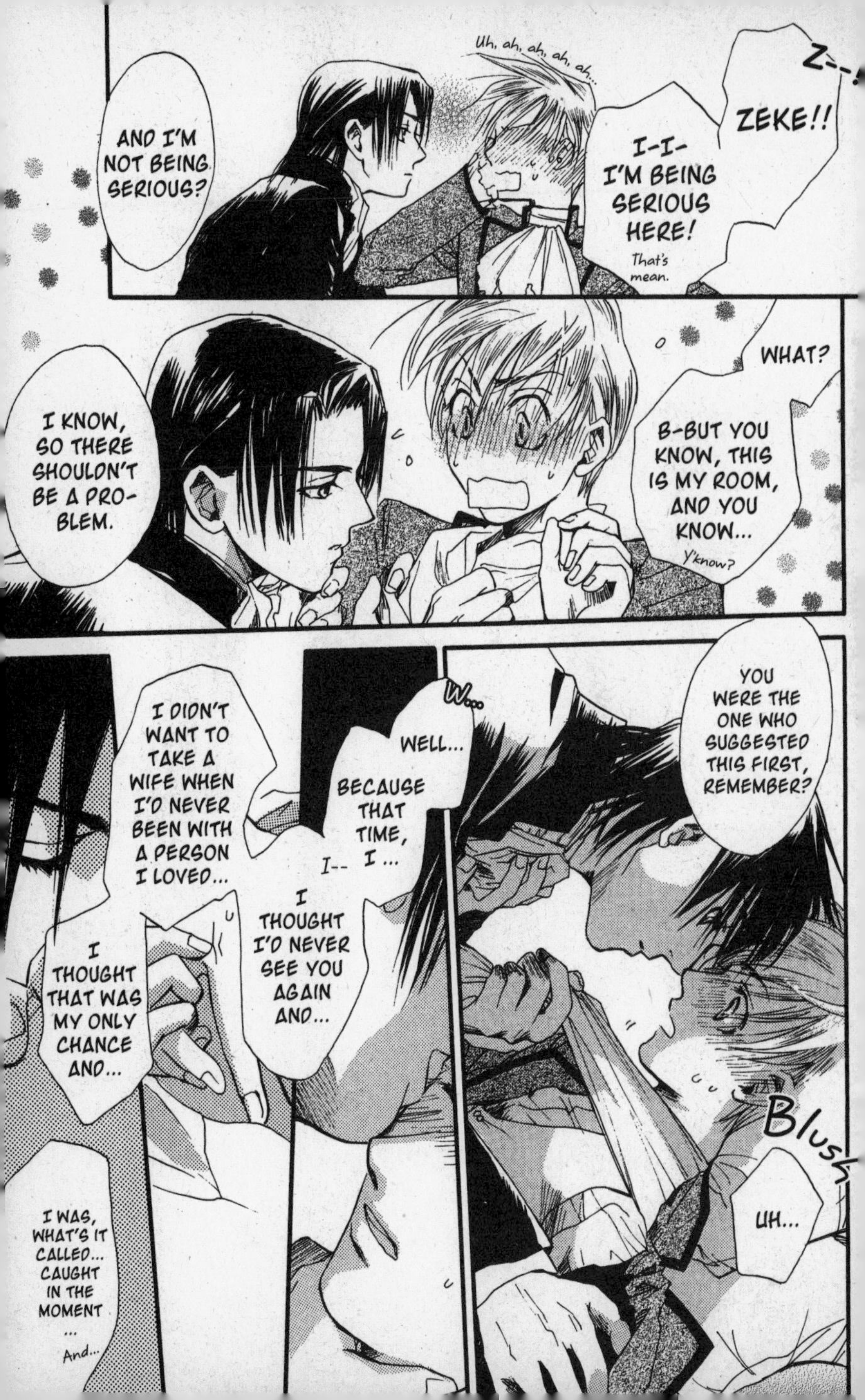
Z--!
ZEKE!!
I-I- I'M BEING SERIOUS HERE!
That's mean.
Uh, ah, ah, ah, ah...
AND I'M NOT BEING SERIOUS?
WHAT?
B-BUT YOU KNOW, THIS IS MY ROOM, AND YOU KNOW...
Y'know?
I KNOW, SO THERE SHOULDN'T BE A PRO-BLEM.
YOU WERE THE ONE WHO SUGGESTED THIS FIRST, REMEMBER?
Blush
UH...
W...
WELL...
BECAUSE THAT TIME, I ...
I--
I THOUGHT I'D NEVER SEE YOU AGAIN AND...
I DIDN'T WANT TO TAKE A WIFE WHEN I'D NEVER BEEN WITH A PERSON I LOVED...
I THOUGHT THAT WAS MY ONLY CHANCE AND...
I WAS, WHAT'S IT CALLED... CAUGHT IN THE MOMENT ...
And...

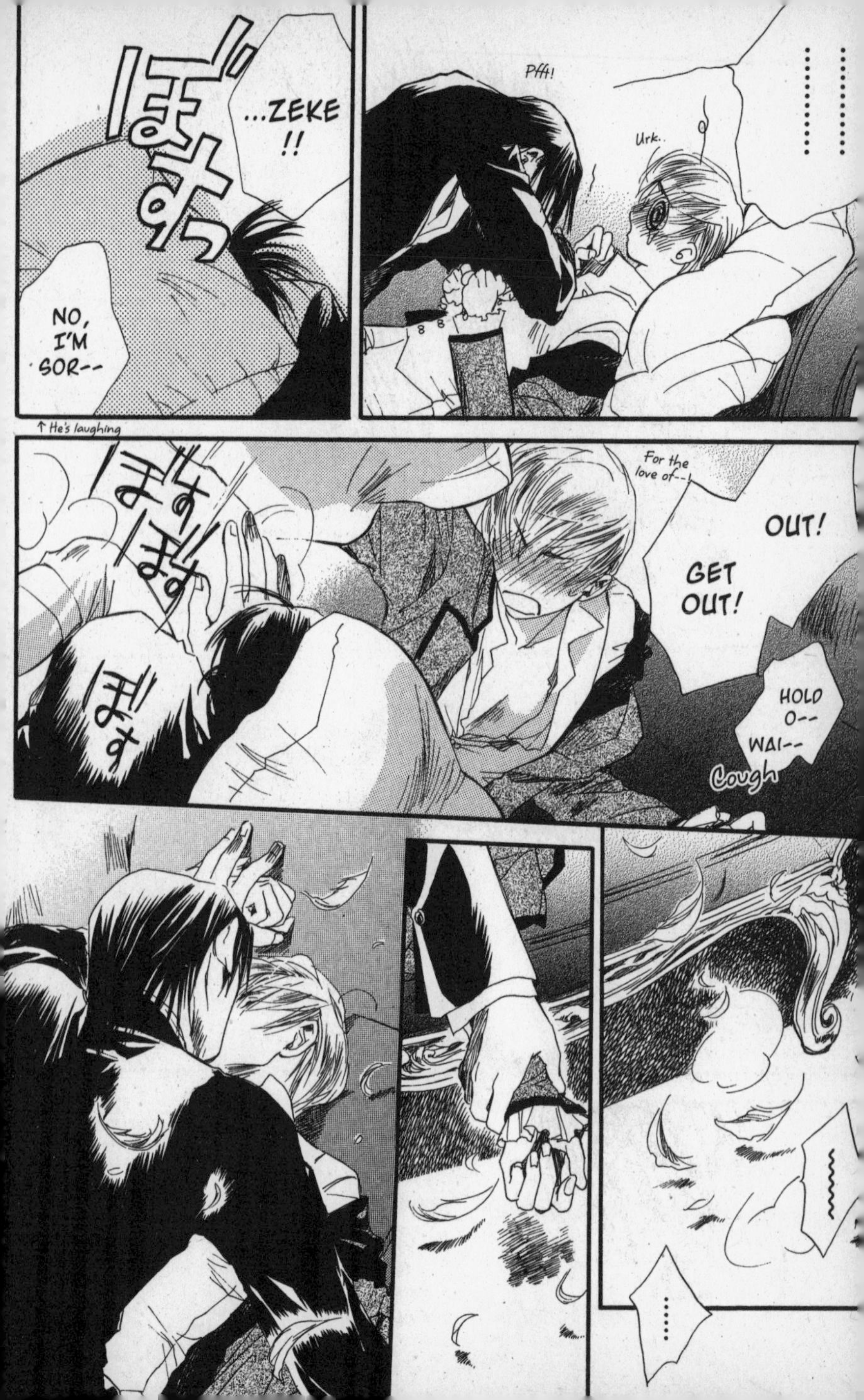
....
Pff!
Urk..
...ZEKE !!
ぼすっ
NO, I'M SOR--
↑ He's laughing
For the love of--!
OUT!
GET OUT!
HOLD O--
WAI--
Cough
ぼすぼす
ぼす
......
......

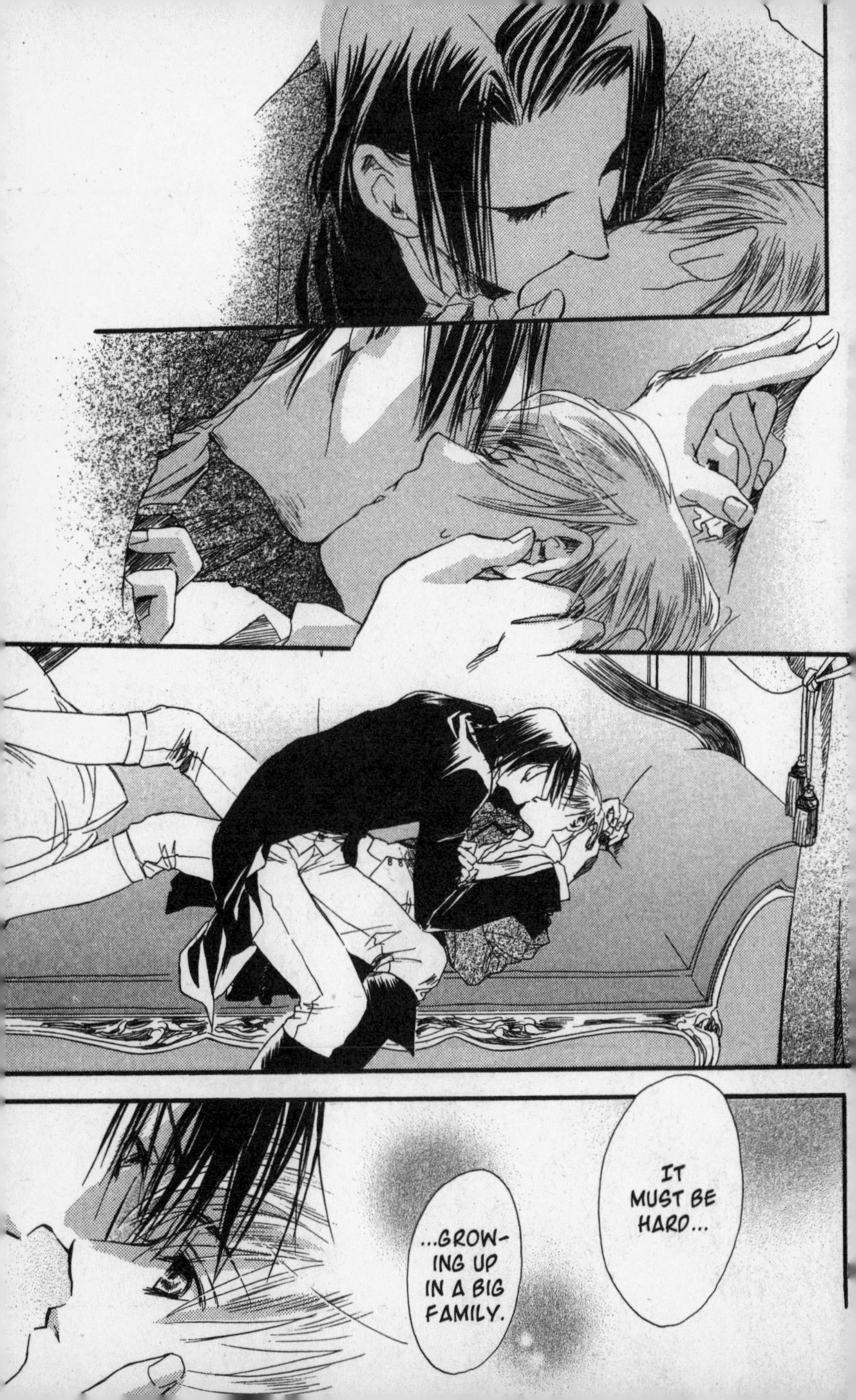
IT MUST BE HARD...
...GROWING UP IN A BIG FAMILY.

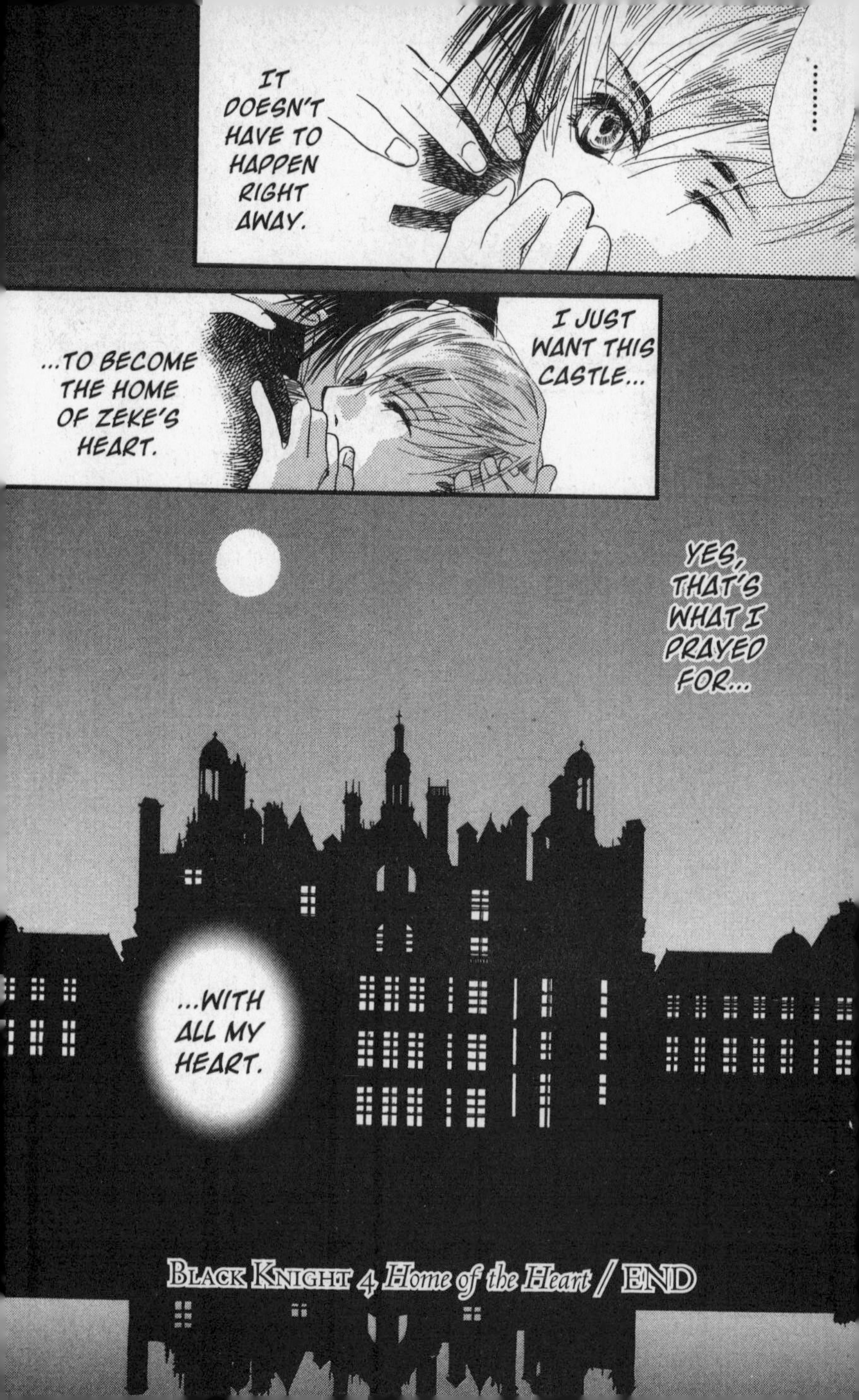
......
IT DOESN'T HAVE TO HAPPEN RIGHT AWAY.
I JUST WANT THIS CASTLE...
...TO BECOME THE HOME OF ZEKE'S HEART.
YES, THAT'S WHAT I PRAYED FOR...
...WITH ALL MY HEART.
BLACK KNIGHT 4 Home of the Heart / END

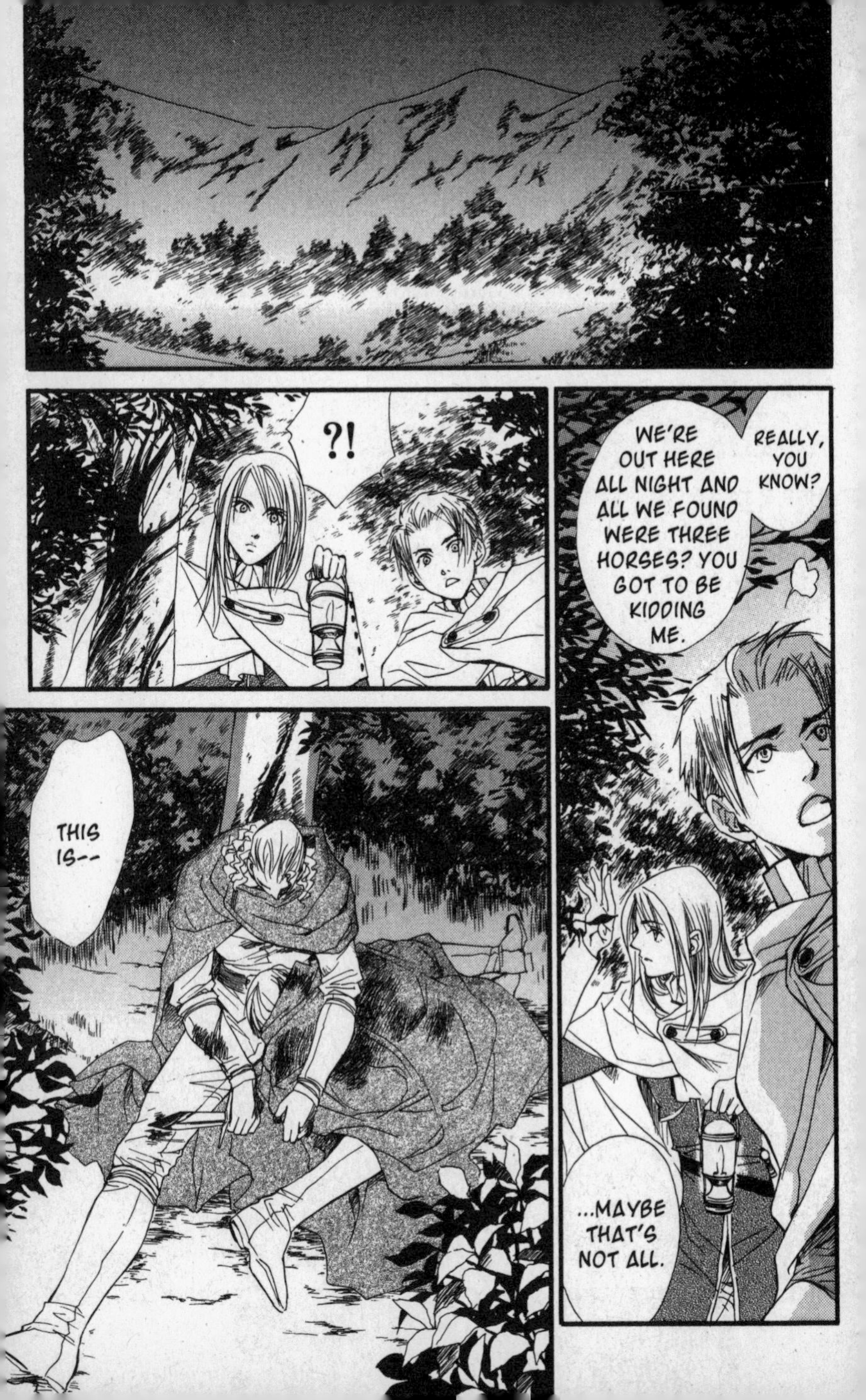
REALLY, YOU KNOW?
WE'RE OUT HERE ALL NIGHT AND ALL WE FOUND WERE THREE HORSES? YOU GOT TO BE KIDDING ME.
...MAYBE THAT'S NOT ALL.
?!
THIS IS--

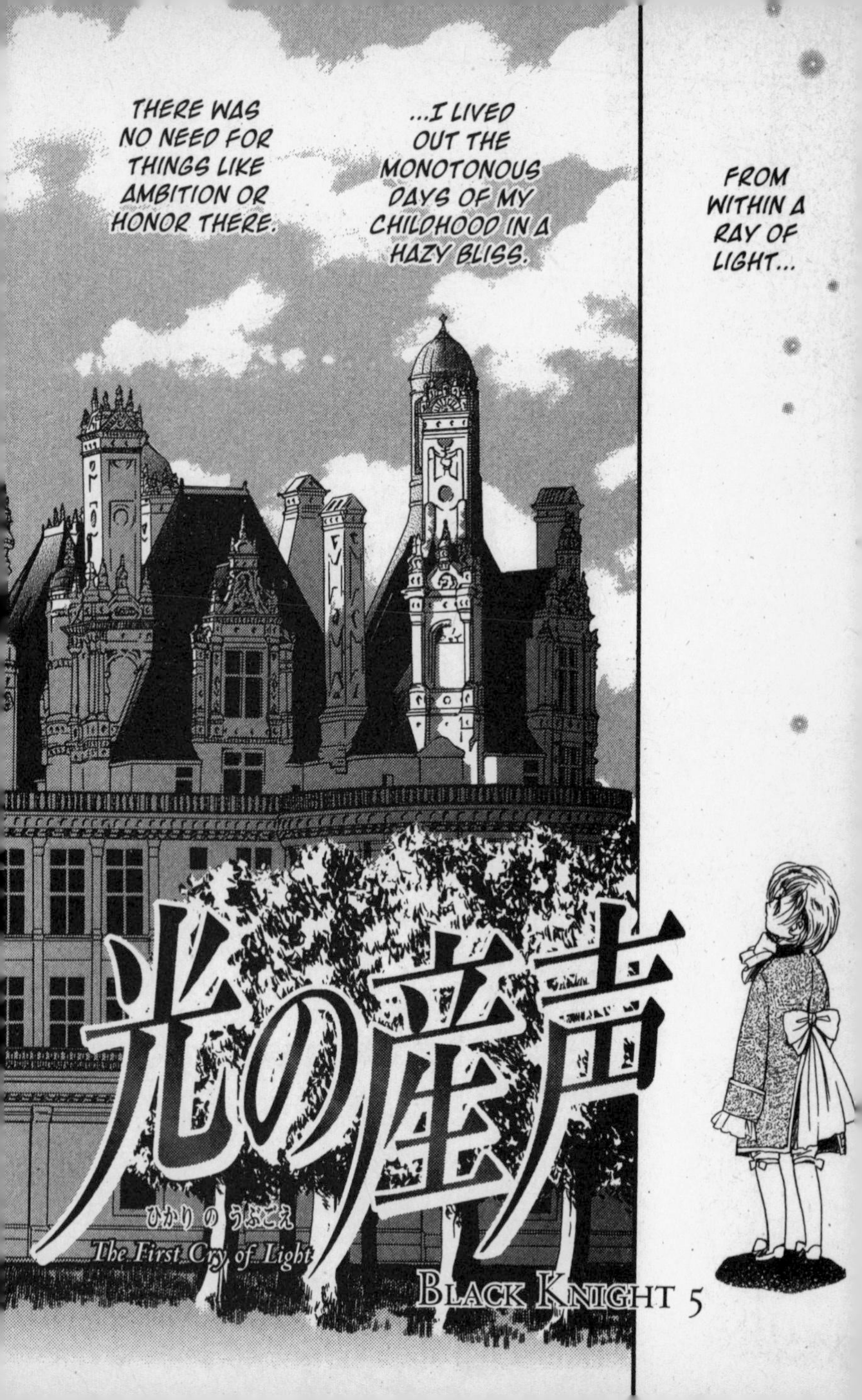
FROM WITHIN A RAY OF LIGHT...
...I LIVED OUT THE MONOTONOUS DAYS OF MY CHILDHOOD IN A HAZY BLISS.
THERE WAS NO NEED FOR THINGS LIKE AMBITION OR HONOR THERE.
光の産声
ひかり の うぶごえ
The First Cry of Light

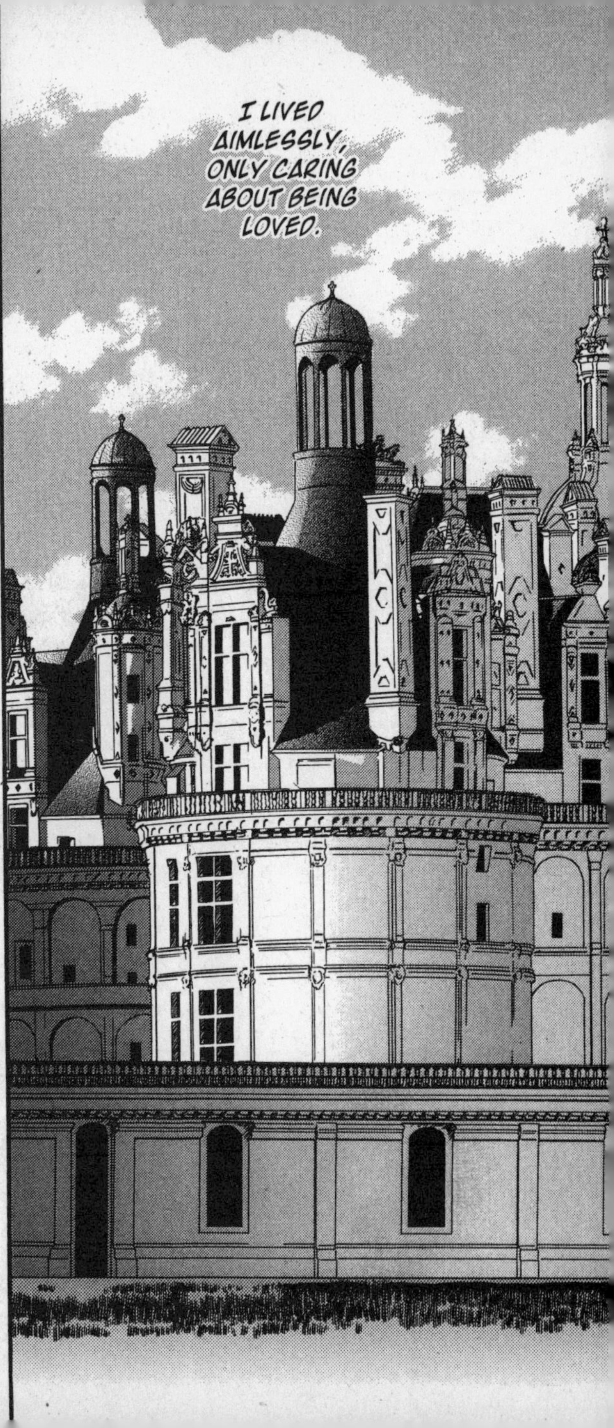
I LIVED AIMLESSLY, ONLY CARING ABOUT BEING LOVED.
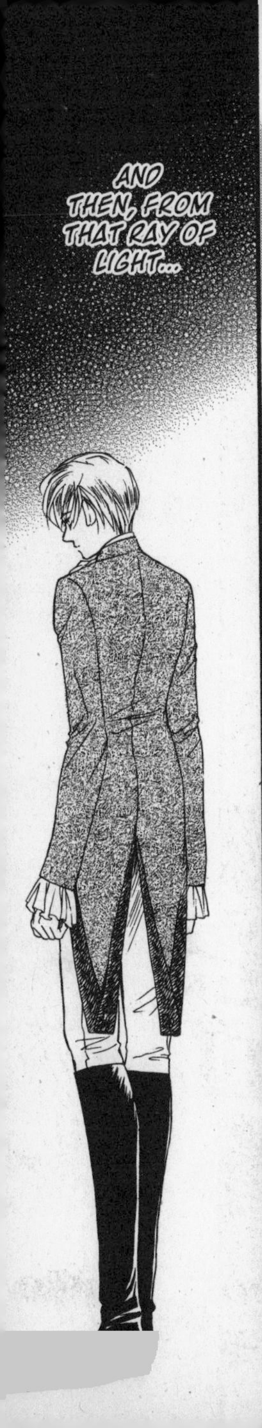
AND THEN, FROM THAT RAY OF LIGHT...

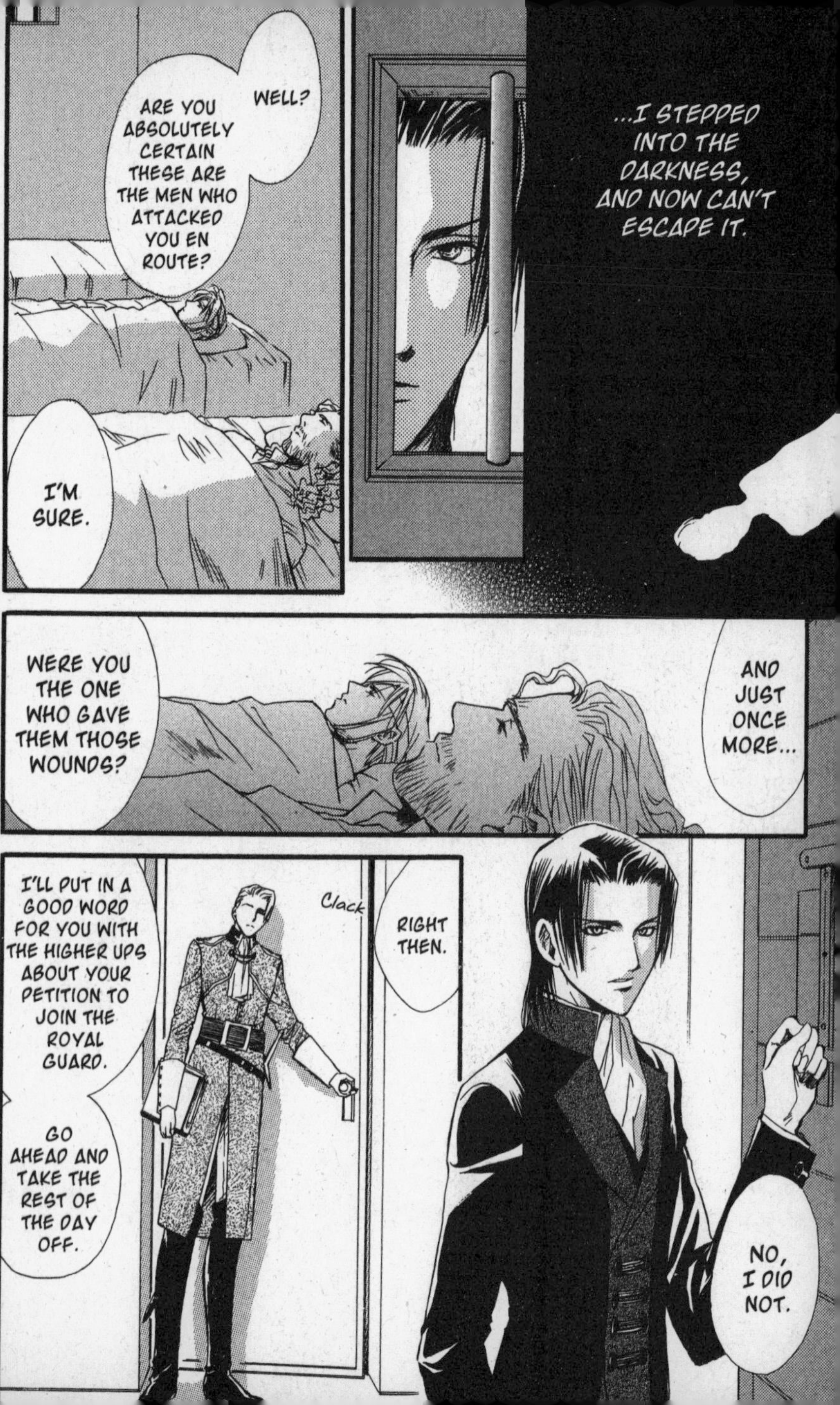
...I STEPPED INTO THE DARKNESS, AND NOW CAN'T ESCAPE IT.
WELL?
ARE YOU ABSOLUTELY CERTAIN THESE ARE THE MEN WHO ATTACKED YOU EN ROUTE?
I'M SURE.
AND JUST ONCE MORE...
WERE YOU THE ONE WHO GAVE THEM THOSE WOUNDS?
NO, I DID NOT.
RIGHT THEN.
Clack
I'LL PUT IN A GOOD WORD FOR YOU WITH THE HIGHER UPS ABOUT YOUR PETITION TO JOIN THE ROYAL GUARD.
GO AHEAD AND TAKE THE REST OF THE DAY OFF.

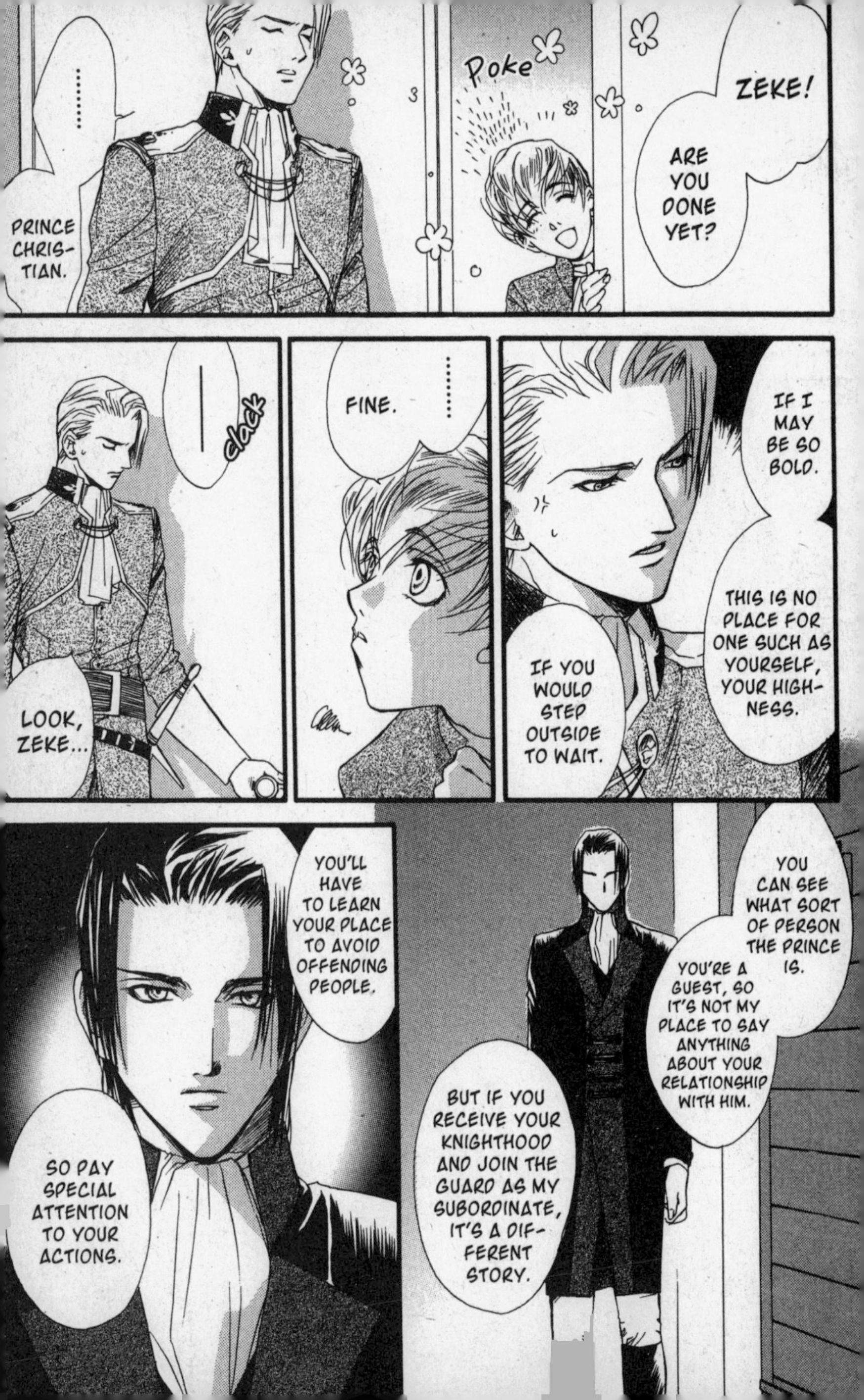
Poke
ZEKE!
ARE YOU DONE YET?
......
PRINCE CHRIS-TIAN.
IF I MAY BE SO BOLD.
THIS IS NO PLACE FOR ONE SUCH AS YOURSELF, YOUR HIGH-NESS.
IF YOU WOULD STEP OUTSIDE TO WAIT.
......
FINE.
—
clack
LOOK, ZEKE...
YOU CAN SEE WHAT SORT OF PERSON THE PRINCE IS.
YOU'RE A GUEST, SO IT'S NOT MY PLACE TO SAY ANYTHING ABOUT YOUR RELATIONSHIP WITH HIM.
BUT IF YOU RECEIVE YOUR KNIGHTHOOD AND JOIN THE GUARD AS MY SUBORDINATE, IT'S A DIF-FERENT STORY.
YOU'LL HAVE TO LEARN YOUR PLACE TO AVOID OFFENDING PEOPLE.
SO PAY SPECIAL ATTENTION TO YOUR ACTIONS.

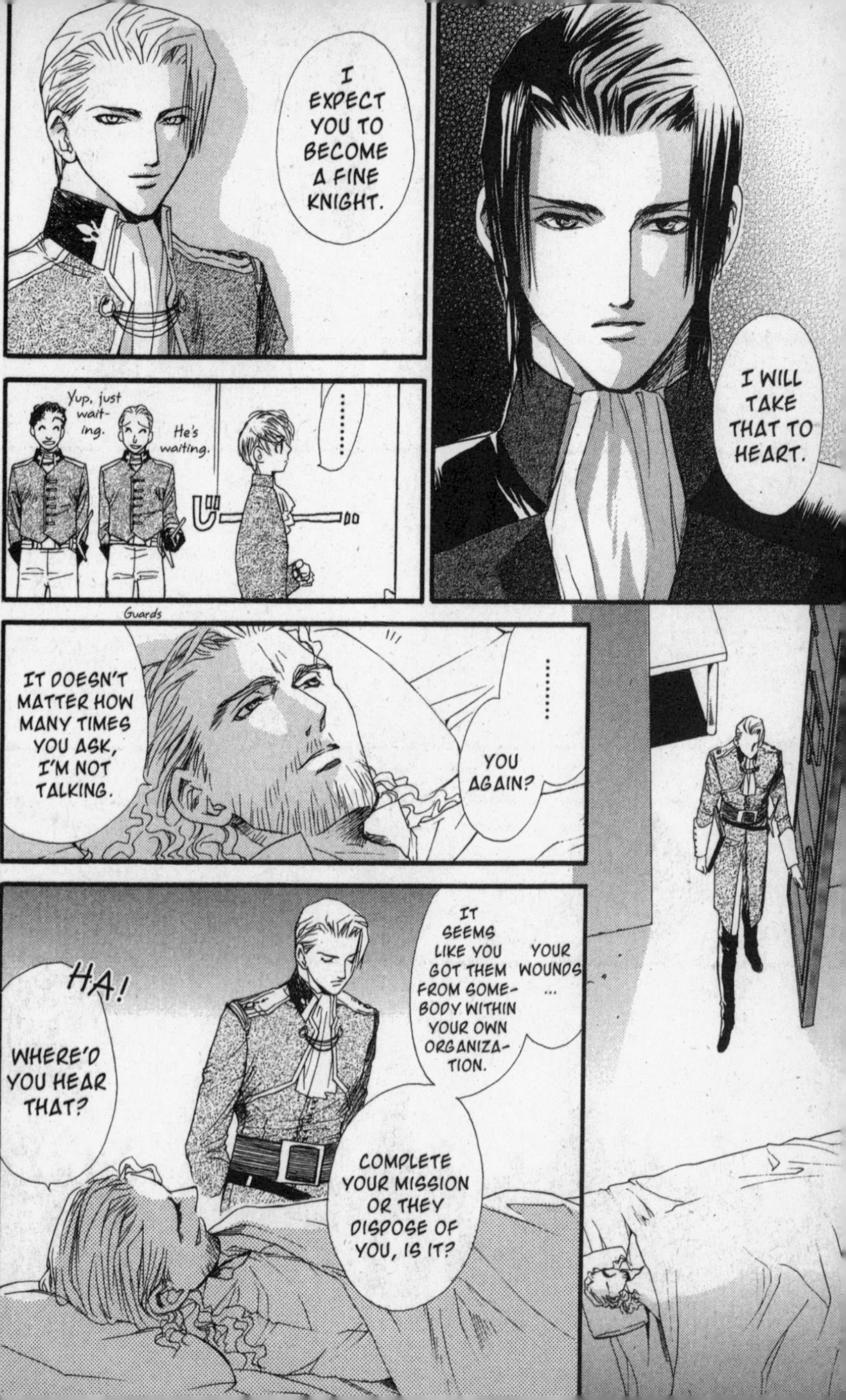
I WILL TAKE THAT TO HEART.
I EXPECT YOU TO BECOME A FINE KNIGHT.
......
He's waiting.
Yup, just wait-ing.
Guards
......
YOU AGAIN?
IT DOESN'T MATTER HOW MANY TIMES YOU ASK, I'M NOT TALKING.
YOUR WOUNDS ...
IT SEEMS LIKE YOU GOT THEM FROM SOME-BODY WITHIN YOUR OWN ORGANIZA-TION.
HA!
WHERE'D YOU HEAR THAT?
COMPLETE YOUR MISSION OR THEY DISPOSE OF YOU, IS IT?

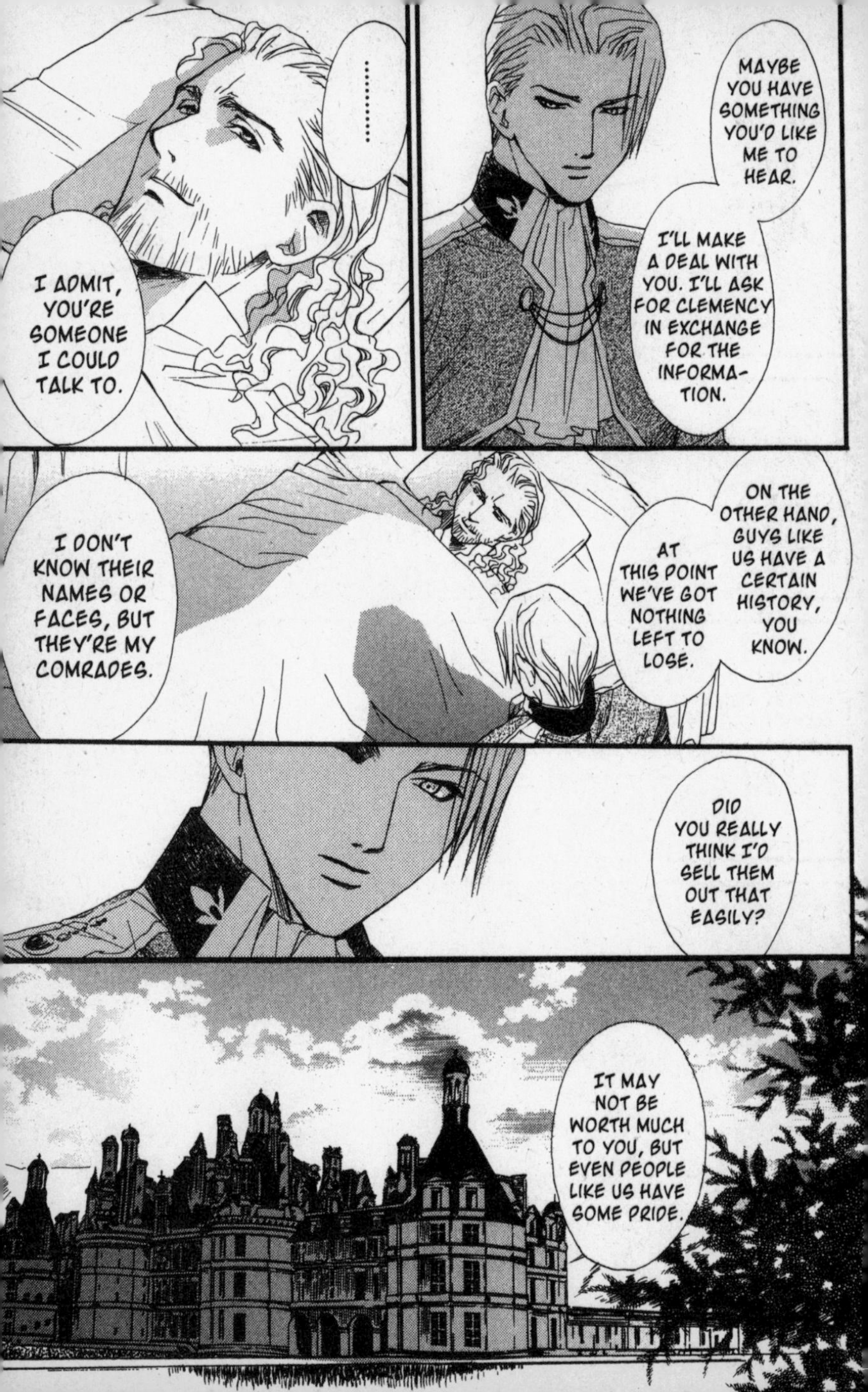
MAYBE YOU HAVE SOMETHING YOU'D LIKE ME TO HEAR.
I'LL MAKE A DEAL WITH YOU. I'LL ASK FOR CLEMENCY IN EXCHANGE FOR THE INFORMATION.
......
I ADMIT, YOU'RE SOMEONE I COULD TALK TO.
ON THE OTHER HAND, GUYS LIKE US HAVE A CERTAIN HISTORY, YOU KNOW.
AT THIS POINT WE'VE GOT NOTHING LEFT TO LOSE.
I DON'T KNOW THEIR NAMES OR FACES, BUT THEY'RE MY COMRADES.
DID YOU REALLY THINK I'D SELL THEM OUT THAT EASILY?
IT MAY NOT BE WORTH MUCH TO YOU, BUT EVEN PEOPLE LIKE US HAVE SOME PRIDE.

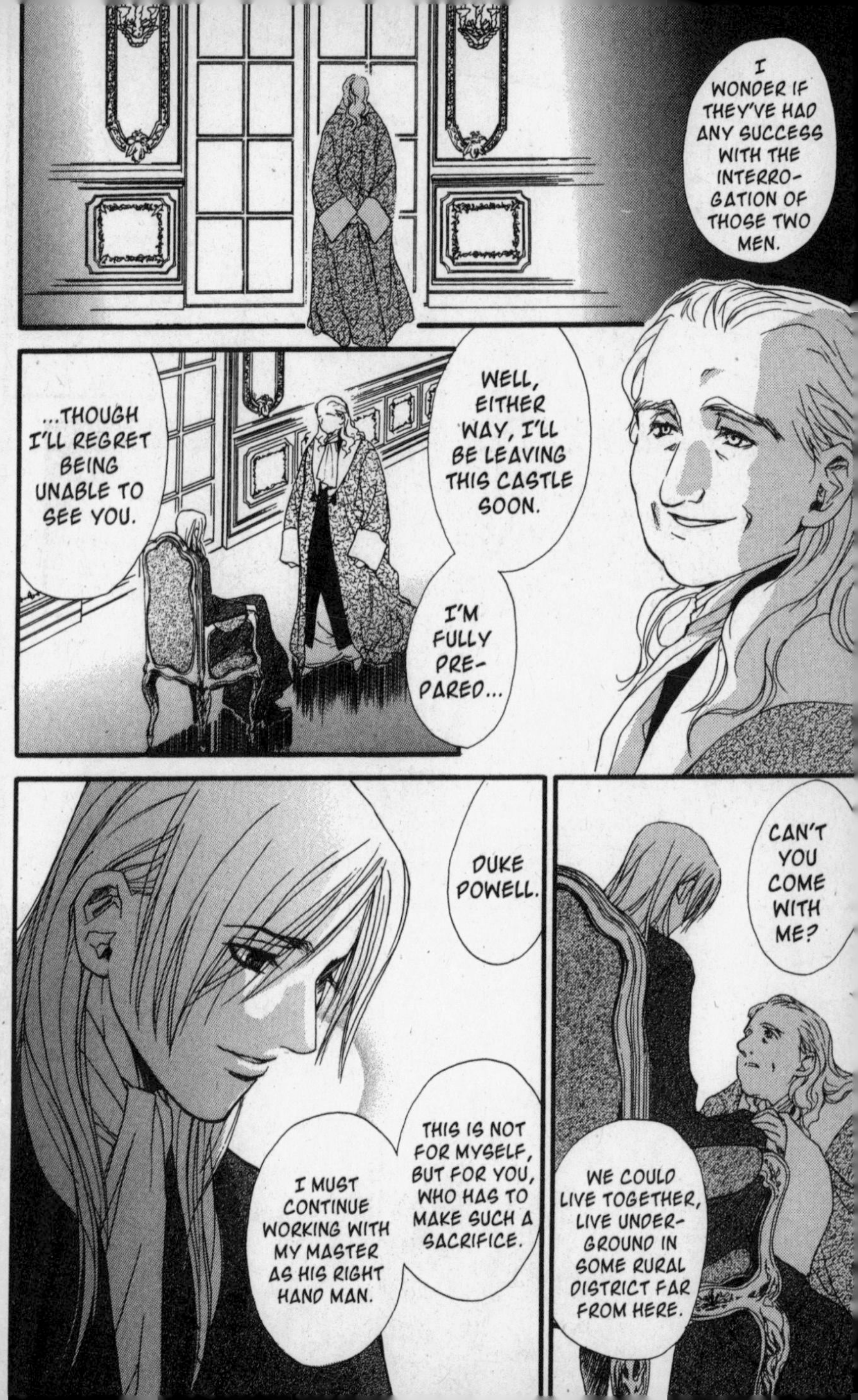
I WONDER IF THEY'VE HAD ANY SUCCESS WITH THE INTERRO-GATION OF THOSE TWO MEN.
WELL, EITHER WAY, I'LL BE LEAVING THIS CASTLE SOON.
I'M FULLY PRE-PARED...
...THOUGH I'LL REGRET BEING UNABLE TO SEE YOU.
CAN'T YOU COME WITH ME?
WE COULD LIVE TOGETHER, LIVE UNDER-GROUND IN SOME RURAL DISTRICT FAR FROM HERE.
DUKE POWELL.
THIS IS NOT FOR MYSELF, BUT FOR YOU, WHO HAS TO MAKE SUCH A SACRIFICE.
I MUST CONTINUE WORKING WITH MY MASTER AS HIS RIGHT HAND MAN.

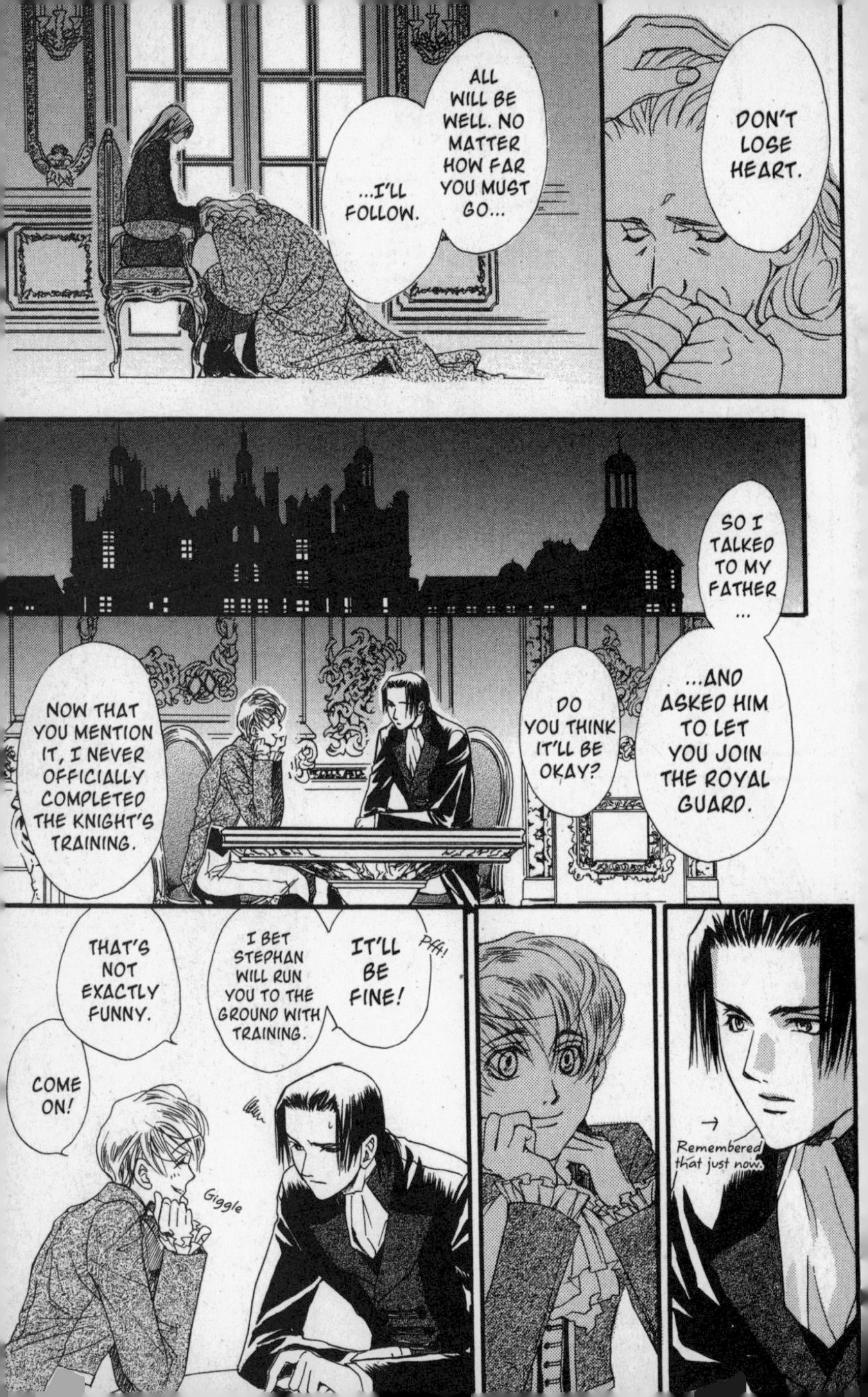
DON'T LOSE HEART.
ALL WILL BE WELL. NO MATTER HOW FAR YOU MUST GO...
...I'LL FOLLOW.
SO I TALKED TO MY FATHER...
...AND ASKED HIM TO LET YOU JOIN THE ROYAL GUARD.
DO YOU THINK IT'LL BE OKAY?
NOW THAT YOU MENTION IT, I NEVER OFFICIALLY COMPLETED THE KNIGHT'S TRAINING.
→ Remembered that just now.
Pfft!
IT'LL BE FINE!
I BET STEPHAN WILL RUN YOU TO THE GROUND WITH TRAINING.
THAT'S NOT EXACTLY FUNNY.
COME ON!
Giggle

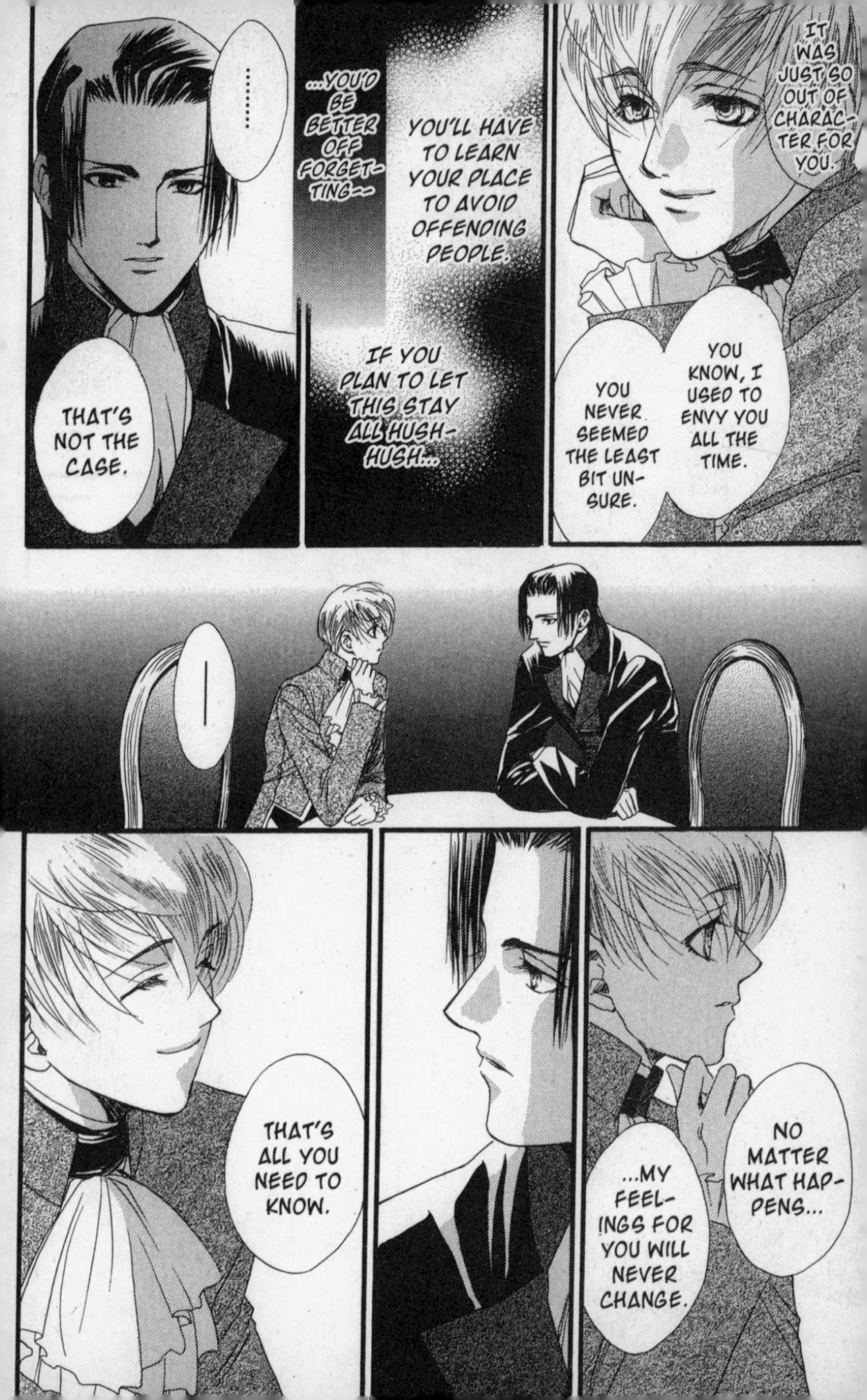
IT WAS JUST SO OUT OF CHARACTER FOR YOU.
YOU KNOW, I USED TO ENVY YOU ALL THE TIME.
YOU NEVER SEEMED THE LEAST BIT UNSURE.
YOU'LL HAVE TO LEARN YOUR PLACE TO AVOID OFFENDING PEOPLE.
...YOU'D BE BETTER OFF FORGETTING--
IF YOU PLAN TO LET THIS STAY ALL HUSH-HUSH...
......
THAT'S NOT THE CASE.
—
NO MATTER WHAT HAPPENS...
...MY FEELINGS FOR YOU WILL NEVER CHANGE.
THAT'S ALL YOU NEED TO KNOW.

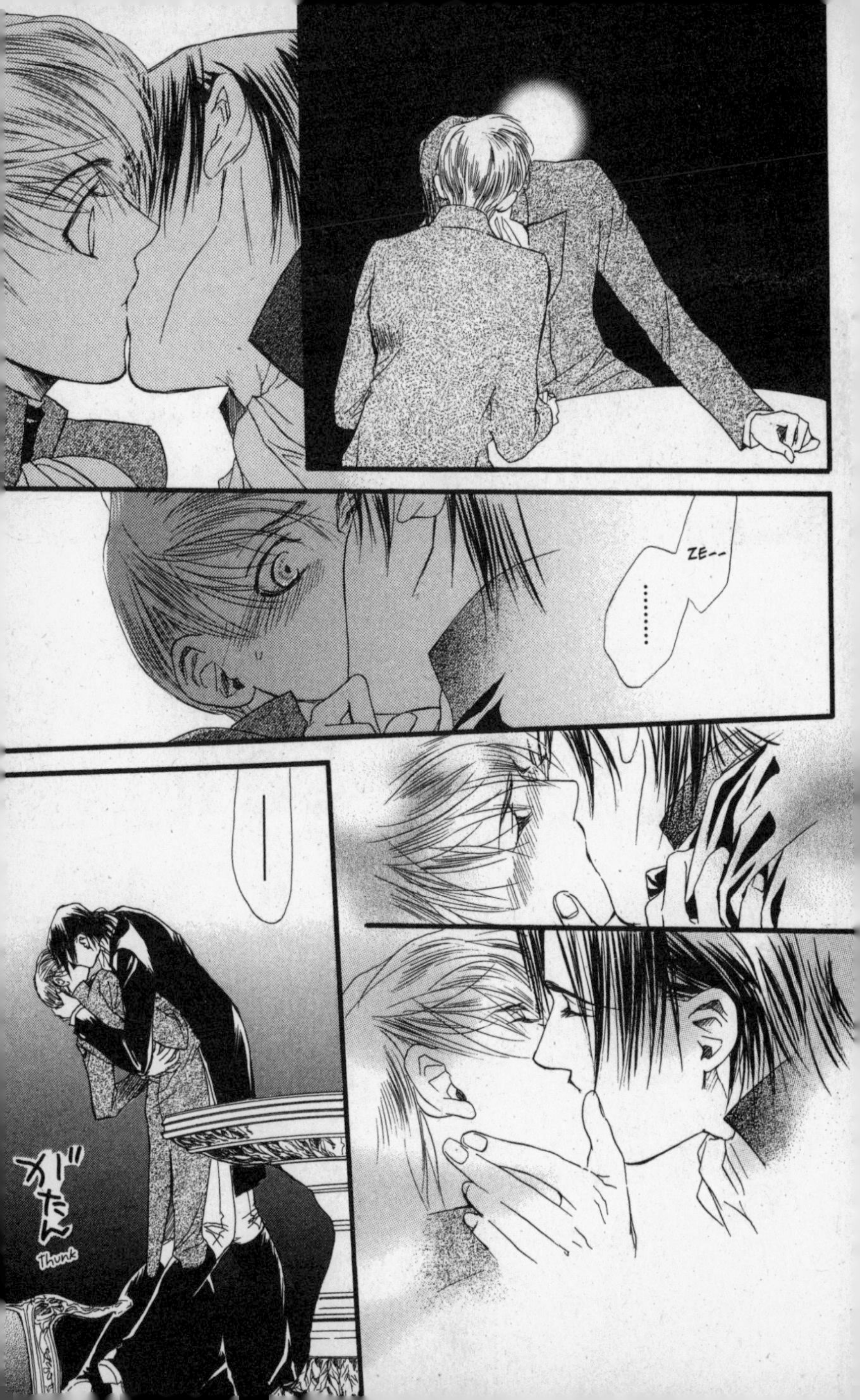
ZE--
....
—
ガたん
Thunk

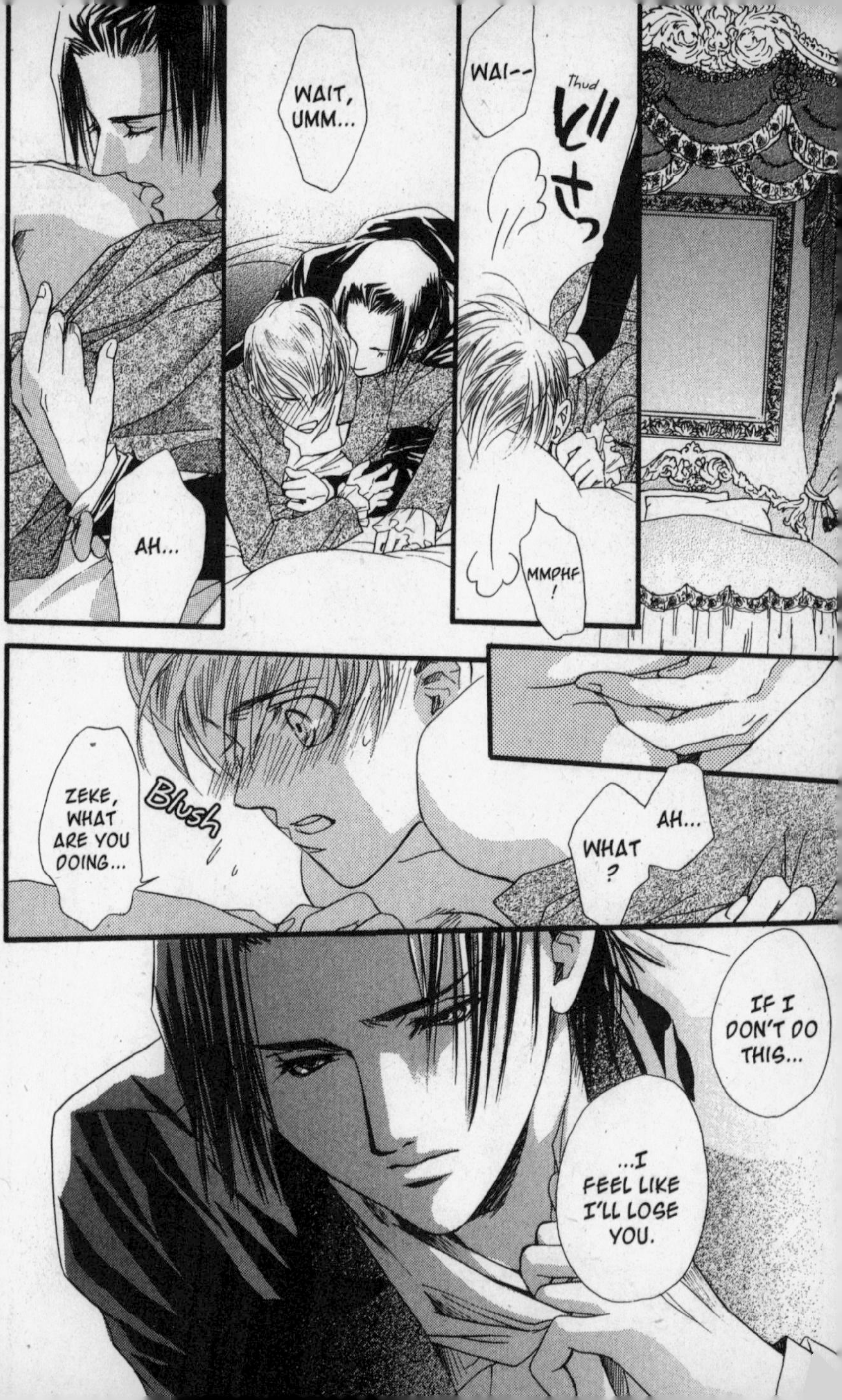
WAI--
Thud
どさっ
MMPHF!
WAIT, UMM...
AH...
AH... WHAT?
ZEKE, WHAT ARE YOU DOING...
Blush
IF I DON'T DO THIS...
...I FEEL LIKE I'LL LOSE YOU.

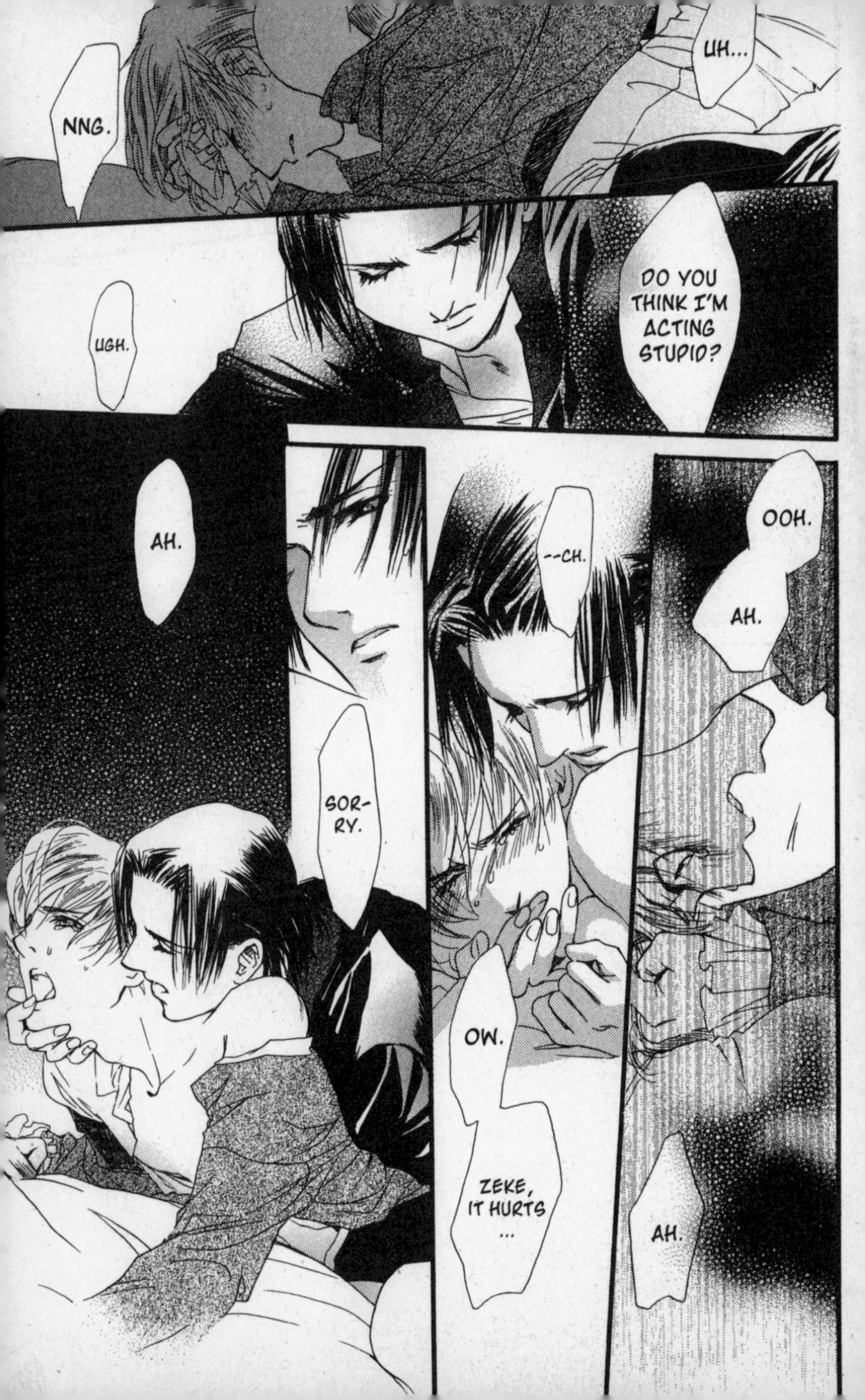
UH...
NNG.
DO YOU THINK I'M ACTING STUPID?
UGH.
OOH.
AH.
AH.
--CH.
OW.
ZEKE, IT HURTS ...
SOR-RY.
AH.

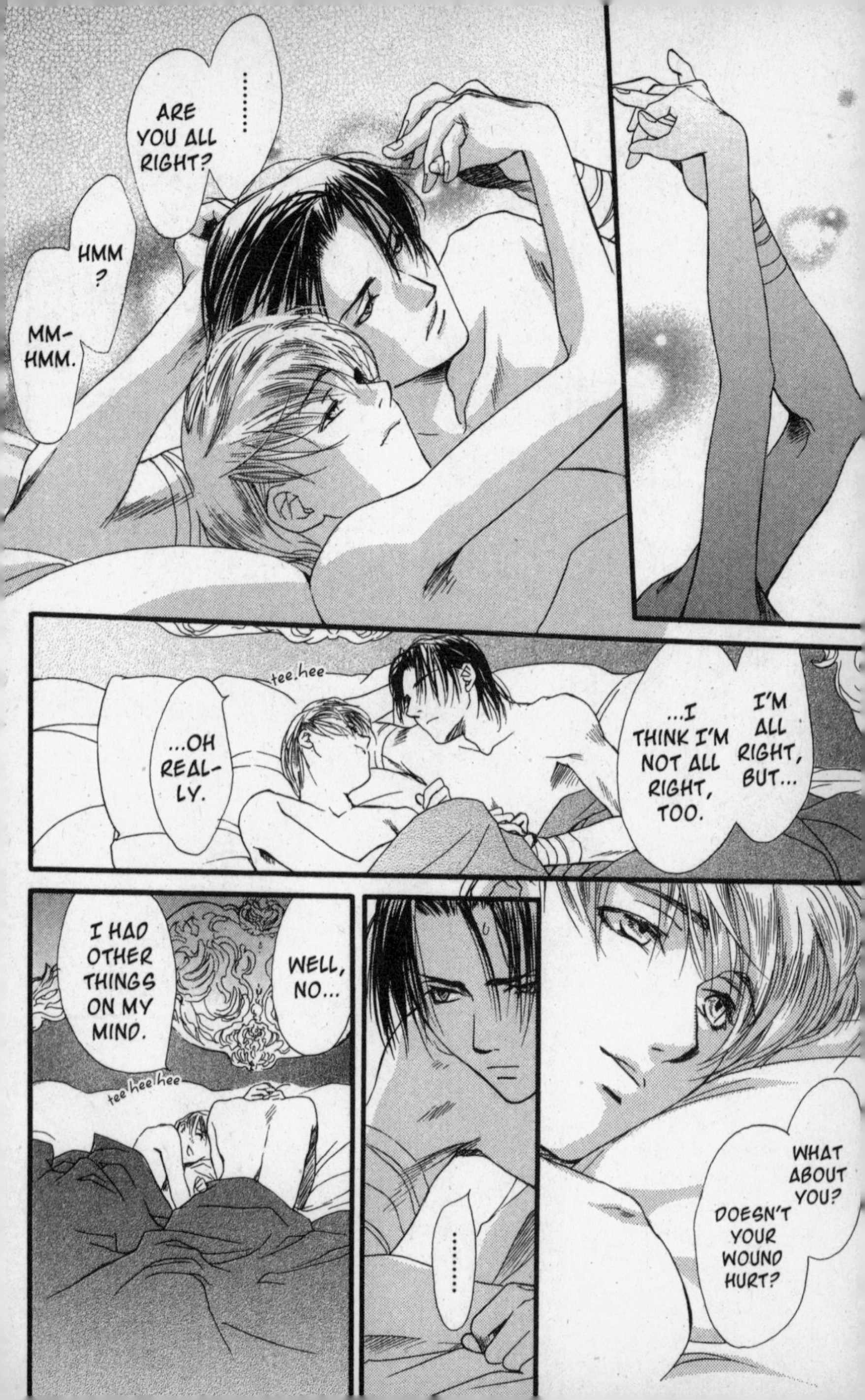
......
ARE YOU ALL RIGHT?
HMM?
MM-HMM.
I'M ALL RIGHT, BUT...
...I THINK I'M NOT ALL RIGHT, TOO.
tee hee
...OH REALLY.
WHAT ABOUT YOU?
DOESN'T YOUR WOUND HURT?
......
WELL, NO...
I HAD OTHER THINGS ON MY MIND.
tee hee hee

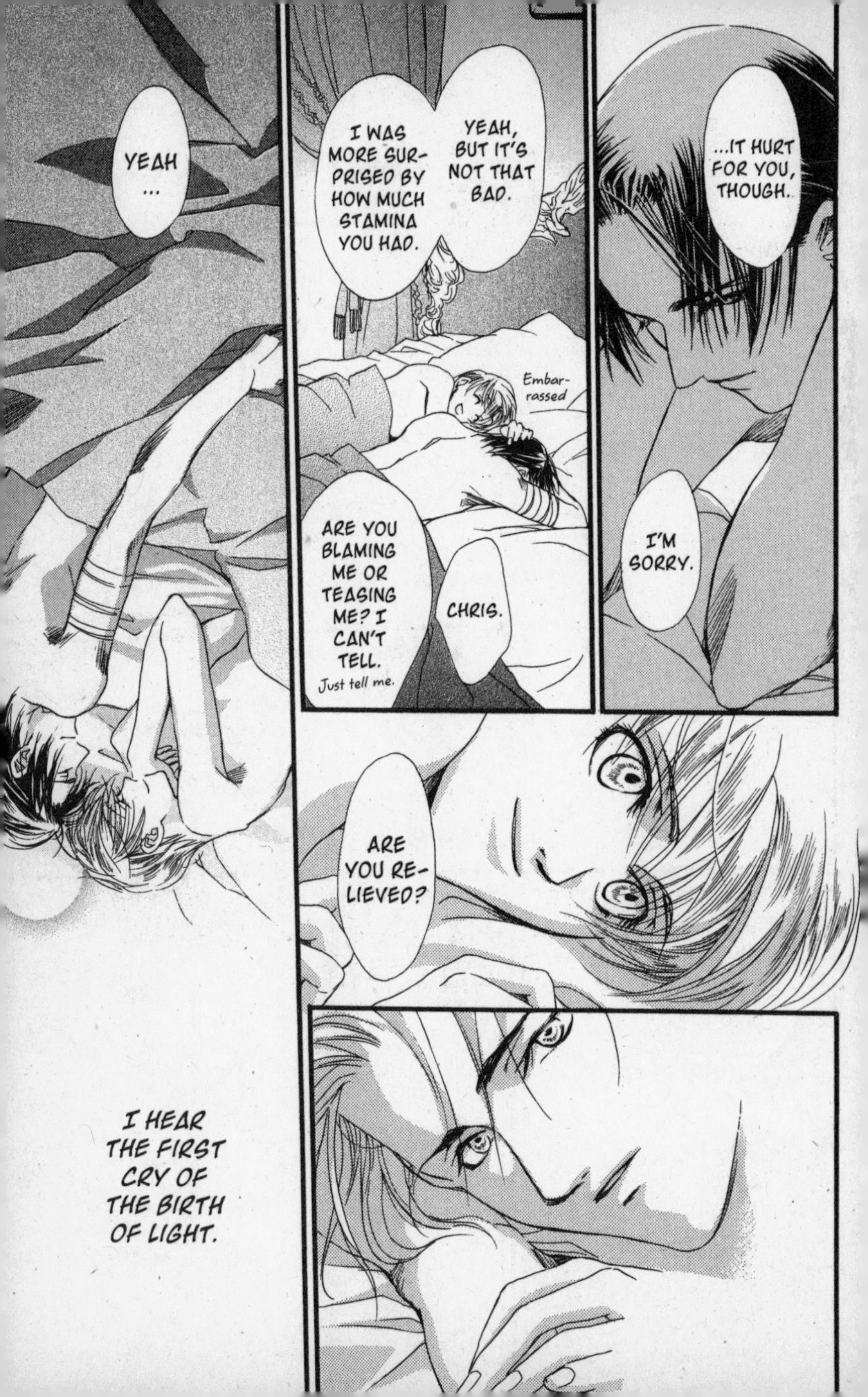
...IT HURT FOR YOU, THOUGH.
I'M SORRY.
YEAH, BUT IT'S NOT THAT BAD.
I WAS MORE SURPRISED BY HOW MUCH STAMINA YOU HAD.
Embarrassed
CHRIS.
ARE YOU BLAMING ME OR TEASING ME? I CAN'T TELL.
Just tell me.
ARE YOU RELIEVED?
YEAH ...
I HEAR THE FIRST CRY OF THE BIRTH OF LIGHT.

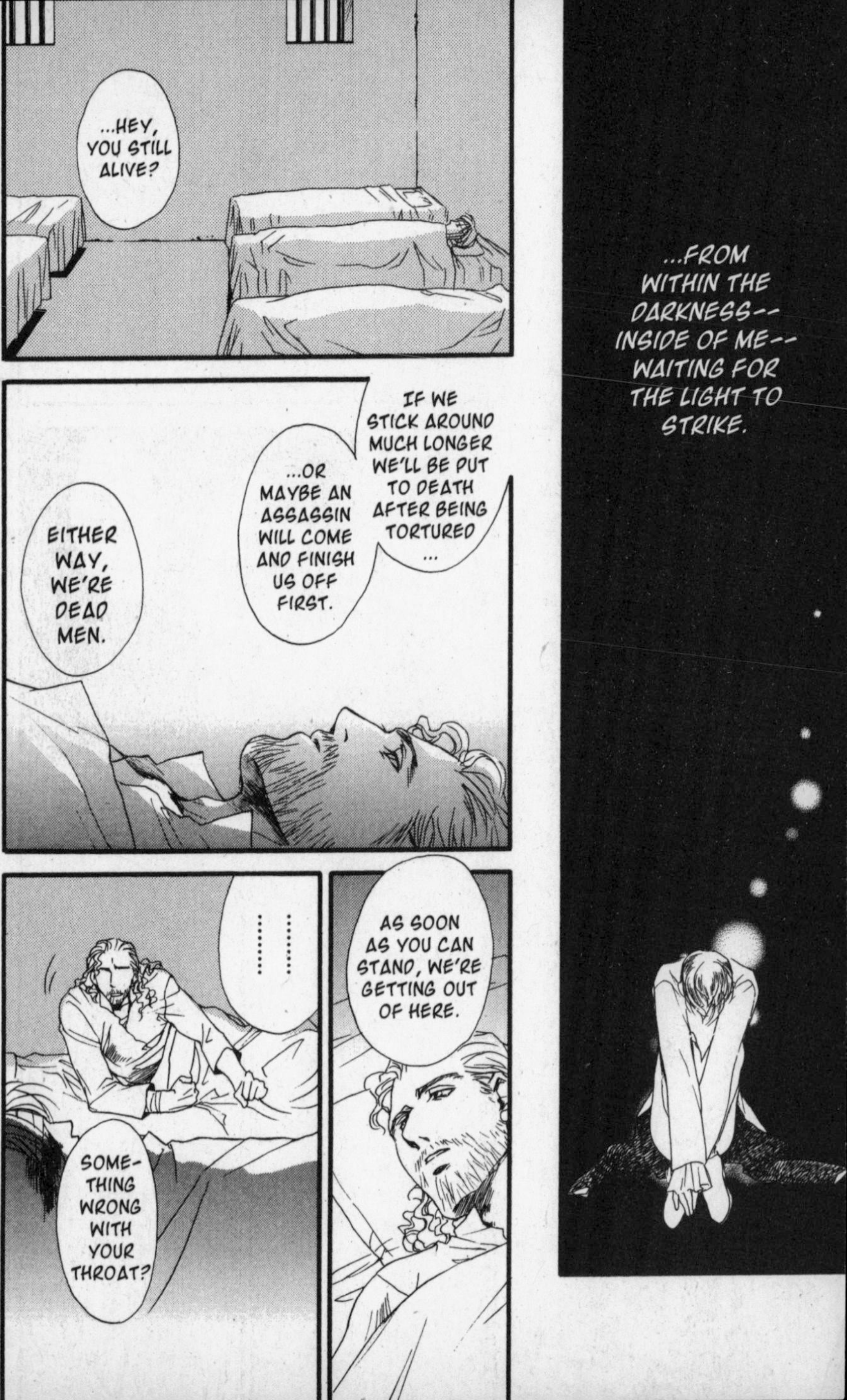
...FROM WITHIN THE DARKNESS-- INSIDE OF ME-- WAITING FOR THE LIGHT TO STRIKE.
...HEY, YOU STILL ALIVE?
IF WE STICK AROUND MUCH LONGER WE'LL BE PUT TO DEATH AFTER BEING TORTURED ...
...OR MAYBE AN ASSASSIN WILL COME AND FINISH US OFF FIRST.
EITHER WAY, WE'RE DEAD MEN.
AS SOON AS YOU CAN STAND, WE'RE GETTING OUT OF HERE.
......
SOME-THING WRONG WITH YOUR THROAT?

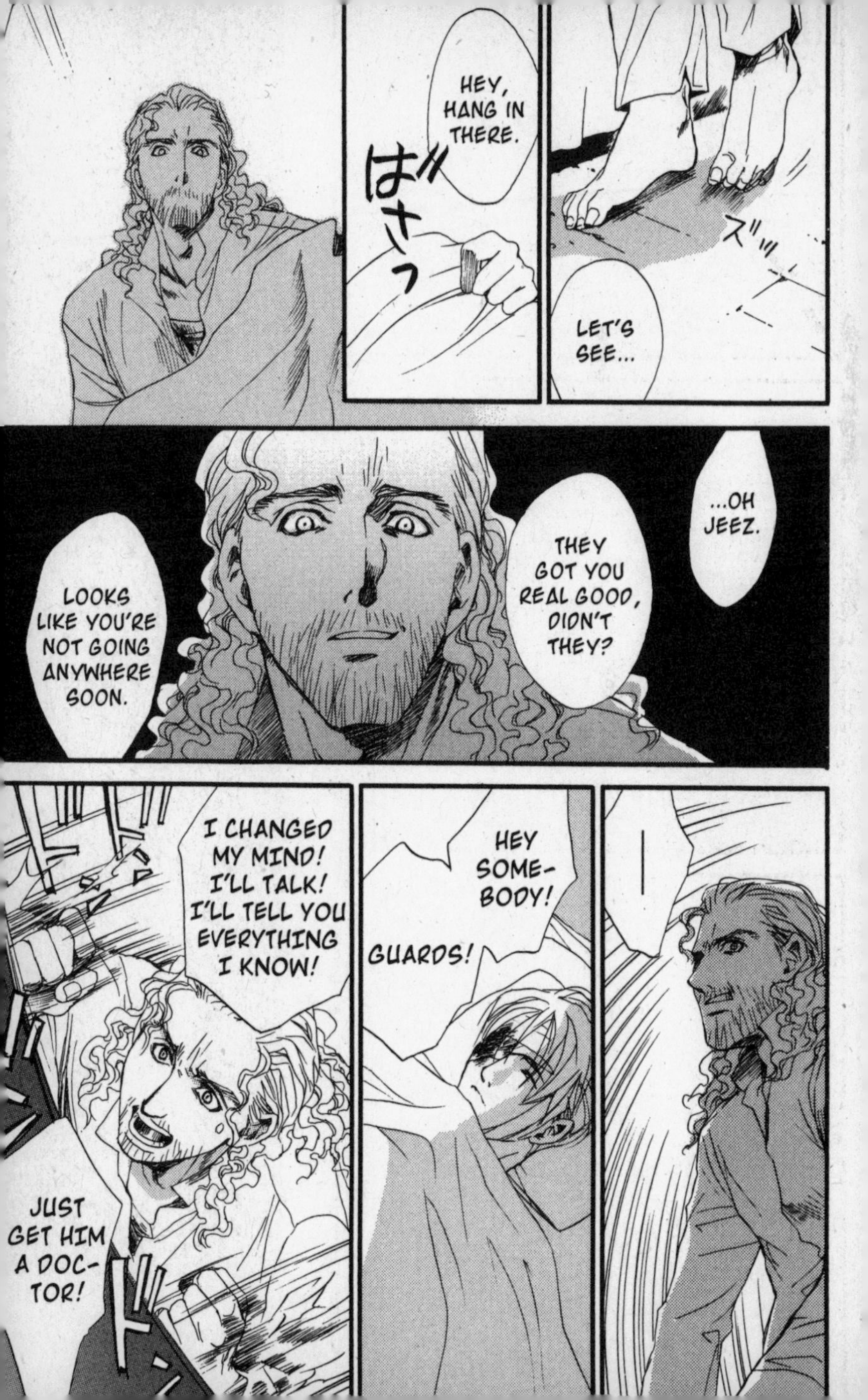
ズッ
LET'S SEE...
HEY, HANG IN THERE.
ばさっ
...OH JEEZ.
THEY GOT YOU REAL GOOD, DIDN'T THEY?
LOOKS LIKE YOU'RE NOT GOING ANYWHERE SOON.
HEY SOMEBODY!
GUARDS!
I CHANGED MY MIND! I'LL TALK! I'LL TELL YOU EVERYTHING I KNOW!
JUST GET HIM A DOCTOR!

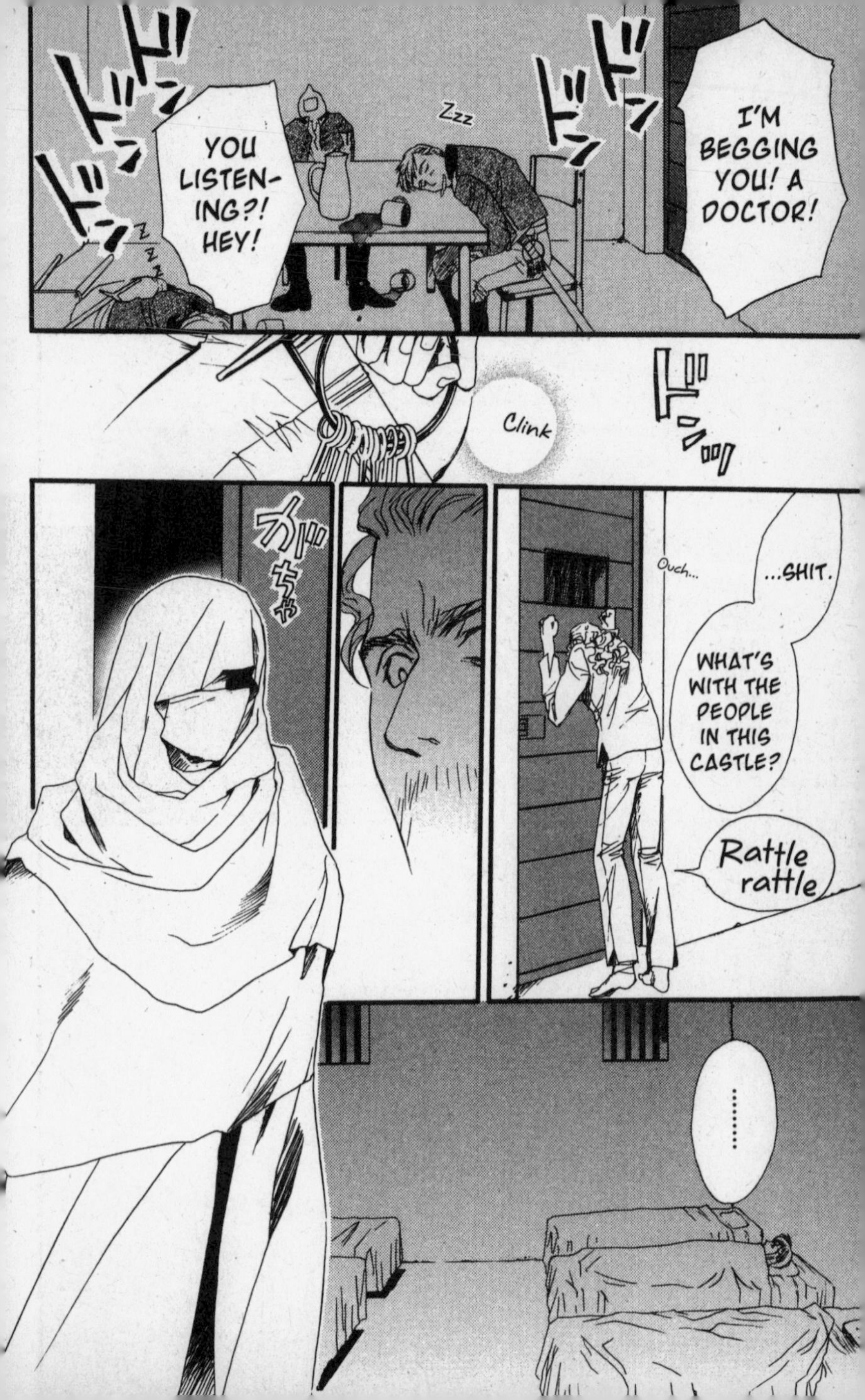
I'M BEGGING YOU! A DOCTOR!
Zzz
YOU LISTEN-ING?! HEY!
Clink
...SHIT.
Ouch...
WHAT'S WITH THE PEOPLE IN THIS CASTLE?
Rattle rattle
がちゃ
......

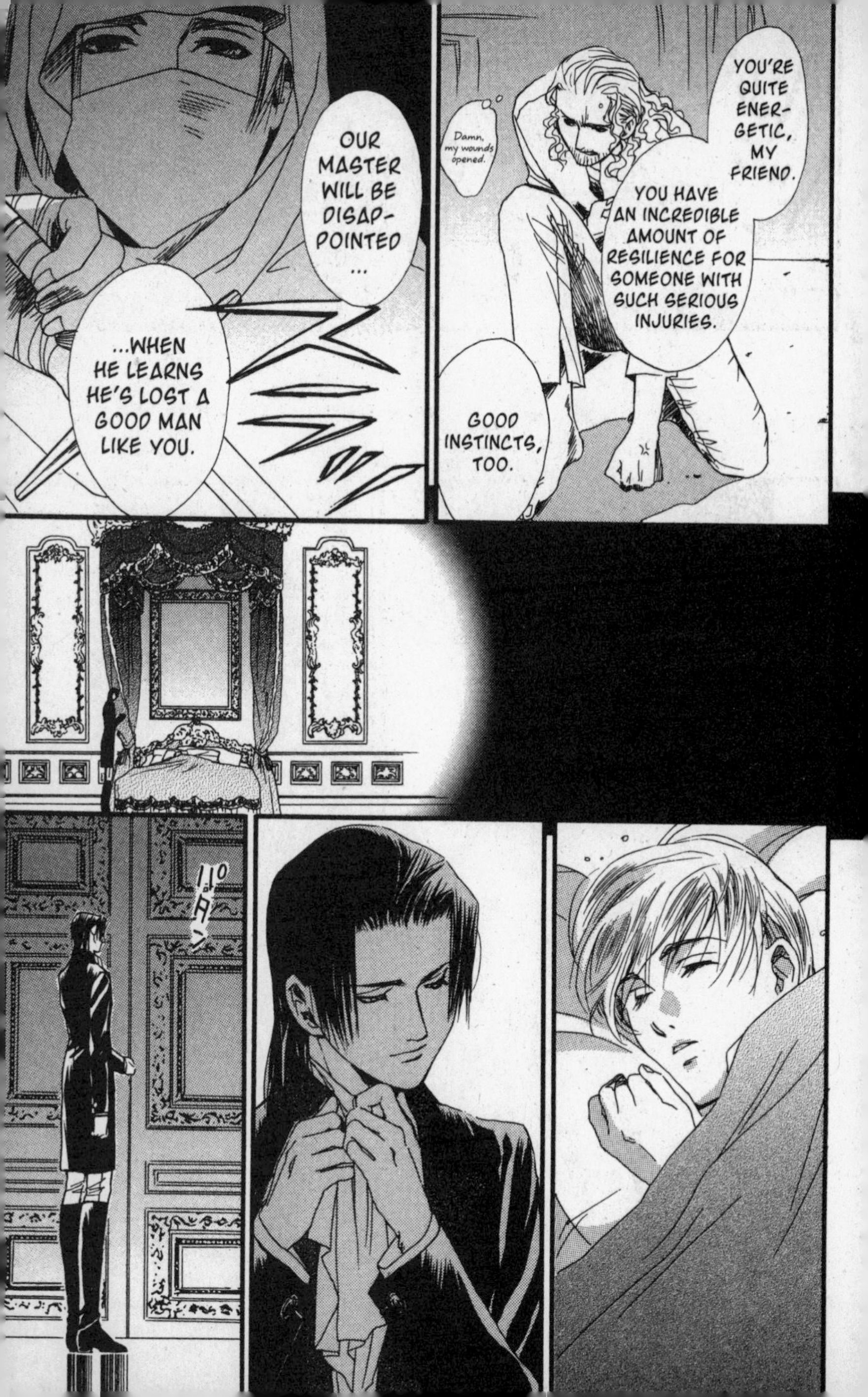
YOU'RE QUITE ENERGETIC, MY FRIEND.
Damn, my wounds opened.
YOU HAVE AN INCREDIBLE AMOUNT OF RESILIENCE FOR SOMEONE WITH SUCH SERIOUS INJURIES.
GOOD INSTINCTS, TOO.
OUR MASTER WILL BE DISAPPOINTED...
...WHEN HE LEARNS HE'S LOST A GOOD MAN LIKE YOU.
パタン

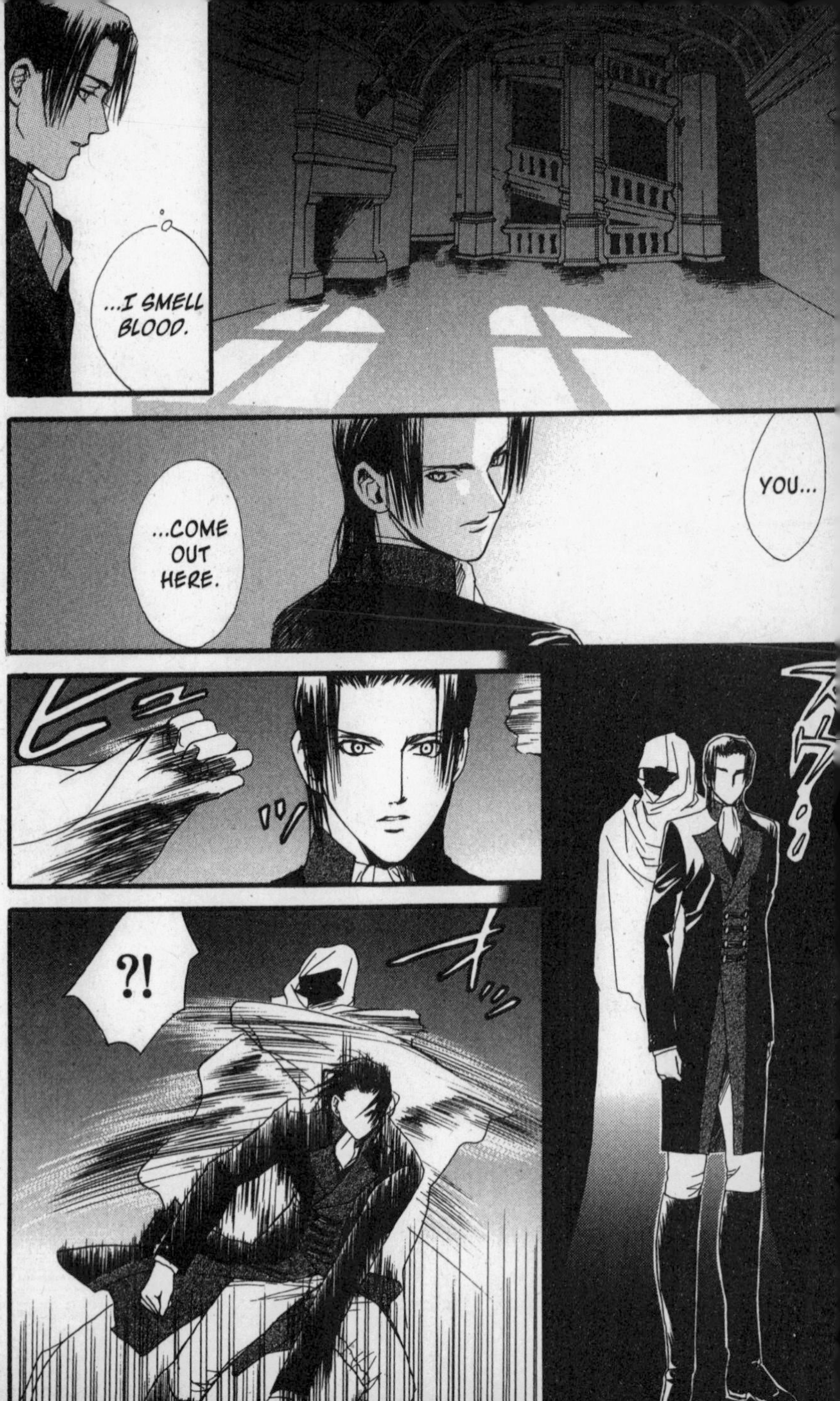
...I SMELL BLOOD.
YOU...
...COME OUT HERE.
?!

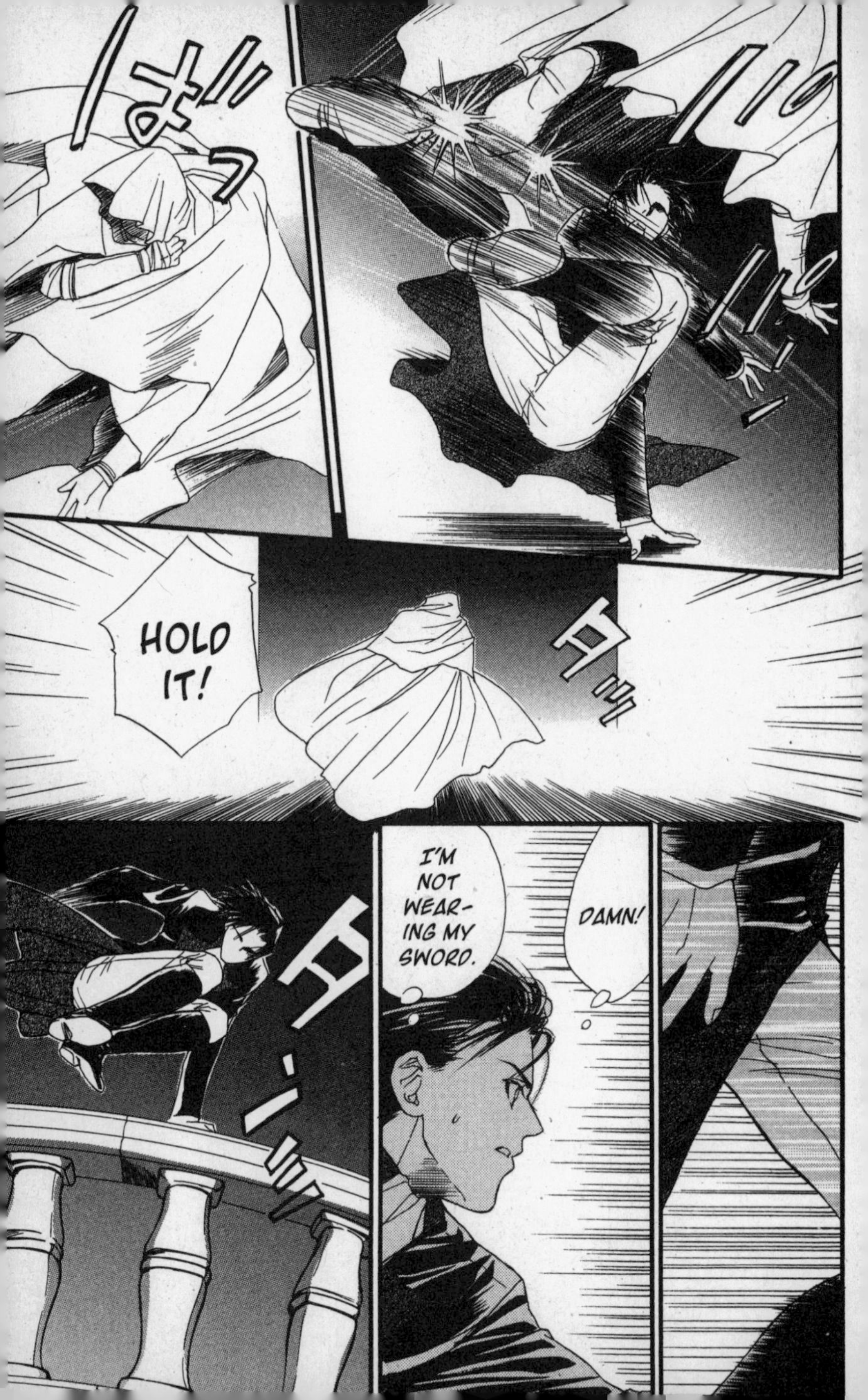
HOLD IT!
DAMN!
I'M NOT WEAR-ING MY SWORD.

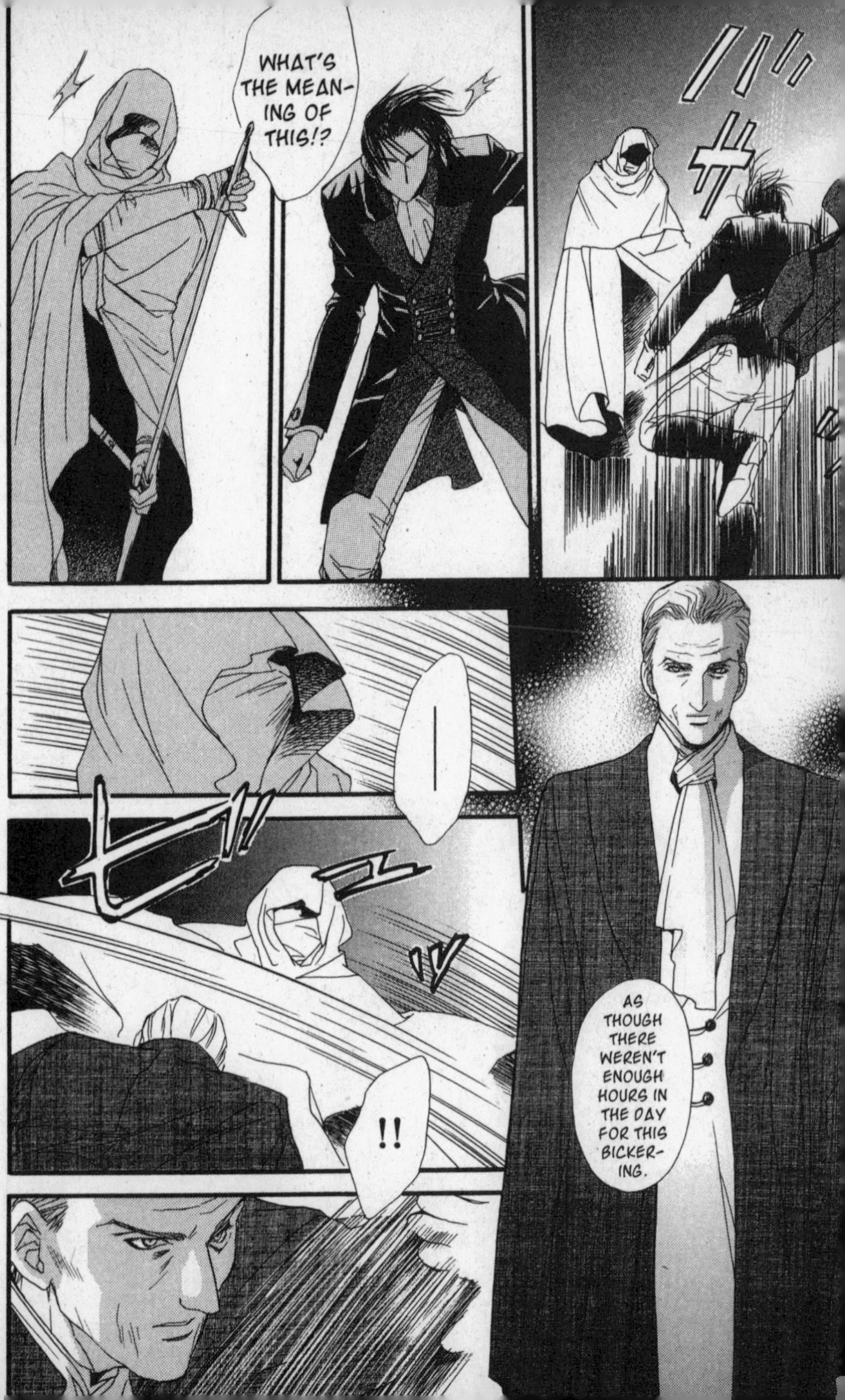
WHAT'S THE MEAN-ING OF THIS!?
AS THOUGH THERE WEREN'T ENOUGH HOURS IN THE DAY FOR THIS BICKER-ING.
!!

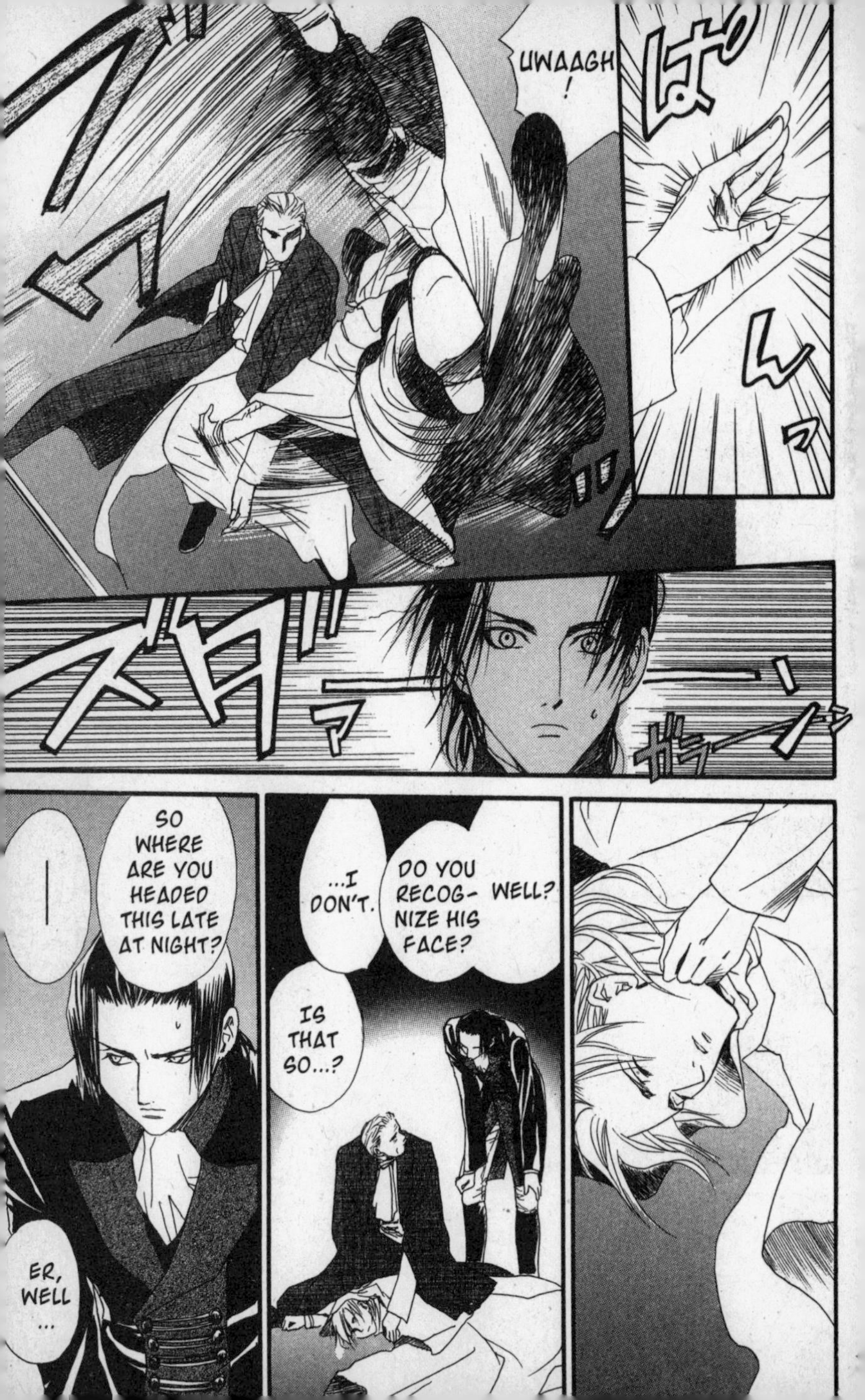
UWAAGH!
WELL?
DO YOU RECOGNIZE HIS FACE?
...I DON'T.
IS THAT SO...?
SO WHERE ARE YOU HEADED THIS LATE AT NIGHT?
—
ER, WELL...

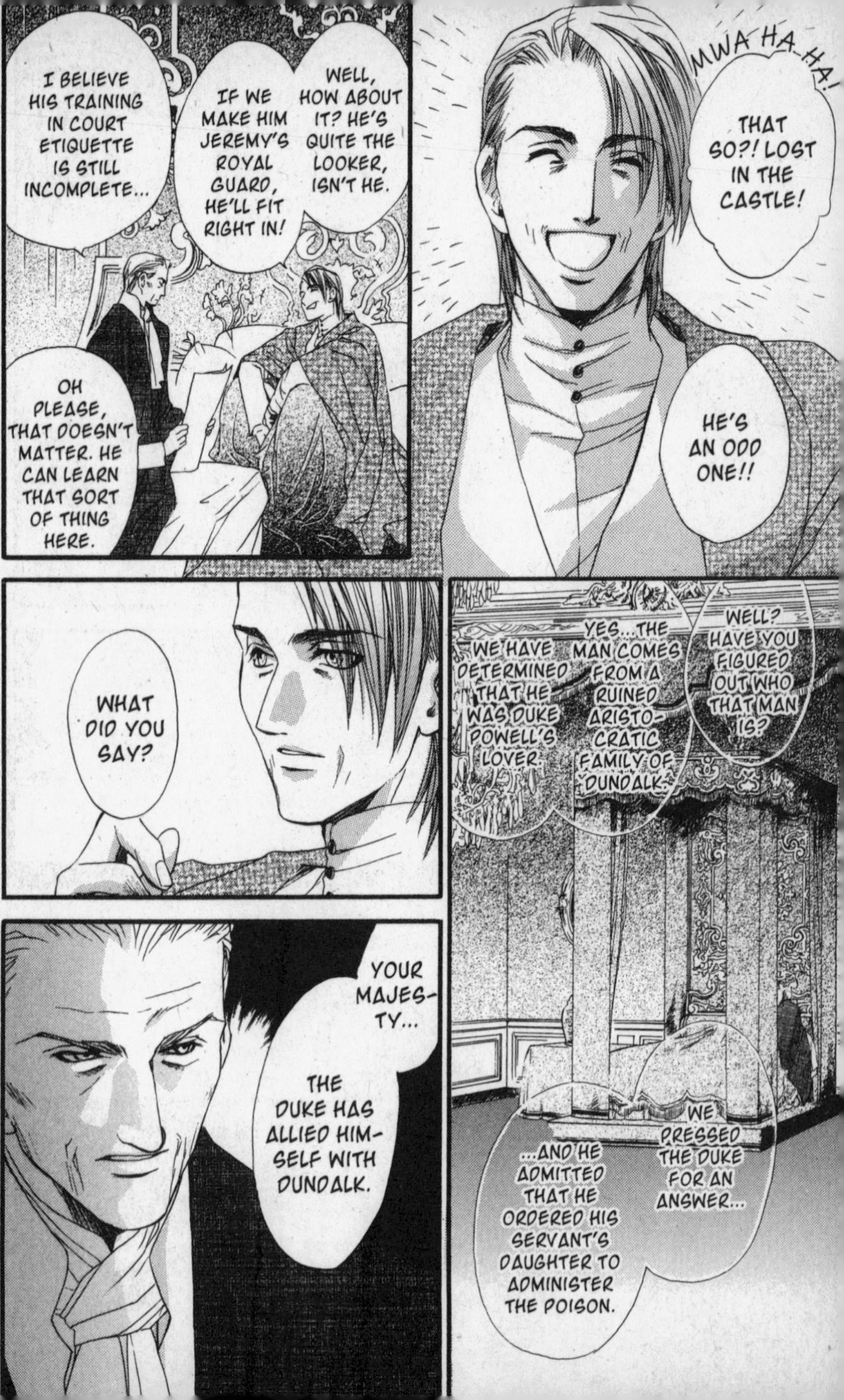
MWA HA HA!
THAT SO?! LOST IN THE CASTLE!
HE'S AN ODD ONE!!
WELL, HOW ABOUT IT? HE'S QUITE THE LOOKER, ISN'T HE.
IF WE MAKE HIM JEREMY'S ROYAL GUARD, HE'LL FIT RIGHT IN!
I BELIEVE HIS TRAINING IN COURT ETIQUETTE IS STILL INCOMPLETE...
OH PLEASE, THAT DOESN'T MATTER. HE CAN LEARN THAT SORT OF THING HERE.
WELL? HAVE YOU FIGURED OUT WHO THAT MAN IS?
YES... THE MAN COMES FROM A RUINED ARISTOCRATIC FAMILY OF DUNDALK.
WE HAVE DETERMINED THAT HE WAS DUKE POWELL'S LOVER.
WE PRESSED THE DUKE FOR AN ANSWER...
...AND HE ADMITTED THAT HE ORDERED HIS SERVANT'S DAUGHTER TO ADMINISTER THE POISON.
WHAT DID YOU SAY?
YOUR MAJESTY...
THE DUKE HAS ALLIED HIMSELF WITH DUNDALK.

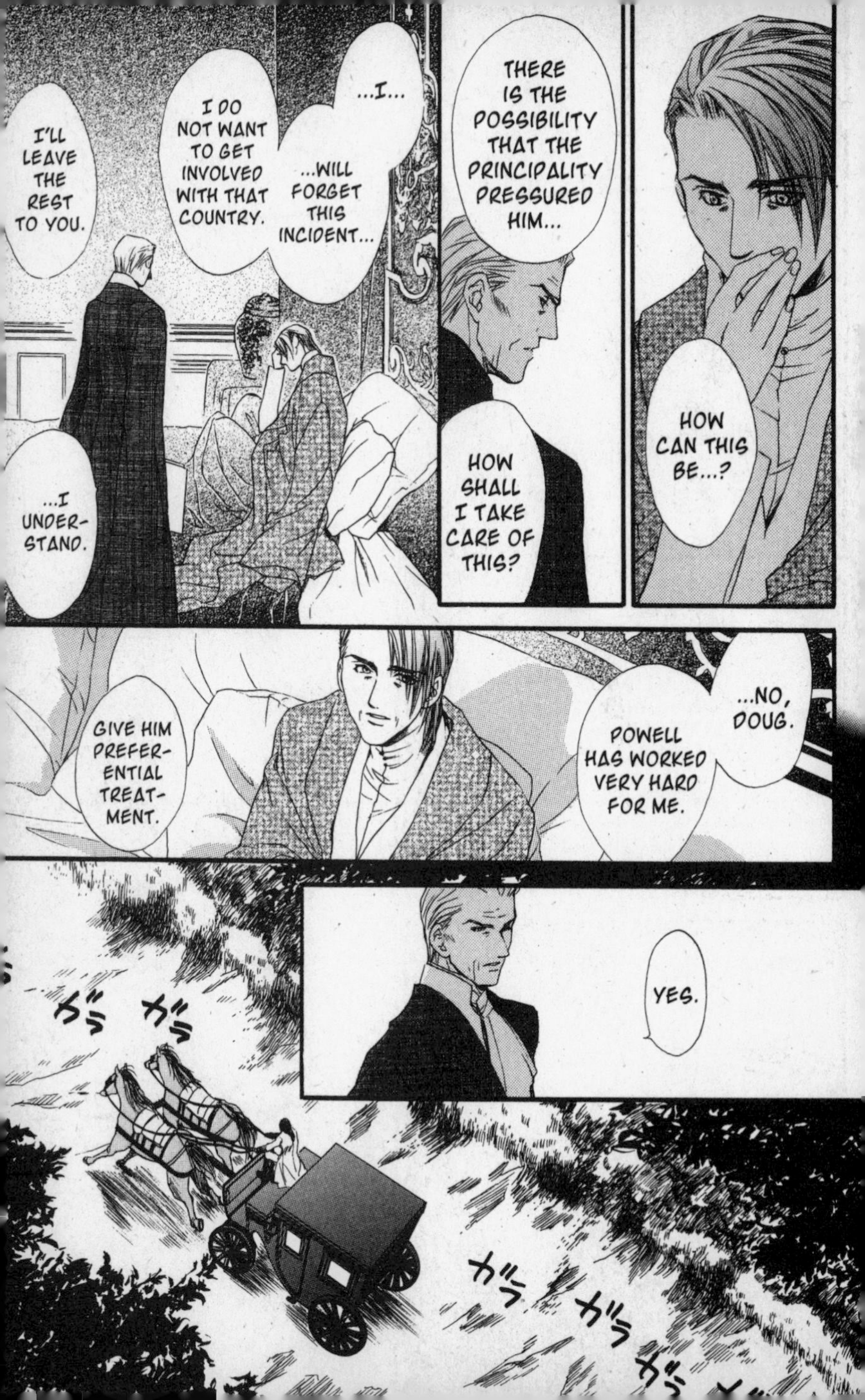
HOW CAN THIS BE...?
THERE IS THE POSSIBILITY THAT THE PRINCIPALITY PRESSURED HIM...
HOW SHALL I TAKE CARE OF THIS?
...I...
...WILL FORGET THIS INCIDENT...
I DO NOT WANT TO GET INVOLVED WITH THAT COUNTRY.
I'LL LEAVE THE REST TO YOU.
...I UNDERSTAND.
...NO, DOUG.
POWELL HAS WORKED VERY HARD FOR ME.
GIVE HIM PREFERENTIAL TREATMENT.
YES.
ガラ ガラ
ガラ ガラ ガラ

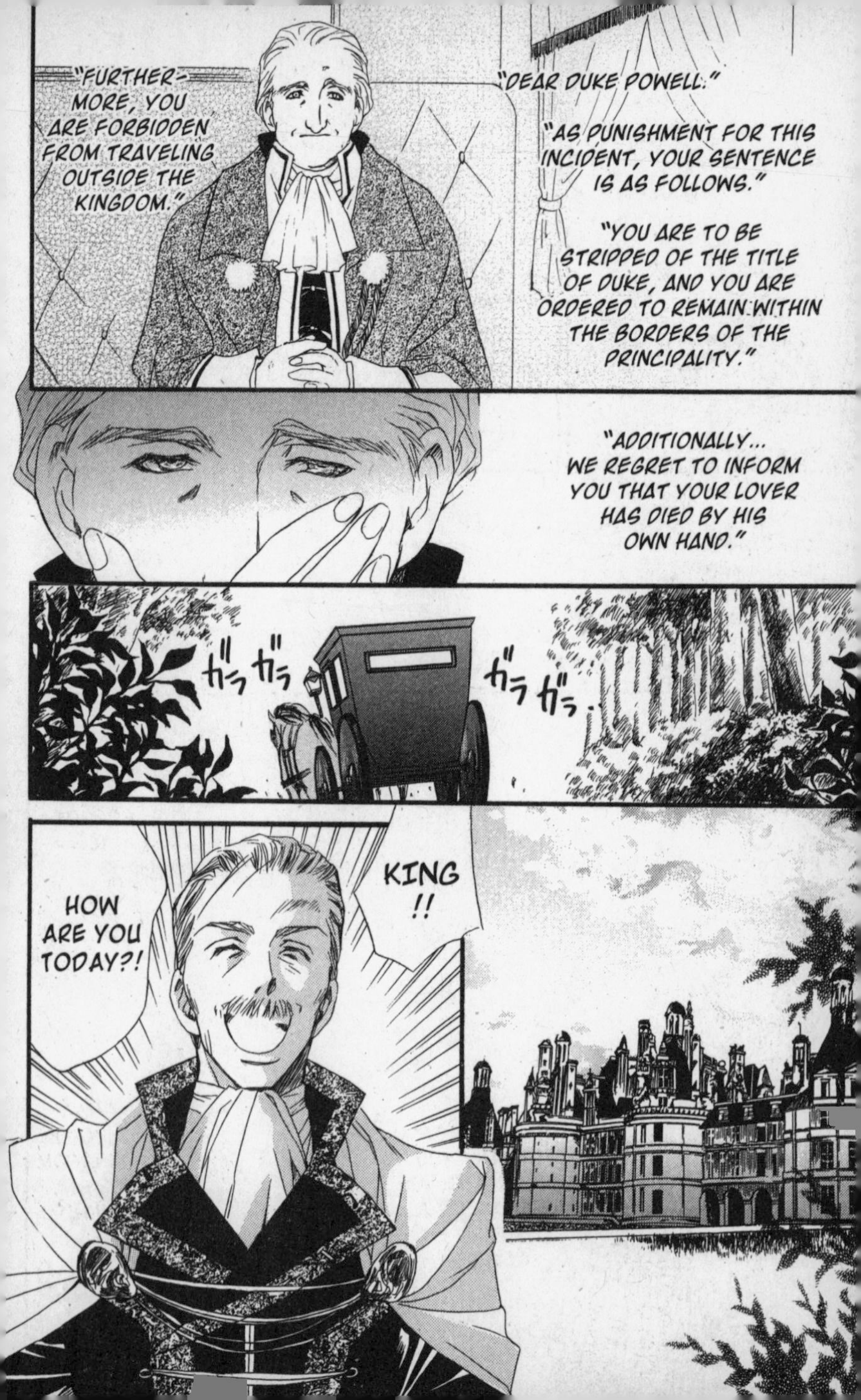
"DEAR DUKE POWELL:"
"AS PUNISHMENT FOR THIS INCIDENT, YOUR SENTENCE IS AS FOLLOWS."
"YOU ARE TO BE STRIPPED OF THE TITLE OF DUKE, AND YOU ARE ORDERED TO REMAIN WITHIN THE BORDERS OF THE PRINCIPALITY."
"FURTHER-MORE, YOU ARE FORBIDDEN FROM TRAVELING OUTSIDE THE KINGDOM."
"ADDITIONALLY... WE REGRET TO INFORM YOU THAT YOUR LOVER HAS DIED BY HIS OWN HAND."
ガラガラ
ガラガラ
KING!!
HOW ARE YOU TODAY?!

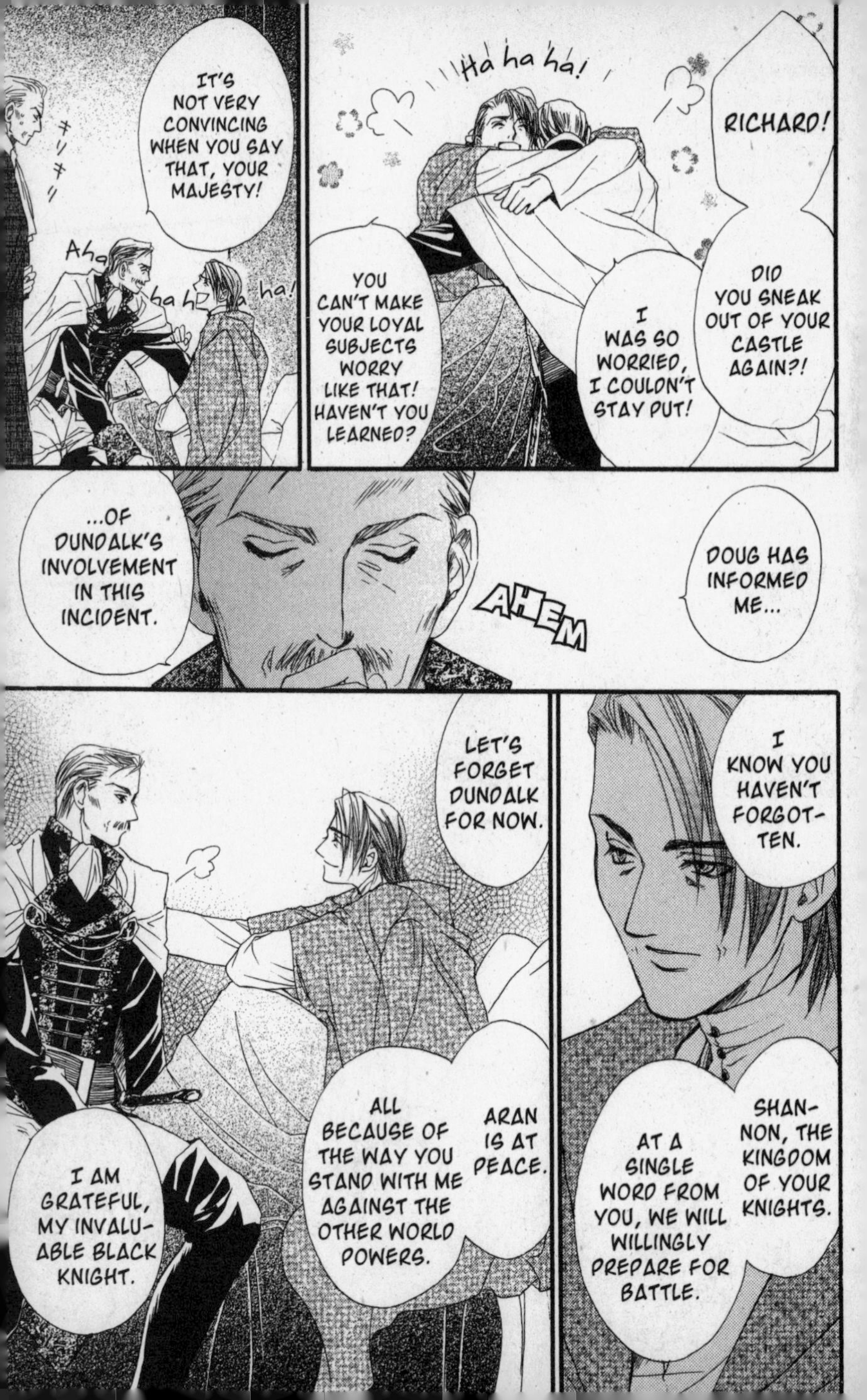
RICHARD!
Ha ha ha!
DID YOU SNEAK OUT OF YOUR CASTLE AGAIN?!
I WAS SO WORRIED, I COULDN'T STAY PUT!
YOU CAN'T MAKE YOUR LOYAL SUBJECTS WORRY LIKE THAT! HAVEN'T YOU LEARNED?
IT'S NOT VERY CONVINCING WHEN YOU SAY THAT, YOUR MAJESTY!
キリキリ
Aha ha h a ha!
DOUG HAS INFORMED ME...
AHEM
...OF DUNDALK'S INVOLVEMENT IN THIS INCIDENT.
I KNOW YOU HAVEN'T FORGOT-TEN.
SHAN-NON, THE KINGDOM OF YOUR KNIGHTS.
AT A SINGLE WORD FROM YOU, WE WILL WILLINGLY PREPARE FOR BATTLE.
LET'S FORGET DUNDALK FOR NOW.
ARAN IS AT PEACE.
ALL BECAUSE OF THE WAY YOU STAND WITH ME AGAINST THE OTHER WORLD POWERS.
I AM GRATEFUL, MY INVALU-ABLE BLACK KNIGHT.

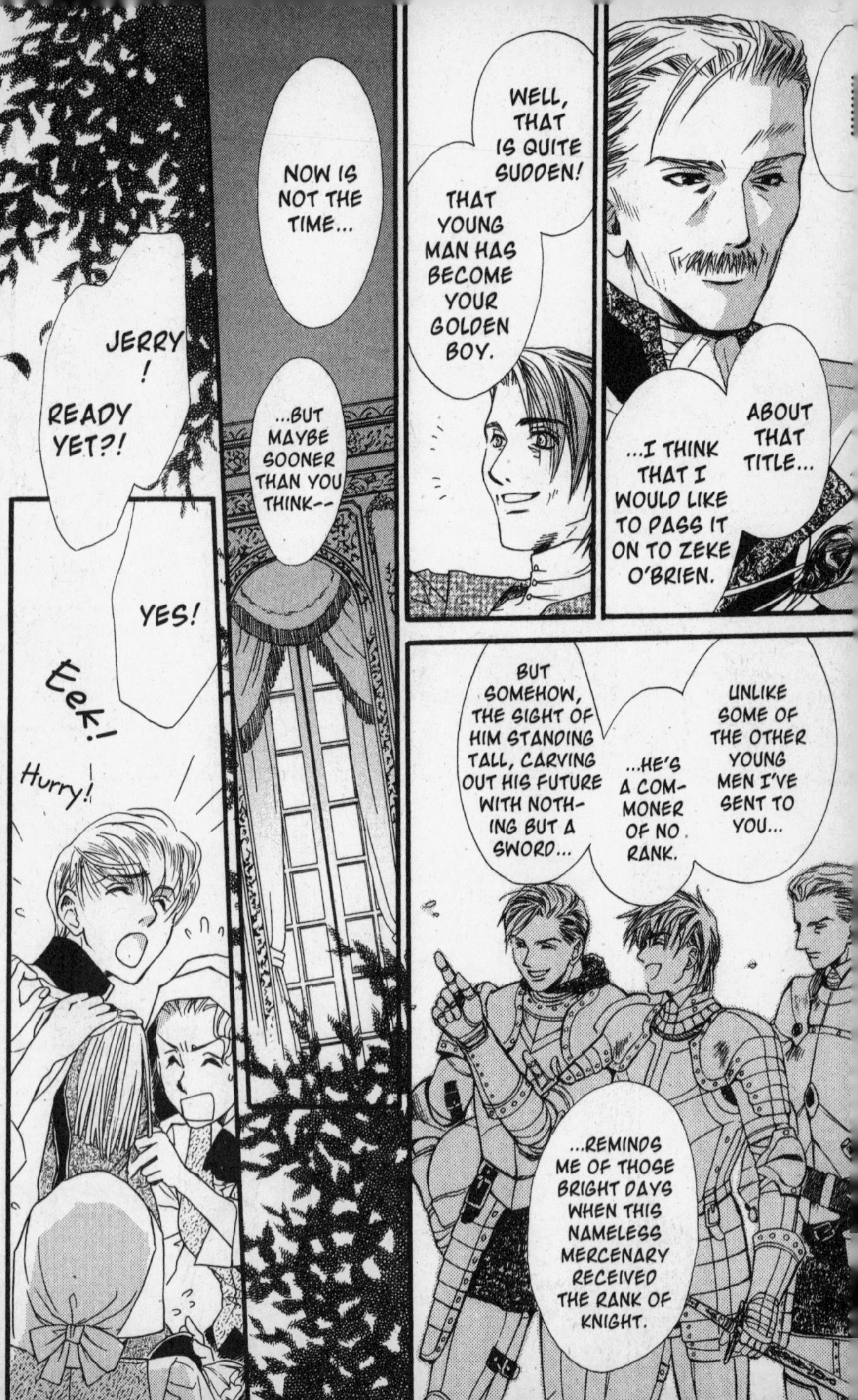
ABOUT THAT TITLE...
...I THINK THAT I WOULD LIKE TO PASS IT ON TO ZEKE O'BRIEN.
WELL, THAT IS QUITE SUDDEN!
THAT YOUNG MAN HAS BECOME YOUR GOLDEN BOY.
UNLIKE SOME OF THE OTHER YOUNG MEN I'VE SENT TO YOU...
...HE'S A COM-MONER OF NO RANK.
BUT SOMEHOW, THE SIGHT OF HIM STANDING TALL, CARVING OUT HIS FUTURE WITH NOTH-ING BUT A SWORD...
...REMINDS ME OF THOSE BRIGHT DAYS WHEN THIS NAMELESS MERCENARY RECEIVED THE RANK OF KNIGHT.
NOW IS NOT THE TIME...
...BUT MAYBE SOONER THAN YOU THINK--
JERRY!
READY YET?!
YES!
Eek!
Hurry!

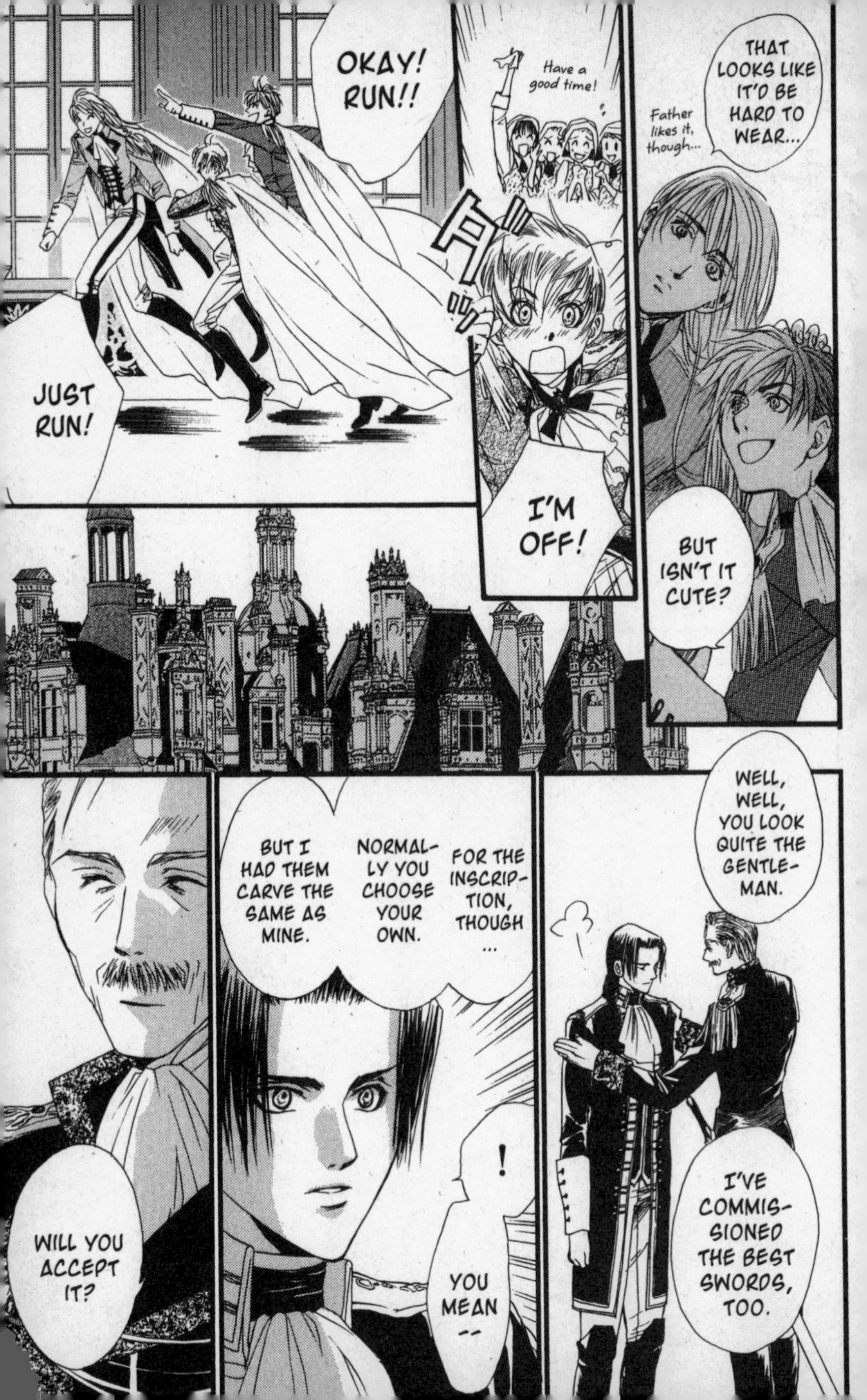
THAT LOOKS LIKE IT'D BE HARD TO WEAR...
Father likes it, though...
BUT ISN'T IT CUTE?
Have a good time!
I'M OFF!
OKAY! RUN!!
JUST RUN!
WELL, WELL, YOU LOOK QUITE THE GENTLEMAN.
I'VE COMMISSIONED THE BEST SWORDS, TOO.
FOR THE INSCRIPTION, THOUGH...
NORMALLY YOU CHOOSE YOUR OWN.
BUT I HAD THEM CARVE THE SAME AS MINE.
!
YOU MEAN --
WILL YOU ACCEPT IT?

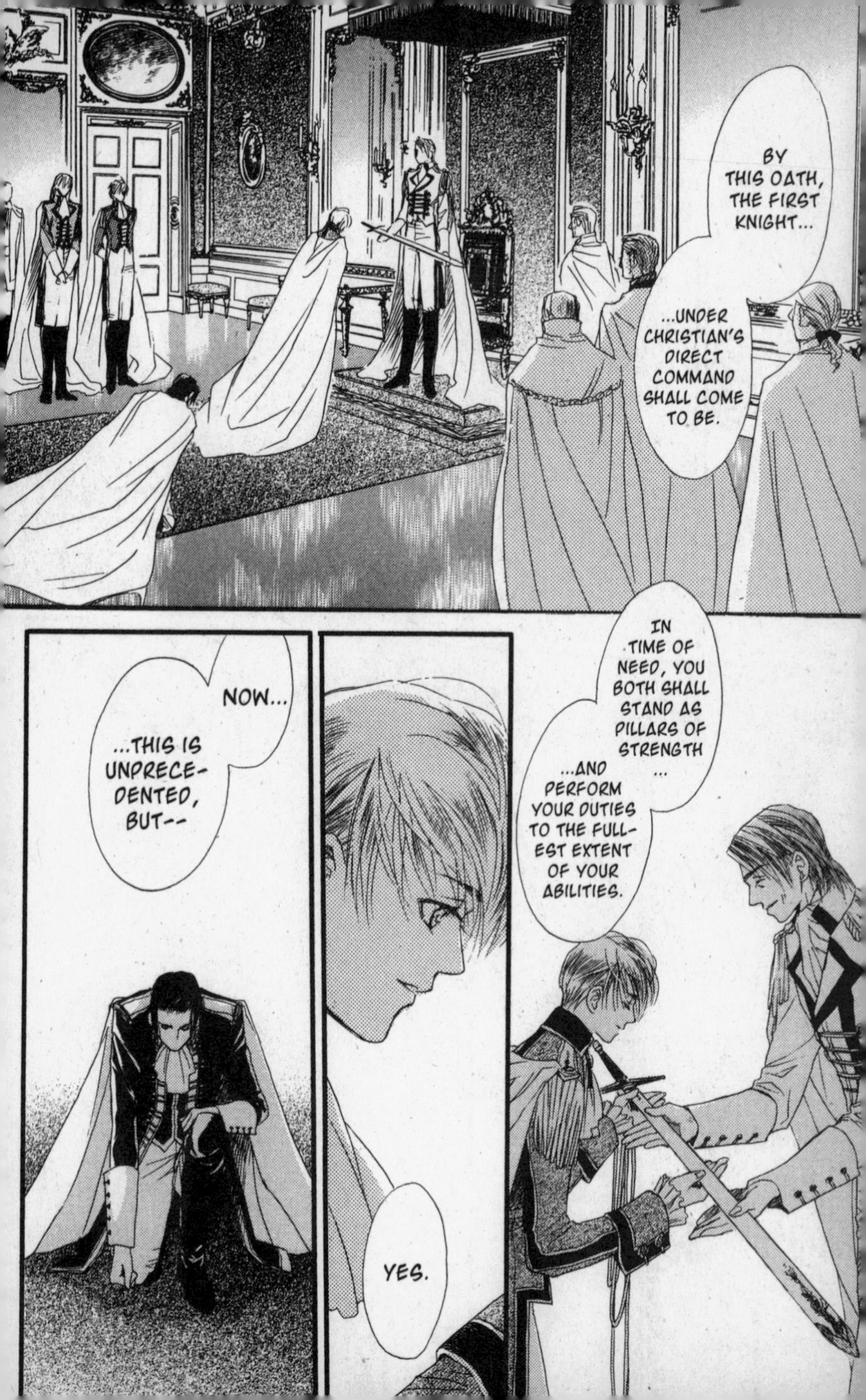
BY THIS OATH, THE FIRST KNIGHT...
...UNDER CHRISTIAN'S DIRECT COMMAND SHALL COME TO BE.
IN TIME OF NEED, YOU BOTH SHALL STAND AS PILLARS OF STRENGTH ...
...AND PERFORM YOUR DUTIES TO THE FULL-EST EXTENT OF YOUR ABILITIES.
YES.
NOW...
...THIS IS UNPRECE-DENTED, BUT--

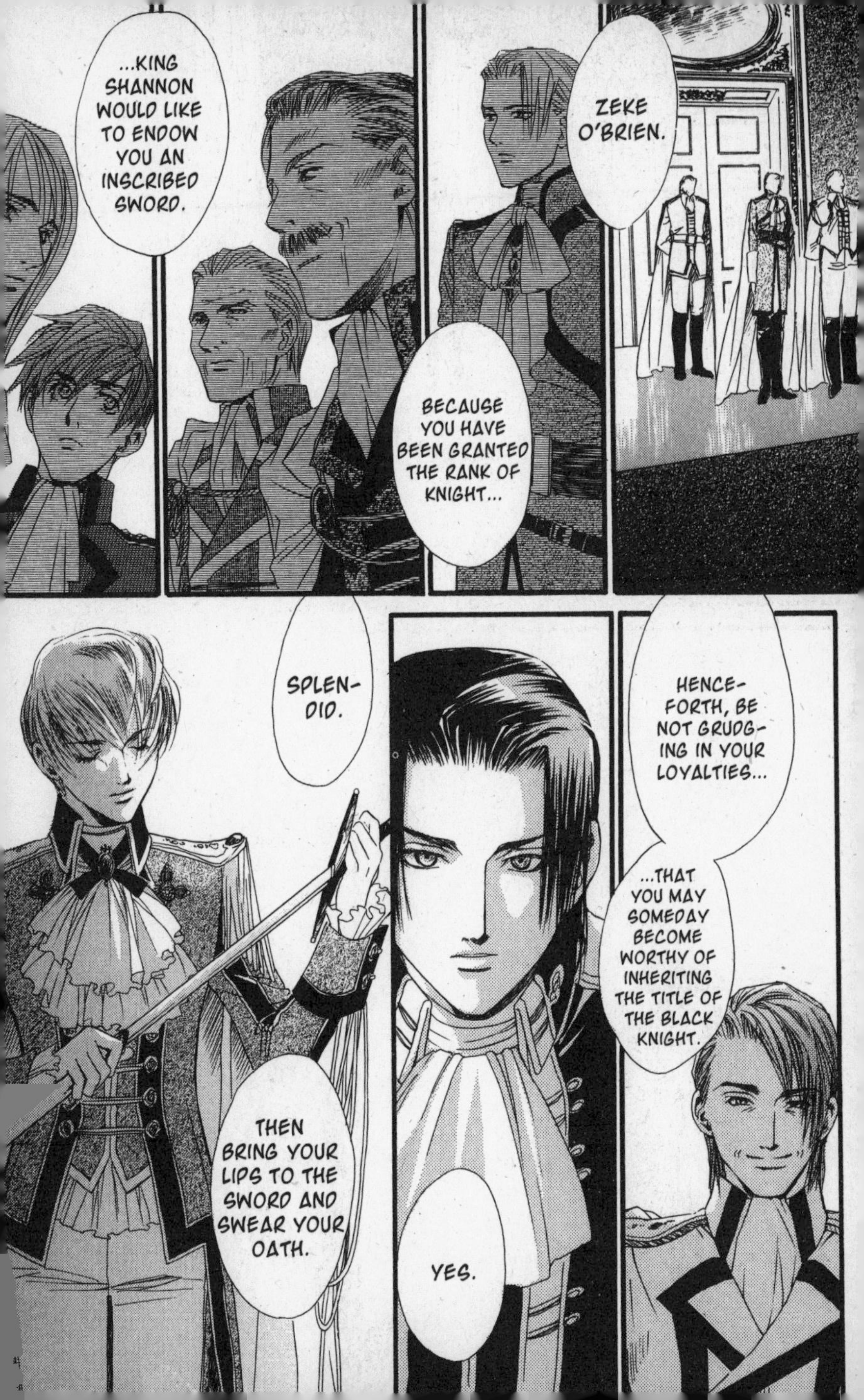
ZEKE O'BRIEN.
BECAUSE YOU HAVE BEEN GRANTED THE RANK OF KNIGHT...
...KING SHANNON WOULD LIKE TO ENDOW YOU AN INSCRIBED SWORD.
HENCE-FORTH, BE NOT GRUDG-ING IN YOUR LOYALTIES...
...THAT YOU MAY SOMEDAY BECOME WORTHY OF INHERITING THE TITLE OF THE BLACK KNIGHT.
YES.
SPLEN-DID.
THEN BRING YOUR LIPS TO THE SWORD AND SWEAR YOUR OATH.

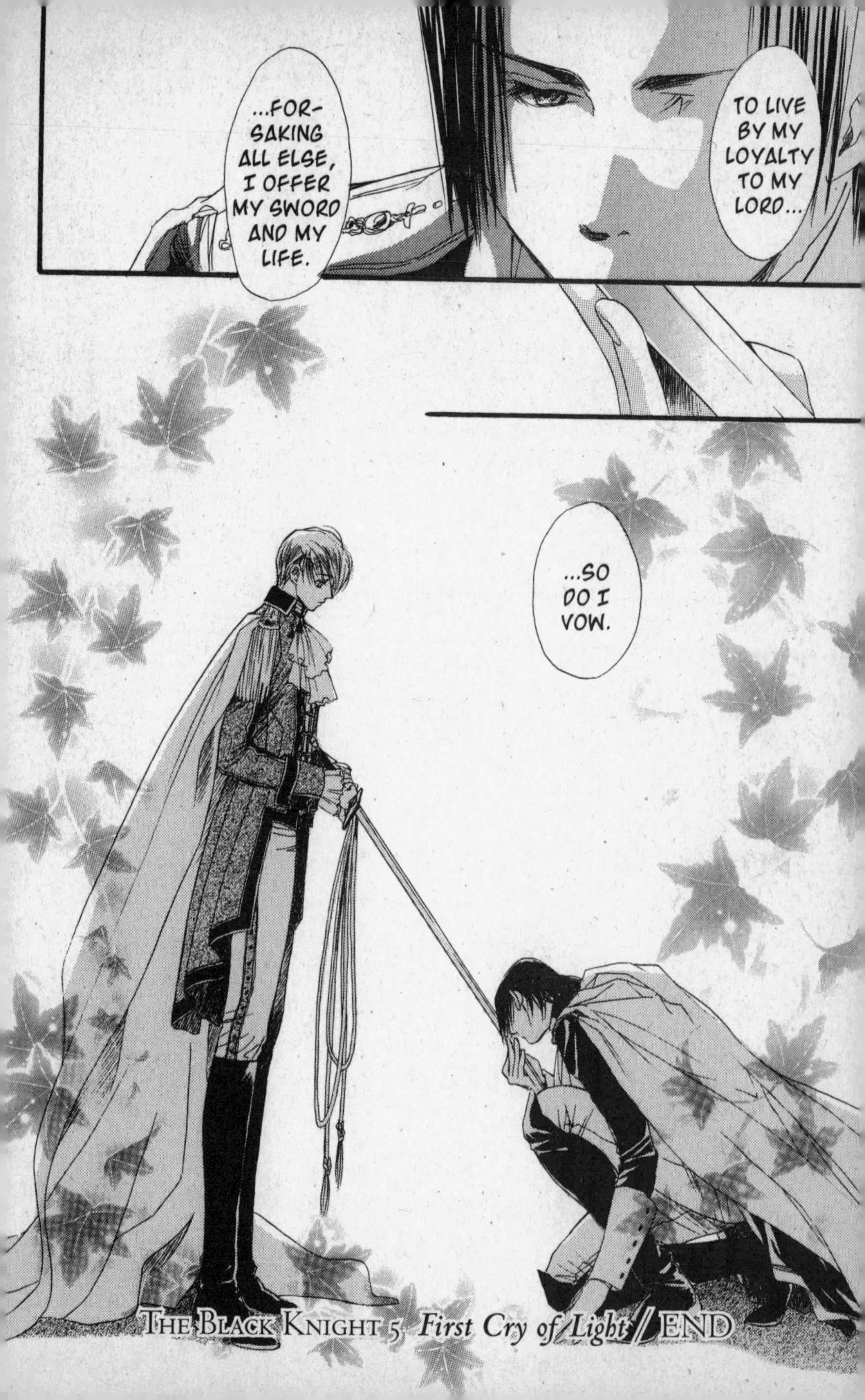
TO LIVE BY MY LOYALTY TO MY LORD...
...FOR-SAKING ALL ELSE, I OFFER MY SWORD AND MY LIFE.
...SO DO I VOW.

THE BLACK KNIGHT 5 *First Cry of Light* / END

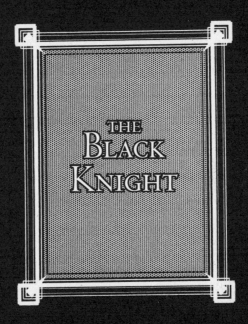

THE
BLACK
KNIGHT

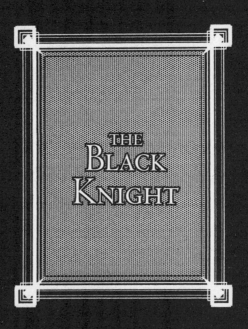

THE
BLACK
KNIGHT

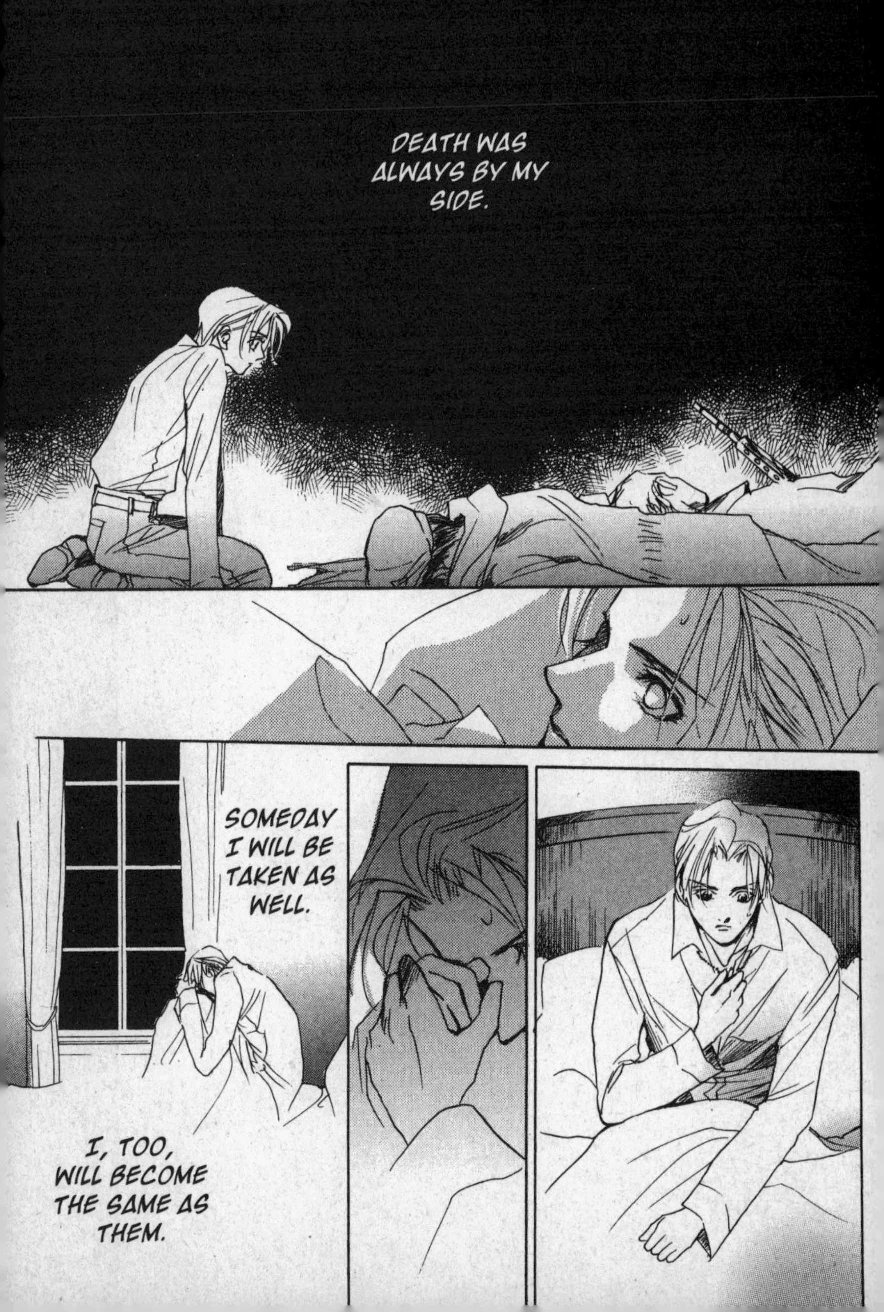
DEATH WAS ALWAYS BY MY SIDE.
SOMEDAY I WILL BE TAKEN AS WELL.
I, TOO, WILL BECOME THE SAME AS THEM.

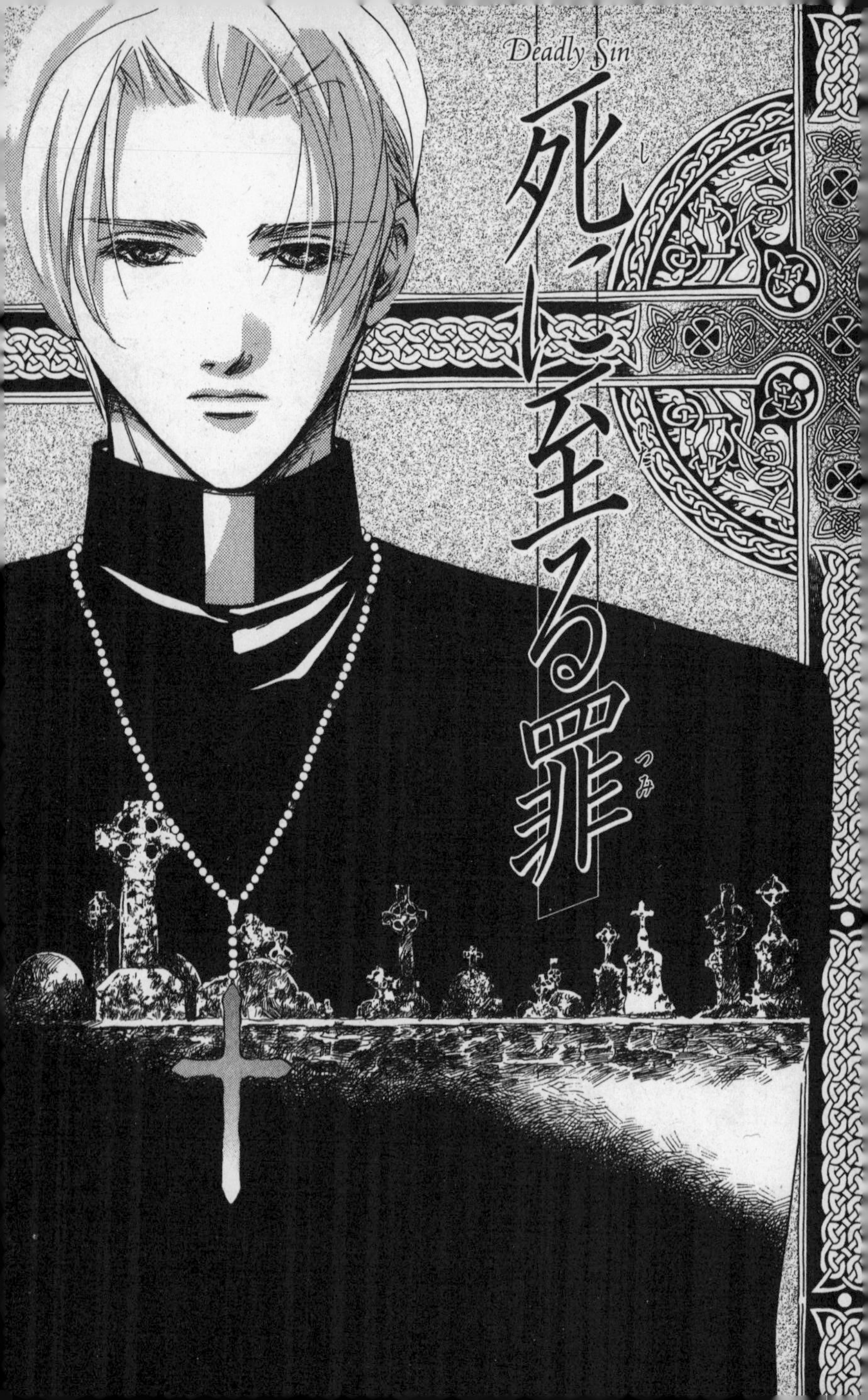
Deadly Sin
死に至る罪

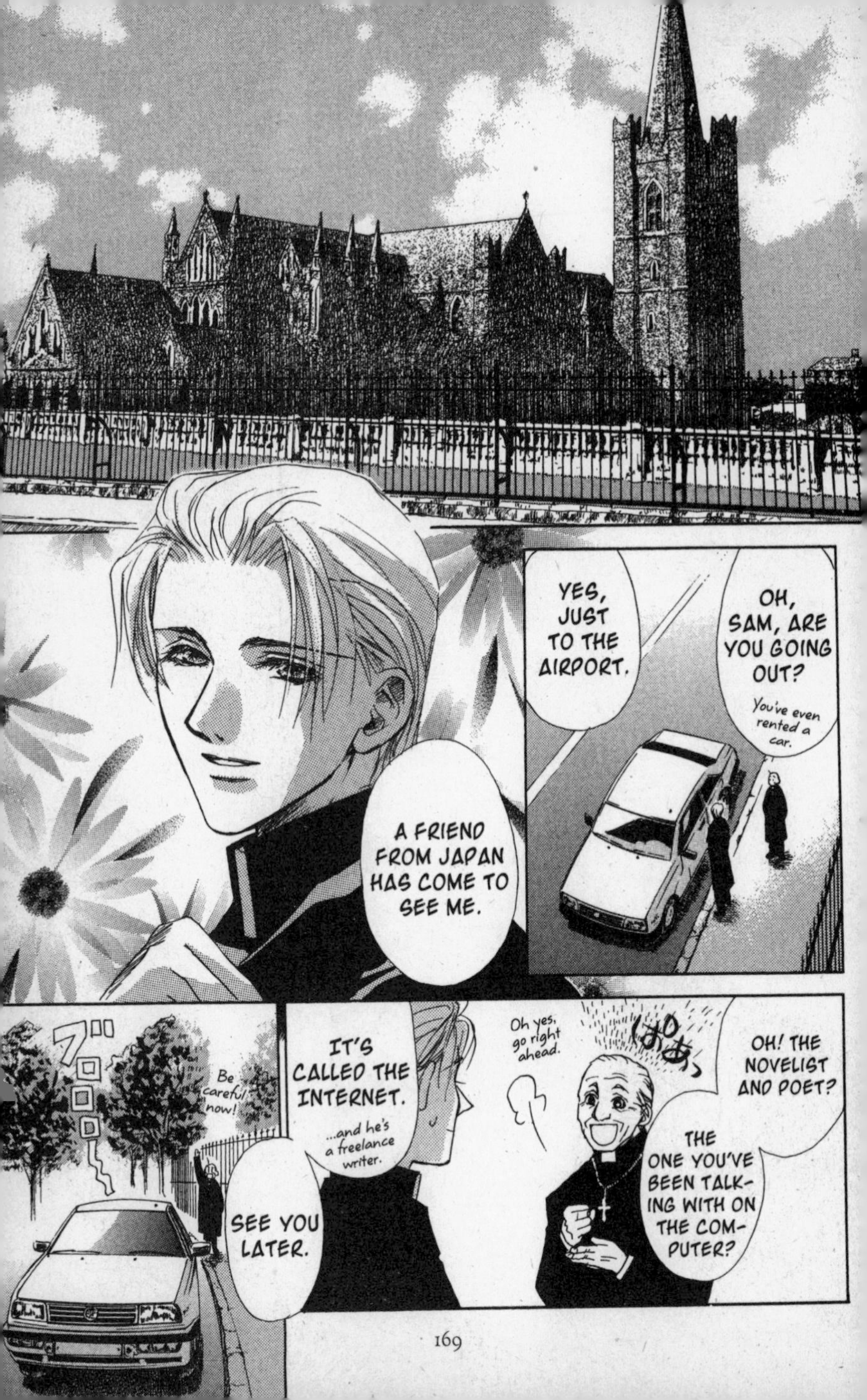
OH, SAM, ARE YOU GOING OUT?
You've even rented a car.
YES, JUST TO THE AIRPORT.
A FRIEND FROM JAPAN HAS COME TO SEE ME.
OH! THE NOVELIST AND POET?
THE ONE YOU'VE BEEN TALKING WITH ON THE COMPUTER?
Oh yes, go right ahead.
IT'S CALLED THE INTERNET.
...and he's a freelance writer.
SEE YOU LATER.
Be careful now!

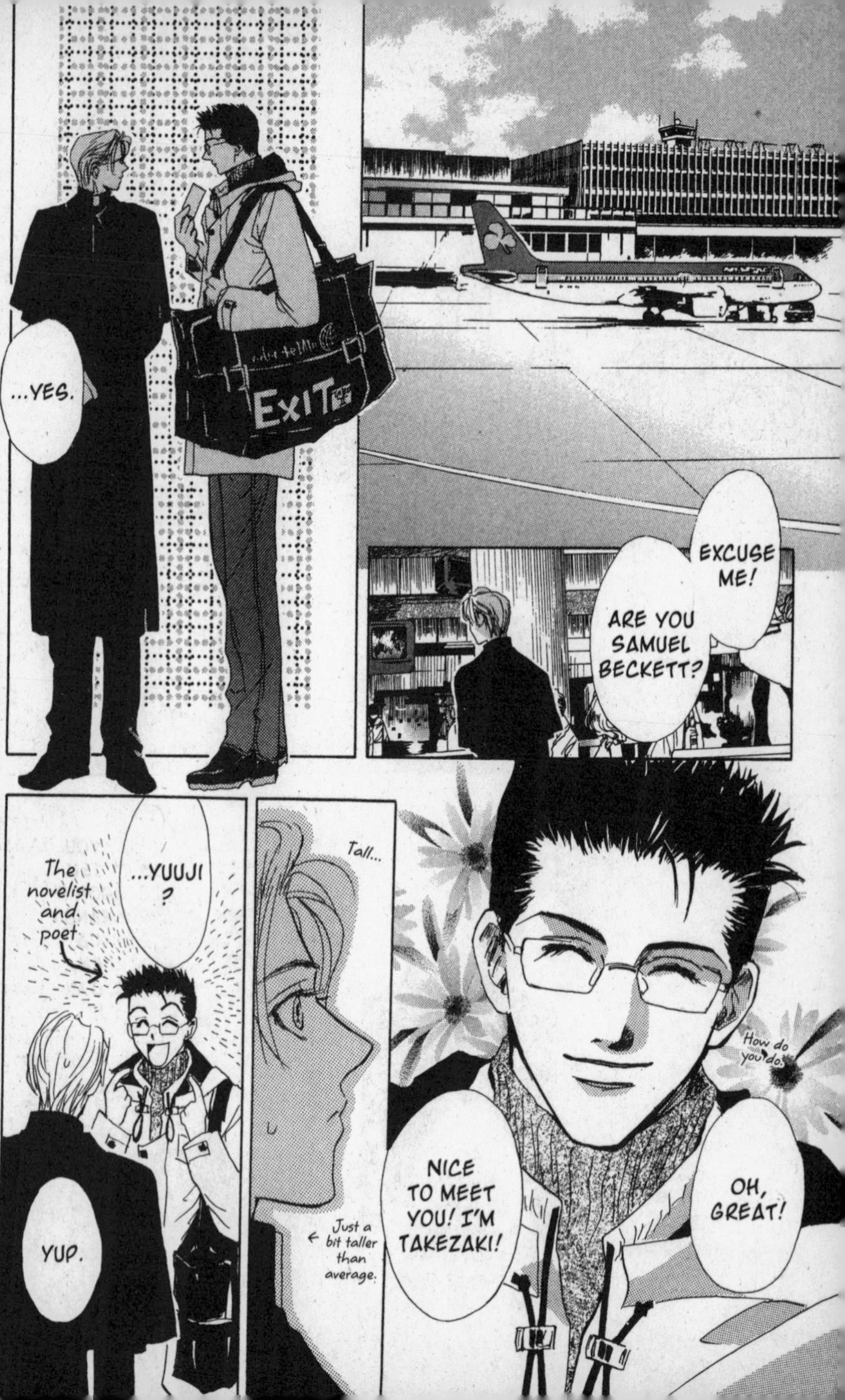
EXCUSE ME!
ARE YOU SAMUEL BECKETT?
...YES.
How do you do.
OH, GREAT!
NICE TO MEET YOU! I'M TAKEZAKI!
Tall...
Just a bit taller than average.
...YUUJI?
The novelist and poet
YUP.

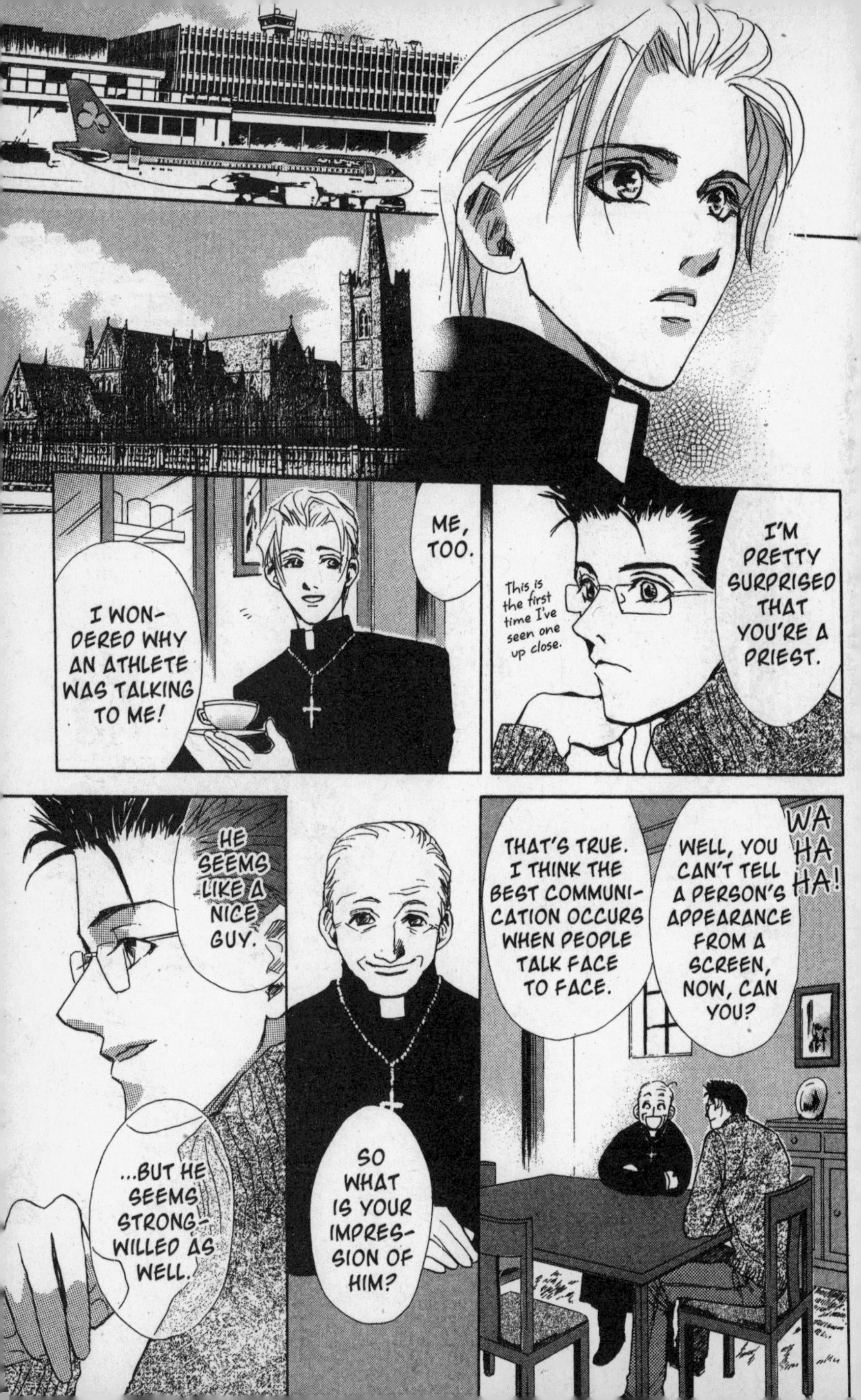
I'M PRETTY SURPRISED THAT YOU'RE A PRIEST.
This is the first time I've seen one up close.
ME, TOO.
I WON-DERED WHY AN ATHLETE WAS TALKING TO ME!
WA HA HA!
WELL, YOU CAN'T TELL A PERSON'S APPEARANCE FROM A SCREEN, NOW, CAN YOU?
THAT'S TRUE. I THINK THE BEST COMMUNI-CATION OCCURS WHEN PEOPLE TALK FACE TO FACE.
SO WHAT IS YOUR IMPRES-SION OF HIM?
HE SEEMS LIKE A NICE GUY.
...BUT HE SEEMS STRONG-WILLED AS WELL.

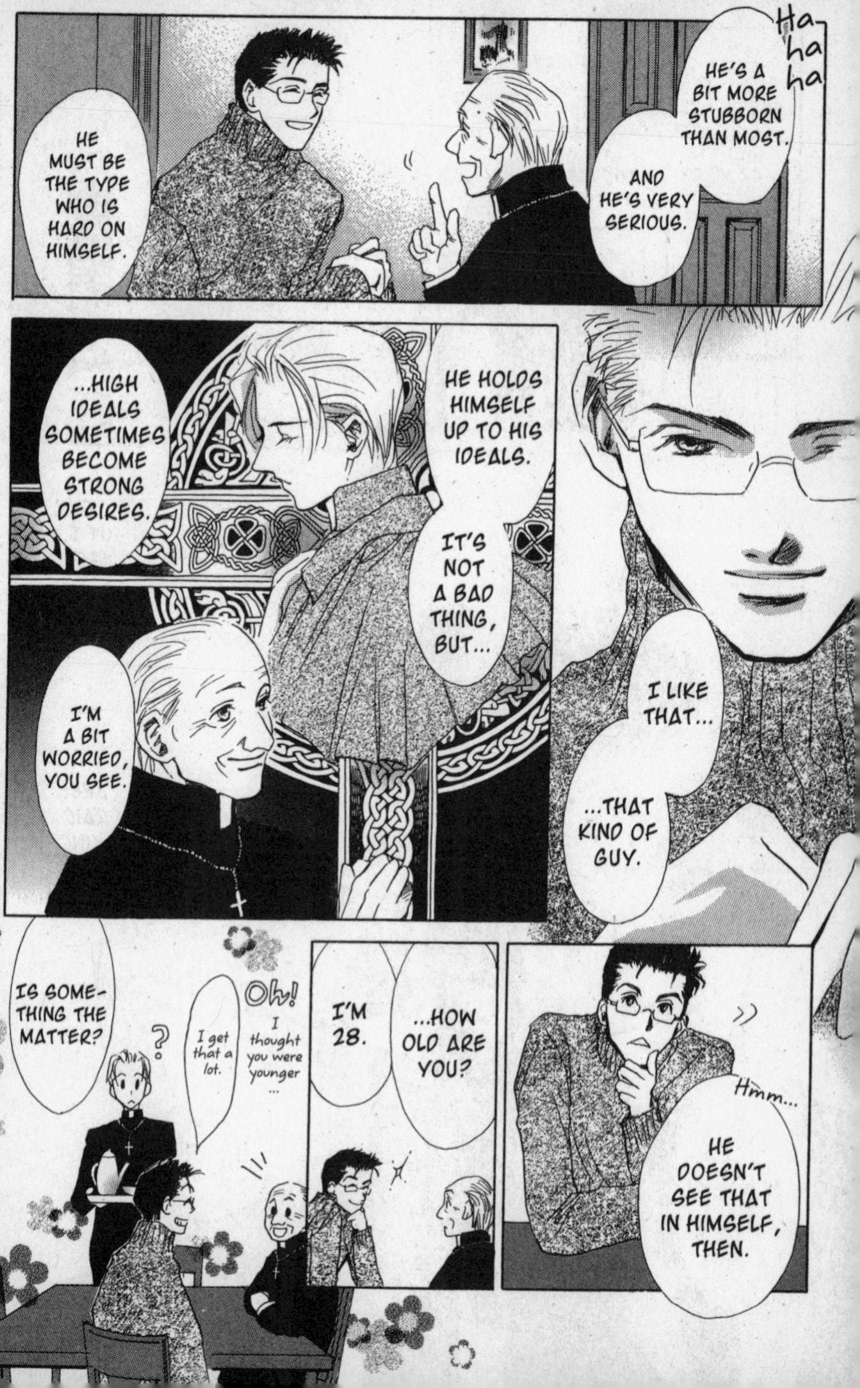

Ha-ha ha
HE'S A BIT MORE STUBBORN THAN MOST.
AND HE'S VERY SERIOUS.
HE MUST BE THE TYPE WHO IS HARD ON HIMSELF.
I LIKE THAT...
...THAT KIND OF GUY.
HE HOLDS HIMSELF UP TO HIS IDEALS.
IT'S NOT A BAD THING, BUT...
...HIGH IDEALS SOMETIMES BECOME STRONG DESIRES.
I'M A BIT WORRIED, YOU SEE.
Hmm...
HE DOESN'T SEE THAT IN HIMSELF, THEN.
...HOW OLD ARE YOU?
I'M 28.
Oh!
I thought you were younger...
I get that a lot.
?
IS SOME-THING THE MATTER?

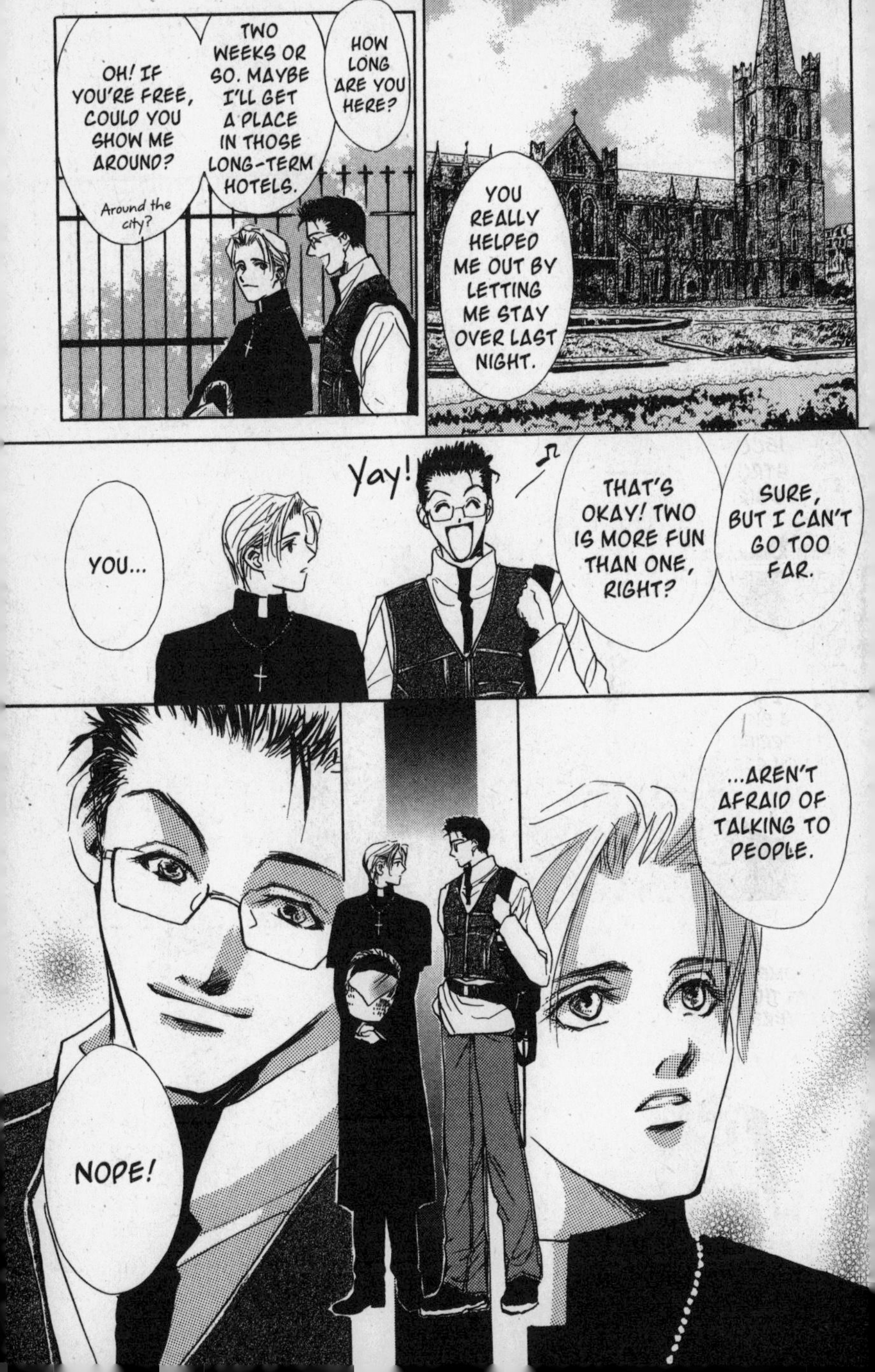
YOU REALLY HELPED ME OUT BY LETTING ME STAY OVER LAST NIGHT.
HOW LONG ARE YOU HERE?
TWO WEEKS OR SO. MAYBE I'LL GET A PLACE IN THOSE LONG-TERM HOTELS.
OH! IF YOU'RE FREE, COULD YOU SHOW ME AROUND?
Around the city?
SURE, BUT I CAN'T GO TOO FAR.
THAT'S OKAY! TWO IS MORE FUN THAN ONE, RIGHT?
Yay!
YOU...
...AREN'T AFRAID OF TALKING TO PEOPLE.
NOPE!

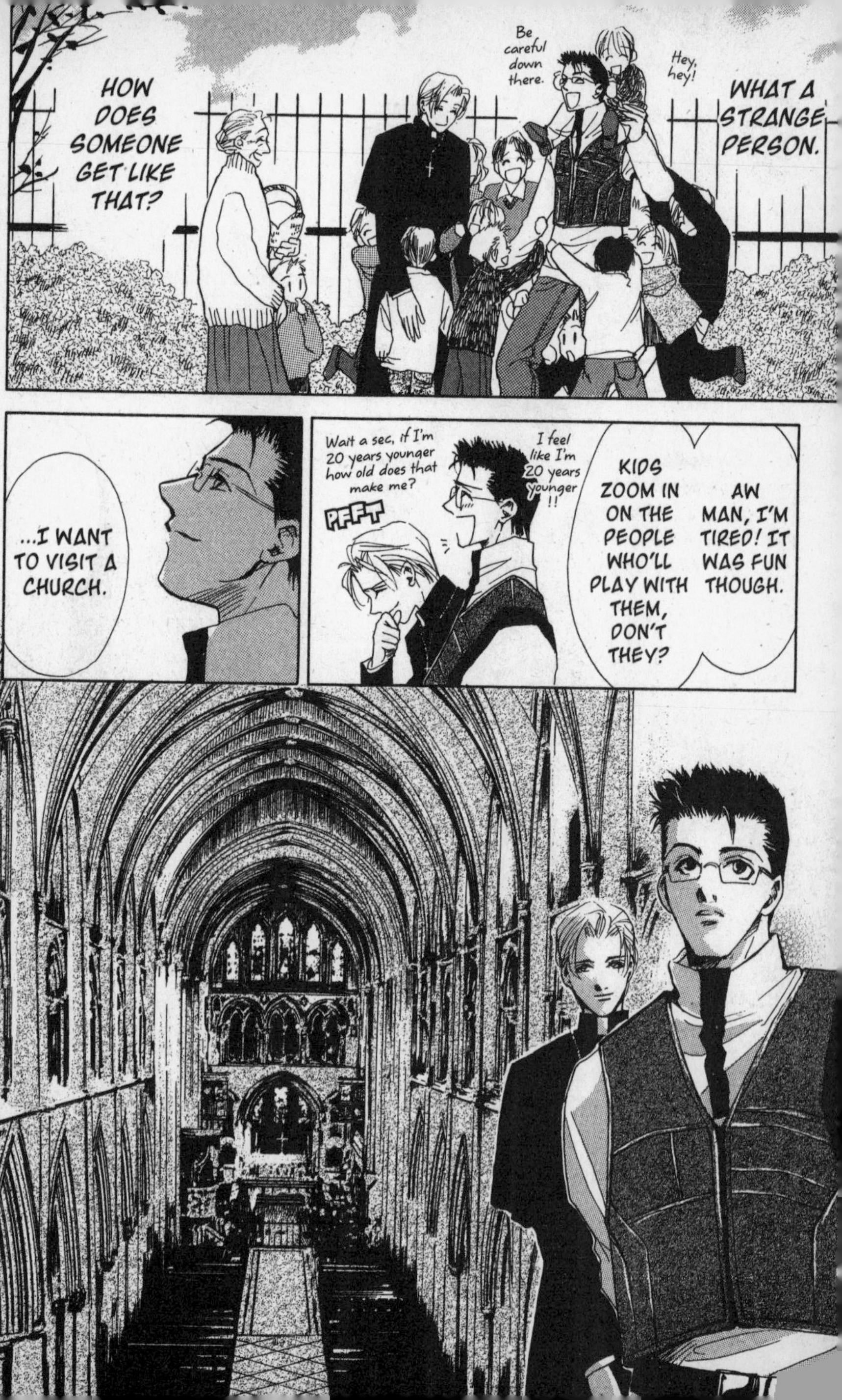
WHAT A STRANGE PERSON.
Hey, hey!
Be careful down there.
HOW DOES SOMEONE GET LIKE THAT?
AW MAN, I'M TIRED! IT WAS FUN THOUGH.
KIDS ZOOM IN ON THE PEOPLE WHO'LL PLAY WITH THEM, DON'T THEY?
I feel like I'm 20 years younger!!
Wait a sec, if I'm 20 years younger how old does that make me?
PFFT
...I WANT TO VISIT A CHURCH.

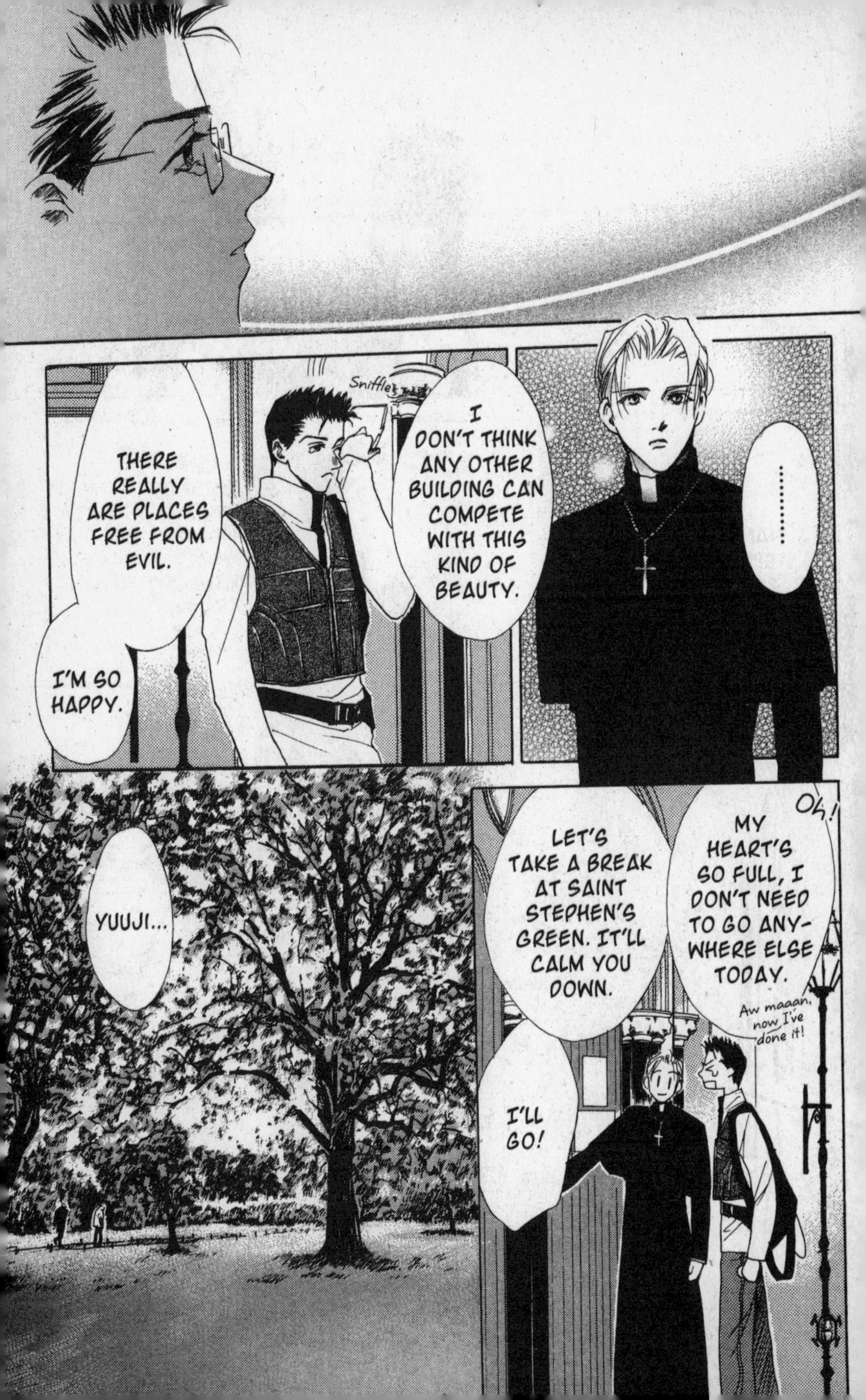
......
Sniffle
I DON'T THINK ANY OTHER BUILDING CAN COMPETE WITH THIS KIND OF BEAUTY.
THERE REALLY ARE PLACES FREE FROM EVIL.
I'M SO HAPPY.
Oh!
MY HEART'S SO FULL, I DON'T NEED TO GO ANY-WHERE ELSE TODAY.
LET'S TAKE A BREAK AT SAINT STEPHEN'S GREEN. IT'LL CALM YOU DOWN.
Aw maaan, now I've done it!
I'LL GO!
YUUJI...

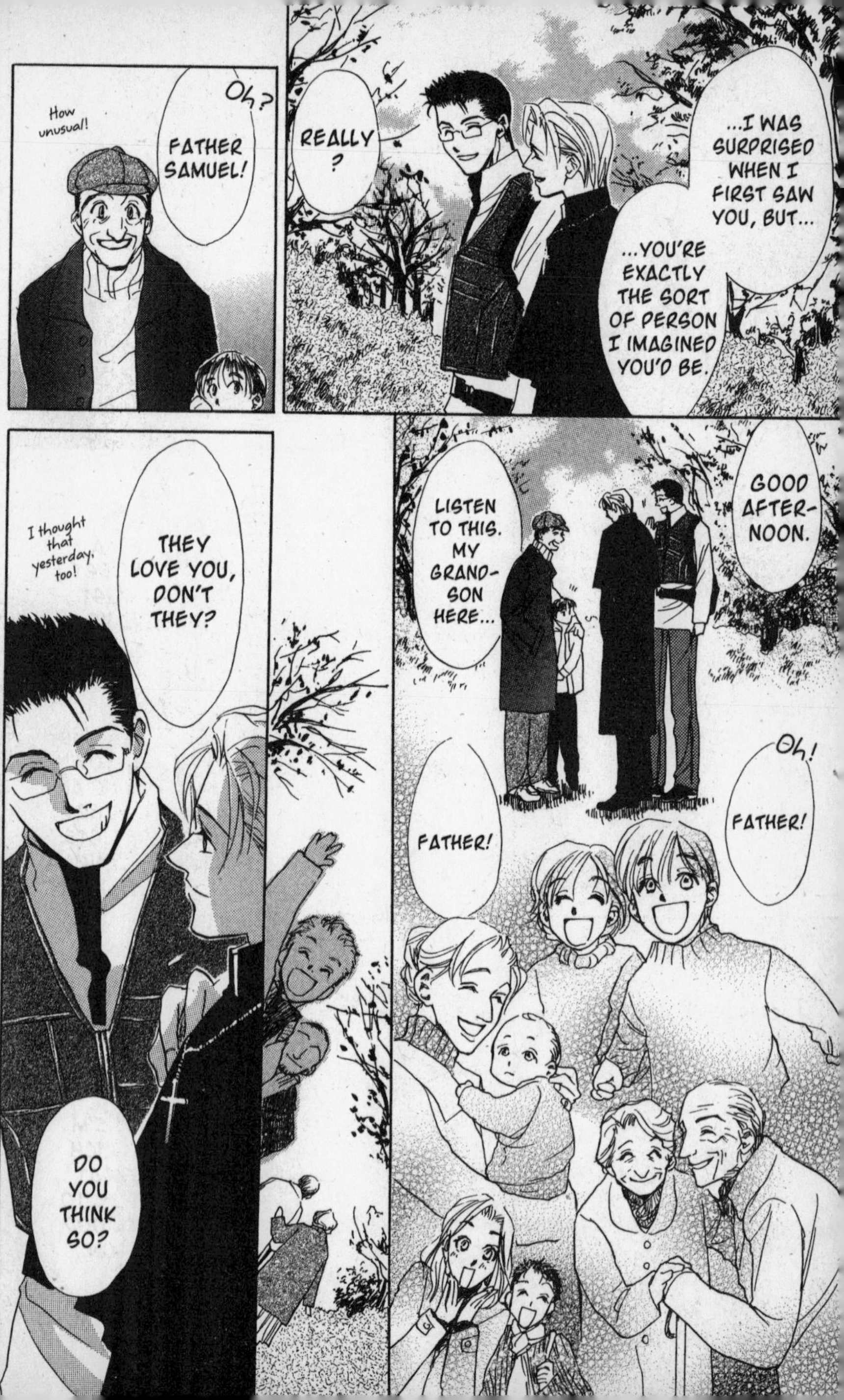
...I WAS SURPRISED WHEN I FIRST SAW YOU, BUT...
...YOU'RE EXACTLY THE SORT OF PERSON I IMAGINED YOU'D BE.
REALLY?
Oh?
FATHER SAMUEL!
How unusual!
GOOD AFTER-NOON.
LISTEN TO THIS. MY GRAND-SON HERE...
Oh!
FATHER!
FATHER!
THEY LOVE YOU, DON'T THEY?
I thought that yesterday, too!
DO YOU THINK SO?

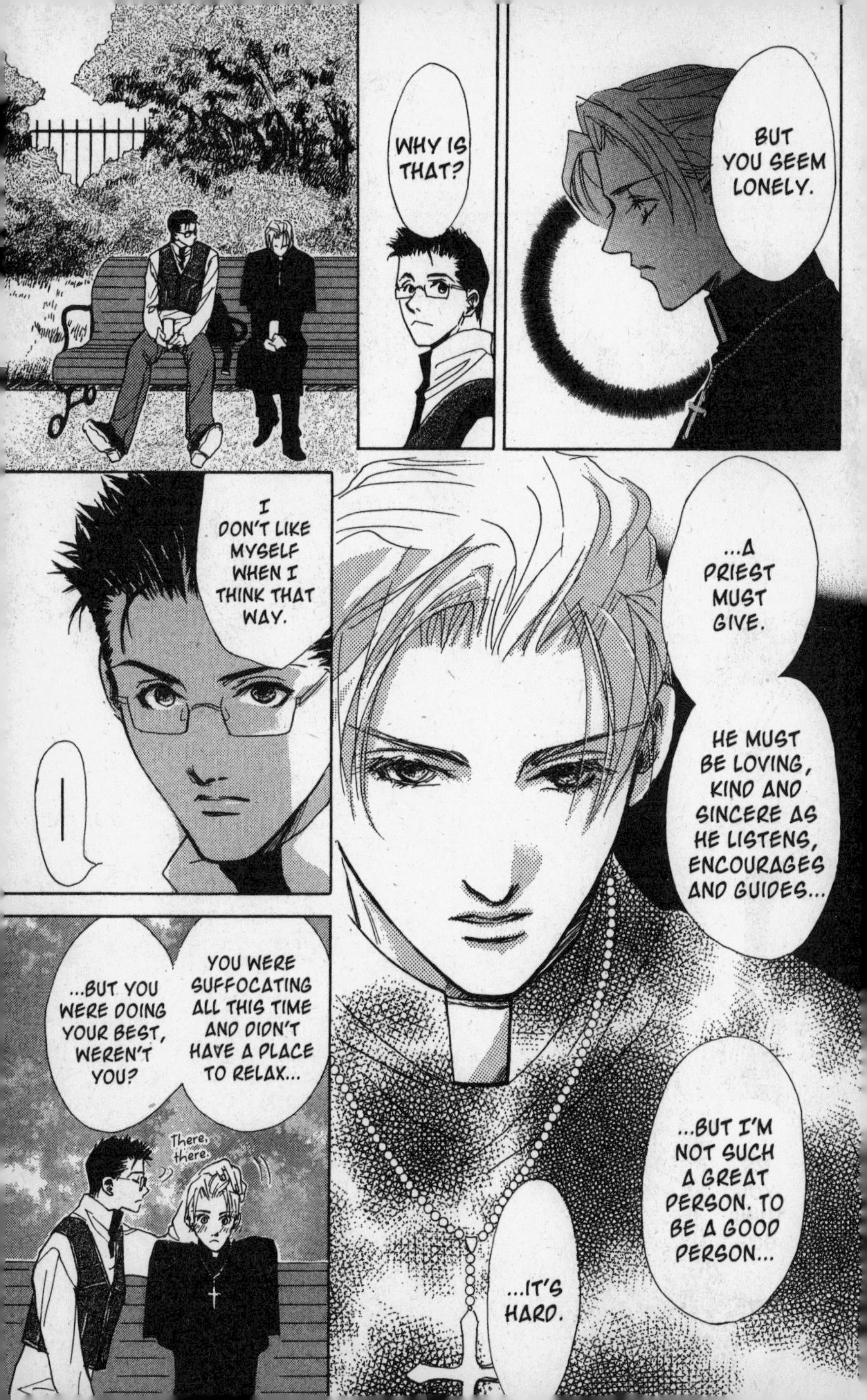
BUT YOU SEEM LONELY.
WHY IS THAT?
...A PRIEST MUST GIVE.
HE MUST BE LOVING, KIND AND SINCERE AS HE LISTENS, ENCOURAGES AND GUIDES...
...BUT I'M NOT SUCH A GREAT PERSON. TO BE A GOOD PERSON...
...IT'S HARD.
I DON'T LIKE MYSELF WHEN I THINK THAT WAY.
YOU WERE SUFFOCATING ALL THIS TIME AND DIDN'T HAVE A PLACE TO RELAX...
...BUT YOU WERE DOING YOUR BEST, WEREN'T YOU?
There, there.

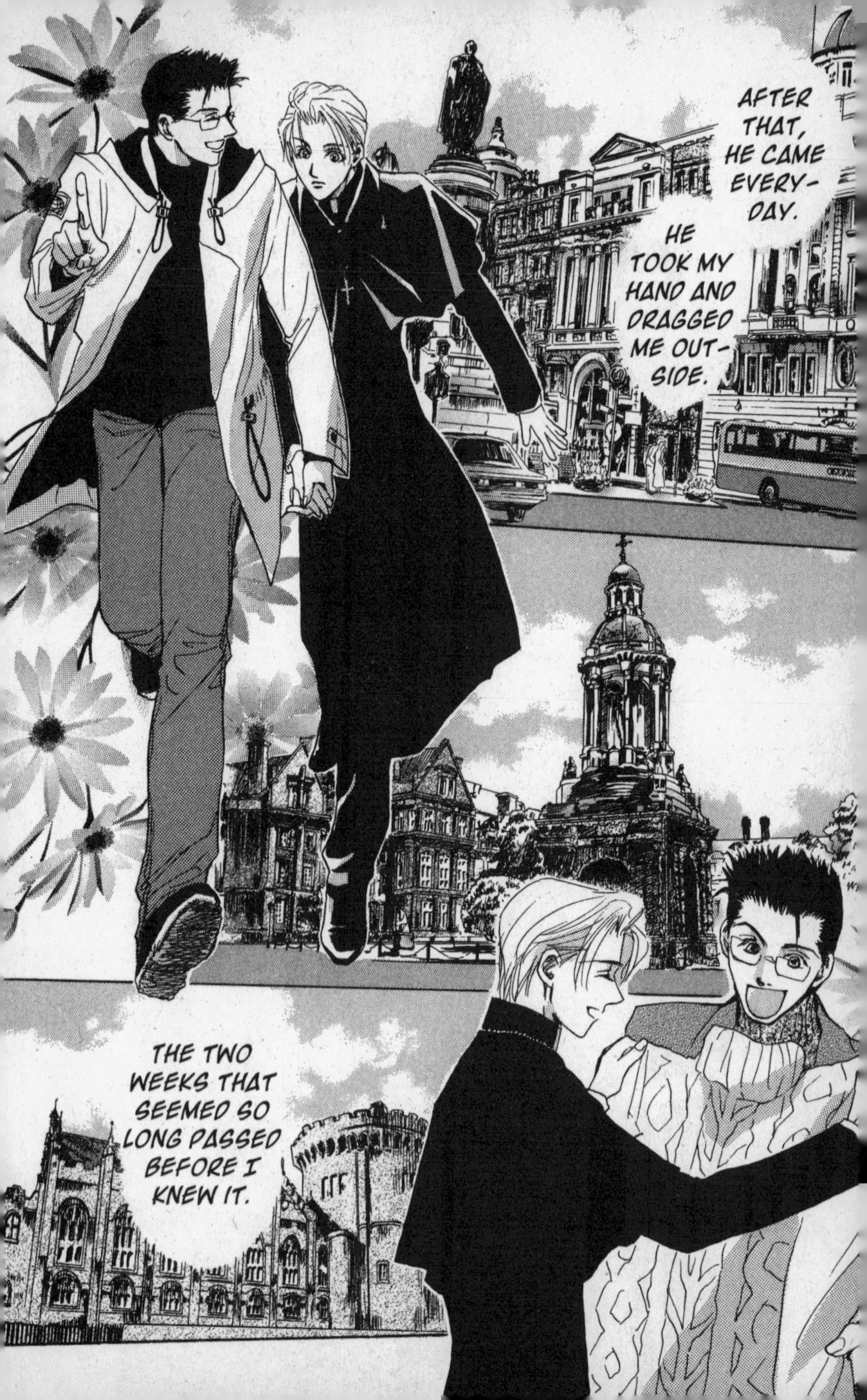
AFTER THAT, HE CAME EVERY-DAY.
HE TOOK MY HAND AND DRAGGED ME OUT-SIDE.
THE TWO WEEKS THAT SEEMED SO LONG PASSED BEFORE I KNEW IT.

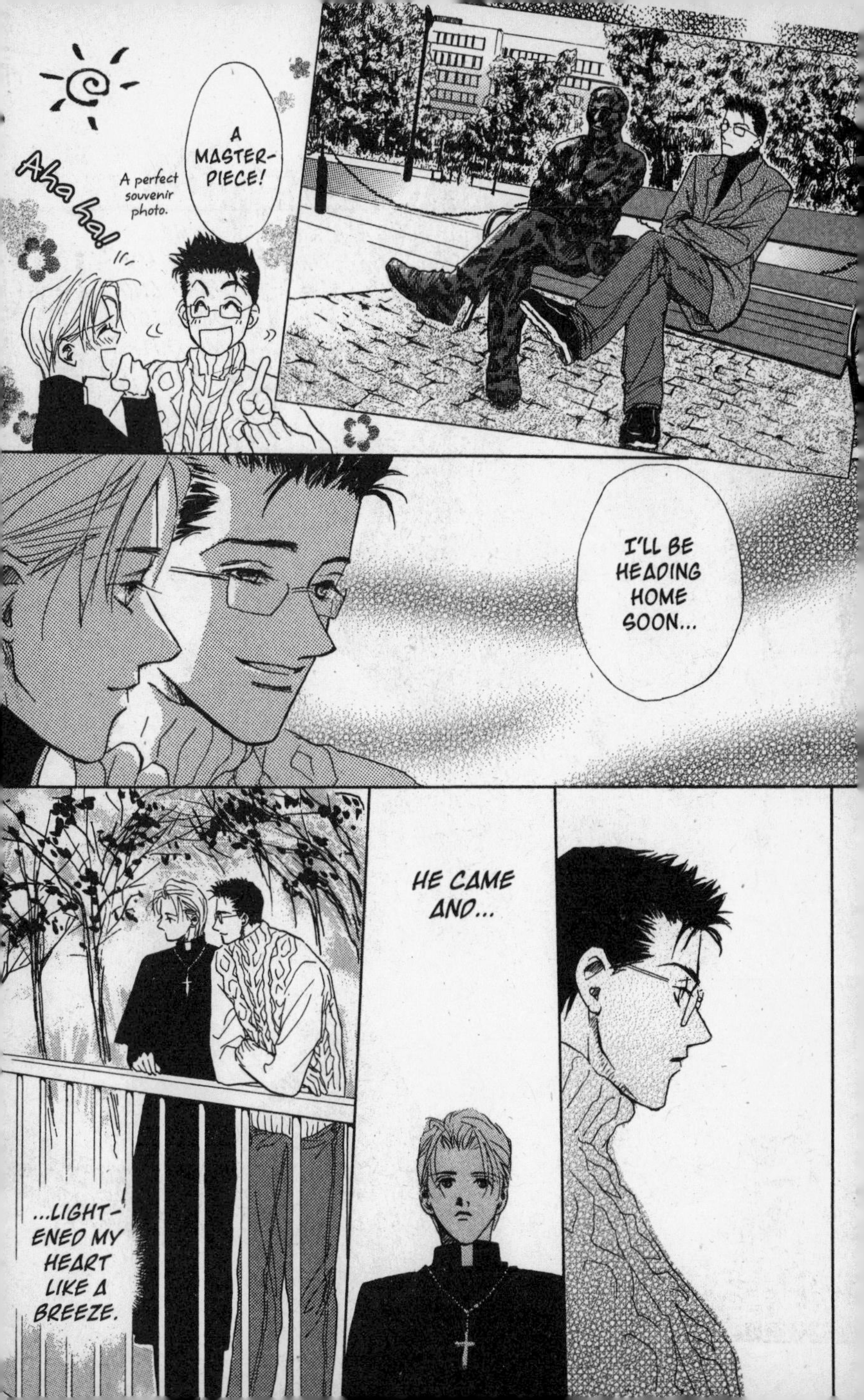
A MASTER-PIECE!
A perfect souvenir photo.
Aha ha!
I'LL BE HEADING HOME SOON...
HE CAME AND...
...LIGHT-ENED MY HEART LIKE A BREEZE.

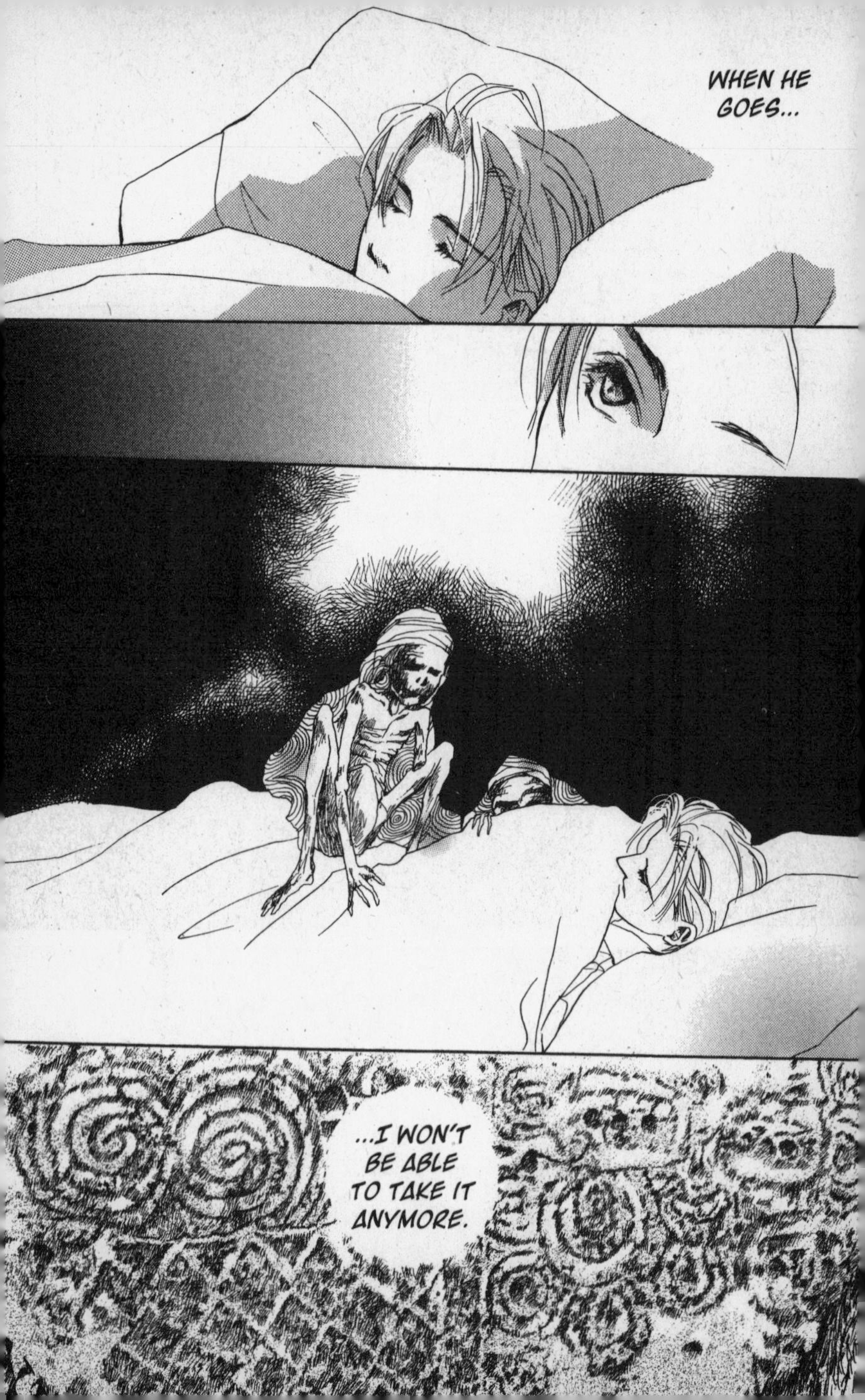
WHEN HE GOES...
...I WON'T BE ABLE TO TAKE IT ANYMORE.

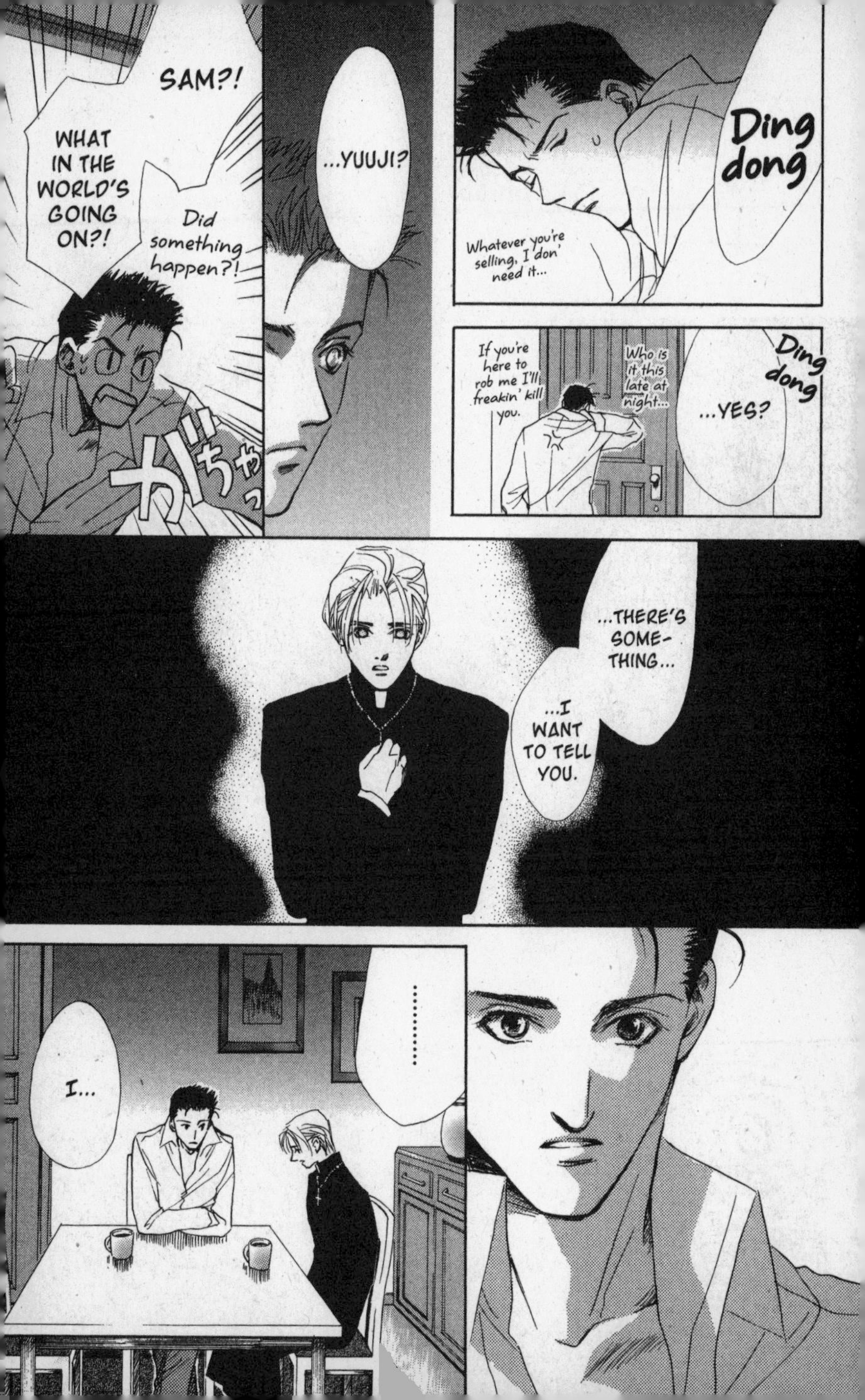
Ding dong
Whatever you're selling, I don' need it...
Ding dong
...YES?
Who is it this late at night...
If you're here to rob me I'll freakin' kill you.
...YUUJI?
SAM?!
WHAT IN THE WORLD'S GOING ON?!
Did something happen?!
がちゃっ
...THERE'S SOME-THING...
...I WANT TO TELL YOU.
......
I...

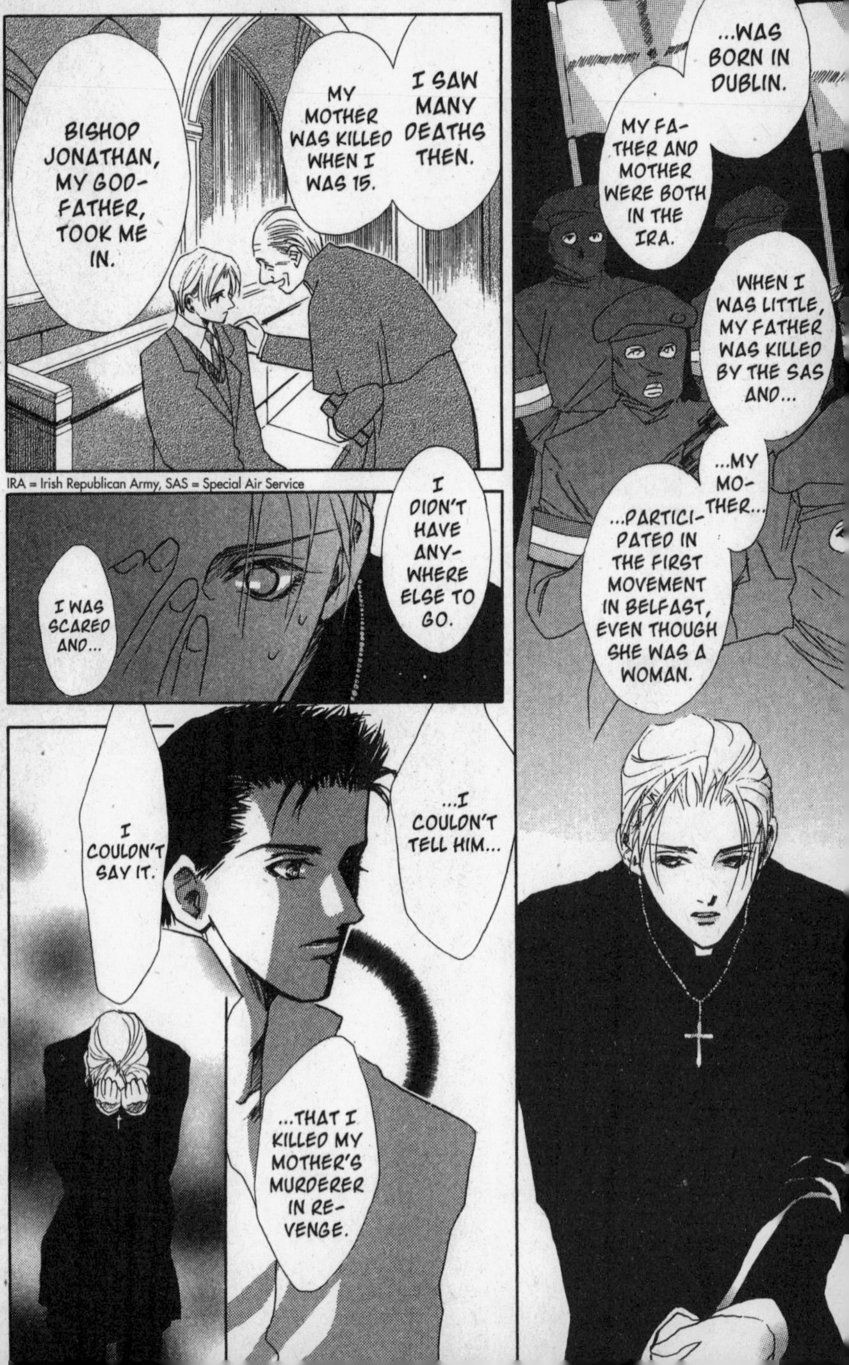
...WAS BORN IN DUBLIN.
MY FATHER AND MOTHER WERE BOTH IN THE IRA.
WHEN I WAS LITTLE, MY FATHER WAS KILLED BY THE SAS AND...
...MY MOTHER...
...PARTICIPATED IN THE FIRST MOVEMENT IN BELFAST, EVEN THOUGH SHE WAS A WOMAN.
I SAW MANY DEATHS THEN.
MY MOTHER WAS KILLED WHEN I WAS 15.
BISHOP JONATHAN, MY GODFATHER, TOOK ME IN.
I DIDN'T HAVE ANYWHERE ELSE TO GO.
I WAS SCARED AND...
...I COULDN'T TELL HIM...
I COULDN'T SAY IT.
...THAT I KILLED MY MOTHER'S MURDERER IN REVENGE.

IRA = Irish Republican Army, SAS = Special Air Service

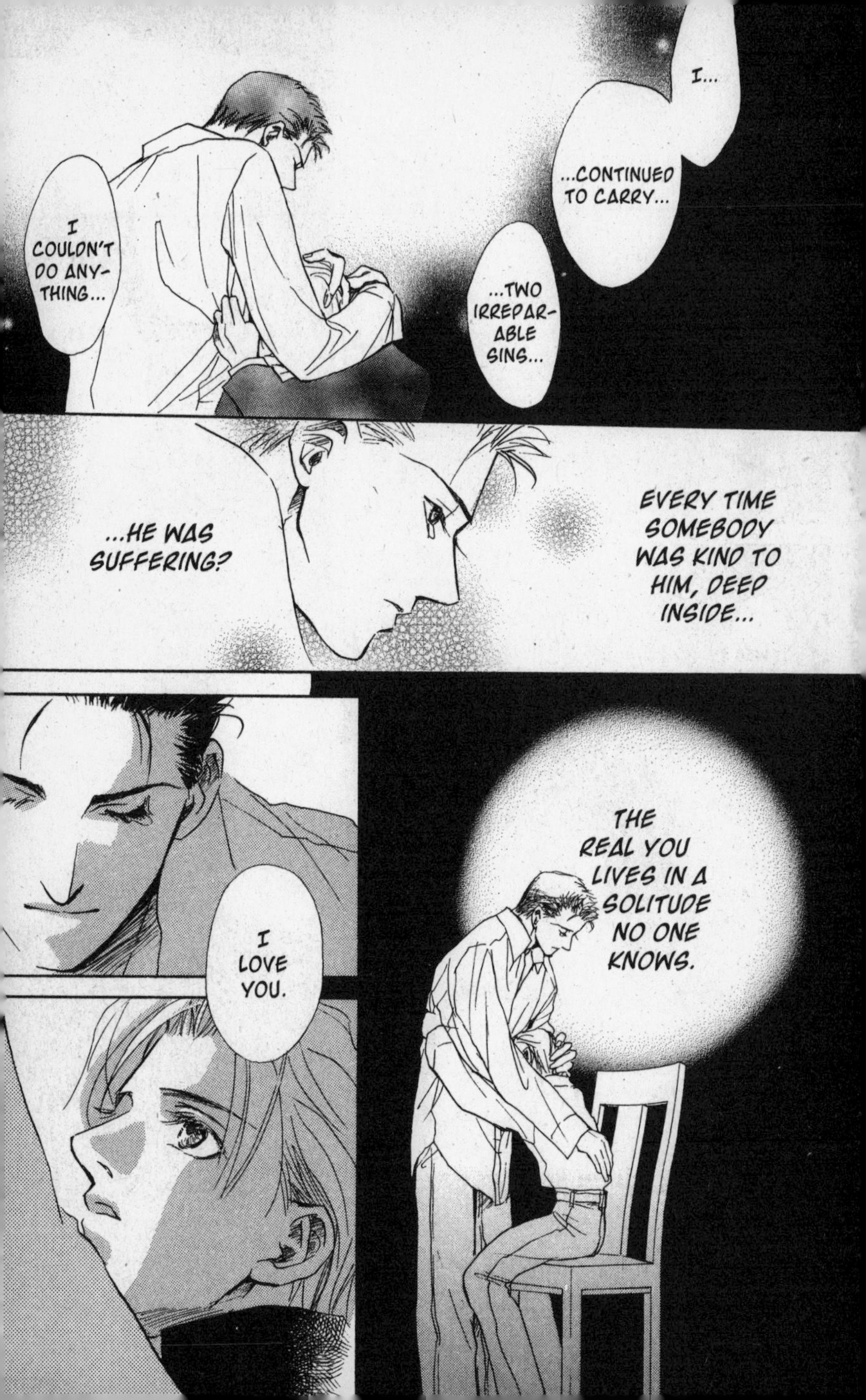
I...
...CONTINUED TO CARRY...
...TWO IRREPARABLE SINS...
I COULDN'T DO ANYTHING...
EVERY TIME SOMEBODY WAS KIND TO HIM, DEEP INSIDE...
...HE WAS SUFFERING?
THE REAL YOU LIVES IN A SOLITUDE NO ONE KNOWS.
I LOVE YOU.

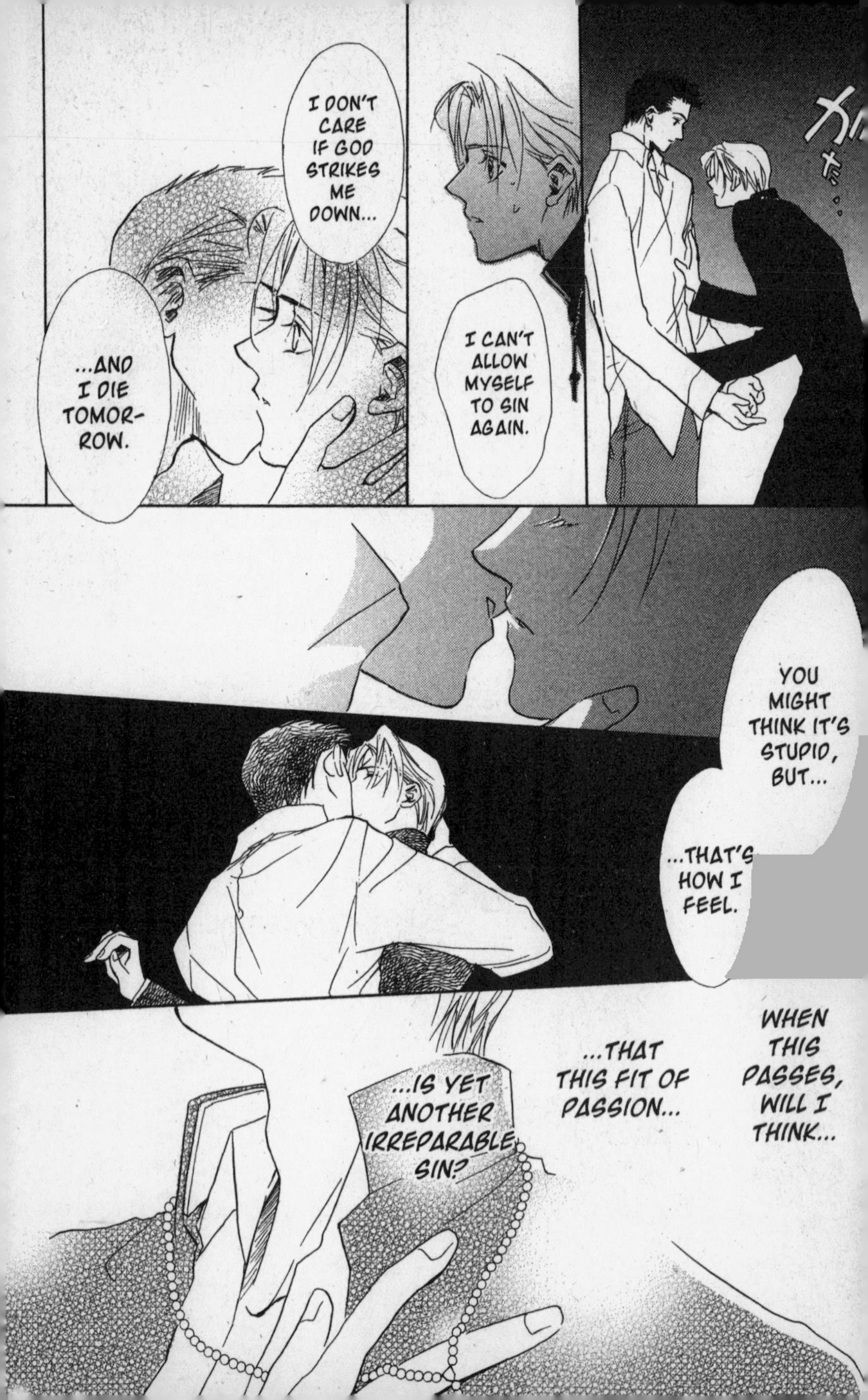
I CAN'T ALLOW MYSELF TO SIN AGAIN.
I DON'T CARE IF GOD STRIKES ME DOWN...
...AND I DIE TOMORROW.
YOU MIGHT THINK IT'S STUPID, BUT...
...THAT'S HOW I FEEL.
WHEN THIS PASSES, WILL I THINK...
...THAT THIS FIT OF PASSION...
...IS YET ANOTHER IRREPARABLE SIN?

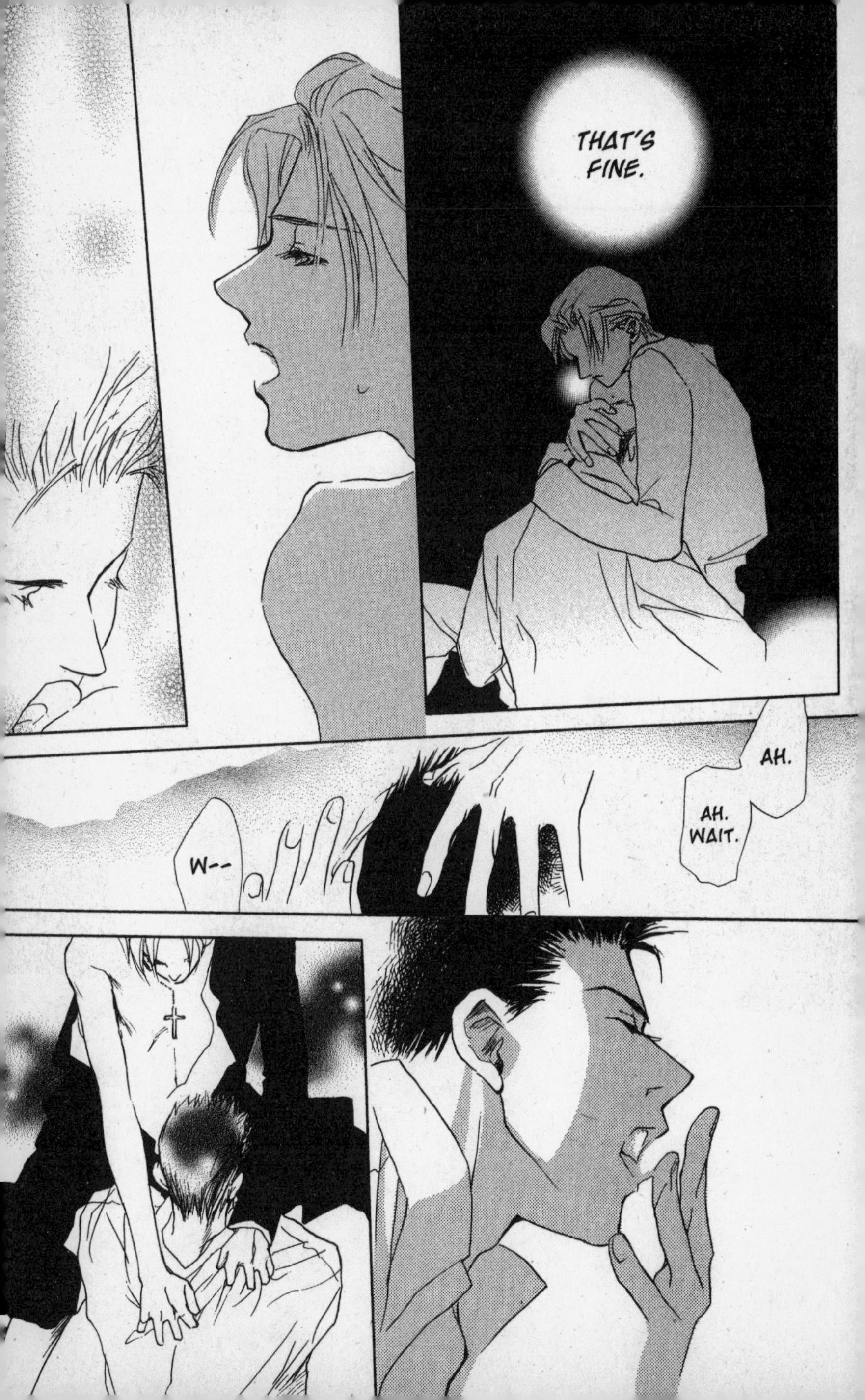
THAT'S FINE.
AH.
AH. WAIT.
W--

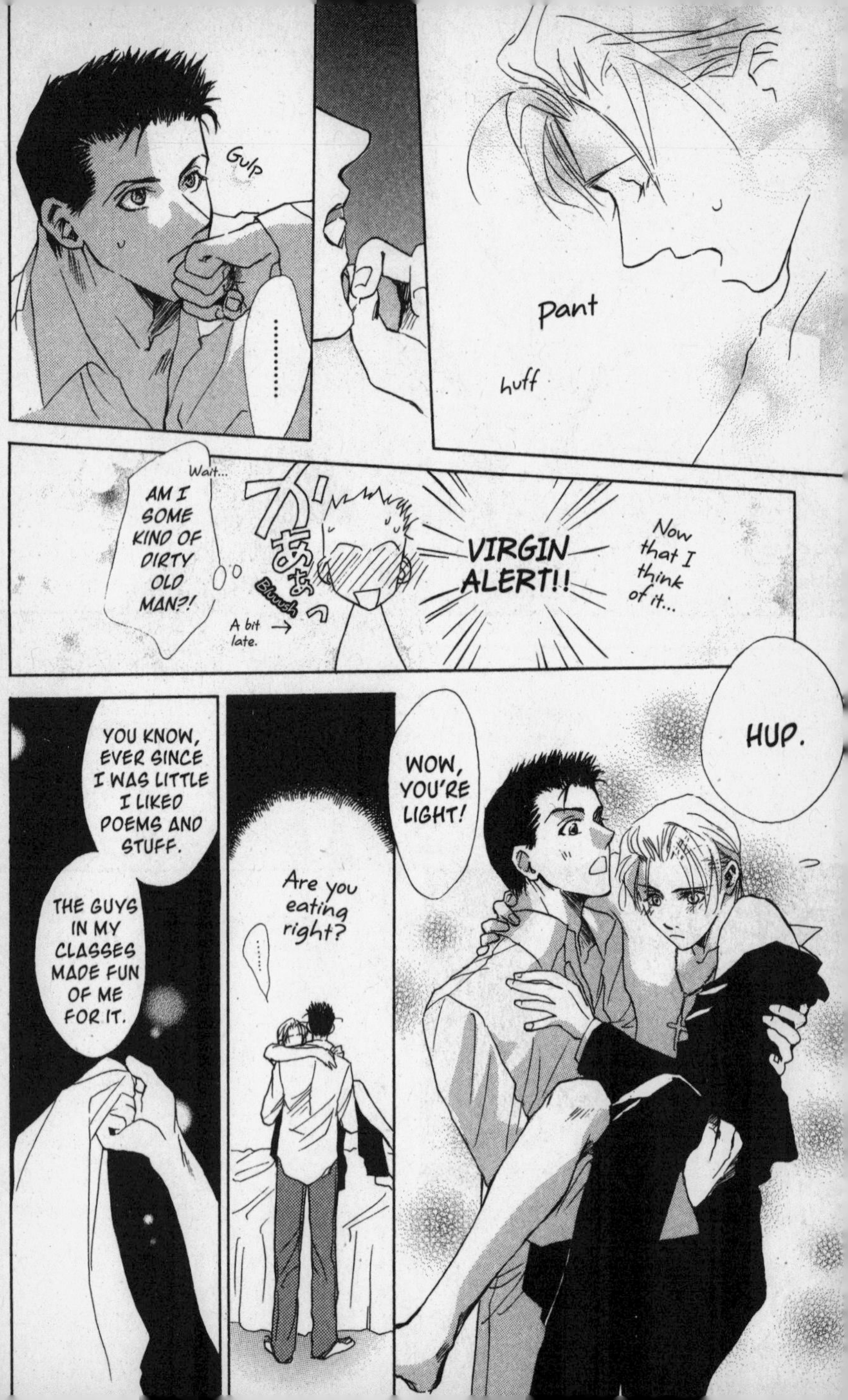
pant
huff
......
Gulp
Now that I think of it...
VIRGIN ALERT!!
Bluush
A bit late.
Wait...
AM I SOME KIND OF DIRTY OLD MAN?!
HUP.
WOW, YOU'RE LIGHT!
Are you eating right?
......
YOU KNOW, EVER SINCE I WAS LITTLE I LIKED POEMS AND STUFF.
THE GUYS IN MY CLASSES MADE FUN OF ME FOR IT.

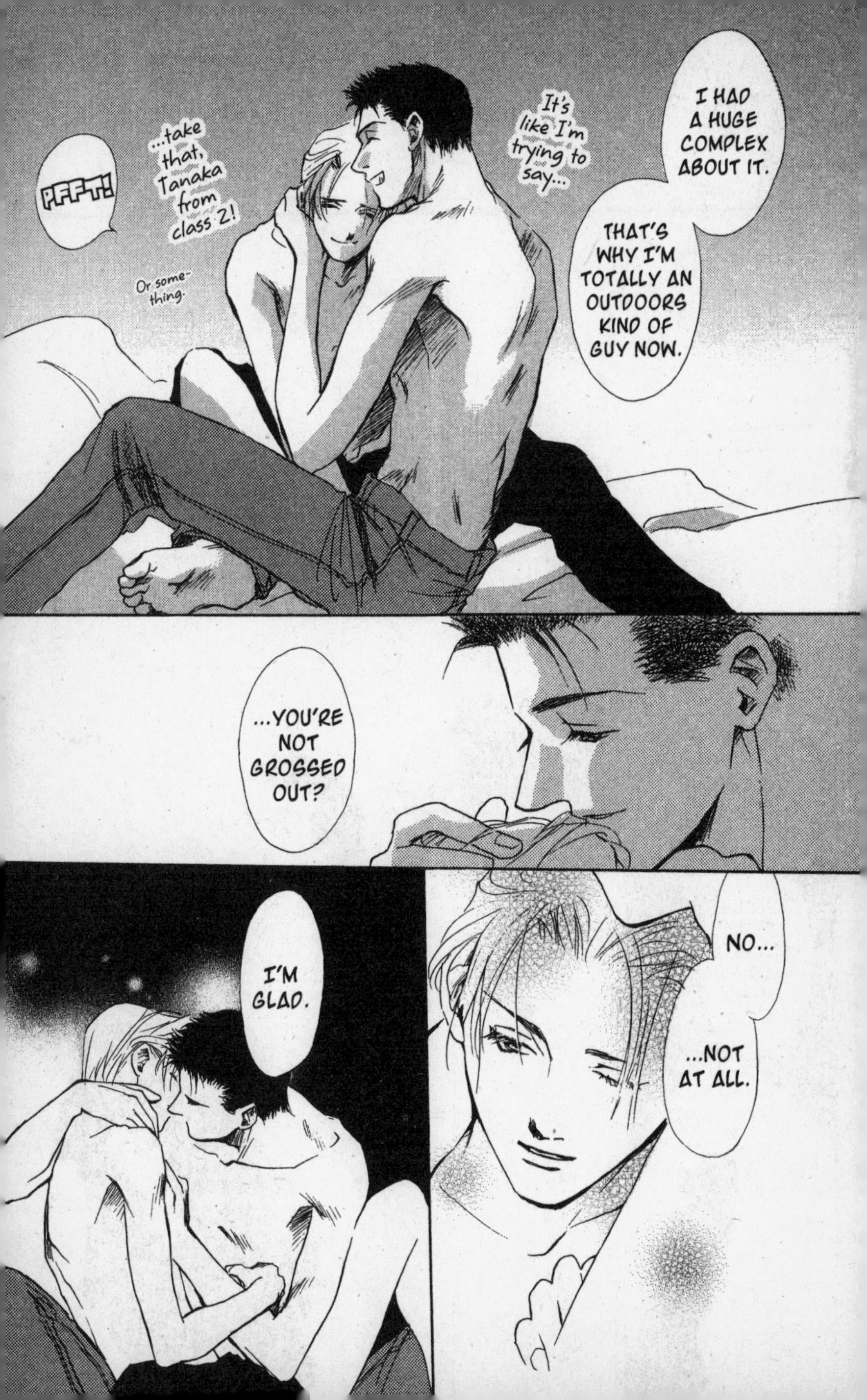
I HAD A HUGE COMPLEX ABOUT IT.
THAT'S WHY I'M TOTALLY AN OUTDOORS KIND OF GUY NOW.
It's like I'm trying to say...
...take that, Tanaka from class 2!
Or some-thing.
PFFT!
...YOU'RE NOT GROSSED OUT?
NO...
...NOT AT ALL.
I'M GLAD.

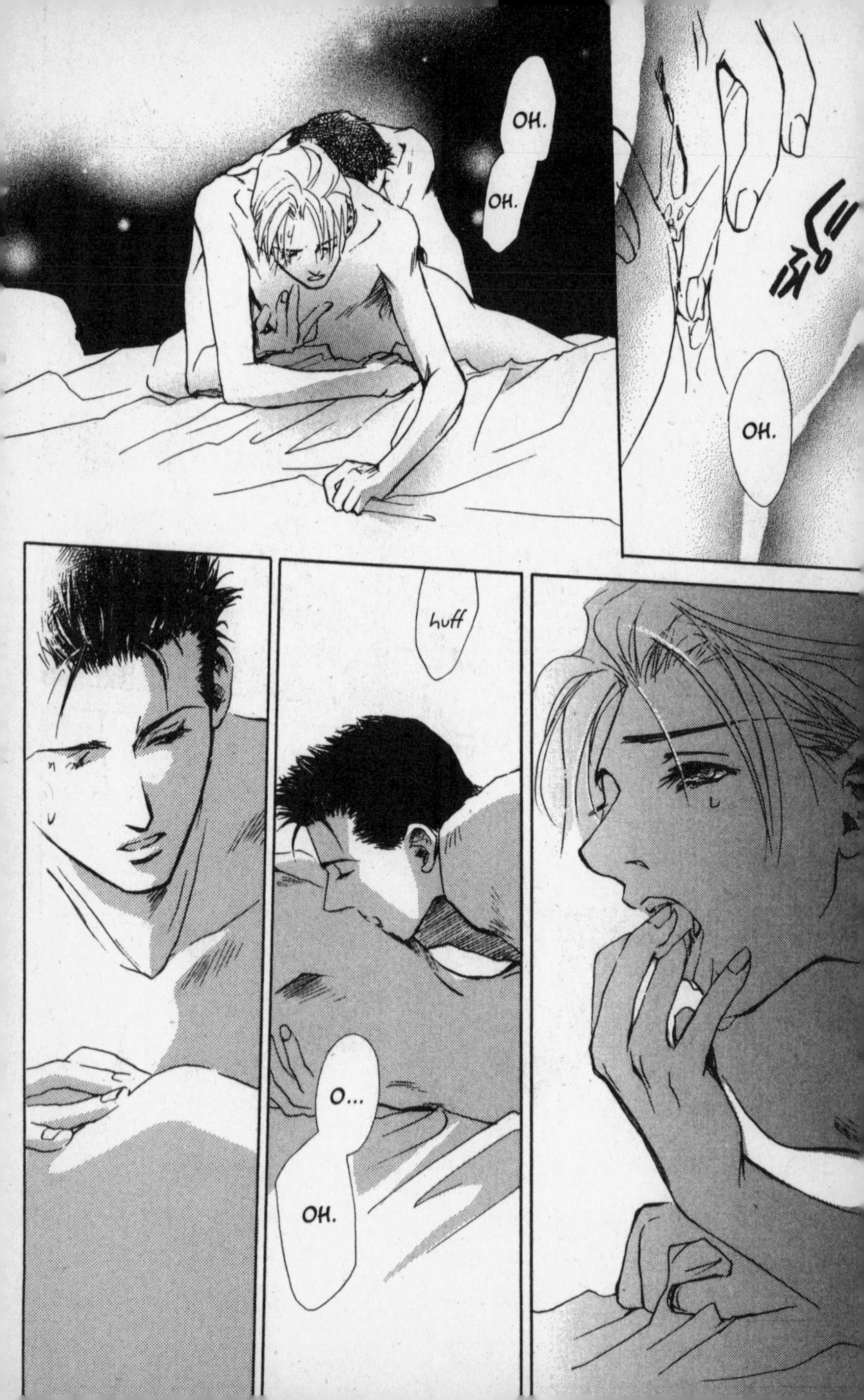
OH.
OH.
OH.
huff
O...
OH.

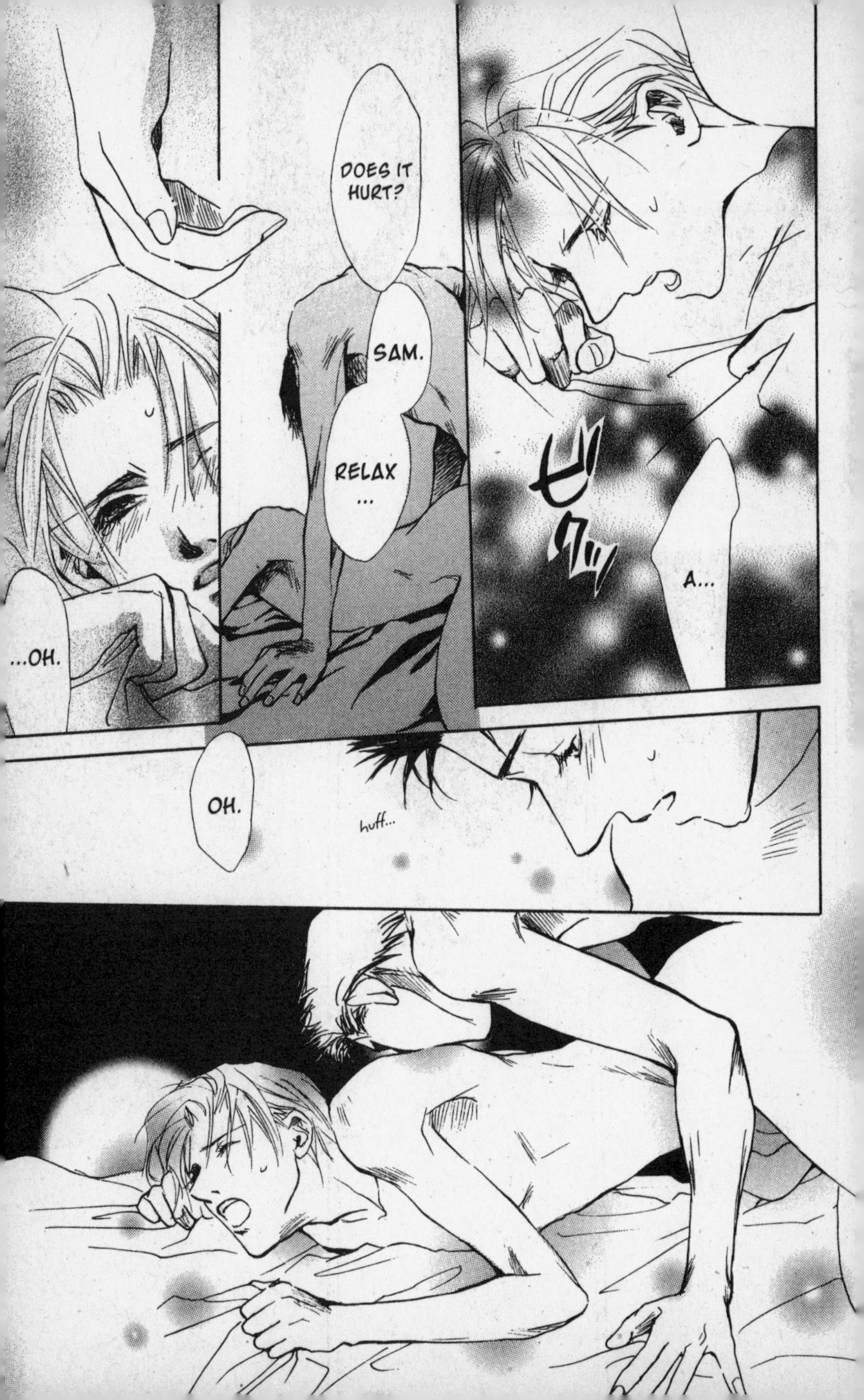
ビクッ
A...
DOES IT HURT?
SAM.
RELAX ...
...OH.
huff...
OH.

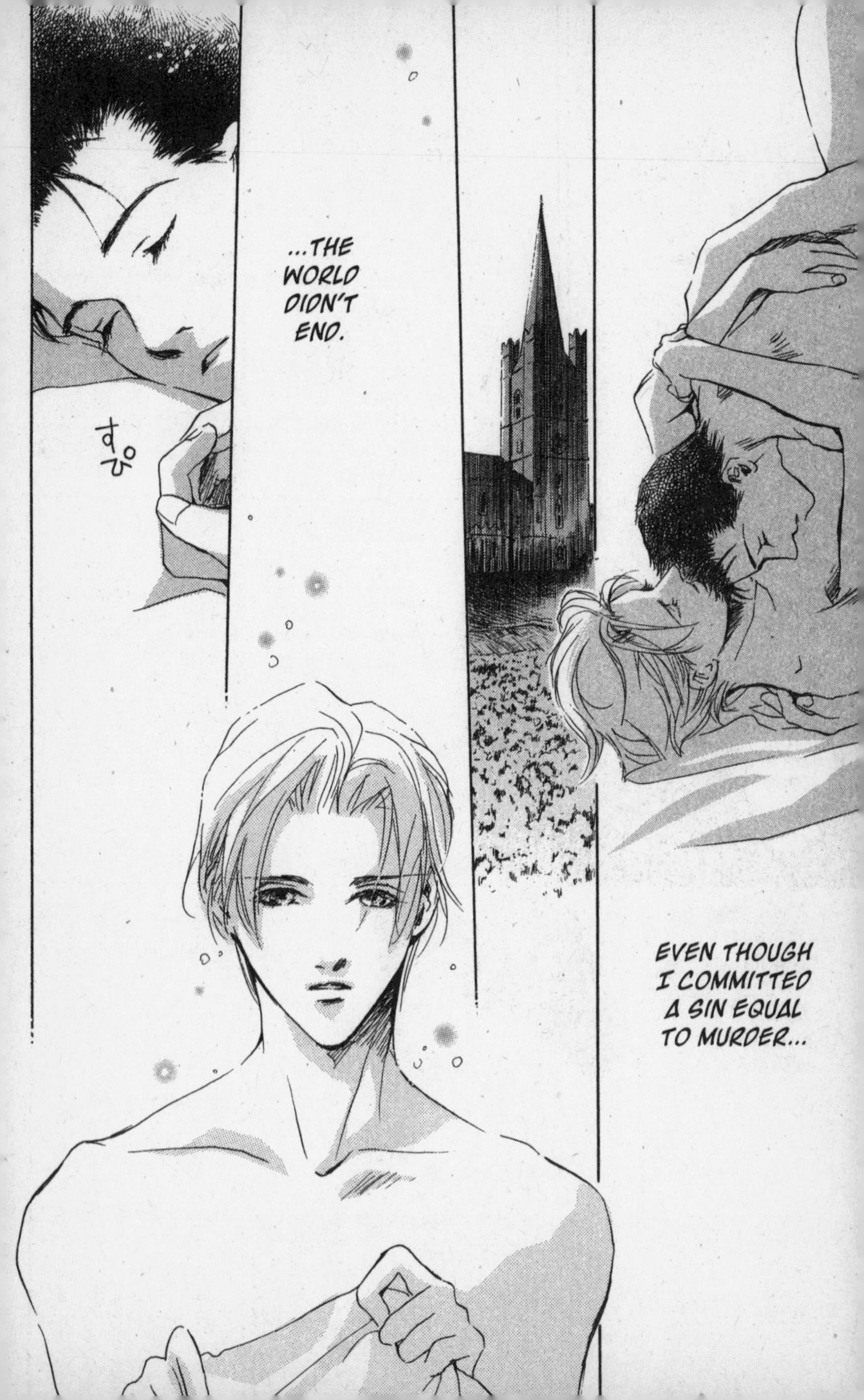
EVEN THOUGH I COMMITTED A SIN EQUAL TO MURDER...
...THE WORLD DIDN'T END.
すぴ

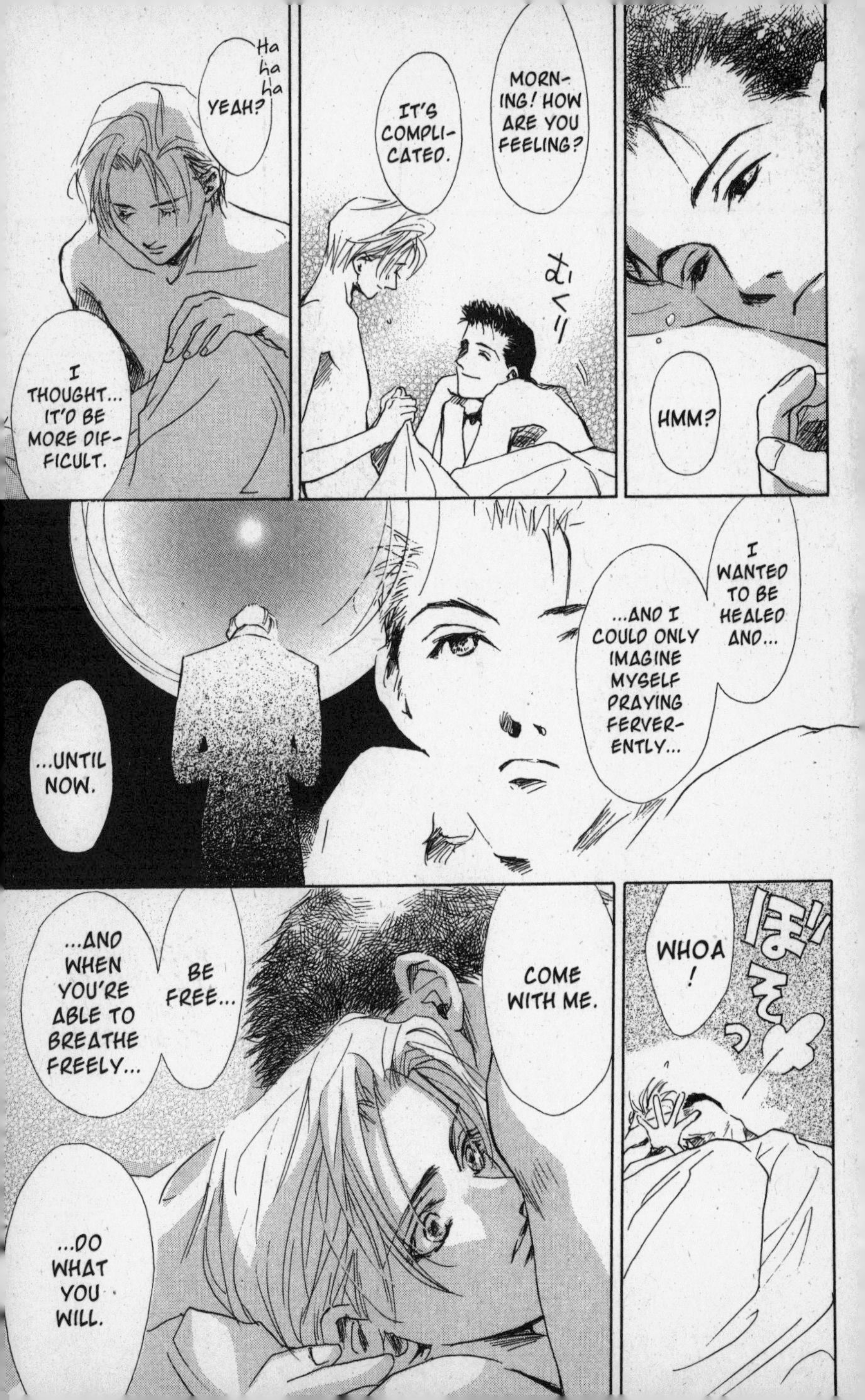
HMM?
MORNING! HOW ARE YOU FEELING?
IT'S COMPLICATED.
むくり
Ha ha ha
YEAH?
I THOUGHT... IT'D BE MORE DIFFICULT.
I WANTED TO BE HEALED AND...
...AND I COULD ONLY IMAGINE MYSELF PRAYING FERVERENTLY...
...UNTIL NOW.
WHOA!
COME WITH ME.
BE FREE...
...AND WHEN YOU'RE ABLE TO BREATHE FREELY...
...DO WHAT YOU WILL.

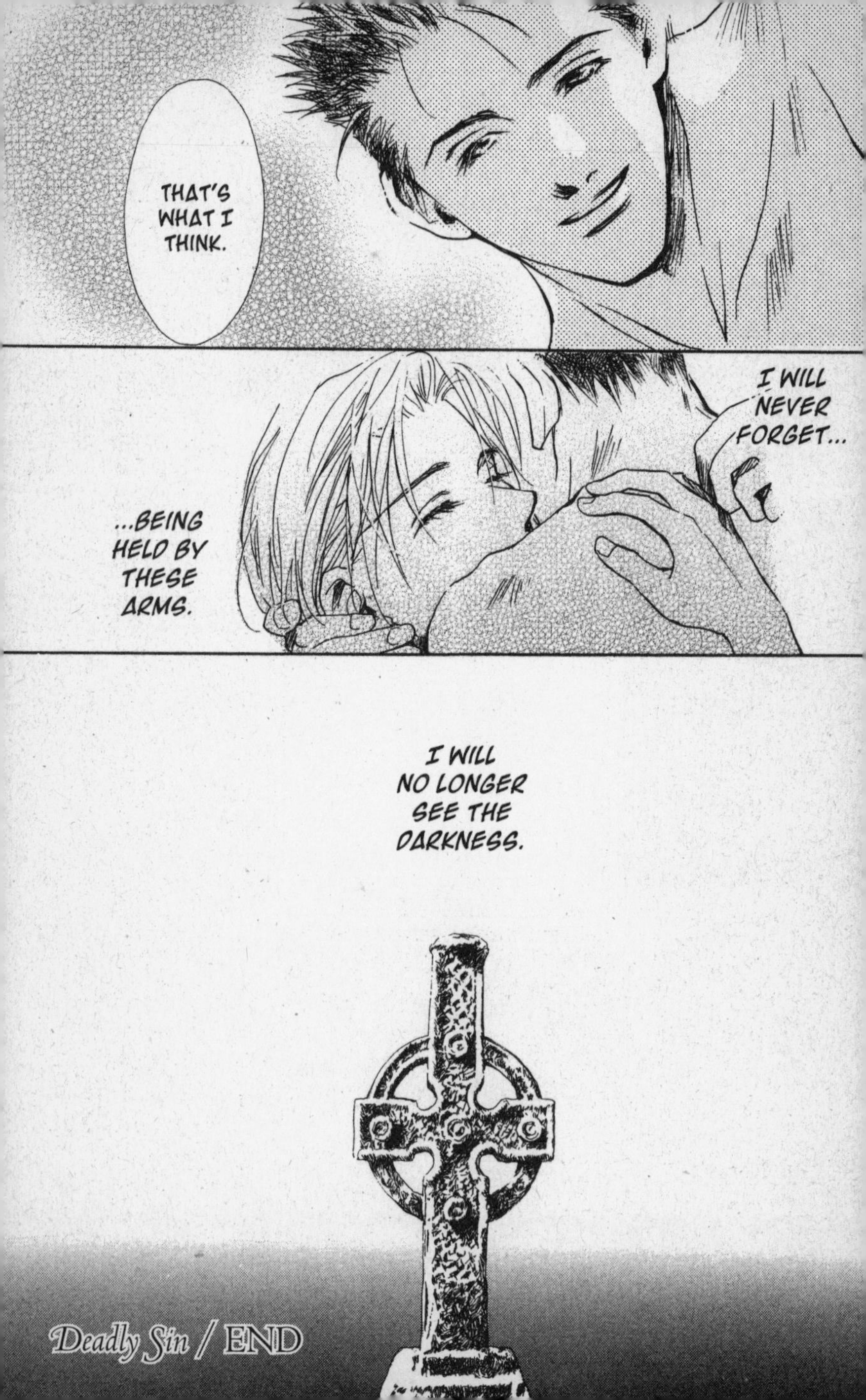
THAT'S WHAT I THINK.
I WILL NEVER FORGET...
...BEING HELD BY THESE ARMS.
I WILL NO LONGER SEE THE DARKNESS.
Deadly Sin / END

I would like to express my feelings of
gratitude to all the people who helped
during the publication of this book.

Manager/Assistant: Hime
Assistants: Asami-san, Mika-rin
Editor: Iwamoto-sama
Comic Editor: K-sama
Helper: Y-sawa-dono
The people at Biblos
The people at the printers
The people who gave me their opinions

And then, to all the people who read
this book, thank you very much from
the bottom of my heart!

BLACK KNIGHT

Zeke is now a knight under his prince and lover and continues working hard to improve his skills in swordsmanship and court etiquette. But when James, Chris's cousin and the second prince of a neighboring kingdom, appears at the castle to beg the king to release his knight, William, from the dungeons, Chris sees this as his opportunity to be useful to his country. With war possibly looming between the two kingdoms, Prince Chris takes a bold move against the wishes of his knight and father.

BLACK KNIGHT VOL.1
Created by Kai Tsurugi

ISBN: 1-59816-522-4

First Printing: July 2006
10 9 8 7 6 5 4 3 2 1
Printed in the USA

Follow the love lives of Izumi, Takamiya and others as they are brought together at a host club called "Blue Boy" that specializes in high-class male escorts. Love lines cross, chances are lost and found, and hearts are broken in this fan favorite boys' love classic.

LOVE MODE
Yuki Shimizu
1

青 BLU

In stores now! $9.99

Hisae Shino is an unemployed anime voice actor who also has to support his son Nakaya, a sophomore in high school. The sweet and naive Shino will take any job he can get—even if it means boys' love radio dramas! When he gets paired up with the supercool Tenryuu, the two bond...to a degree that Shino never intended!

Price: $9.99
In stores now!

Welcome to turn-of-the-century Paris!

GORGEOUS CARAT

Ball gowns swirl, champagne corks pop, and jewels sparkle—
and the amethyst-colored eyes of one particular young man
just might capture the heart and mind of a swashbuckling
jewel thief...

A boys' love action-romance set on the magnificent streets of
gay Pareé, *Gorgeous Carat* follows the breathtaking adventures
of Ray and Florian as they battle crime lords, back-stabbing
family members, and an attraction to each other.

High school is difficult enough, especially when you live the shadow of your stunningly attractive older brother...

Suzuki Tanaka

MENKUI!

Kotori is often teased for being superficial, and with a gorgeous brother like Kujaku, you can't really blame him for thinking that looks are everything. However, once Akaiwa steps into the picture, Kotori's life is heading for a lesson in deep trust, self-confidence, and abiding love.

OT
OLDER TEEN

青 BLU

stop

blu manga are published in the original japanese format

go to the other side and begin reading